THE POPULAR ARTS

STUART HALL: SELECTED WRITINGS

A series edited by Catherine Hall and Bill Schwarz

Contents

Gallery appears after page 258

Introduction to the 2018 Edition
Richard Dyer

The really popular is almost worthless—this applies to newspapers, music, art and most activities except football, horse-racing, and other forms of sport. The trouble about a democratic age . . . is that it generates a strong prejudice against imposing anything on people. [. . .] But of course the imposing goes on all the same. The educational system, the churches, the B.B.C. still, all in their way attempt to raise the masses to the level of the middle class.

Today it is hardly incendiary to admire Raymond Chand'
Holiday and Miles Davis, or John Ford and Gene Kelly, as '
and Paddy Whannel do in *The Popular Arts*.[1] When the b'   ιυ -
lished in 1964, however, it was in a context represent'   view
above, quoted by Whannel (1958: 34) from a front p   in the
Times Educational Supplement.[2] *The Popular Arts*   counter
such views, feeling its way toward a critical positic   ther than
against popular culture. It is poised on the cusp   tradition of
cultural critique that preceded it, Arnold and   way of Hoggart and Williams, and the cultural and '   , that were to
come. Perhaps somewhat neglected subse   onetheless constituted a vital and engaging stage in th   of the latter pair.

Hall and Whannel explicitly place   ?A 15) in a wave of
writing emblematized by the work c   Williams (1958, 1960,
1962) and Richard Hoggart (1957)   ooth how *The Popular*
Arts was taken up in the initial r   , is another book in the
tradition of Richard Hoggart   d Williams," "emphasis
falls on what might crudely '   oggart-Williams approach
to contemporary culture")   later accounts (e.g., Turner
1990: 67–68; Procter 20'   ner books of this wave commonly adduced inclu   , of the *English Working Class*

(Thompson 1963), *Music in a New Found Land* (Mellers 1964), *Discrimination and Popular Culture* (Thompson 1964), and *Understanding the Mass Media* (Tucker 1966).[5]

Behind these is a tradition of engagement with culture, which Williams himself had traced, in his *Culture and Society* (1958), back to the mid-eighteenth century. It is a tradition grounded in philosophical and literary writings, and crucial among these, as far as *The Popular Arts* is concerned, are those of F. R. and Q. D. Leavis, and the journal *Scrutiny* with which they were identified. These critics had established (or been taken to establish) the study of literature—but really English—as the vehicle for developing a critical engagement with life and society. Literary works were evaluated for the ethical depth and complexity made possible for the reader, not in the sense of teaching moral lessons but through involvement in a work's depiction of life. This entailed paying detailed and sustained attention to the literary work. These two elements—the ethical evaluation of a work, the full attention to its properties—are guiding assumptions of *The Popular Arts*.

Although F. R. Leavis had no admiration or enthusiasm for popular art, he had in 1933 collaborated with Denys Thompson on a book, *Culture and Environment*, which at least addressed popular culture in detail. Thompson would go on to edit the collection indicated above, *Discrimination and Popular Culture*. Q. D. Leavis was likewise no fan of such culture, but her *Fiction and the Reading Public* (1932) scrutinized popular fiction in a serious and systematic way and realized that readers' pleasure in it mattered. Like a scattering of others noted by Hall and Whannel (e.g., de Rougemont 1939; Eliot 1948; Rosenberg and White 1957; James 1963) including some specifically dealing with film (e.g., Wolfenstein and Leites 1950; Balázs 1952;[6] Kracauer 1947; Morin 1960; Warshow 1962), the Leavises and *Scrutiny* had addressed themselves seriously to the popular arts and new media, and in 1959 Whannel even declared that "what the cinema needs is a Leavis" (Whannel 1959a: 30). In an interview in 2009, Hall noted that Whannel comes out of—he's not a Leavisite in a narrow sense—but he

comes out of that tradition of attention to these words in this order, which is very much the T. S. Eliot, Leavis tradition . . .

that kind of close criticism applied to popular culture was really what he was wanting to do, and that was sort of what I was wanting to do at that stage too. (Hall with Jaggi 2009: 24[7])

With Terry Bolas in March 2004, Hall was more circumspect, suggesting the Leavisite vocabulary was more strategic, "mindful of the strong influence of Leavis among English teachers," the latter the initial target audience. The Leavisite quality of *The Popular Arts* was widely perceived at the time (the book "offers a number of particularised judgements in the Leavisian spirit . . . within the field of mass civilisation itself" (Bantock 1967: 162)) and in later, historicising accounts (the Thompson collection and *The Popular Arts* "constitute the last significant episode in the *Scrutiny* tradition of cultural criticism" (Hilliard 2012: 174)).

The Leavisite pressure, but also moves beyond it, can be felt in a number of elements. The overall project of the book echoes the subtitle of Leavis and Thompson's *Culture and Environment*, namely *The Training of Critical Awareness*, as well as Thompson's collection: "We should be seeking to train a more demanding audience" (*PA* 35), "It is . . . on a training in discrimination that we should place our emphasis" (*PA* 37).

The Leavisis' stress on a full engagement with the detail of the object of study is several times reiterated, albeit in relation to texts in media they would not have considered: "generalizations are really only useful . . . when supported by reference to detailed examples" (*PA* 14–15), "there is a difference, surely, between vague opinion and the considered view based on close analysis" (*PA* 35)—that "surely" the same rhetorical device as the famous Leavisite phrase for forwarding critical debate, "this is so, isn't it?" Much of *The Popular Arts* puts into practice this dictum of close attention. In a discussion of a furore occasioned by the scene of Nancy's murder in a television adaptation of *Oliver Twist*, Hall and Whannel insist that the only way to come to terms with it is to address "the actual presentation and handling of the episode" (*PA* 115); similarly, in discussing changes in the tropes of romantic fiction they argue that it is not "the simple presence of these themes, tensions and experiences which deserves attention, it is the way in which, in each period, they are being handled" (*PA* 169). The stress on the specificities of the text at hand is not to be formalist, but always about how they shape a perception of the world, and offer a response to it. In this too Hall and Whannel are Leavisite, even quoting F. R. approvingly at one point: "a serious interest in literature can[not] confine itself to the kind of intensive local analysis associated with "practical criticism" [. . .]: a real literary interest is an interest in man, society and civilization" (*PA* 40).[8]

Training in "discrimination" implies the making of value judgements. Hall in 2009 noted that *The Popular Arts* "was still at the point of being fascinated by value judgments, recognizing that we were applying critical procedures which had developed in relation to serious literature and high culture and philosophy to the underground culture" (Hall with Jaggi 2009: 25[9]) and Hall and Whannel note their intention to focus in their discussion of examples on "work of some quality, material with the power to last" (*PA* 15). Some of the terms of judgement are recognizably Leavisite, notably the opposition of the authentic with the meretricious, the latter a key term in the period indicating not just superficiality but something easily and immediately pleasing, as if ease and immediacy are themselves reprehensible. Elsewhere notions such as originality, intensity, and subtlety as well as crudity and the ersatz are deployed. At other points, however, other less evidently Leavisite criteria peep out. Raymond Chandler is valued over Spillane and Ian Fleming by the modernist yardstick of self-reflexivity: "Chandler never disguised the conventions of his form [and] is continually reminding the reader of them" (*PA* 160), "He inverts the thriller conventions, draws attention to their artificiality" (*PA* 163). They value the arts they consider for their very modernity, their use of new technologies, their accord with the world as it is now: the cinema, notably, "is a *modern* medium, not simply because it belongs to an advanced technological stage in society, but because its characteristic forms—its immediacy, its continual shifts of focus and perspective—are themselves aspects of the modern sensibility" (*PA* 46).

In one of their statements of intent, the authors observe: "A true training in discrimination is concerned with pleasure" (PA 38). The move to pleasure marks an extension, even a break with, the

Leavisite purview. There is sometimes a direct embrace of pleasure: "there will always be a need for films that merely affirm, which offer a fantasy of delight and genuine release in a celebration, rather than a criticism, of life" (*PA* 224). Sometimes, as in the discussion of the novels of Mickey Spillane, the embrace is more cagey. The account of the way the pleasures of sex and violence are conveyed is detailed and evocative (*PA* 143–151) and they conclude (*PA* 151):

> As one ploughs through a succession of novels in which the elements of the form are crudely welded together, with the drool of pleasure of the supposed readers already written into the novel, one begins to develop a perverse respect for Spillane himself. At least, in his novels, the incidents are given some pattern overall by Hammer's philosophy of life, repellent though it may be. Moreover, they are written with a certain cold-hearted gusto and drive.

Here a Leavisite negativity ("ploughs through," "crudely," "drool") gives way to a version of the positive notion of organic form (the narrative pattern is given a wider sense by the underlying worldview) and winds up in affective enthusiasm ("gusto and drive"—even the "cold-hearted" is a way of being more precise about the feeling quality of the work). This is not unabashed, postmodern hedonism, nor is it dismissive of or unresponsive to the pleasures of violence and nastiness. They are less equivocal in their discussion of romantic fiction in Chapter 7, noting the collapse of issues of honor that inform classic works such as those of Richardson, Austen, Brontë, and D. H. Lawrence, "leaving the reader [in contemporary romances] totally exposed to the events [which] give them their full sensational impact," with "sensational" here by no means used enthusiastically. Nonetheless, it is remarkable that they wrote about such fiction at all, and seriously and in detail, and much of their argument concerns the implications for women's emancipation. Their discussion was published eleven years after the first translation of Simone de Beauvoir's *The Second Sex*[10] and only a year after Betty Friedan's *The Feminine Mystique*, with its critique of romantic fiction, and it seems to anticipate the debates over pleasure, romance, and pornography that were to be so central to second-wave feminism less than ten years later.

Important as the Leavisite dimension is to *The Popular Arts*, there are also other, more immediate contexts that shaped and distinguished it, political, pedagogical, disciplinarian, and personal.

The Popular Arts was also a New Left project. In addition to its rejection of the imperialism and authoritarianism of much actually existing socialism, the New Left had sought to break with the economic reductionism of the established left, seeing cultural issues, in the broadest sense, as at least as determinant and important. Its chief organ was first (1957–59) *Universities and Left Review* and then from 1960 *New Left Review*. Hall and Whannel had both contributed to the former, and then Hall edited the first twelve issues (1960–62) of the latter and Whannel wrote for it and was on the advisory board. In the editorial to the first edition, Hall made clear the importance of popular culture (Hall 1960: 1):

> The purpose of discussing the cinema or teen-age culture in *NLR* is not to show that, in some modish way, we are keeping up with the times. These are directly relevant to the imaginative resistances of people who have to live within capitalism— the growing points of social discontent, the projections of deeply-felt needs.

The Popular Arts is shot through with just such a sense of social urgency about popular culture, of it mattering.

The actual coverage of the popular arts in *New Left Review* was little. There was an article by Whannel with Brian Groombridge about pop music that was at times (Groombridge and Whannel 1960b: 52) bilious ("noise of an unbelievable ugliness is wrung from saxophones and guitars with sadistic cruelty and finally processed in the laboratory"), elsewhere (ibid.: 53) open to its possibilities ("The response to the surly aggressiveness of Presley contains within itself valuable sources of non-conformism"), a veering found in *The Popular Arts*. Whannel contributed to a supplement on television that was addressed to the Pilkington Committee, reporting on the state and future of television (and to which Richard Hoggart made a decisive contribution), and here (Coppard et al. 1961: 35–36) popular culture was strongly spoken up for:

It is only when the concept of popular culture is treated with the respect—and enthusiasm—it deserves, and when the same care, seriousness, awareness of the human dignity of the audience that is apparent in a few of the best "minority" programmes spreads through the whole range of production, that we are likely to get good television in this country.

In an article titled "The New Frontier" in the eighth issue of *New Left Review* (Hall 1961), Hall stressed the centrality of education to a new socialist politics, and *The Popular Arts* very clearly places itself on this political frontier. Hall and Whannel had both been secondary school teachers; at the time of writing Hall was teaching film and media at Chelsea College of Science and Technology as a supplementary subject to students taking largely vocational courses, and Whannel was the Education Officer at the British Film Institute (BFI) and traveling the country speaking on film mainly within an adult education context.[11] Whannel had co-organized an eight-day forum at the National Film Theatre in London on "The Visual Persuaders," linking the BFI's educational work with social, cultural, and intellectual debates of the day (see Bolas 2012: 136), and had been involved in shaping the agenda of a conference held by the National Union of Teachers (NUT) in 1960 under the title "Popular Culture and Personal Responsibility," which had identified the importance of addressing popular media in education.

The Popular Arts was originally intended as a handbook for teaching popular culture in schools, and its last eighty pages (not reproduced here) consisted of curriculum and classroom plans and guidance on reading and audiovisual teaching materials. The book begins by referencing the authors' experience of teaching in secondary modern schools.[12] The first chapter engages with the concerns expressed in the resolution produced by the NUT conference and other institutionally based statements such as the Nuffield Foundation television inquiry in 1958, conducted by Hilda Himmelweit and published as *Television and the Child*, the Crowther Report 1959, produced for the Central Advisory Council for Education and dealing with educational provision for fifteen to eighteen year olds, and the pamphlet,

Sex and Violence in Modern Media, published by the Educational Institute of Scotland in 1961. What all these share is an anxiety about popular media and young people, a panic related not only to a long established worry about the power of the media over young minds in general but more specifically the appeal of what were seen as newly forceful and available forms of media presentations of sex and violence, not least in the culture surrounding rock 'n' roll and the emergent social category of the teenager.

The general urgency of *The Popular Arts*'s concern with popular culture is intensified and darkened by this background, an example of what social scientists would come to call a "moral panic." This term was used probably first by Marshall McLuhan in *Understanding Media* (1964) and taken up in the early seventies by Jock Young (1971) and Stan Cohen (1972); Hall and Whannel do not use the term, but there is clearly a germ here of some of Hall's most celebrated later collaborative work on youth cultures (e.g., Hall and Jefferson 1975; Hall et al. 1976). At points in *The Popular Arts* there are echoes of the concern signaled in Hall's *Universities and Left Review* article, "Politics of Adolescence?," where young people are not the problem but perhaps a glimpse of the solution to society's ills. "Instinctively, young people are radical," he argues. "They may understand superficially: but they feel in depth" (Hall 1959: 2), and he gives a rather moving evocation of an intuitive hatred among young people of the class system and bland politics. In *The Popular Arts*, young people are seen as "pioneering" about sexual morality (*PA* 273), and teenage culture as a "contradictory mixture of the authentic and the manufactured" (*PA* 276).

Some commentators emphasize this strand in the book, and it is certainly important to note its prescient presence, but it seems overstating the case to argue that "Hall and Whannel emphasized how young men from working-class backgrounds developed forms of cultural expression that enabled them to resist commercial culture" (Horowitz 2012: 235). The book is rather more propelled by the teacherly concern over how to respond to the wider worry about young people. On the whole Hall and Whannel are not enthusiastic about teen romance magazines or rock 'n' roll, but they have a teacher's, and new left activist's, commitment to starting from where people are, a concern "not with the giving of knowledge but with the evaluating of experience," as Whannel put it at the NUT conference.[13] The wrinkle in the approach is that implicitly the authors hope that pupils will come to the same evaluations as them and learn to prefer a better—and older—popular culture than the ones they prefer at present, that is, Ella Fitzgerald and Frank Sinatra rather than Adam Faith and the Twist.

Toward the end of *The Popular Arts* (394–395), Hall and Whannel surmise that "cinema might be given separate and specialist treatment," away from a general popular arts curriculum, for its special "quality of achievement" and at any rate the beginnings of a developed aesthetics. Whannel at the time was developing the education department at the British Film Institute, sometimes defining it as an "academy in waiting," preparing the ground for film as a discipline to be taken up in the universities (see Bolas 2009: 145–146). Hall was not only teaching film, including in extramural classes and for the British Film Institute (BFI) as well as at Chelsea College; he also contributed an account of doing so to a booklet, *Film Teaching*, edited by Whannel and Peter Harcourt (Hall 1964). The bulk of this essay is what would become, and still is, standard material in introductory film studies courses, looking at what was then called the "language of the cinema"; in the first part however, Hall states (p. 11) that what he understands film studies to be about is the training of intelligence and sensibility, explicitly citing F. R. Leavis and saying the only difference is that he is applying these precepts to film, while toward the end he turns away from the then canonical cinema he has so far drawn on (Eisenstein, *Twelve Angry Men*, Wajda) to the matter of popular cinema. He argues (p. 26) that it is not enough just to consider the work of the great directors:

> The study of cinema would be wholly incomplete without that great body of work, done in the most popular forms, and reaching far wider audiences. This takes us into the realm of the commercial cinema proper; and, of course, a great deal of trash has been produced there. But can one understand the full potential

of the medium until one has accounted for the real qualities of some westerns, some thrillers, some comedies, and some musicals? For these are where the cinema has been *fully* creative—making out of unpromising material and debased conventions a quite original contribution to the art form. (Emphasis in original.)

Here it is not, as in *The Popular Arts*, a question of bringing out the artistic quality in popular works, but rather the centrality of the popular to understanding and appreciating the film medium itself. Given the commitment of both Hall and Whannel to film as film, it's not surprising that *The Popular Arts* should give a special place to it.[14] Only jazz is of equal importance, and lovingly as it is written about, the perennial problem of how to write rigorously about music, and a fortiori popular music, is probably what holds the authors back from advocating it too as worthy of "separate and specialist treatment."[15]

The enthusiasm for film and jazz in *The Popular Arts* stems partly from a modernist embrace of a new medium or form, but also directly from Paddy's and Stuart's love of them.[16] This is one of the personal elements that made the character of the book possible. However much it is informed by a sense of the political and pedagogical importance of their subject, it is not merely dutiful. They themselves, and others who knew them, have attested to their unabashed delight in jazz and Hollywood movies. Stuart came at jazz more through contemporary jazz and learnt much about the earlier history from Paddy ("He liked mainstream, and I liked modern jazz . . . I really discovered Billie Holiday with him").[17] As for Hollywood, Stuart recalled, "I always had a passionate addiction to the movies and . . . as a youth in Kingston, I saw on Saturday afternoon matinees at the Carib Theatre everything from Hollywood that found its way to Jamaica [. . .] This passion continued in Oxford. We often went to the cinema two or three times a week."[18] Peter Wollen and Laura Mulvey (Mulvey and Wollen 2008: 219), who knew Paddy at the BFI, both stress the difference between him and Hoggart and Williams because "he loved Hollywood cinema" (Wollen). Mulvey (ibid.) suggests that standing up for Hollywood was also "a provocative stand against dominant cultural values"; somewhat similarly, David Horowitz (2012: 243) speculates that watching Hollywood films in Jamaica was perhaps for Stuart "a counterweight to British influence."

The readiness to remain true to their pleasure in the popular cultural forms of their childhood and youth may also have been made possible from the fact that both were inside outsiders, people in established positions with a fair degree of cultural capital and yet for different reasons somewhat displaced from inhabiting those positions straightforwardly. Stuart was an Oxford graduate about to take up a position in a major red-brick university, but also a Jamaican in the United Kingdom, from a family that was among the upper echelons of Jamaican society but who was now living in a country that largely did not recognize such niceties in its attitudes toward black and immigrant peoples. Paddy was Scottish but working in London; he had worked as a projectionist on leaving school at age fifteen and got back into education after the war, earning a teaching diploma from Alnwick College of Education in 1946 and a diploma in art history from the University of London in 1948. Both had been teachers but in the least prestigious parts of the secondary and tertiary education sectors. Quite apart from their socialist convictions (probably less outlandish then than in post-Blair Britain), they were influential, established, and socially skilled men who nonetheless carried histories and experiences that enabled them to speak outside of conventional lines and embrace the culture that had also made them.

The Popular Arts had a mixed reception on publication. The British press, tabloids and broadsheets alike, tended to scorn the absurdity of taking popular culture seriously, though the educational and left-wing journals were more welcoming. Later commentators have praised it as a significant step toward the serious engagement with the popular (it "remains one of the most diverse and sustained accounts of popular culture ever written" (Procter 2004: 19)) and film in particular (it "was the first book to use what you might call a theoretical approach to a subject that had no academic standing" (Mulvey and Wollen 2008: 218)). Yet there is generally a feeling that the Leavisite legacy sometimes results in "a degree of elitism" (Procter 2004: 23). Indeed there are occasionally surprising formulations ("It would, of course, be foolish to make large claims for this popular culture" (*PA* 40), "The best cinema—like most advanced jazz—seems to push towards high art: average films or pop music are processed mass art" (*PA* 78)) and a palpable dislike throughout of the popular press, most television, and advertising. Even cinema, "by far the most mature and expressive" form of popular art, "cannot be compared to literature either in volume or *quality of achievement*" (ibid., my italics), and jazz "is still—compared with the classical forms—a simple music" (*PA* 72). The notions of originality, newness, and surprise that Hall and Whannel deploy at points are argued to prevent them valuing convention, repetition, and familiarity, characteristics of popular (and also classical) aesthetics (see Turner 1990: 67–68); Eric Hobsbawm, in a teasing contemporary review, suggested that they simply hadn't come to terms with the fact of the industrialization of culture. [19]

The impact of *The Popular Arts* beyond the United Kingdom is hard to determine. In most countries, even English-speaking ones, by the time cultural studies had been discovered, it was Hoggart and Williams who constituted the founding texts.[20] It was translated and published in Italy in a series ("Cultura e Società") edited by Richard Hoggart and Fernando Ferrara, part of the development of cultural studies within English studies at the "Orientale" in Naples and used there in research and teaching for many years.[21] This was, as far as I can tell, the only language into which it was ever translated. In an article published in 1987, Karin Barber argued that *The Popular Arts* could offer "a promising application to African arts" (p. 71), implying that it was not in fact already a known text.

The book was published by Pantheon in the United States, perhaps a few months after its appearance in the United Kingdom and with an additional subtitle—*A Critical Guide to the Mass Media*—that registers the already considerable presence of mass media research in the United States while holding on to a humanistic notion of analysis. An early review by Roger Brown of the University of Illinois noted that "although a good deal of the output examined is British rather than American, anyone interested in improving his critical awareness of this sort of material ought to benefit from working carefully through the distinctions that are made" (1965: 430). A similar enthusiasm, yet with the sense of a need to take into account geocultural difference, was registered ten years later by Richard E. Barbieri in an article in *The English Journal*, published by the National Council of Teachers of English. Arguing that the emergence of "Pop culture [is] not only a growing but an eminently worthwhile field for students and teachers," he observed, "Though British, [*The Popular Arts*] contains much of value for American culture, and its teacher orientation, strong rationale, specific curriculum suggestions and excellent annotated bibliography make it a prime resource" (1976: 35).

A quick trawl of national and university libraries in Anglophone countries indicates that the book is in their holdings, often in both the British and American editions. The former ran to three editions. However, a history has yet to be written about how it was taken up, either by individual scholars in their work or in curricula and syllabi. Although Whannel himself published little after *The Popular Arts* (and died in 1980 at the age of fifty-eight), the book clearly informed the thinking of many of the film studies graduates at Northwestern in his time. Jane Feuer (1980, 1982), for instance, draws on Hall and Whannel to discuss the complex position of the Hollywood musical between folk art and mass art, while Jerome Delamater (1976, 1981) linked the work of Busby Berkeley with that of the French surrealists, thus placing a mass cultural product unapologetically in the context of canonical avant-garde ones.

For Grant Farred (2007: 85), *The Popular Arts* is a text "that has long since fallen into disuse, if not disrepute"; for David Horowitz (2012: 235) it is "a landmark book on mass media, albeit one to which scholars have paid relatively little attention." Philip Bounds (2016: 100), on the other hand, refers to it as a "seminal investigation." Farred and Horowitz are probably right to say that it has been to a considerable extent forgotten, except by those with an interest in the history of cultural studies, but, if it is hard to show in a precise way its influence on later work, Bounds may also be right to discern already in it much that followed.

The book's title words, which accurately state its contents, also cue some of the ambiguities of its legacy. The notion of the popular it pursues situates it between folk, autochthonously produced culture of the people, and mass, centralized, production line culture. The former has all but disappeared from Western societies (and Hall and Whannel are wary of sentimentalizing it), the latter seeks to hold sway. Somewhere between can be discerned cultural production that is still rooted in ordinary people's lives and experiences, even though produced within a commercial imperative and on a large scale. Chandler, Chaplin, Miles Davis, John Ford, Billie Holiday, Gene Kelly, Marie Lloyd, and *Z Cars* are among the examples of "the really popular work" (*PA* 78) the authors seek out. This particular notion has fallen into desuetude, although it did inform the popular culture course that ran at the UK's Open University from 1982 to 1987, led by Tony Bennett under Hall's aegis. What remains on the agenda is the popular as an issue, the notion evoking as it does both the autochthonous ("jazz is of the people," *PA* 73) and the box office and how we are to pick our way through these opposed notions.[22]

Farred (2007: 96) observes that *The Popular Arts* introduces "the vexed and difficult issue of the aesthetic into cultural studies." Much of the trajectory of cultural studies qua cultural studies seems to be a move away from the implications of the "arts" of the book's title, though if one considers the latter in relation to film studies and musicology, its prescience is striking. Partly through the way that Whannel's involvement in the development of film studies in the United Kingdom and the United States shaped the discipline, the contours of an aesthetics of popular art emerge: genre, star, representation (supplemented by authorship, a notion implicit but unexplored in *The Popular Arts*). These concerns have been extended and modified in later years with work looking beyond Hollywood, notably and rather late in the day at Hindi cinema as well as the popular cinemas of Africa, South America, Asia, and Europe. Similar trajectories might be traced in musicology (see Laing 1994) and art history (the latter often in its reinvention as "visual culture"), although literary and television studies seem to have made less headway, the former wary of the popular, the latter of art.

Seen from the perspective of departments, journals, and publishers, lists of cultural studies, *The Popular Arts* seems part of a pre-history of the discipline offering only passages and glimpses of what was to follow. Seen in relation to developments in arts and humanities disciplines in the past fifty years, and with its ethics wearing identity politics garb, its paradigms of popular aesthetics are ubiquitous. Everyone's doing cultural studies now, something suggested by the way the word "studies" is appended to so many disciplines. And not only. Broadsheet newspapers, weekly and monthly journals of comment, museums, niche TV and radio stations (think, to take only British examples, of *The Observer*, the Victoria and Albert Museum, Radio 4, Sky Arts), all routinely take popular culture seriously along the lines set out by Hall and Whannel. When I began rereading *The Popular Arts* for the purposes of this introduction and its place in an edition of Hall's work, it seemed to open up a path not taken; now looking around I wonder where it did not lead.

NOTES

1. Reference citations in the text will use the abbreviation *PA*.
2. Published in response to a forum organized by the Joint Council for Education through Art.
3. It is not stated in the book whether or which parts of *The Popular Arts* are more the work of one or the other man. Garry Whannel has a copy of the book, almost certainly his father's, with chapters initialed as follows: 1. The Media and Society, PW; 2. Minority Art Folk Art and Popular Art, SH; 3. Popular Art and Mass Culture, SH; 4. Popular Forms and Popular Artists, SH/PW; 5. Violence on the Screen, SH; 6. The Avenging Angel, PW/SH; 7. Falling in Love, SH; 8. Fantasy and Romance, PW; 9. Friends and Neighbours, SH; 10. The Young Audience, PW; 11. The Big Bazaar, SH; 12. The Institutions, PW; 13. Mass Society: Critics and Defenders, PW; 14. The Curriculum and the Popular Arts, PW. In a much later interview Hall referred to "my chapter on advertising . . . Paddy Whannel's chapter on the Western" (Hall with Jaggi 2009: 25). As noted elsewhere, there are echoes of Hall's writings on adolescence in the book, and David Horowitz (2012: 238–242) shows how many of the topics covered in it were also covered by Whannel writing a regular column for the NUT journal *The Teacher* from 1962 to 1966 under the rubric "Albert Casey's Entertainment Guide" (the pseudonym a reference to one of his jazz favorites, the guitarist Al Casey).
4. Quotations in parentheses are from Flew (1964: 876) and Coleman (1964) respectively.

5. Bolas (2009: 112) notes that Tucker had seen *The Popular Arts* in manuscript.

6. See Carter (2010) for the relation of this book to Balázs's original publications.

7. I am grateful to Marina Vitale for drawing my attention to this interview.

8. The quotation is from Leavis (1952: 200).

9. It is clear in the context that by "underground" here Hall means popular mass culture, not the avant-garde.

10. First published in France in 1949 (*Le Deuxième sexe*. Paris: Gallimard), first English translation, by Howard Parshley (New York: Alfred A. Knopf).

11. On the importance of adult education for the development of cultural studies, see Steele (1997). In a review of *The Popular Arts* in the journal *Adult Education*, Roy Shaw described the BFI Education Department as "one of the most off-beat extra-mural departments in the country, and quite the most adventurous in the past decade."

12. In the prevalent two-tier system, secondary modern schools were more vocationally, and less academically, oriented. Part of Hall's agenda in "The New Frontier" is the abolition of this system in favor of comprehensive schools.

13. This is from a verbatim report of the conference published by the National Union of Teachers, quoted here from Bolas (2009: 103).

14. For further discussion of the privileging of film in *The Popular Arts*, see Farred (2007: 92).

15. In a review of Francis Newton's *The Jazz Scene* in *Universities and Left Review*, Whannel (1959b: 70) did urge educationists to take jazz into consideration, "not because I want to see our schools setting up courses on the story of jazz [. . .] but because an understanding of the urban popular arts will help us to get the task of teaching in a better focus."

16. Stuart Hall was my PhD supervisor and we remained friends until his death. Paddy Whannel facilitated my PhD thesis by okaying the private screening of an unusually large number of musicals for me at the BFI (in pre-video days) and acting as the external examiner on it. I met him only a couple of times, as he moved to Northwestern University in 1971. Rereading *The Popular Arts* now I am astonished—and rather embarrassed—to realize just how much a child I am of it, without quite realizing it. Much of what I have written—on entertainment, musicals, stars, thrills—is all there in embryo and yet I must have so imbibed it and made it mine that I nowhere formally registered the fact.

17. From an unpublished interview with Bill Schwarz.

18. Ibid.

19. Storey (2000: 55) draws attention to the modernist implications of the authors' use of the term "surprise." The Hobsbawm quote was published in

the *Times Literary Supplement*, 3277, December 17, 1964, reprinted in Hobsbawm (2013: 261–271); I am grateful to Rosalind Brunt for drawing this to my attention.

20. I am grateful to Graeme Turner, Tom Waugh, Anu Koivunen, Maxime Cervulle, Erica Carter, and Jane Gaines and Ted Striphas for discussion of the mainly non-presence of *The Popular Arts* in, respectively, Australia, Canada, Finland, France, Germany, and the United States.

21. Hall and Whannel (1970). My thanks to Martina Vitale for discussing this with me.

22. The introduction by Ginette Vincendeau and myself to our collection on popular European cinema exemplifies this (Dyer and Vincendeau 1992). In seeking to wrest European film from both art house and national cinema problematics, we were treading in Hall and Whannel's footsteps.

REFERENCES

Balázs, Béla. 1952. *Theory of Film*. London: Dennis Dobson.

Bantock, G. H. 1967. *Education, Culture and the Emotions*. London: Faber and Faber.

Barber, Karin. 1987. "Popular Arts in Africa." *African Studies Review* 30:3, 1–78.

Barbieri, Richard E. 1976. "Resources for the Study of Popular Culture." *The English Journal* 65:3, 35–40.

Bolas, Terry. 2009. *Screen Education: From Film Appreciation to Media Studies*. Bristol: Intellect.

Bolas, Terry. 2012. "Paddy Whannel and BFI Education." In Nowell-Smith and Dupin 2012: 133–151.

Bounds, Philip. 2016. "From Folk to Jazz: Eric Hobsbawm, British Communism and Cultural Studies." In Philip Bounds and David Berry (eds.), *British Marxism and Cultural Studies: Essays on a Living Tradition*. Abingdon: Routledge, 87–105.

Brown, Roger. 1965. "*The Popular Arts* by Stuart Hall and Paddy Whannel." *AV Communication Review* 13:4, 429–435.

Carter, Erica, ed. 2010. *Béla Balázs: Early Film Theory*. Oxford: Berghahn.

Cohen, Stan. 1972. *Folk Devils and Moral Panics*. London: Routledge.

Coleman, John. 1964. "Pop Project." *The Guardian*, December 18, 7.

Coppard, Kit, Paddy Whannel, Raymond Williams, and Tony Higgins. 1961. "Television Supplement." *New Left Review* 1:7, 33–48.

Delamater, Jerome. 1976. "*Busby Berkeley:* An American *Surrealist*." *Wide Angle* 1:24–29.

Delamater, Jerome. 1981. *Dance in the American Musical.* Ann Arbor, Mich.: UMI Research Press.

Dyer, Richard, and Ginette Vincendeau, eds. 1992. "Introduction" to *Popular European Cinema.* London: Routledge, 1–14.

Eliot, T. S. 1948. *Notes towards a Definition of Culture.* London: Faber and Faber.

Farred, Grant. 2007. "'The First Shall Be Last': Locating *The Popular Arts* in the Stuart Hall Oeuvre." In Brian Meeks (ed.), *Culture, Polities, Race and Diaspora: The Thought of Stuart Hall.* London: Lawrence & Wishart, 85–97.

Feuer, Jane. 1980. "Hollywood Musicals: Mass Art as Folk Art." *Jump Cut* 23, 23–25.

Feuer, Jane. 1982. *The Hollywood Musical.* Bloomington: Indiana University Press.

Flew, Antony. 1964. "The Great Pop Show." *The Spectator*, December 25, 18.

Groombridge, Brian, and Paddy Whannel. 1960. "Something Rotten in Denmark Street." *New Left Review* 1:1, 52–54.

Hall, Stuart. 1959. "Politics of Adolescence?" *Universities and Left Review* 1:6, 2–4.

Hall, Stuart. 1960. "Editorial." *New Left Review* 1:1, 1–3.

Hall, Stuart. 1961. "The New Frontier." *New Left Review* 1:8, 47–48.

Hall, Stuart. 1964. "Liberal Studies." In Paddy Whannel and Peter Harcourt (eds.), *Film Teaching.* London: British Film Institute Education Department, 10–27.

Hall, Stuart, and Paddy Whannel. 1970. *Arti per il Popolo. I media sono i mostri.* Trans. Maria Palermo Concolato. Rome: Officina.

Hall, Stuart, and Tony Jefferson, eds. 1975. Resistance Through Rituals: Youth Subcultures in Post-war Britain (Working Papers in Cultural Studies, 7–8), Birmingham: Centre for Contemporary Cultural Studies, University of Birmingham.

Hall, Stuart, Chas Critcher, Tony Jefferson, John Clarke, and Brian Roberts. 1976. *Policing the Crisis: Mugging and Law 'n' Order.* Birmingham: University of Birmingham.

Hall, Stuart, with Maya Jaggi. 2009. *Personally Speaking: A Long Conversation with Stuart Hall.* Northampton Mass.: Media Education Foundation (DVD, transcript at http://www.mediaed.org/transcripts/Stuart-Hall-Personally -Speaking-Transcript.pdf).

Hilliard, Christopher. 2012. *English as a Vocation: The "Scrutiny" Movement.* Oxford: Oxford University Press.

Hoggart, Richard. 1957. *The Uses of Literacy.* London: Chatto and Windus.

Horowitz, David. 2012. *Consuming Pleasures: Intellectuals and Popular Culture in the Post-war World.* Philadelphia: University of Pennsylvania Press.

James, Louis. 1963. *Fiction for the Working Man, 1830–50.* Oxford: Oxford University Press.

Kracauer, Siegfried. 1947. *From Caligari to Hitler: A Psychological History of the German Film.* Princeton, N.J.: Princeton University Press.

Laing, Dave. 1994. "*Scrutiny* to Subcultures: Notes on Literary Criticism and Popular Music." *Popular Music* 13:2, 179–190.

Leavis, F. R. 1952. *The Common Pursuit.* London: Chatto and Windus.

Leavis, F. R., and Denys Thompson. 1933. *Culture and Environment: The Training of Critical Awareness.* London: Chatto and Windus.

Leavis, Q. D. 1932. *Fiction and the Reading Public.* London: Chatto and Windus.

McLuhan, Marshall. 1964. *Understanding Media: The Extensions of Man.* New York: McGraw Hill.

Mellers, Wilfred. 1964. *Music in a New Found Land: Themes and Developments in the History of American Music.* London: Barrie and Rockliff.

Morin, Edgar. 1957. *Les Stars.* Paris: Seuil. (English translation by Richard Howard: New York: Grove Press, 1960.)

Mulvey, Laura, and Peter Wollen. 2008. "From Cinephilia to Film Studies" (interview). In Lee Grieveson and Haidee Wasson (eds.), *Inventing Film Studies.* Durham N.C.: Duke University Press, 217–232.

Newton, Francis [Eric Hobsbawm]. 1959. *The Jazz Scene.* London: MacGibbon and Kee.

Nowell-Smith, Geoffrey, and Christophe Dupin, eds. 2012. *The British Film Institute, the Government and Film Culture, 1933–2000.* Manchester: Manchester University Press.

Procter, James. 2004. *Stuart Hall.* London: Routledge.

Rosenberg, Bernard, and David Manning White, eds. 1957. *Mass Culture; the Popular Arts in America.* Glencoe, Ill.: Free Press.

Rougemont, Denis. 1939. *L'Amour et l'Occident,* Paris: Plon. (English translation (Montgomery Belgion): *Passion and Society.* London: Faber and Faber, 1940 / *Love in the Western World.* New York: Harcourt, Brace and Company, 1940.)

Steele, Tom. 1997. *The Emergence of Cultural Studies: Adult Education, Cultural Politics and the "English" Question.* London: Lawrence and Wishart.

Storey, John. 2000. *Cultural Theory and Popular Culture: An Introduction.* New York: Longman.

Thompson, Denys, ed. 1964. *Discrimination and Popular Culture.* Harmondsworth, England: Penguin.

Thompson, E. P. 1963. *The Making of the English Working Class.* London: Victor Gollancz.

Tucker, Nicholas. 1966. *Understanding the Mass Media.* Cambridge: Cambridge University Press.

Turner, Graeme. 1990. *British Cultural Studies.* London: Unwin Hyman.

Warshow, Robert. 1962. *The Immediate Experience.* New York: Doubleday.

Whannel, Paddy. 1958. "Artist, Critic and Teacher." *Universities and Left Review* 4, 33–35.

Whannel, Paddy. 1959a. "Towards a Positive Criticism of the Mass Media." *Film Teacher* May 17, 28–30.

Whannel, Paddy. 1959b. "Jazz and Its Publics." *Universities and Left Review* 7, 69–70.

Williams, Raymond. 1958. *Culture and Society, 1780–1950.* London: Chatto and Windus.

Williams, Raymond. 1960. *The Long Revolution.* London: Chatto and Windus.

Williams, Raymond. 1962. *Communications.* Harmondsworth, Penguin.

Wolfenstein, Martha, and Nathan Leites. 1950. *Movies: A Psychological Study.* Glencoe, Ill.: Free Press.

Young, Jock. 1971. *The Drugtakers: The Social Meaning of Drug Use.* London: MacGibbon and Kee.

THE POPULAR ARTS

Introduction

The origins of this book can be traced back to the period when we were both teaching in secondary modern schools. This is a sobering experience for any teacher—a time in which he is made acutely aware of the conflict between the norms and expectations of formal education and the complexities of the real world which children and young people inhabit. Some attempt on our part to come to terms with those areas of life and experience which did not fall within the boundaries of 'education' naturally led to many discussions about their cultural and leisure interests. At the same time we felt an urgent need, as teachers, to bring into relation with the concerns of the school our own interests in some of the modern arts, especially the cinema and jazz. During the succeeding years we have been lecturing on and arguing about the cinema and the mass media with a variety of audiences—film societies, teacher training colleges, youth clubs and youth leaders, adult education classes, students in further and higher education. The arguments in this book grew directly out of that experience.

In recent years there has developed an interest in the social and cultural aspects of the mass media. This is both a debate about the media themselves—about the place and nature of art and communication—and about, broadly, the 'quality of life' in our society. Naturally we have been involved with both aspects of this debate—with the general discussion about cultural change, and with the problems of relating these topics directly to the classroom. Our original intention was to produce a book which could have been used by a teacher who already had some idea of what he was trying to do in this field. This would have contained examples with some guidelines for discussion, together with lists of available materials—a practical handbook. But the more we looked at the problem, the clearer it became to us that the gap between the general debate and the classroom was still too wide.

We have therefore produced a book which tries to bridge this gap. We have not tried to advance general and theoretical arguments about 'mass culture', the 'mass society' or 'mass communication'. On the other hand, this book cannot be used directly with a class, though we move some way towards this by proposing a number of teaching projects, and by offering sources and materials and a selective reference section which we hope can be of immediate service to teachers. But the book is now aimed more widely— to the teacher and the educationist, of course, but also to the general reader who is concerned about these problems in an 'educational' sense, using the term in its broadest context. Thus we have dealt with a wide range of material, but our selection of themes has been guided by their educational relevance. We have discussed a host of examples, but we have paid attention to those which might have special meaning and significance for a young audience. Where we have touched on the more general or theoretical aspects of the problem, we have tried to give the discussion an educational slant. In the central section, where we make a critical examination of various examples of material offered by the media, grouped in terms of particular themes, we have tried to suggest connections and to conduct the critical argument in such a way as to indicate the educational approach which we believe ought to underpin any work in this area. Both the detailed examples and the extensive use of quotations and references to other work will, we hope, suggest particular teaching approaches, though we have reserved more practical proposals for the end.

One of the problems facing anyone writing about the mass media is that so much of the material is ephemeral. The danger of going rapidly out of date could have been avoided by writing in more general terms, but this is precisely the approach which we believe to be least helpful; generalizations are really only useful in this field when supported by reference to detailed examples: already, far too much written on this subject has behind it nothing of the direct response to watching a film, or the actual experience of listening to a pop song òr looking at television. The risk that these references will be wasted because the material is often so weak and transient is somewhat minimized by the approach adopted, since within each of the themes discussed we have stressed work of some quality, material with the power to last. This is not an opportunist tactic; it is central to the main thesis of the book. In terms of actual quality (and it is with this, rather than with 'effects', that we are principally concerned) the struggle between what is good and worth while and what is shoddy and debased is not a struggle *against* the modern forms of communication, but a conflict *within* these media. Our concern is with the difficulty which most of us experience in distinguishing the one from the other, particularly when we are dealing with new media, new means of expression, in a new, and often confusing, social and cultural situation. This book attempts to develop a critical method for handling these problems of value and evaluation in the media. We have had, of course, to deal extensively with inferior work, but even when the specific examples discussed may soon vanish, the formulae on which they are based are likely to remain for some time.

The debt we owe to many writers in this field is recognized in the use we have made of their ideas in our argument and the direct references we have made to their work in our text. Our hope is that the reader will study this body of work for himself. But we wish to make specific reference here to the work of Richard Hoggart and Raymond Williams. They have made a major contribution to this whole debate, and our debt, directly and indirectly, to them is immense. We have gained a great deal from discussions with colleagues engaged in lecturing, teaching and writing about the media, especially Brian Groombridge, Alan Lovell, Peter Harcourt, Lawrence Burton, Boleslaw Sulik, Jim Kitses, Laurie Stenhouse, Anne Mercer, Norman Fruchter and Roy Knight. We owe another kind of debt to those who have sponsored classes, courses, seminars and discussions in this area, and who were bold enough to encourage and initiate work before the subject itself had become so popular: in particular, Stanley Reed of the British Film Institute, Fred Flower, Principal of Kingsway Day College, Gerald Collier, Principal of the College of the Venerable Bede, Durham, and Norman Arnold, Principal Lecturer in Liberal Studies at the Chelsea College of Science. The chapter on the thriller novel was strengthened by access to an unpublished study by Harold Silver. We are especially grateful to Roy Shaw, Graham Martin and Marghanita Laski for the valuable criticisms and suggestions they made to us during the early stages of writing. Our thanks are due to Jeannie Semple, Barbara Negri and Brenda Davies for checking some of the factual details, to Margaret Shields for helping with the bibliography and to Charles Marshall for making detailed corrections to the manuscript. We should like to acknowledge the immense amount of work, time and energy put into the project by Kay Whannel and Suzy Benghiat, who typed numerous drafts and collected many of the examples. With Garry Whannel, now aged fourteen and a sharper television critic than the authors, they watched more bad TV programmes, suffered more noisy records and sat through more bad films than even the most dedicated critics ought to expect.

Finally, we owe a great deal to Ann Howgate of Hutchinson, who did some ruthless editorial work on a first draft and made many useful criticisms at all stages of writing, and to John Stevens who accepted with such calm the fact that he commissioned one book and received another.

PW and SH

PART ONE

Definitions

I

The Media and Society

I have only reached the stage of firmly opting for any straight hour's worth of mass-culture in preference to again being told about it.

KINGSLEY AMIS, *Encounter*, July 1960

The story is told of an ancient tribe whose people lived a comfortable and unchanging existence. The children of the tribe were brought up in the traditions of their fathers and were taught how to fish in clear streams and how to hunt the sabre-toothed tiger. Then the snows came and the streams became muddy and the sabre-toothed tiger moved south. But the tribe preserved their traditional ways. They cleared a small part of the stream so that the children could continue to fish, and they stuffed a tiger's head so that they could learn to hunt. Then a radical young tribesman approached the council and asked why, instead, the children were not taught to fish in muddy streams and hunt the polar bear, which had recently begun to ravage the villages. But the council was angry. 'We have always taught how to fish in clear streams and how to hunt the sabre-toothed tiger. These are the classical disciplines. Besides,' they added, 'the curriculum is overcrowded.'

In recent years two social changes have excited considerable comment and controversy in the educational world. The first is the revolution in communications brought about by the development of sound recording, cinematography, sound broadcasting and television, and the use of these media to provide information, art and entertainment. The second is the change in the attitudes of young people—the so-called 'teenage' revolution—which has been particularly marked since the end of the war.

19

The first is the direct outcome of the industrial revolution—the application of the techniques of multiple transmission and wide dissemination to the printed word and the reproduced sound and image. This technical transformation has been paralleled by a general growth in democracy and the spread of literacy. Yet the process has been a long and continuous one: it began with the invention of printing. The second is a more recent development and can be identified, not so much with the industrial revolution as a whole, but rather with one particular phase of that revolution—the phase of high consumption and increased leisure which has become a feature of some societies in the middle of this century. During this phase a widespread change in attitudes and style reveals itself among the younger generation—a change which reflects partly their enhanced economic status and partly the changing design of social values in the society as a whole.

Increasingly we are coming to see how the two processes interact. At the simplest level the media do touch the lives of a great number of people in the society. If we take the coverage of sound radio, the two television services, the national press and the sale of magazines and popular papers, and the cinema distribution chains, we have *four* major national communication grids—variable, it is true, for different parts of the country, but covering roughly every area to some degree, and every sector of the community. More particularly, the increased spending power of the younger generation, and the development of something approaching a discernible 'youth culture', means that a fairly direct connection can be made between the younger generation and the media. In some fields the media are sustained economically by the adolescent market, and much of the material communicated is intended for that age group. The media provide young people with information and ideas about the society into which they are maturing. They can test few of these descriptions and interpretations against their own experience. At the deeper level, the use of the media to provide imaginative experiences through various forms of art and entertainment has a modifying impact upon young people's attitudes and values.

These changes cannot be held apart from education. They are bound to alter its character and modify its content and may even force us to re-examine its aims. Part of the teacher's task is to give his pupils some understanding of the world in which they live. But the media are changing the world in ways important enough for a study of these changes to become part of formal education. More than that; the attitudes of young people are changing. They mature earlier, in some ways their response is more sophisticated, and they are more acutely conscious of the differences between the world of the classroom and that of work and leisure. This alters their expectations of, and their attitudes towards, education. Changes are involved, therefore, not only in what we teach but in how we teach.

There is, in fact, a growing recognition that the media of mass communication play such a significant role in society, and especially in the lives of young people, that the school must embrace the study of their organization, content and impact. But there is little agreement about how such studies should be carried out. Just what shall be studied? With what precise purpose? In what relationship to the established subjects? Ultimately the answer will depend upon our attitude towards these media, our social thinking about the kind of society in which they wield their influence and, in particular, our response to the things the media offer—individual films, television programmes, popular songs, etc.

Many teachers feel that the media represent a threat to standards and traditional values. 'School and home', said Sir Ronald Gould, Secretary of the National Union of Teachers, 'are often oases constantly threatened by the surrounding desert.' It is easy to see how this attitude has developed. The teacher is at the point of interaction between many conflicting social and cultural pressures. He may regard education as justifying itself, a means towards securing individual fulfilment, but he will be made aware of the social pressures for education to provide 'good citizens' or 'skilled producers', and he will be conscious of the fact that for many of his pupils what they are taught seems little related either to their emotional needs or to the kind of work they are likely to do. He is asked to be the guardian of a cultural tradition to which he does not always wholly belong. As the entry to the teaching profession widens, we see new tensions arising—tensions between the teacher's own background (which may be closer to that of his pupils than he would care to admit), the goals of the professional class to which he is a newcomer, and the culture of the school. The last of these no longer represents the coherent body of knowledge and standards it once did. The cultural map is no longer so clearly defined. The older culture has been put under pressure, not only from the new media, but also from the art and experiment of the *avant-garde*. But with the erosion of the old academic standards how is he to distinguish what is really new and original from the meretricious? How is he to separate the real line of continuity in culture from the many *ersatz* offerings? How is he to distinguish serious intellectual work from mere shifts in taste and fashion? An intellectual minority works to clarify the situation but is itself subject to the same confusions, and its concerns and debates frequently seem remote from the insistent demands of the classroom. Given this situation (which many training colleges have all too inadequately prepared him for) the teacher has to fend for himself, with the result that much that is taught in the school is an uncertain mixture of the progressive and the middlebrow.

These problems are intensified by the material situation—the out-of-date buildings, the understaffed schools, the overcrowded classrooms. Such conditions add to the psychological strain of teaching and intensify the teacher's feeling that the society has left him rather unmercifully exposed, that the community is unwilling to accord him the status and rewards he deserves. Experiencing this clash of values, uncertain of his place in society and of the traditional role of teaching, his task appears the more difficult because of the vigorously publicized products of the entertainments industry which appear, at times, so completely to engage the attention of his pupils. In his response to the new media there is considerable justice in the teacher's antagonism. Much that is produced under the name of 'entertainment' is shoddy and third-rate, and some of it is profoundly debased. Yet one can understand Kingsley Amis's remark (at the head of this chapter). So much of the criticism against the mass media seems uninformed, the attacks mis-directed, at times little more than an outburst of irritation and anger at a *whole* situation, where the products of the media serve as a scapegoat.

If we are going to deal adequately with the problem as it affects the classroom we must define it carefully; even the more considered statements contain assumptions that should be carefully examined. These assumptions appear to group themselves around three broad and seemingly contradictory approaches. As an example of the first approach we might take the Resolution passed at the NUT Annual Conference in 1960:

Conference whilst recognizing the vital part played by teachers in developing the moral and cultural standards of the nation and its children, considers that this is a task in which others must co-operate.

Although today more young people than ever are actively engaged in intellectual pursuits and appreciate or participate in the creation of art, literature, music or drama, Conference believes that a determined effort must be made to counteract the debasement of standards which result from the misuse of press, radio, cinema and television; the deliberate exploitation of violence and sex; and the calculated appeal to self-interest.

It calls especially upon those who use and control the media of mass communication, and upon parents, to support the efforts of teachers in an attempt to prevent the conflict which too often arises between the values inculcated in the classroom and those encountered by young people in the world outside.

This was an important Resolution. It was the first time the issue had arisen in such a form at a major conference and it led directly to the NUT Special Conference, *Popular Culture and Personal Responsibility*, which attempted intelligently to bring together teachers, critics, controllers of the media and creative artists working within them. But it is unfortunate that the Resolution puts the entire blame on the providers. The prime responsibility of the providers should, of course, be clear. Nevertheless, it would have been encouraging if the Resolution had recognized that teaching has a more positive role, and that there are educational inadequacies to account for as well. No doubt if the Conference had listed the 'values inculcated in the classroom' they would have been unexceptionable. However, we could benefit from a more precise statement of what those values are, and of how they have stood the passage of time. And there is surely something to say about the *way* those values are handled, and of what often prevents them from making a serious impact upon young people. It is not only that these values are under pressure from newer, perhaps more meretricious, ones. It is that they are often handled in such a way that they fail to connect. They are offered as valid because they fell within a tradition, not because they are still active and alive and relate to contemporary experience. One of the reasons why the Special Conference itself was only a partial success was that many teachers present were too eager to think in terms of censorship and control, to defend the *restrictionist* approach, and to attribute to education a purely passive role.

In this respect the terms used in the Crowther Report are preferable:

There is undoubtedly a duty on those who wield such great power to use it responsibly. That is a matter for the whole community, and not especially for educationalists. There is also in our view a duty on those who are charged with the responsibility for education to see that teenagers, who are at the most insecure and suggestible stage of their lives, are not suddenly exposed to the full force of the 'mass media' without some counterbalancing assistance.

The Crowther Report does establish a better balance of blame than the NUT Resolution. But a more fundamental objection can be made to both statements in the way they define the problem itself. Both passages imply a clear distinction between the two cultures—the culture of the mass media and the traditional culture of the sophisticated arts. And both see these as standing in opposition to each other.

The language of the Crowther Report is that of threat and menace—young people 'exposed to the full force of the mass media'. In the NUT Resolution, the 'counter-balancing assistance' is defined exclusively in terms of the traditional culture—'art, literature, music or drama'. The opposition is expressed in even sharper form in a Report on *Sex and Violence in Modern Media* published by the Educational Institute of Scotland:

> It should not be forgotten that while sales of 'pop' music grow so do sales of records of good music, and the increasing attendance of teenagers at classical concerts is no less a sign of the times than the yelling bobby-soxers waiting at the stage door for their latest rock-and-roll idol. The theatre too in Scotland, though not exactly flourishing, is in a healthier condition than it has been for some years. From these and other indications of a vigorous cultural life we conclude that many of the younger generation are well able to find worth-while leisure interests for themselves.

'Pop' music is seen here as universally the opposite of—implicitly the enemy of—'good' music. There is no recognition that popular music is of different kinds which vary in achievement and aim, or that each may have its own standards. 'Pop' here may well cover anything from jazz to dance music: 'good' music anything from the light classics to Bach. Much of this kind of writing is too generalized to be useful. It is not really in touch with its subject. The use of an old-fashioned term, 'bobby-soxer', is as revealing as the way some educational journals still use the word 'crooner'.

It would be unfair to suggest, however, that either the NUT Resolution or the Educational Institute betray an outright and unqualified hostility to the mass media. The NUT Resolution refers rather to the 'mis-use of press, radio, cinema and television'. Even so, the *right* use goes unstated. The tone of the Resolution suggests a rather narrow definition; we suspect it would be improving and didactic. Here, too, the implied assumption is of a clearly defined and unchanging traditional culture. A not uncommon attitude among teachers is that the media ought to be used essentially as transmitters of that traditional culture—more documentary on television, and more respectful adaptations of the classics in the cinema. Again, the Educational Institute Report makes the point explicit:

> There are of course honourable exceptions to the ruling trend. We still have quality newspapers which uphold the best traditions of British journalism, and the British Broadcasting Corporation, which has been animated by a high sense of public duty from its birth, has struggled hard to preserve its standards in the face of competition from commercial television.

We need hold no special brief for the *Mirror* or the *Express* to see that there is a peculiar blindness here to the faults and shortcomings of the quality press. It was, after all, *The Times* that made one of the most open appeals to snobbery in its 'Top People' advertising campaign—a campaign which, in its opening phase, was seriously intended and only later took on the defensive tone of irony. In its treatment of the Pilkington Report—a document close, one assumes, to the point of view of the Institute —the *Daily Telegraph* was distinguished from the *Sketch* by its typography and layout, but hardly at all by the quality of its arguments. The tribute to the BBC is, perhaps, better earned. All the same, there is a very limiting conception of broadcasting implied in the phrase 'animated by a high sense of public duty'. This was hardly the impulse behind *The Goon Show*, for example. Yet *The Goon Show* is very relevant here; the success of broadcasting should be judged not simply in terms of making the established works available to a wider public but also by the achievement of people like Spike Milligan who have used the medium in original ways. (This applies with even more force to the cinema.) The Educational Institute Report indeed recognizes that there is a body of popular work that has its own value:

> Detective stories, thrillers and westerns, for example, have long been respectable and many of the great as well as the humble have owned that reading of this kind provides their favourite form of relaxation.

What is probably in mind here, though, is the old-style mystery story or the clean-living outdoor adventure yarn—tolerated because they are diversions, strictly for 'relaxation', as harmless as crossword puzzles or playing bridge, and somewhat grudgingly included, it seems, because they have been made 'respectable'—and by the 'great' rather than the 'humble'. Again, the tone excludes any kind of vigorous popular art that might challenge or excite. More relevant references might have been made to the singing of Ella Fitzgerald, the novels of Raymond Chandler or the musical films of Stanley Donen. But the moment we make such specific references we can see how the sharp distinction between traditional and popular culture begins to break down.

In opposition to these rather limiting standards are the views of those who seem willing to accept almost anything provided it is called entertainment. There is usually an assumed distinction between the serious matters which call for study and discrimination and those classed as escapist diversions. On the one hand there is serious art designed to educate, and on the other there is entertainment which provides distraction for our idle moments. It would therefore be foolish, it is argued, to bring to bear on the latter the language of critical analysis. The label 'entertainment' is assumed to absolve us from making judgements. In some youth clubs, for example, there is a striking contrast between the 'activity' periods where there is an attempt to apply standards, and the 'leisure' periods when the juke-box uninhibitedly blasts forth the values of Tin Pan Alley. Sometimes the distinction is underlined by applying a rule that club members are only allowed the privilege of a jive session if they also attend one of the more improving and approved activities.

The composer Malcolm Arnold, speaking at the NUT Conference *Popular Culture and Personal Responsibility*, said:

Nobody is in any way a better person morally or in any other way for liking Beethoven more than Adam Faith. . . . Of course the person who likes both is in a very happy position since he is able to enjoy much more in this life than a lot of other people.

One can see the honest intention here to be fair to pop music, but the random use of Adam Faith as an example reveals how prevailing standards can be adopted uncritically. Adam Faith has an interesting personality, but as a singer of popular songs he is by any serious standards far down the list. By serious standards we mean those that might be legitimately applied to popular music—the standards set, for example, by Frank Sinatra or Ray Charles. But this is to introduce the element of judgement, bringing with it, inevitably, questions of value; and the idea of making such judgements about entertainment is often resisted; they are seen as a rather stuffy application of critical methods that do not really apply.

Such resistance often springs from the wider belief that there is a clear difference between the way we respond to art and the way we respond to situations in life. There is assumed to be a real world of work understood in political and economic terms and then, independently, we have descriptions of this objective reality in the form of art and other kinds of communication. The point is made by Raymond Williams:

> We degrade art and learning by supposing that they are always second-hand activities: that there is life, and then afterwards there are these accounts of it . . . the struggle to learn, to describe, to understand, to educate, is a central and necessary part of our humanity. This struggle is not begun, at secondhand, after reality has occurred. It is, in itself, a major way in which reality is continually formed and changed. What we call society is not only a network of political and economic arrangements, but also a process of learning and communication.
>
> *Communications*

The divorce between art and life is often reflected in school as a distinction between the 'work' subjects, which prepare us for making a living and in which there is an emphasis on intellectual discipline, and the 'recreative' subjects which prepare us for our leisure time and in which the emphasis is on 'creativity' and 'appreciation'. The arts come to be regarded as sugar on the pill, relegated to the fringes of our lives, rather than as essential ways in which we can articulate experiences. Good Taste is acquired as an additional accomplishment in a kind of finishing-school process once the business of understanding the real world has been completed. This is the *well-rounded-man* view of culture which always involves the separation of moral values from what are called the aesthetic qualities. It is a view that has its ready allies in some of the providers of mass entertainment and is very clearly expressed in the following quotation from Norman Collins:

> There is a good jazz and bad jazz. Good classical music and bad classical music. Good music-hall and bad music-hall. Good sermons and bad sermons. Good football and bad football. And, no matter how bad the jazz, the classical music, the music-hall, the sermons or the football no element of *moral* badness is involved. It is purely an aesthetic and not an ethical term. Prigs are of both kinds. There is no hard dividing line. It is strange, however, how frequently the aesthetic prig begins invoking the ethical values. Dire social consequences are predicted where none will accrue. Phrases like 'morally enervating' are used when morality simply does not happen to be involved.
>
> *Twentieth Century*, November 1959

With the argument taken to this point we are, it would seem, a long way from the language of moral censure used in the NUT Resolution and the Educational Institute Report. Standing somewhat between these attitudes of hostility and acceptance is the strategy defined by Brian Groombridge as 'cultural opportunism'. Many teachers, youth workers and churchmen, having become highly conscious of the gap between the generations, seek to make contact with the young by embracing their leisure interests. The popular press carries regular features on the more lurid examples such as juke-boxes at the altar and rocking-and-rolling parsons. The underlying intention is, of course, to develop in the young people a wider range of interests and to lead them towards an appreciation of 'better things'. But the interest in popular entertainment is often an assumed one and the danger for those who adopt this strategy is that in their anxiety not to be thought 'square' they will come to accept not merely the valid place of entertainment but the standards provided by publicity and the mass-production machine. An ATV programme, characteristic of a current trend, brought together Adam Faith and the Archbishop of York, Dr Donald Coggan, to talk about young people and religion. An interesting confrontation: Adam Faith is obviously a sincere and intelligent young man, the Archbishop is known to be outspoken; religion is a controversial subject. As it turned out, however, there was no confrontation. Faith's rather earnest questions were continually side-stepped by what appeared to be the Archbishop's anxiety to prove that they were both really on the same side. The gap between the generations evaporated. The conflict between the teenager and religious faith never emerged. The lasting impression was that, for the teenager, believing in God and being in love were practically the same thing.

The opportunist approach, although seemingly more open-minded, is basically a modified version of the idea that the art and entertainment provided by the new media are a threat to the traditional culture. The educational tactics are different but the description of the cultural scene is the same. We have seen that this description is uninformed by a considered response to specific examples, that it fails to make the necessary distinctions as to value and kind, that it adopts too readily large and misleading generalizations and that it employs moral categories too clumsy to catch the subtleties of style. But if we reject such a hostile attitude, equally we must reject the uncritical acceptance of the products of the media merely because they can be classed as entertainment. These extreme positions are two sides of the same coin: in neither case is there any attempt at judgement. The sharp distinction between ethical and aesthetic qualities assumed by Norman Collins does not exist. The moral statements made by art are made in aesthetic terms; that is to say they are embodied in the manner of presentation. To discover the moral meanings in art and entertainment we must first respond to them in their own terms. The point will emerge more clearly if we look at a particular example.

The Third Man series (BBC Television) is a fairly characteristic piece of 'escapist entertainment'. Apart from the theme music and the name of the hero, Harry Lime, it has little to do with the original film. In the TV series, Lime is a reformed character who has set up as a private investigator. He does very well and in one of the programmes remarks, 'Honesty is a great racket.' He is in fact Harry Lime Inc.—one of the essentials of the plot is that large sums of money change hands. The series combines opulence (butlers bringing in the tea, old masters on the wall) with cosmopolitan gloss (cocktail bars and international airports). At the end of one programme the heroine appears with her fifth husband—a prince. 'I chase money—she chases men,' comments Lime. Earlier he has said to the girl, 'You're merchandise like diamonds or a Rembrandt'—a remark which more or less sums up the value the series places on both women and art, and which was once enshrined in a concluding image of a woman caressing her cheek with a bag of diamonds.

Harry Lime is one of the few heroes who prefers cash to getting the girl at the end. This is not to say that sex is absent, only that it is firmly dissociated from love or any permanent relationship. Lime goes through his affairs with a dead-pan dreariness that perfectly matches the clichés of the décor. In one programme he meets a girl (who has nothing to do with the plot) at an airport bar. They indulge in what is no doubt meant to be sophisticated talk. 'Talk to me,' she says, 'maybe we'll fall in love or something.' She tells him that she never eats because food bores her. At the end of the episode they meet again while Lime is waiting for his plane, and she tells him that she never sleeps either. When asked what she does do, she makes no reply but slowly runs her hand over Lime's lips, chin and expensive suit. He misses his plane.

The production values of these films, with their drum rolls, zither clangs and crude camera movements for dramatic effects, and their glossy picture of life, are similar to the values of the commercials. It is impossible to describe *The Third Man* in neutral terms. The values and moral attitudes are embodied in the style itself; they are not imported from the outside in the process of judgement. In television and the cinema, as in literature, style carries the meaning; it is not the neutral dressing-up of subject matter. The point was made admirably clear by Karel Reisz when talking about the shooting of a jive sequence in his film about a youth club, *We are the Lambeth Boys*. He showed that such a sequence could be treated in a number of ways. It could, for example, be given excitement by the use of large close-ups of feet and faces edited together to produce a fast rhythmic shower of images on the screen. Reisz rejected this method on the grounds that it would falsify his own experience—the dancing in the youth club was more relaxed and informal. A contrast of style is provided by the stills from *We are the Lambeth Boys* and *Violent Playground* (Plate 1). In the second film the dancing is presented as a rather frenzied and orgiastic affair. In both cases the style clearly reveals the attitude of the film-maker.

Because questions of value are bound up with the style of a film, because they are deep in its texture and not simply to be found in the manipulation of plot or the choice of subject, they enter into films of all kinds. Most cinema-goers will remember with pleasure the barn dance in *Seven Brides for Seven Brothers*, the opening scene of *Guys and Dolls*, and Gene Kelly's dance in the rain in *Singing in the Rain*. The quality of these and other sequences in good musicals is only achieved through sheer professional skill based on hours of rigorous training and rehearsal. But this by itself does not account for our pleasure. What we respond to is the sense of spontaneity in the performances. The dancers seem to be spontaneously expressing their feelings. *The quality of these feelings is therefore an element in our pleasure.* It is only when a style emerges which is shaped by feeling as well as by skill and technical ability that we get a liberating response.

The argument advanced so far is based on the assumption that art and entertainment have some effect on us. But this is something that is frequently challenged on the grounds that such evidence as exists proves little either way. Dr Mark Abrams has argued that the 'consumption of the mass media' has been at a high level for a long time and that the emergence of television, for example, has made little difference because watching TV has merely replaced similar types of activity such as the reading of comics. He has further argued that the content of the media has remained stable throughout this period. It is true, of course, that in any comparison of the inter-war years with today, the pop songs show the same preoccupation with love, movies still deal in boy-meets-girl stories, and the cowboy and the gangster have been with us all the time. But this is very superficial. A closer, more detailed, examination would reveal significant differences in all these fields. *M Squad* is not the same thing as a Douglas Fairbanks adventure film. There is a difference between Henry Hall's dance orchestra and *Juke Box Jury*, and a particularly significant difference between the stars of the pre-war period (Garbo, Gable, Taylor, etc.) and those of the post-war years (Brando, Dean, Bardot, etc.). Another point made by Dr Abrams is that 'mass communication acts usually as an agent of reinforcement of existing predispositions and not as an agent of change'. But this seems to be saying more than it does. Reinforcing (or undermining) 'existing predispositions' is surely an important part of change. All of us have predispositions which we would prefer not to have reinforced. Nevertheless it is worth keeping in mind that the media have a secondary rather than a primary role. We should beware of leaping from content analysis to effects and of assuming any direct and mechanistic connection between the media and social behaviour. Greed, envy, snobbery and so on are in us all; they are not the invention of advertising agencies.

There *is*, however, evidence about the way in which the media can affect attitudes and values. We will draw upon some of this research in later chapters. Sufficient here to take two examples from the fullest existing study, the Nuffield Foundation research into the effects of television on children, which was conducted by Dr Hilde Himmelweit.

Viewers seem to be affected by the materialistic outlook inherent in many television plays. When considering what sort of adult they themselves would like to be, they tend to think more of the things they would like to own than of personal qualities or the work they would like to do.

Television and the Child

The second quotation also concerns the young person's image of adult life:

> Our data show that, compared with controls, adolescent viewers, especially girls, were more worried, indeed were even frightened about growing up, leaving school, leaving home, taking up their first job and getting married.

ibid.

How we interpret such evidence is another matter. It could well be argued that it is no bad thing for adolescent girls to be disturbed by the thought of marriage. Marghanita Laski has suggested that researchers might well investigate the distinction between useful and harmful disturbance. The quotation illustrates the way in which research evidence can conceal value judgements.

The discussion about effects is bedevilled by the assumption, so frequently made, that they are *bound* to be bad. This distorts the argument and encourages people to think in the crude and negative terms of censorship. Sir John Wolfenden, former Vice-Chancellor of Reading University and Chairman of the ITA Children's Advisory Committee, has been quoted as saying:

> Westerns shared with historical costume plays the status of being possibly real but outside the child's own experience. This degree of unreality made them, for all practical purposes, aseptic.

Times Educational Supplement, 6 April 1962

But it is an odd defence of the time and money spent on TV westerns to argue that they make no impact. It is the merit of the superior westerns of the cinema that they are not aseptic. Surely the value of art and entertainment is that it does affect us? It is the quality of the effect that matters. The fact that no one has proved a TV programme positively harmful is not by itself sufficient justification for continuing it. We should be asking of these new means of communication not what harm they might be doing, but how they can be used more creatively. We should be seeking to train a more demanding audience. In these terms the argument about research and effects is frequently a red herring so far as the teacher is concerned. There is no reason why our attitude here should differ fundamentally from that which we adopt in our approach to the older forms of communication. No one has yet suggested that we conduct a research programme to prove scientifically that Shakespeare, Dickens and Lawrence have an effect upon us before we approve the teaching of literature.

The debate about mass communications is all too frequently conducted at the level of generalities, and much of the writing on the subject has little sense of a personal response. It is not even clear what is meant by terms like 'mass media' or 'mass communications'. Experiences, attitudes and values are communicated in a variety of ways. Which of these do we include when we speak of mass communications? Do we, for example, include—along with the cinema, TV, press, etc.—the large chain stores like Marks and Spencers which have so obviously influenced taste? Indeed, if we put the emphasis on the mass or multiple production of cultural goods, we must include all books, newspapers, gramophone records, etc., Tolstoy as well as Spillane, *The Times* as well as the *Daily Mirror*, Beethoven as well as The Beatles.

Even if we think in terms of numbers, of the size of the audience, the distinction is not a sharp one. The sales of the Bible exceed those of James Hadley Chase; many pornographic books certainly reach fewer people than does the *Spectator*. The problem is further complicated by the fact that some of the media, printing for example, are exclusively means of reproduction; whereas others contain within themselves the possibility of entirely new art forms. In the end we are driven back to a qualitative definition based on critical judgements of individual pieces of work. Such judgements are often dismissed by sociologists as 'subjective' or 'impressionistic'; but there is a difference, surely, between vague opinion and the considered view based on close analysis which presents itself for debate and discussion controlled by 'evidence' from the work in question. True, it is only an opinion, but many of our most important judgements are of this kind. A mental life that did not allow free play to imagination and intuition, that denied the role of speculation and was confined to what could be scientifically proved, would be not merely impoverished but paralysed. The methods of sociological and psychological research are relatively crude and it is often the most important qualities that defy measurement. No one has yet come up with any way of 'proving' that *The Third Man* is bad and *Crime and Punishment* good. There is even a danger in the idea that such a thing is possible; that we might be able to evolve from a body of evidence about effects a formula for producing good art. That this is not a fantasy is proved by the case of the special feature films produced for children, many of which have suffered by being confined in a set of assumptions about how the young respond to movies and what they require from their screen entertainment.

When we leave behind the broad sociological categories and use the evidence of critical judgements we realize that what must be embraced by the term 'mass culture' is art that is machine-produced according to a formula. This has been admirably defined by Clement Greenberg in his essay 'Avant-Garde and Kitsch' (quoted by Dwight MacDonald in *Against the American Grain*) as a formula which 'pre-digests art for the spectator', which 'spares him the effort, provides him with a short cut to the pleasures of art, that detours what is necessarily difficult in the genuine art'. This formula, as Dwight MacDonald adds, 'includes the spectator's reactions in the work itself instead of forcing him to make his own responses'. The important point about such a definition is that it cuts across the commonplace distinctions. It applies to some films but not all, to some TV but not all. It covers segments of the traditional as well as the popular culture. Much academic painting, for example, is produced according to such a formula and so is a good deal of modern art. MacDonald himself has used the definition with considerable force on Hemingway's *Old Man and The Sea* and Thornton Wilder's *Our Town*.

The idea of a uniform mass culture standing in bleak hostility to the traditional virtues is not based on fact, and teaching derived from such an idea is bound to be purely defensive. Its tone will be nagging and disapproving. A teacher fired with the desire merely to expose the second-rate can blunder, resented, into what the young person may regard as his world of private pleasure. At one point the Educational Institute Report makes this revealing comment:

One possible disadvantage of such teaching is, of course, that it requires teachers to be more familiar with the contents of the popular press and of television programmes than many of them would wish to be.

The opportunist teacher who embraces the leisure interests of his pupils in the hope of leading them to higher things is as frequently unsympathetic to the really valuable qualities of popular culture as his colleague who remains resolutely hostile. In neither case is there a genuine response, nor any basis for real judgements. Young people are especially sensitive to the insincerity that is often at the root of such opportunism. Even when this doctrine is presented in its more progressive dress as 'beginning with the child's interests' it remains unsatisfactory. The assumption is that we can begin with jazz but with the intention of moving towards concert music; we can begin with the cinema but only as a stage in developing an interest in the theatre. Now jazz music and the movies have their own special virtues but it is doubtful if these can be revealed when they are regarded only as stepping-stones in a hierarchy of taste. If these virtues are not revealed, if in handling jazz and films we do not confront their essential qualities, then their study will not result in a real growth of awareness.

It is, therefore, on a training in discrimination that we should place our emphasis. We should think of this as a training for a greater awareness, for a sharper attention to subtle meanings. In this sense it should be distinguished from 'raising the level of taste'. Taste-changing goes on all the time. Calendars with kittens in baskets are replaced by prints of Van Gogh's *Sunflowers* and these in turn by Buffet reproductions. But these shifts in fashion can take place without any great increase in pleasure or understanding.

We must also stop talking about the various kinds of art and entertainment as if they were necessarily competitive. Popular music, for example, has its own standards. Ella Fitzgerald is a highly polished professional entertainer who within her own sphere could hardly be better. Clearly it would be inappropriate to compare her to Maria Callas; they are not aiming at the same thing. The popular singer, especially one with a jazz background, uses her voice in ways that would be illegitimate for a concert singer. Equally it is not useful to say that the music of Cole Porter is inferior to that of Beethoven. The music of Porter and Beethoven is not of equal value, but Porter was not making an unsuccessful attempt to create music comparable to Beethoven's. Different kinds of music offer different sorts of satisfaction. If we can begin to recognize different aims and to assess varying achievements with defined limits we shall get rid of much of the mishmash in between.

A true training in discrimination is concerned with pleasure. It places its emphasis on what can be gained from the best that is available. It is careful not to define the best in narrow terms: by 'best' it will mean Tony Hancock rather than the *Brains Trust*, *The Gunfighter* rather than the filmed classic, *Born Yesterday* rather than *Lust for Life*. Already useful work is being done in this field in a number of schools and colleges, particularly in relation to the cinema. (We will draw upon this in later chapters.) There is, however, an earlier tradition derived primarily from the text book *Culture and Environment*, written by F. R. Leavis and Denys Thompson and published in 1933. Within this tradition a great deal of valuable work has been done, especially in the teaching of English, and anyone concerned with the problems of education and the cultural environment owes an immense debt to these pioneers. But this work is based on a conservative, indeed pessimistic, view of society. It contrasts the organic culture of preindustrial England with the mass-produced culture of today. This is a perspective that has produced a penetrating critique of industrial society but as a guide to action it is restrictive. The old culture has gone because the way of life that produced it has gone. The rhythms of work have been permanently altered and the enclosed small-scale communities are vanishing. It may be important to resist unnecessary increases in scale and to re-establish local initiatives where we can; but if we wish to re-create a genuine popular culture we must seek out the points of growth within the society that now exists. With the growth of larger political and economic units, the increase in social mobility and the declining role of the family, the media might be made to provide a range of imaginative experiences which could help young people to grapple with some of the problems they face as a result of maturing quickly and moving at an early age into a more open society. At any rate, we cannot begin to conceive of creative uses of the media if we are thinking wistfully of a past age which it is all too easy to picture in dangerously romantic terms. 'All that can be done, it must be realized,' wrote Q. D. Leavis, 'must take the form of resistance by an armed and conscious minority.' This is too limiting a view—especially for those who teach the majority school population. To be fair, of course, *Culture and Environment* dealt exclusively with the written word, and its destructive criticism of advertising and popular reading-matter has to be seen in the context of the positive teaching of literature. But once we take in the cinema, for example, we can no longer think in defensive terms. No one has to be defended against de Sica, Bergman or Antonioni.

What continues to be important in the *Culture and Environment* tradition is the emphasis on analysis and the concern for humane values. Analysis as a discipline and method is still rather suspect in the teaching profession. It is true that some of the work done under the heading of literary analysis is niggling and mean-spirited. But we should not spurn a method merely because it has been misapplied. It is sometimes assumed that analysis with its insistence on close attention to the text and its preoccupation with style turns the study of literature into an exercise for pedants, excluding all the values that make it a humanizing influence. But the text is studied to see what the writer has to say, the style is examined to reveal those very values. The point is made by Dr Leavis in his essay 'Sociology and Literature':

> For to insist that literary criticism is, or should be, a specific discipline of intelligence is not to suggest that a serious interest in literature can confine itself to the kind of intensive local analysis associated with 'practical criticism'—to the scrutiny of the 'words on the page' in their minute relations, their effects of imagery, and so on: a real literary interest is an interest in man, society and civilization, and its boundaries cannot be drawn; the adjective is not a circumscribing one.
>
> *The Common Pursuit*

Alongside this kind of analysis the teacher will, of course, make provision for all sorts of practical and creative work—painting, imaginative writing, drama, film-making and so on. But in the hands of a teacher generous and open in his own responses analysis can also be creative. The work of David Holbrook in English teaching is relevant here; also articles in the journal, *The Use of English*. Raymond Williams's *Reading and Criticism* provides a useful introduction to its application at adult education level. Some work along these lines is also being carried out in the study of the cinema, and the British Film Institute pamphlet *Film Teaching* describes four courses. We need not accept either the particular judgements of these writers and teachers or the social philosophy that underlies them to see the value and relevance of their work and how it can guide our handling of the art and entertainment provided by the more recently developed communications media. It would, of course, be foolish to make large claims for this popular culture. The cinema, by far the most mature and expressive of these forms, has produced remarkable work in its short history; but it cannot be compared to literature either in volume or quality of achievement. Nevertheless, the best films do offer experiences comparable in kind to those offered by literature, and they can be discussed with similar profit. This can be established by looking at an example in detail.

The Polish film *A Generation*, directed by Andrej Wajda, provides a direct commentary on some of the issues we discuss in this chapter, particularly as they affect young people. It handles experiences ranging from the personal and private to the social and public. It is sufficiently rich and subtle to make a detailed discussion worth while.

A Generation is set in wartime Poland. The hero is a boy called Stach who, with his friends, leads a shiftless existence in a derelict suburb of Warsaw. As the film opens we see them stealing coal from a passing German train in a spirit of adolescent adventure. But the reality of war breaks through and one of the boys is shot. Stach is befriended by Sekula, an older man, who finds him a job in a workshop and introduces him to Dorata, a young girl who leads a Youth Resistance Group. Stach joins the group and takes part in its actions during the rising of the Jews in the Ghetto. Stach and Dorata fall in love; but later she is captured by the Germans, and he is left alone to form a new group of young resistance fighters.

What has surprised a number of teachers who have used this film is the response of young audiences and the extent to which they identify with the hero. Despite the gap between their own experience and the world of occupied Poland they recognize this boy. The film dramatizes some of the tensions and doubts they feel within themselves. The Generation of the title has references beyond national frontiers. The response is perhaps, first of all, to simple expressions of youthful energy—the enthusiasm with which Stach and his friends embark on the enterprise of stealing a lorry. But Stach finds himself in a world that has lost its bearings. The adventure with the lorry ends in death and tragedy. The film records the boy's growth to manhood, a maturing quickened by the tragedies of war in which he discovers not merely a cause but an inner strength and dignity. But the affirmation is not a simple one, and in the discussion of motive and behaviour young people can become articulate about their own allegiances. When they talk about the quality of Stach's idealism and the way such an impulse can be satisfied or frustrated, they will also be talking about some of the problems of their own lives.

Wajda is a romantic artist but the images of war are not glamorized. In the opening shot of the film the camera moves over the dilapidated shacks where a group of workmen are aimlessly kicking a ball about on a piece of waste ground. Later, the Germans visit the workshop, and to distract and appease them an old workman bounces up and down on a bed. As they leave and he moves his bulk from the bed, we see the tired self-disgust on his face. In such scenes, in the shots of the bare walls of factories with their fragments of posters, and run-down cafés with hints of black-marketeering, we are made to feel the draining away of the energy and self-respect of an occupied people. The handling of the ever-present violence of the war is controlled and disciplined. A mere handful of images impresses upon us the tragic heroism of the Ghetto uprising. Through a hole in a wall a pall of smoke is seen rising in the distance as Sekula walks towards it. This is followed by a closer shot of the burning buildings beyond the motionless line of waiting German soldiers. Later, a young Jew seeks and is refused shelter and walks away into the night. Finally, as the young resistance fighters meet at the fair-ground, we see past the swings the smoke from the Ghetto now dying to a wisp in the air.

These images of loss and defeat are contrasted with the poignant idealism of the resistance group: the two elements are interwoven in one of the most memorable sequences (Plate 2). After Stach and Dorata have met for the first time (in a beautifully organized scene outside a church in the market-place) we are introduced to a meeting of the resistance group. They take an oath in a spirit of romantic dedication. This is followed by a series of stark and compelling images of the meaning of resistance. A line of German soldiers holding dogs guard a street. Opposite them, against the grey sky, hang the bodies of Polish patriots. People gather in groups to read the warning notices, and the camera moves behind the steel helmets slowly revealing a great fresco of the peasant faces of city workers.

Shortly afterwards Stach is driving a horse-drawn cart. We

look up at Stach's bright face as he shouts at the horses whose heads turn and twist as they gallop down the street. It is morning. The light floods the cobble-stones and we see the horses' breath in the air. The images are full of energy and youthful ardour. Suddenly both we and Stach are confronted with the black arch of a bridge below which passes a line of broken-spirited workers being taken away to the labour camps. Immediately after this, Stach is interrogated by the Germans, accused of theft, and beaten up. The beating is given no special emphasis. A blow from a cane draws blood from his cheek; the soldiers rather jovially push him about. As he falls to the ground we observe his face. We are made conscious not so much of his physical pain as of the hurt to his pride. We are made aware of what it means not to be free.

Such a sequence can be used to discuss different experiences of war. It can also be compared to the picture of war presented by other films or the paperback adventure stories. At the same time as we discuss its different meanings we are also being made aware of how these meanings are expressed. The attitude of the film-maker comes across to us in his way of seeing—in his style. The quality of idealism is not merely established in plot or dialogue, nor is it something external to the way the film is constructed. It springs from the internal rhythms of the work itself; it suffuses the images we see on the screen. The sequence with the horses, for example, is not offered as an arbitrary symbol of Stach's temperament and feelings. It has its logical place in the telling of the story. Rather, the images on the screen are charged with poetic force and we must respond almost physically to grasp their meaning.

A Generation is not simply a social drama. It is also a love story so beautifully and tenderly conveyed that when the two young people make love for the first time the camera can turn away not in the spirit of reluctant censorship but as a movement of respect towards a private moment.

These two elements, the social commitment and the personal relationship, are not presented to us as antagonistic in the conventional manner of a love-versus-duty romance but as separate strands in the same process. At the end of the film, when Dorata is taken away to prison and death, Stach sits waiting in the open country for his young comrades to join him. Slowly they approach and Stach, brushing away a tear, turns to face them. In the final shot we see them as Stach sees them. The camera has been placed below eye-level so that we are looking slightly upwards at them. They are very young and they look out innocently upon the world. The spirit evoked is one of hope and idealism. At the same time the rather formal grouping tragically recalls one of those posed photographs of soldiers before they go into battle. In this way the two dominant moods of the film are embraced in a powerful concluding image (Plate 3).

When we say that in discussing a film like *A Generation* we can draw upon the methods employed in teaching literature, we do not mean that a film can be understood as literature. In a film the important meanings are conveyed visually and it is to these that we must pay attention. A literary interpretation based on a response mainly to plot and dialogue would not only miss most of what *A Generation* has to offer but would radically misrepresent the film. It would be likely, for example, to interpret it in political terms, stressing the hero's conversion to Communism, whereas the way the actual images of the film are composed and handled puts the stress on the quality of the boy's conversion rather than on the ideological content. The kind of attention we must pay to these visual qualities is the equivalent of the attention we give to the verbal images, rhythms and so on, in our reading. As with literature, such a study forces us to make connections with experiences outside the work itself. In discussing *A Generation* we would be talking about the process of growing up, the attitudes of the different generations towards each other, falling in love, our responsibilities to others, war, work, idealism, freedom and authority. Such a discussion would be informed and held in check by the experience of the film itself, at its most valuable when it sprang from a full awareness of the film's texture of meanings. Also, by constantly referring back to the film, it would itself help to train this awareness. And it is by offering this sort of training that education can most effectively act as an agent of change.

2

Minority Art, Folk Art and Popular Art

In principle, it seems clear that the dramatic conventions of any given period are fundamentally related to the *structure of feeling* in that period. I use the phrase *structure of feeling* because it seems to me more accurate, in this context, than *ideas* or *general life*. . . . But while we may, in the study of a past period, separate out particular aspects of life, and treat them as if they were self-contained, it is obvious that this is only how they may be studied, not how they were experienced. . . . And it seems to be true, from the nature of art, that it is from such a totality that the artist draws; it is in art, primarily, that the effect of the totality, the dominant structure of feeling, is expressed and embodied.

RAYMOND WILLIAMS, *Preface to Film*

We often write and speak as if the new media—the cinema, television, radio, record, popular printed-matter—had simply extended the means available for communicating between groups of people. Had this been true, their impact on our social life would have been far less direct than it has turned out to be. But when the means of communication are extended on this scale the development cannot be judged in simple quantitative terms. People are brought together in a new relationship as audiences, new kinds of language and expression are developed, independent art forms and conventions arise. The media are not the end-products of a simple technological revolution. They come at the end of a complex historical and social process, they are active agents in a new phase in the life-history of industrial society. Inside these forms and languages, the society is articulating new social experiences for the first time. In fact, the emergence of new art forms is closely linked with social change. We can see this more clearly in a period which is not so close to our own. The development of the morality play and of Elizabethan drama from the older kinds of religious drama—the miracle and mystery plays—was related in a complex way to the emergence of the 'new world' of Tudor society out of feudalism. The cinema is a *modern* medium, not simply because it belongs to an advanced technological stage in society, but because its characteristic forms—its immediacy, its continual shifts of focus and perspective—are themselves aspects of the modern sensibility. It is equipped, in some special way, to apprehend experiences which are no longer easily contained within existing forms, such as the novel, poetry or even traditional drama.

Within the media, then, meanings are constantly attributed to contemporary life, information—not only about 'what happens' but also about 'how it happens'—is passed from source to audience, in a context of attitudes and values which are 'new' in some significant way. Certain patterns of life and some structures of feeling are strengthened and affirmed as against others. Contemporary life may not receive its fullest expression here, but it is likely to be pictured or expressed in these channels first. It is for this reason that the purely sociological approach to a study of the media, with its proper objective bias, is never wholly satisfactory, helpful as this approach is in showing us the functional uses to which the media are put. We need the critical and evaluative approach precisely because the media themselves, their content and forms, are not neutral: we have to attend to the forms within which the new experiences are being presented, to discriminate between values, and to analyse our responses to them carefully. In educational terms at least, this is the only kind of moral control which we can apply to the sudden expansion that has taken place. This process of evaluation is the proper business of education, and begins within the formal system itself, though of course it cannot end there.

We examined in the preceding chapter some of the representative attitudes in teaching towards this growth, and some of the 'classroom' consequences of adopting a critical and evaluative attitude towards the media. In doing so, however, we were trying to move beyond the application, in a dead and insensitive way, of conventional ethical attitudes towards the new media. In particular, we were concerned to break with the false distinction, maintained from apparently different vantage points in education, between the 'serious' and the 'popular' and between 'entertainment' and 'values'. These distinctions, we suggested, offer us a false framework for reference and judgement. Attention to style and form—the *way* the communication is made, and its internal and implied rhythms and emphases—is the only way of rendering fully our response to the material, and to the values and attitudes confirmed or neglected within it.

We tried to illustrate this by detailed reference to Wajda's film, *A Generation*. That illustration, however, now serves to take us a stage further in the argument. In the wake of *Fiction and the Reading Public* and *Culture and Environment*, and other works following in that tradition, the practice of discrimination in this field has gradually been brought into some—though not many—schools as part of English or General Studies. Much more could be done in this way, and there are signs that some imaginative teachers are designing new courses along such lines of growth. Unfortunately, many teachers still see this as a *defensive* educational tactic, although throughout his work, and especially in *Education and the University*, F. R. Leavis has argued convincingly that criticism, with its attention to a whole response and its concern for the life of the mind and the tone of civilization, is a creative activity in the true sense. Some of the material handled in the detailed studies in later chapters in this work is in line with the educational work which has been done in this tradition.

But, as we argued, no young person has to be defended against a film like *A Generation*. The point then arises—what sort of 'art' is this? What is its relation to the traditional culture; or, to put the question a different way, what claims are being made for the new media, and what general standards are being invoked?

In one sense, the media are *merely means of transmission*. They make it possible to transmit work of high quality of a traditional kind. Of course, adaptation is often involved, and where a work of art has been adapted it need not necessarily retain its original force. There is no necessary connection between the quality of a work in one art form and its quality in another. The invention of printing did not alter the nature of the Bible, though it altered the conditions for its dissemination: but the translation of the Bible into the English of King James did, in certain important ways, alter its character. *Hamlet* on the screen, Michelangelo on television, *Jane Eyre* on radio involve transcription from one medium to another, and this process can quite radically alter the quality of the work transmitted. Dickens's or Jane Austen's novels, or Shakespeare's plays, have, on the whole, made rather mediocre films. They have not been fully transcribed. They tend to be literary films, or filmed plays, rather than films. On the other hand, some transcriptions can be wholly successful on their own terms—the radio adaptation of Sillitoe's *The Loneliness of the Long Distance Runner*, for example (more successful than the film of the novel). Given effective adaptation, the new media are significant new means for transmitting good work, 'high culture', to wider audiences.

This use of the media extends, by means of the cinema or television screen, the radio or record, what print and literacy first began. A complex society such as ours needs the new media, provided they are properly used, since they offer experiences and explore relationships which, given the variety and pace of modern life, cannot be prepared for or recapitulated within the microcosm of the modern family. But this is essentially a sociological argument: the media are seen here as agents of socialization, standing beside the family and complementing one's school, one's groups of friends and the community itself.

A Generation, however, is not a film with a social message; nor, indeed, is it of sociological significance, except in very complex ways. Nor, although based on a novel, is it a valued work of art merely transmitted by a new medium. It is a work created *by* and *in* the new medium. It exists *as a film*, a rich and intensive human statement. Its qualities have been realized wholly by the cinema, rendered by the director in visual terms. The point of each scene is carried by the very balance of image, sound, gesture and composition characteristic of the film as a form of art. A good play could be made from such a film, but there would be no guarantee of its quality: precisely the same problems of adaptation would arise—though here it would be a question of adaptation from a new to an older art form.

In films of the quality of *A Generation* we see the potentialities of some of the new media, not merely for the transmission of existing forms of art, but as, themselves, a *means of creating art.* Perhaps the most positive effect of the revolution in communications we have been describing has been the real extension of the means available to us for making art, and the discovery of wholly new art forms, with their own laws of composition. Few of the media have fully realized this potential; the claims of the cinema are clear and beginning to be admitted, the claims of television are much more doubtful. The very existence of works of quality affects our judgement of the capacities of the media, since they give us rough but measurable standards. In literature the existence of *Anna Karenina* modifies altogether our sense of what is possible in the art of the novel and reshapes our judgements retrospectively. The same is true of films like *La Règle du Jeu, Viridiana, Living, L'Avventura* or *The Silence.*

What happens when a new work of art is created is something that happens simultaneously to all the works of art which preceded it. The existing monuments form an ideal order among themselves, which is modified by the introduction of the new (the really new) work of art among them. The existing order is complete before the new work arrives; for order to persist after the supervention of novelty, the *whole* existing order must be, if ever so slightly, altered; and so the relations, proportions, values of each work of art are readjusted; and this is conformity between the old and the new.

T. S. Eliot, *Selected Essays*

Really creative work in the cinema or in television reshapes 'the existing order'. It brings all that the medium offers to the threshold of its potential. Once a medium or art form has been brought to such a pitch of achievement, with its audience raised to such a level of expectation, it cannot evade the challenge offered to it. Creative work not merely alters, it *clarifies* the order of achievement. We know better how to deal with the medium, what to ask of it. The form has been touched by human excellence.

Both the cases so far discussed—the transmission of art and the creation of new serious art in new forms—develop a relationship between the new media and the realm of 'high culture'. There is a great deal of argument about the relative merits of the best in different forms—is *La Grande Illusion* as 'great' as *War and Peace*? This is by no means a new argument (is *War and Peace* as 'great' as *Henry IV* or *The Iliad*?) but essentially a critical argument confined to comparisons between one work of art and another which are all roughly at the same level. Whatever the medium, really creative work presents no problem in the wider sense. Such work bears the stamp of an original imagination; its power depends upon its capacity to force us 'out of ourselves' to attend to the range and quality of someone else's mind. Our ways of feeling can actually be extended, as Lawrence has proved in the novel. New social experiences are brought to consciousness, as in the novels of George Eliot or Balzac. Or we are disturbed simply by the texture of the created life, as in the work of Jane Austen or Tolstoy. Such work is often, necessarily, difficult, as is that of Henry James or Thomas Mann. Its formal and symbolic content will be high. Indeed, it may set out quite deliberately to break existing forms, as Joyce did, and by undermining these forms to dissolve the images of life and the social stereotypes supported by them. The question of which new works we may validly bring into this 'existing order' is difficult, but we can understand the claims of Renoir, Buñuel, Kurosawa and Antonioni to this area of 'high culture'.

Throughout this study we shall be referring to creative work at this level in the new media, where it exists. But so much—the great bulk—of what is offered bears no relation to this body of creative work. Much of it does not even have the *intention* of art behind it. Is it, then, simply a question of disposing *all* that the media offer along a simple spectrum stretching from good to bad, art to non-art, and reconciling ourselves to the enormous disparity between the volume of the shoddy and the scarcity of the great? Or is some other cultural relationship between the media and art registered by our uneasiness in the face of this simple dichotomy?

Hannah Arendt argues:

> Culture relates to objects and is a phenomenon of the world; entertainment relates to people and is a phenomenon of life. An object is cultural to the extent that it can endure; its durability is the very opposite of functionality, which is the quality which makes it disappear again from the phenomenal world by being used and used up.
>
> *Between Past and Future*

The precise quality of much mass-media material is effectively described there—its transient relation to 'people' and 'life', its rapid expendability, what Miss Arendt calls its 'functionality' (an instrument of entertainment, relaxation, diversion, even vicarious escapism). She is right to point out, as she has earlier, that this process of reducing art-work to the level of mass culture is a continual process threatening 'high culture' itself:

> Of course I am not referring to mass distribution. When books or pictures in reproduction are thrown on the market cheaply and attain huge sales, this does not affect the nature of the objects in question. But their nature is affected when these objects themselves are changed—rewritten, condensed, digested, reduced to kitsch in reproduction, or in preparation for the movies.
>
> ibid.

We shall discuss this particular process in mass culture later. But Miss Arendt seems to be conferring, retrospectively, a permanence on 'high art' which, though true of some of its artefacts, is false to its actual manner of creation. Is there, in fact, a body of cultural work which can be discussed and judged in creative terms, but which does not 'resist' time in quite the way she suggests?

Such forms did exist in what we now refer to as folk culture.

This term has been applied to the communal artefacts of a primitive or rural 'folk'. It also includes the anonymous folk culture created by the industrial classes after the Industrial Revolution, when they were shut out from official 'high culture' by the barriers of class, money, literacy and education. This folk culture was part of communal ways of life or 'organic' communities (a deceptive phrase, since it includes not only primitive peoples and country dwellers but also the urban slums of commercial and industrial cities, country backlands, ethnic ghettos and slave plantations). We would include, for our purposes, traditional rural songs and airs, but also urban broadsides and ballads, work songs and songs of protest; not only medieval shows, spectacles and chronicles, but work, games and dances, and traditional crafts. As James Reeves says:

The poetic and musical inheritance was far from homogeneous: it contained ballads four centuries old, side by side with the street songs of Victorian peddlers, medieval lyric fragments of perhaps French origin, seventeenth- and eighteenth-century urban broadsides and tavern songs, and the products of Georgian concert-rooms and pleasure-gardens. Yet the collective mind assimilated everything, adding much and discarding much, exercising a selective instinct in retaining what it felt it could make its own. In choosing from the mass of available material, I have taken what seems to me most vigorous, most direct, most economical in language, most imaginative in expression, and most truly and deeply felt. This traditional verse is unique and valuable because it is lively, energetic, concrete, idiomatic, rhythmically vital, natural, without meretricious artifice, and capable at times of amazingly imaginative utterance. In Keats's phrase, it can 'surprise by a fine excess'. At its most intense it seems to draw upon a fund of imagery which belongs not to the mind of a single poet but to the hidden emotional life of all who speak and know English.

The Idiom of the People

These arts were very close indeed to 'life' and 'people'. Often, what we see now as 'crafts' were simply traditional forms of 'work', and what we refer to as 'arts' were really ritual celebrations of folk or community. Folk art survived the coming of the cities—though not, in the mind of collectors like Cecil Sharp, without loss of quality. There was certainly a vigorous urban and early industrial 'folk' culture. Gradually, however, much of it has disappeared with the development of industrialization, as the close communities have been dispersed and the rhythms of work have been altered by the development of technology and the machine, and (most important from our point of view) as 'tastes and cultural activities, hitherto existing as modes of behaviour, have been brought into the realm of literacy and communication' (Raymond Williams, *Culture and Society*).

Since this folk culture and the way of life were so nearly interchangeable, we cannot now wish to revive the culture without restoring the way of life. The desire to return to the organic community is a cultural nostalgia which only those who did not experience the cramping and inhuman conditions of that life can seriously indulge. It is, incidentally, a defensive reaction which often slips in when the mass media are being criticized and bewailed, and we must beware of it. On the other hand, there is no need to substitute for it a simple-minded progressivism. We need not wish to revive the 'rural idiocy' of English village life in order to understand what were the human costs of its disappearance— the novel, itself the product of that change from a rural to an urban society, has made this loss one of its most eloquent themes. Nor does it follow that the culture which replaces folk art must necessarily be, in some simple sense, better. It is worth while, therefore, to remind ourselves of the essential quality of this folk culture.

The two key characteristics of folk art are suggested by Oscar Handlin in his essay in the collection, *Culture for the Millions*. Folk culture, he suggests, 'dealt directly with the concrete world intensely familiar to its audience'. It dealt with common situations within a familiar pattern of life. This is as true of primitive folk art, such as the Heroic Lays, songs and legends, as it was of industrial folk art, such as ballads and broadsides. Secondly, there was a direct relationship between performer and audience: the threshold of participation was high, the material familiar, since it had been repeated and handed down, with slight variation, from one generation to the next, the forms simple or traditional. Writing of the early epic 'poets and reciters', Jan de Vries says:

> The man who gave the *Niebelungenlied* its final and most perfect shape knew very well that he was merely a link in the long chain of poets and reciters who had carried the legend through the centuries. One may therefore speak of a folk-epic if one bears in mind that it is not a spontaneous product of collective poetry-making, and that moreover (certainly in earlier times) the word 'people' meant something different from what it means today. Yet it is an epic of the people in the sense that the subject-matter, the legend, is actually the property of a popular tradition. . . . Who preserved this matter through the centuries if not an endless row of bearers of a common popular tradition, who sometimes did no more than communicate a text that they had learnt by heart but who sometimes (with more or less talent) gave a new shape to a legend?
>
> *Heroic Song and Heroic Legend*

One sees many of the characteristics of this kind of folk-poetry tradition surviving the coming of print in the history of the broadside and the ballad. The earliest printed ballad sheets date from the mid-fifteenth century, but the popular ballad survives through the Industrial Revolution until the coming of the penny press at the end of the nineteenth century. 'The act of printing', comments Leslie Shepard, 'was, so to speak, merely superimposed on an oral tradition that had already found new directions.'

Thus we see that the broadside ballad brings together many different strains. The true past history includes the ballads that were *not* written down or printed but sung and learnt traditionally, and the perennial popular interest in such 'song histories' was the mainspring for the successful form of the printed ballad. Traditional and topical ballads were sung side by side, and some topical ballads even became 'folk' by passing into oral tradition.

The Broadside Ballad

Though industrial folk art was sometimes a deliberate resistance

to 'high culture', and although it often came, as Dwight Mac-
Donald suggests, to 'take its cue from high culture', it was in
origin and feeling close to the oral traditions and forms of an
earlier culture; in this sense a communal art, and 'popular' in that
it belonged to the culture of the whole people.

In total perspective, however, popular culture was not justified by
such by-products so much as by the function it served. Millions of
people found in this culture a means of communication among themselves and the answers to certain significant questions that they were
asking about the world around them.

Oscar Handlin, 'Mass and Popular Culture'
in *Culture for the Millions*

Now, Miss Arendt might well argue that, vigorous as some of
these popular arts of the industrial period were in comparison
with contemporary mass culture, they were essentially of the same
order of creation: their functional or instrumental element was
always too high in comparison with their individual richness of
content to place them in the same category as 'high culture'. They
were not made to endure—even if some of them did—but to be
expended, used up. They were not objects of contemplation like
the works of high art, but communal artefacts, part of a whole
rhythm of life. And now that they have been replaced by the
much more debased products of the mass media, the separation
which Miss Arendt makes between 'culture' and 'entertainment'
has been made complete.

Yet such a sharp distinction breaks down when we come to
examine particular works or when we look more carefully at a
particular piece of cultural history. If we examine how some of
these urban folk arts developed into popular entertainments, we
detect a significant line of growth and change. The best example
here is the music hall, which flourished in the later stages of this
industrial-urban culture. Music hall was illegitimate popular
theatre. The traditions behind it included popular spectacles and
shows and the street drama, as well as the gin-palaces, the pleasure

gardens and song-and-supper rooms of the late Victorian era. By its hey-day, in the Edwardian period, it had achieved a distinctive existence as a popular form.

The music hall maintained many elements in common with earlier folk culture. It was, in many ways, a truer reflection of the life and culture of the urban classes than was to be found in any other artistic form. It dealt, by means of spectacle, song, comedy, with a whole range of familiar experiences, framed by common references and attitudes. These attitudes were, to a large extent, shared between audience and artist, and the rapport was high. The music hall was, for a time, part of the very life of 'the community' —though that community was now much more stratified than any of the earlier 'organic' societies. On the other hand, the music hall was, in essence, an art of the performer, rather than the art of a community. The community had become an 'audience': the art had been individualized. It would be easy to sentimentalize the music hall—a late expression of the 'folk' in our culture—but it would be closer to the truth to say that the music hall was a transitional form—in a transitional society—between earlier 'folk' and later 'popular' art. A great deal of the music hall was poor and second-rate, but there seems certainly to have been a company of outstanding performers who established their reputation in the halls by the very force of their personal style. Dan Leno, George Robey, W. G. Ross and Marie Lloyd were not 'stars' in the Hollywood or pop-music sense, but they were not the 'anonymous folk poets' or 'communal creators' of Reeves's *Idiom of the People* either. Folk culture had been gradually individualized into something else. The music hall was not simply poor-quality legitimate theatre—nor was it simply an 'occasional' entertainment. The source of its peculiar strength—and the core of the 'act' of its most distinguished performers—remained the closeness of audience and artist to certain shared experiences and moral attitudes, and a shared quality of humour and pathos. T. S. Eliot wrote that 'Marie Lloyd's audiences were invariably sympathetic, and it was through this sympathy that she controlled them'. As a popular artist, she became a 'stand-in' for the audience—yet she was at the same time a professional, and part of the music-hall business—the commercial culture and the entertainment world:

> Whereas other comedians amuse their audiences as much and sometimes more than Marie Lloyd, no other comedian succeeded so well in giving expression to the life of the audience, in raising it to a kind of art. It was, I think, this capacity for expressing the soul of the people that made Marie Lloyd unique, and that made her audiences, even when they joined in the chorus, not so much hilarious as happy.
>
> T. S. Eliot, *Selected Essays*

'Raising it to a kind of art.' But what kind of art was this? Certainly not 'high art' as we have defined it. There was no durable creation there, in Miss Arendt's terms, capable of withstanding the flux of time. Exactly the reverse, in fact—a performance intense, expendable, momentary. Perhaps it was an artistic experience rather than art—but the line is almost impossible to draw. It was, as all art is, a selection from experience, shaped, compressed and intensified. The art of the music hall was a stylized art, a conventional art. So, too, is 'high art'. But whereas high art in our times will often consciously create its own conventions—'make it new'—or deliberately break the conventions already made, the music hall depended for its impact upon the conventions being known and accepted and endlessly repeatable. Certainly innovations were made; but they, too, rapidly became part of the pattern. Indeed, the quality of the performance seems to have increased directly with the degree of familiarity with, or recognition of, the conventions which could be expected. M. C. Bradbrook has argued that

> A convention may be defined as an agreement between writers and readers, whereby the artist is allowed to limit and simplify his material in order to secure greater concentration through a control of the distribution of emphasis.
>
> *Elizabethan Tragedy*

In the music hall, the 'area of agreement' in the performance was extensive, and this was connected with a more complex and implicit agreement in attitudes to life between audience and artist. Of course, there is great use of conventions of presentation in, say, the novels of Joyce or Henry James, but these do not, on the whole, lead—as in the music hall—to a simplification of the material offered. In Joyce or James the conventions are employed so as to shape and control the material in their novels (it is a condition of their *art*). In the more popular arts, the conventions also serve to bring the artist more immediately in touch with his audience (it is a condition of their *performance*).

The writer, poet or painter today, engaged in a work of 'high art', is concerned with the primacy of his own experience: he wrestles directly with his material. Ultimately, his respect for his readers or audience will show through, but as an implicit or subsumed effect of his art, part of his 'good faith' as an artist. The writer or poet who consciously handles his material with the audience continually in the forefront of his mind is, often, the producer of 'mass' art: by trying to write too deliberately for his readers and his market, he ends up by writing for no one in particular. For the artists of the music hall the making of rapid connections with the audience was not—as it may have been for the second-raters—a quick way of ingratiating themselves with their fans, but something else, *a condition of the kind of art* in which they were engaged. They worked deliberately, as artists, for what Daniel Bell has called 'an eclipse of distance'. And whereas Bell assumes—as we all do about high art—that

> The disruption of distance means that one has lost the control over the experience—the ability to step back and conduct one's 'dialogue' with the art.
>
> *Encounter*, May 1963

this disruption of distance, for the popular artists, seems to have been an essential requirement of their control over the experience or attitude which they were dramatizing in their acts.

Finally, where we now associate quality in the high arts with an extension of experience, and the discovery of new ways of feeling (it has not always been so—at least, not to the same extent; cf. a great deal of eighteenth-century poetry and the whole notion of 'decorum'), the art of the music hall seemed to depend upon *confirming known* experiences and values. The attitudes common to artist and audience were enriched and deepened by being affirmed again within the conventions of the art. Where high art, today, is judged by its capacity to disturb and challenge us, the popular arts confirm—even reassure.

I consider her superiority over other performers to be in a way a moral superiority: it was her understanding of the people, and sympathy with them, and the people's recognition of the fact that she embodied the virtues which they genuinely most respected in private life, that raised her to the position she occupied at her death. And her death is itself a significant moment in English history.

T. S. Eliot, *Selected Essays*

We have not tried, so far, to define the quality of this kind of popular art, but to establish its identity by drawing quite sharp distinctions between it and high art. It is not that popular art tries to do what difficult art work succeeds in doing, but that they have different qualities. The relationships within them between content, audience and artist are different, too. The significance of the music-hall example discussed here is that, while retaining much in common with folk art, it became an *individual* art, existing within a literate commercial culture. Certain 'folk' elements were carried through, even though the artist replaced the anonymous folk artist, and the 'style' was that of the performer rather than a communal style. The relationships here are more complex—the art is no longer simply created by the people from below—yet the interaction, by way of the conventions of presentation and feeling, re-establishes the rapport. Although this art is no longer directly the product of the 'way of life' of an 'organic community', and is not 'made by the people', it is still, in a manner not applicable to the high arts, a popular art, for the people.

We have now to take account of some arguments and objections. The music hall, it will be argued, was a 'sport', a transitional form, peculiar to late Victorian and Edwardian culture, and appeared at one of those freak moments when, under very special conditions, the community yields up a communal art and style for a brief period just when it is on the brink of major change. Certainly much of this is true, though it would be too simple to say that the music hall then 'disappeared'; especially when we bear in mind the many lines of continuity which lead into our period through the variety theatre, the mainstream of British comedy, *ITMA*, such recent theatrical 'events' as Joan Littlewood's *Oh What a Lovely War* and echoes in the work of Pinter and Osborne. Art forms do not arise, develop and dissolve in quite this way.

Two significant points remain. The first is that the rise of the music hall marks a very special stage in the development of popular entertainment. This stage can be identified with the emergence of the individual performer and the importance of his personal style. This phase in the evolution of entertainment from 'folk' art to 'popular' art cannot be accounted for in broad historical terms, such as the transition from Victorian society to the modern age; it is an aspect of the internal development of the *form* itself. Something similar happened in the sixteenth century with drama, and in the seventeenth with the novel. The change belongs to the chronology of art as well as the chronology of society.

The second point is that the new media do not mark as decisive a break in the cultural development of 'popular' art as we might imagine from the death of the music halls at the hands of, say, television. The media did change. But within the new forms we find many of the same distinctive qualities which distinguished the art of the halls. In the cinema, in television, in radio, a great deal depends upon the impact and *immediacy* of the performance. Unlike classical music, painting or sculpture, these are almost, by definition, the *immediate and spontaneous arts*. The development in the direction of these qualities (as against the more formal, composed and distanced qualities of classical traditional high art) has not in fact been limited to the new media: it has invaded and made its mark in the high arts as well. In the article referred to earlier, Daniel Bell suggests that

the common elements [in the modern period] lie in the effects which culture (the expressive symbolization of experience) seeks to produce, and in contemporary society these effects I would identify as *novelty, sensation, simultaneity, immediacy* and *impact.*

Encounter, May 1963

And, later in his argument, referring to the 'eclipse of distance', he says

Perhaps the starkest illustration of this is in the innovation of the cinema. There the event, the distance (close-up or long shot), the duration of the 'clip', the concentration on one character or another— the entire pace—is 'imposed' upon one, as one sits enveloped . . . in the darkness of the movie house. And the influence of cinematic technique has become so pervasive—the rapid cutting, the flashback, interweaving of themes and break-up of sequence—as to overwhelm, almost, the novel as well.

ibid.

Between popular art of the music hall and this 'cinematic' art a further evolution has of course taken place. Emphases have altered, new terms have appeared (e.g. sensation), there is a new weighting in the word *novelty*. Certain other elements are underplayed in his account—especially, for our purpose, the interaction between artist/performer and audience which, in the music hall, was really central. In the modern media, the relationship between artist and audience, already formalized in the music hall to some extent, has become even more distant. Nevertheless the element of continuity is there.

This line of growth can now be strengthened by an example. If we are thinking of ways in which popular art re-emerged within the modern 'mechanical' media, we ought to look at Chaplin, his art and his relation to his audience. For Chaplin's art grew directly out of an 'entertainment'—the film style of the Keystone studio and the Mack Sennett team. Sennett himself was no artist. But he gathered about him a troupe of zany acrobat-comics, including 'Fatty' Arbuckle, Ford Sterling, Chester Concklin, Ben Turpin, the indefatigable Mabel Normand and, among others, Chaplin. The essence of Sennett comedy was the ability of cinema to set images in motion. The Keystone team erupted on the screen in rapid-sequence turns: their films included slapstick comedy, swiftly performed acts of violence, above all fantasies of speed and chase. These were almost all improvised:

> There was no text, there was no plot. They were shot 'off the cuff', that is to say, a director, a cameraman, a group of actors went out with a few properties—perhaps a step-ladder, some painter's supplies, and a wheel-barrow; they proceeded to a street or a park or a lake, and with nothing more than a general idea of an action in their minds, created their picture.
>
>   Gilbert Seldes, *Movies for the Millions*

This was a kind of comedy with a long, comic tradition in entertainment behind it. Many of the basic situations were already popular in music-hall farce—misunderstandings, disguises, anger at imaginary hurts, pursuits. The slapstick, however, had been made 'indigenously filmic'. Sennett's fantasies, and the speed at which they were performed, dissolved all reason and logic—as Seldes says, 'destroyed the solemn framework in which everyday man had his existence'. Sometimes, as in *A Small Town Idol*, Keystone parodied the serious drama. But the films which are most often remembered were 'mechanical thrills', or episodes built around one of his star performers (see Knight, *The Liveliest Art*). Sennett's sense of timing, his editing, his inventiveness, were supreme. But it needed Chaplin to make that style of invention an art.

At the age of seven Chaplin was dancing in a music-hall act entitled *The Eight Lancashire Lads*. In 1912 Sennett saw him in

New York in an act performed by the Karno Comedy Company called 'A Night in an English Music Hall'. Shortly after, Sennett hired Chaplin as a substitute for Ford Sterling. The Chaplin costume was improvised for a Keystone film:

> Sharing a dressing room with Arbuckle and Mack Swain, Chaplin borrowed 'Fatty's' outsized trousers and, from Swain, a prop moustache. The floppy shoes came from Ford Sterling. The derby, the cane, the too tight coat—all were unerringly chosen in one short afternoon. During the shooting of *The Kid Auto Races at Venice* Chaplin instinctively fell into the sore-footed shuffle that was also to remain part of the character—the remembered gait of an old peddler he had observed during his days on the London streets.
>
> Arthur Knight, *The Liveliest Art*

Chaplin put together the 'tramp' character out of these bits and pieces. When he moved from the Keystone studio to Essanay, he slowed down the pace of his act so that the more intimate and subtle qualities—irony and pathos—had room to develop. From *The Tramp, Easy Street* and *The Kid* to *The Gold Rush, City Lights* and *Modern Times* we see a deepening of this central figure, the emergence of a transcendent comic style which united the timing and ingenuity of Keystone with the slower, sadder arts of mime. The character acquired depth and shading. The little gestures of extravagance or bravado, the jaunty disappointment, the qualified defeat take on a vibrancy which outdistances and sets in perspective the skills and thrills of the earlier period. The style transforms the individual gags and turns, welds them together into a totally created type—the little man against the world. It was this personal style in performance—most notably in *City Lights* and *The Gold Rush*—which recreated a bond between Chaplin and his audiences. At this point, he ceased to be simply a fine and inventive comic entertainer and became a *popular* artist.

It is important to notice that the quality of art we distinguish here is not a matter of dramatic acting as it is known in the legitimate theatre. Balazs makes a forceful distinction:

Such world-wide adulation as that which surrounded these legendary stars cannot be evoked by the most brilliant stage performance in itself. . . . If Charlie Chaplin came to be the best-beloved darling of half the human race, then millions of men and women must have seen in his personality something that means much to them; Charlie Chaplin's personality must have expressed something that lived in all of them as a secret feeling, urge or desire, some unconscious thought, something that far transcends the limits of personal charm or artistic performance. The golden-hearted, shiftless, blundering, cunning little tramp, the victim of mechanization and capitalism, who hits back with grotesquely resourceful pinpricks—Charlie, with his melancholy optimism, expresses the opposition of all of us to an inhuman order of society.

Bela Balazs, *Theory of the Film*

If we think of the best of Chaplin, of the high fantasies of *The Goon Show* on radio (closer perhaps to the best Sennett than the best Chaplin), or Hancock on television (very variable in performance, but, at its best, with something of the silent art of Chaplin), we begin to understand more clearly the place of popular art in the new media. Such art accounts for a very small proportion of what is produced but, when it does exist, it is indigenous to media which have wide appeal and varying, extensive audiences. It is radically different from the uses which may be made of those same media for transmitting works of high art, for it persuades by the depth and intensity of its feelings and values, rather than by the range of the experience. It is often improvised—put together directly out of the 'props' and materials of the form, adapted to the limitations of the medium—the visual quality of the cinema or television screen, perhaps, or the element of sound and noises on radio. It is in another sense improvised out of the common experiences which audience and performer share, and those experiences, known and familiar, are deepened when re-enacted. But, in the modern media, that re-enactment is necessarily performed by the true popular artist who does, with the force and imprint of his personal style, what 'folk poets' of an earlier period did 'instinctively' (a shorthand method of accounting for what, in its own way, was a highly complex process for making art communally). The common qualities are heightened and strengthened in performance by the use of familiar conventions and compression and stylization—Charlie's regalia or his walk, for example. And the quality of style suggests not only the way in which the popular artist makes *art* of the welter of experiences which he draws on, but the *respect* which he always holds both for his art and his audience. It is expressive of popular taste, but does not exploit it. Though this kind of art never reckons its audience strictly in terms of numbers—the relationship is too close for that kind of abstraction—it is an art which thrives only when widely varied audiences find something common and commonly valued in their appreciation of it; one of the preconditions for this being that the institutions which carry this art should be open institutions widely available—as the music hall was, in comparison with the legitimate theatre today, or as Chaplin's films were and are for the cinema audience in comparison with the audience for Truffaut or Antonioni or Bergman in the cinema art houses today. It is not an art created for everybody, calculated to reach as many as possible: but it is a kind of art which has the pressure behind it to be widely available and understood.

3

Popular Art and Mass Culture

Shakespeare and his audience found each other, in a measure they
created each other. He was a quality writer for a quality audience. . . .
The great Shakespearean discovery was that quality extended vertically through the social scale, not horizontally at the upper genteel,
economic and academic levels.

ALFRED HARBAGE, *As They Liked It*

In the previous chapter we tried to show the continuity between
folk art and popular art. Then, by following the line of continuity
into the early cinema and Chaplin, we indicated the way in which
this popular art emerged within the new media.

We were also concerned to make some important distinctions
between the older kind of folk culture and popular art. Popular
art, we suggested, is essentially a conventional art which restates,
in an intense form, values and attitudes already known; which
reassures and reaffirms, but brings to this something of the
surprise of art as well as the shock of recognition. Such art has in
common with folk art the genuine contact between audience and
performer: but it differs from folk art in that it is an individualized
art, the art of the known performer. The audience-as-community
has come to depend on the performer's skills, and on the force of
a personal style, to articulate its common values and interpret its
experiences. The turning point is the emergence of the artist, and
the music hall is only one of many instances where one can pin-
point the transition. But this emergence of the individual performer, when set in context, is itself part of a larger process which
can be traced elsewhere. We see it in the personal ascendancy of
the 'star actors' of the Shakespearean school in the late eighteenth
and nineteenth centuries—Kean, Siddons, Macready. These his-

trionic figures used Shakespeare's plays as personal vehicles for a style of acting which embodied certain shared values, a certain structure of feeling in their audience, as clearly as the art of Marie Lloyd did for her audience at the end of the century. Another ·case-study might be found in Dickens—the interplay between the theatricality of his style and characterization in his novels and the urge to make more direct contact with his audience through the stage and the dramatic performance (see *Dickens the Dramatist*, F. D. Fawcett). More generally, we can trace this process in the emergence of the novel itself as a literary form (see Ian Watt's chapter, 'Individualism and the Novel', in *The Rise of the Novel*). It is through the popular artist and his art that some part of the values, attitudes and experiences of the common audience survives into and through the era of bourgeois individualism. Dickens, Marie Lloyd and Chaplin are three instances, at three different points in time and in three different media, of the popular artist working his way back within himself to a more immediate and direct continuity between art, audience and experience.

The example of Sennett and Chaplin was used to show that popular art could survive the change from the more traditional to the new media, and that it is in the new media especially, which are more widely available to audiences than the traditional forms, that we should expect to find popular art today. It should *not* be thought, however, that what we are offered as the typical product of the mass media today is popular art. A very sharp distinction has to be drawn at this point between popular art and the 'art' of the mass media.

It is true that the modern mass media have replaced many of the earlier institutions such as the music hall. But the distinction which we want to make is based not on the institutions but on the quality of the work done within them. Such distinctions have always been possible—there is no point in sentimentalizing the tradition: for every popular novelist of quality there must have been a hundred literary hacks, serving up stereotyped characters, routine plots and situations; for every Marie Lloyd there must have been a score of imitators of little or no quality in the halls;

for every balladeer with a poetic gift in the common idiom there were a thousand 'cheapjacks' and hucksters of bad verse.

The distinction we are trying to make, however, goes beyond this important discrimination between good and bad popular art. It is essentially a distinction between two *kinds* of art. The typical 'art' of the mass media today is not a continuity from, but a *corruption of*, popular art. We want to suggest the sharp conflict between the work of artists, performers and directors in the new media, which has the intention of popular art behind it, and the typical offering of the media—which is a kind of mass art. Perhaps we can define this conflict by contrasting the typical qualities of popular art with the qualities—often deceptively similar—of mass art.

Where popular art in its modern forms exists only through the medium of a personal style, mass art has no personal quality but, instead, a high degree of personalization. Chaplin indelibly imprints his work with the whole pressure of his personality, which is fully translated into his art. By contrast, mass art often destroys all trace of individuality and idiosyncrasy which makes a work compelling and living, and assumes a sort of de-personalized quality, a no-style. The personal element then becomes detached— a way of marketing the personality of the artist. Where Chaplin or Hancock create their personalities through comic invention, the run-of-the-mill television comic uses his personality as a prop or support to the performance, which altogether lacks a true style. A style of sorts often emerges in mass art, but where Chaplin's style develops out of his grappling with the experiences of his audience through the material and creations of his art, the mass style develops as a set of technical tricks for projecting an image. The popular artist is, in this respect, closer to the high artist, since he has the capacity—once the rapport with the audience is made— to lose himself in his material. In mass art the 'teller' is never lost in the 'tale'. The 'man behind the work' is 'sold' to the audience— the element of manipulation is correspondingly high—instead of, as in Chaplin's case, the man *within* the work.

Next, the quality of stylization and convention which, we

suggested, was especially important in popular art, becomes a kind of stereotyping, a processing of experience, a reliance upon formulae. For the popular artist stylization is necessary, and the conventions provide an agreed base from which true creative invention springs. In mass art the formula is everything—an escape from, rather than a means to, originality. The popular artist may use the conventions to select, emphasize and stress (or alter the emphasis and stress) so as to delight the audience with a kind of creative surprise. Mass art uses the stereotypes and formulae to simplify the experience, to mobilize stock feelings and to 'get them going'. If we compare the handful of great westerns with the majority of mediocre ones, we can see how the conventions of the western form can be exploited to 'get the audience going' without offering anything creative or worth while within the conventions (cf. the discussion of the western and the work of John Ford later). This point is crucial. Chaplin's 'Charlie' is a familiar figure—in one sense, he tells us nothing 'new'. He differs from the characters in, say, Antonioni's *L'Avventura*, who are helping us for the first time to articulate feelings we have 'never had', or did not know we had, until Antonioni embodied them in his film. Yet, in another sense, each Chaplin film is an original—it helps us to know the feelings we have more intensely, and to realize them more subtly. By responding to these films the audience finds its own experience enhanced; the Chaplin figure puts them in touch again with feelings and values they had forgotten they possessed. In mass art, the type is restricted by the conventions, and becomes a stereotype. Of course, if the formula is a compelling one, it will still evoke a response—how often have we cried at 'weepie' films we know to be bad. But, in retrospect, we feel cheated emotionally—unrewarded. And underneath there will be a slackening or weariness of attention as we feel ourselves persuaded to give our assent to it. We believe this is what Macdonald meant when he said (of mass art) that it 'includes the spectator's reactions in the work itself instead of forcing him to make his own responses', or Adorno (speaking of pop music), 'The composition hears for the listener', or Hoggart (referring to popular novelists), 'They act as picture-makers for what is behind the reader's day-dreams.'

This distinction between popular and mass art will be clearer if we take an example of the difference between a popular artist and a mass performer in their attitudes towards their audience and their work. Both are more 'aware' of their audience than the high artist. But whereas the popular artist, feeling his audience in his bones, concentrates everything on making anew and creating, the mass artist seems to be in total subjection to his audience, nervously aware of it, desperately afraid of losing touch. Compare this statement by the banjo player, Johnny St. Cyr:

> The more enthusiastic his audience is, why the more spirit the work-ing man's got to play. And with your natural feelings that way you never make the same thing twice. Every time you play a tune new ideas come to mind and you slip that one in.
>
> ed. N. Shapiro and N. Hentoff, Hear Me Talkin' to Ya

with this by Liberace:

> My whole trick is to keep the tune well out in front. If I play Tchaikovsky I play his melodies and skip his spiritual struggles. Naturally I condense. I have to know just how many notes my audience will stand for. If there's time left over I fill in with a lot of runs up and down the keyboard.
>
> reported in Jazz Monthly

The difference here is not simply between two artists of different abilities, but between two *kinds* of art, two attitudes. Liberace speaks throughout of 'my whole trick'. St. Cyr, however, talks about 'natural feelings'. Liberace has calculated exactly how many notes his audience 'will stand for'. St. Cyr speaks of the relation-ship between the enthusiasm of his audience and the 'spirit the working man's got to play'. Where Liberace has hold of a formula which he can endlessly repeat, St. Cyr says 'you never make the same thing twice'. Consider the nourishing relationship between artist and audience implied in the words of the trombone player, Jim Robinson:

> If everyone is in a frisky spirit, the spirit gets to me and I can make my trombone sing. If my music makes people happy I will try to do more. It is a challenge to me. . . . When I play sweet music I try to give my feelings to the other fellow. That's always in my mind. Everyone in the world should know this.
>
> ed. N. Shapiro and N. Hentoff, *Hear Me Talkin' to Ya*

Of course, modern jazz is no longer a simple music in the sense in which St. Cyr or Robinson speak of it. It is much more a musicians' or performers' music. In the early days of modern jazz, an important element was the desire to make the music more difficult to play, musically more complex. In some ways, modern jazz was a deliberate attempt to get away from the primitive or 'folk' quality of earlier jazz. It was also an attempt to 'defeat' the white audiences whom the new generation of jazz players suspected of liking New Orleans just because it was primitive, naive and unsophisticated. There is an interesting change of stress if we compare Jim Robinson's remarks with, say, those of the trumpet player, Miles Davis:

> I figure if they're missing what Philly Joe Jones is doing it's their tough luck. I wouldn't like to sit up there and play without anybody liking it, but I just mainly enjoy playing with my own rhythm section and listening to them.
>
> *Esquire*, March 1959

Or, with more deliberate impishness:

> If I can play good for eight bars, it's enough for me. It's satisfaction. The only thing is I don't tell anybody which eight bars are the good ones. That's my secret.
>
> ibid.

The attitudes which link Miles Davis with Robinson and St. Cyr,

but which Liberace does not share, are the significance which the
jazz players give to 'never making the same thing twice' (St. Cyr),
'playing sweet music' (Robinson), 'playing good for eight bars'
(Davis); and their common respect for the audience, their refusal
to flatter or underestimate it. On the other hand, look at
the similarity in tone and attitude between Liberace's phrase, 'I
have to know just how many notes my audience will stand for',
and the remarks of one of the providers of commercial television:

> We have a very good idea of the intelligence quotient of what we call
> our 'Nellies', our typical viewers, and we take that I.Q. into account in
> arranging programmes and programme content.
>
> Philip Dorte (Midlands Controller, ATV)
> reported in *The Schoolmaster*, 1 December 1961

The line between Robinson, St. Cyr and Davis, and Liberace
and Dorte is the crucial boundary between popular art and mass
art.

In considering the possibility of making popular art in the
modern world and through the modern media, it is natural to turn
to jazz and the cinema. As a music, jazz has much of the expressive
intensity of folk art. It is no longer, of course, a folk music, but
neither is it an art music, for it has maintained many folk elements
even while developing as a sophisticated urban form. Despite the
advances in technique and complexity, jazz is still—as compared
with the classical forms—a simple music. Emotions may be subtle,
but they are expressed frankly and directly. This is as true of the
music of Davis, Gillespie, Parker and Monk as it was of Armstrong, Bechet or Jelly Roll Morton. Individual players still aim
for a sound and tone which are characteristic of their personalities
and feelings, rather than a standard, classical purity of tone:
Davis's withdrawn introspection, Gillespie's wit and buoyancy,
Parker's rich, explosive, sudden emotions. The core of profes-
sionals is surrounded by a number of semi-pros and amateurs.
The audience itself is varied, shading from those who enjoy in a
relaxed, occasional way through to the expert and dedicated.

Improvisation and spontaneity are still paramount, in spite of the attempts to compose directly for jazz orchestras. The audience responds with direct feeling and warmth. It would surprise many teachers to hear former pupils, whom previously they felt possessed little power of discrimination, arguing about the merits of different groups, styles and performers, open and sensitive to the range of emotions which jazz so powerfully expresses.

As well as the character of the music, the social context is important. With the modern movement, the idea of attentive listening is more common, and jazz is often now performed in the concert hall. Nevertheless, it is still largely a functional music, a music of mood, a music to dance to—and part of its popular appeal lies in the relaxed and informal atmosphere that surrounds it. The best jazz is still nightclub, rehearsal or 'jam-session' jazz. Jazz, of course, is a minority music. But it is popular in the sense of being *of the people*, and while it is no longer the exclusive property of a small, depressed and exploited community the link there has been miraculously preserved. The jazz ethos is still tolerant and non-conformist. Lively, radical and creative groups of young people in quite different cultures have, during the short period of its history, found in it a common, international language. It costs money to go to a jazz club or concert, and art galleries are usually free: but for many young people jazz is more available than the traditional art forms.

This question of availability is crucial when we are considering the openness of the modern media to popular art. Young people are often unused to responding directly to a great deal of serious art, and have not learned to talk about their own responses, or to articulate their own experiences through it. But this cultural inexperience is reinforced by a feeling, quite widely held by a majority of young people today, that the whole world of high culture is 'not for them'. This more-or-less active hostility to high art—including the serious high art offered in the new media—must be taken account of here, since it impinges directly upon the question of available popular forms, and the quality and range of work which can be offered at this level.

'In this country', wrote Sir William Emrys Williams, then Secretary General of the Arts Council (*Observer*, 28/10/62), 'the arts are equally available to steel-workers and stockbrokers, and I believe this classless basis of provision is the best.' Of course, there are no formal restrictions. Access to the arts can, in the strict sense, be had on equal terms. People are 'free', as C. A. R. Crosland said (*Encounter*, November 1962), to choose 'between the *Observer* and the *News of the World*, between serious and frivolous paperbacks, between experimental and horror films, between an art gallery and a leg show'. But such choices seem more real to those who are already readers of the *Observer* or serious paperbacks than they are in practice. The argument ignores the severe lines of division within our system of education, the identification between 'culture' and 'class', and the question of distinct cultural climates in different sections of our stratified society. It is not only a matter of social class, although it is an obvious fact that the audience for classical music and legitimate theatre is predominantly middle class and grammar school. In a variety of ways—a style of architecture, a tone of voice, a manner of dress or address—the practical exclusion of large numbers of people from any effective participation in high culture is sustained. In this situation the school, as much as any other cultural institution, can sometimes make many young people feel that the arts belong to an alien world—that what should be available to all has been taken over by a small group who then, by a number of familiar signals, keep trespassers away. Resentment of this is often bound up with a suspicion that the adult world is all too ready to impose its own standards. Such a sense of active deprivation can often turn into outright hostility. 'Mozart,' said one teenager, 'should take a long run off a short pier.'

It is doubtful whether, at any stage, the identification of culture with certain social classes ever did much for the creation of serious art. Certainly, where this identification still persists, and is supported by the structure of education, real damage is being done to the whole society. As Hannah Arendt has written:

The point of the matter is that as soon as the immortal works of the past became the object of 'refinement' and acquired the status which went with it, they lost their most important and elemental quality, which is to grasp and move the reader or spectator, throughout the centuries. . . . In society, culture, even more than other realities, had become what only then began to be called a 'value', that is, a social commodity which could be circulated and cashed in on as social coinage for the purpose of acquiring social status. . . . Cultural values, therefore, were what values have always been, exchange values; in passing from hand to hand they were worn down like an old coin.

Arendt, 'Society and Culture'
in Culture for the Millions

This process—the practical exclusion of groups and classes in society from the selective tradition of the best that has been and is being produced in the culture—is especially damaging in a democratic society, and applies to both the traditional and new forms of high art. However, the very existence of this problem makes it even more important that some of the media which are capable of communicating work of a serious and significant kind should remain open and available, and that the quality of popular work transmitted there should be of the highest order possible, on its own terms.

Like jazz, the cinema is an available popular form. Although attendances have declined sharply, the current rate of approximately 8 million admissions per week shows that the cinema habit is still a strong one. It is possible to 'drop in' to the movies in a way that one cannot to the theatre—even where there is a theatre to go to. And the public for the movies is predominantly a young one.

The capacity of the film as a vehicle for the self-expression of the artist—popular or otherwise—is less apparent than in jazz. The complicated technical procedures of making films, the dependence on a large team of craftsmen and technicians, the pressures of heavy investment, all combine to make it difficult for film-makers to impress their personalities on their work (see the detailed analysis of the cinema industry offered in Part Three). What is indeed remarkable is the number of those who *have* been able to evolve a personal style. Even more relevant for us is the achievement of the cinema as a popular art. In the early days, the cinema drew heavily on popular drama, stage spectacles and the music-hall comedy. The early films in Britain were often first shown in the halls, and the audiences for these earlier forms became the audience for the cinema. Indeed, long before critics spoke about Chaplin and D. W. Griffiths, the work of these artists was immensely popular. The early film comedies, in the way they defended the underdog, burlesqued authority and inflicted indignity on the rich and pompous, reveal something of the way the cinema reflected popular tastes and attitudes. So did the unabashed sentiment, the pathos and the full-blown romance of the 'melodramas of the heart'.

This popular quality of the cinema as an institution is now threatened from both ends. As the cinema begins to move towards high art, it caters more naturally for the educated, middle-class audience familiar with the more traditional forms. This development is good, in so far as it brings the cinema in touch with the standards of high art, and makes it a medium of complex and subtle communications: but it can help to stratify the audience, and affect adversely the quality of its more popular work. At the other end is the growth of the 'blockbuster' film or spectacular. Those endlessly long, tedious and over-blown productions—a risky gamble by the film studios to hold on to a declining audience —with their printed programmes, booked seats, non-continuous showings, are 'films for people who don't go to the pictures'. If *L'Année Dernière à Marienbad* and *Vivre sa Vie* represent the evolution of a popular art towards high art, *Ten Commandments*, *Around The World in 80 Days*, *King of Kings* and *South Pacific* mark the decline of a popular art into mass art. Bearing in mind the general distinction which we tried to draw earlier between popular art and mass culture, consider the remarks of Penelope Houston on the 'blockbuster':

If the blockbuster banks on its difference from other films, however, it must at the same time assume universality. It must break through *all* the audience barriers, so that it can be sure of an all-class, all-income, all-nationality public. To this end, it must be carefully and deliberately disinfected, as a matter of production policy, of any attitudes which might annoy anyone, anywhere. War films must be neutralized (like *The Longest Day*); religious films must keep in mind religious minorities (like *King of Kings*), though they can afford the luxury of rebuking Imperial Rome; producers, remembering that half their prospective audience is outside America, must be wary of any theme which bears so directly on the American scene that it lacks appeal for foreigners. Westerns, of course, are exempt: Hollywood long ago converted the western into international currency.

The word *must*, in this context, really is a categorical imperative: once the investment has been made, and the initial risk taken, the film is committed to certain box-office demands.

Sight and Sound, Spring 1963

Nevertheless, a number of popular cinema forms—such as the western, the thriller and the musical—have developed; and although most examples of these genres are banal, routine treatments of well-worn formulae (as is common in mass art), a number of gifted popular artists have been able to fulfil themselves while working within this popular tradition and using the familiar conventions. Even the spectacular can, at times, be made to work in this way. This line of work, which we mark off as distinct from either high art or mass art in the cinema, is a continuing thread of creative achievement in a mass medium. It is also a thread which links together a good deal of the work which we discuss favourably in this study. And where more debased work is critically examined, popular art represents a kind of touchstone of quality which informs our criticism. In the following chapter we offer a study of popular work in two such forms (jazz and the cinema), and two popular artists working in two genres (Billie Holiday and the blues, John Ford and the western), as a way of detailing the general argument.

A final point should be made about the cinema in particular. There is a quality about the medium of film which makes it peculiarly accessible as a popular art. It is, as John Grierson said, a *physical* medium. The experience of watching a film makes a direct impact on us—the 'darkened auditorium, the dominating screen, with its very large, moving figures, its very loud sound, its simultaneous appeal to eye and ear' (Williams, *Preface to Film*). This has its dangers—allowing 'inferior artists to gain apparent effects by a process of powerful suggestion rather than of artistic expression'. But it also has compensating advantages: the film, which we feel so directly and immediately, can often by-pass some of the social and cultural barriers that cut off audiences from material in the more traditional arts. Modern media like the cinema, though so frequently misused, do have this potential for undermining the established hierarchies of culture, simply because they hold an effective bridgehead of communication between cultures or classes, and access to them cannot be tightly controlled. We have yet to see what would happen if these channels of communication were really cleared for work of quality: the cultural leap could be enormous. It would be foolish to exaggerate. The best cinema—like most advanced jazz—seems to push towards high art: average films or pop music are processed mass art. But this only makes the really popular work in both forms the more significant.

Once the distinction between popular and mass art has been made, we find that we have by-passed the cruder generalizations about 'mass culture', and are faced with the full range of material offered by the media—a range in television stretching from serious drama to the sociological soap-operas and the lysol dramas like *Emergency Ward 10* and *Dr Kildare*, from *Panorama* and *Your Life in their Hands* to *Candid Camera* and *This is Your Life*. Occasionally, the intention of popular communication in our sense can be felt behind some of this material—but very rarely indeed. A small proportion of it may be acceptable entertainment, or it may have what Graham Martin has defined as 'survival value' —it reminds us, in an affirmative way, of the continuities of life and nature (some nature films or science documentaries have this quality—e.g. the programmes series by Gerald Durrell), or confirms our common humanity (feature documentaries about unfamiliar people and places), or is genuinely informative, in a direct, committed or personal way (e.g. René Cutforth's fine BBC television script and film on the Ramadan Festival in the Arab societies). This is not popular *art*, but there are real qualities in such communication which we have to account for (the quality which distinguishes the truly popular piece of journalism as compared with the familiar packaged journalese of the 'popular' papers).

Another kind of quality—this time, closer to popular art, but not yet art since it is not imaginatively created—seems occasionally to 'happen' in the media. These moments of spontaneous break-through are rarely calculated by artist or producer: they grow out of typed and formula-ridden material, live for a moment, only to be defeated in the end by quite other routine and trivialized qualities. This occurs in popular art, too, when a release of feeling emerges, not from the 'over-all motions of the plot' but in 'the briefer passages', or when 'the simple vitality explosively asserts itself' (*The Structure of Literature*, Paul Goodman). But because these fragmentary moments of delight or passion or revelation are not imaginatively *made*, and because the qualities are not sustained throughout the whole of the parts, with the shape, sequence and balance of structure which we associate with art, they cannot survive. Richard Hoggart gives an excellent account of this kind of experience in his lecture, *Schools of English and Contemporary Society*:

Who can listen to a programme of pop songs, or watch *Candid Camera* or *This is Your Life*, without enduring a complicated and complex mixture of attraction and repulsion, of admiration for skill and scorn for the phoney, of wry observations of similarities and correspondences, of sudden reminders of the raciness of speech, or of the capacity for courage or humour, or of shock at the way mass art can 'process' anything, even our most intimate feelings.

But the popular work which deserves serious attention, and which provides a touchstone for criticism of the material of the mass media, is imaginative work: it must have creative intention behind it, though it is communicated in a popular form in an accessible medium. The popular artist has the source of feeling or insight within him, it is to this that he is responsible, it is this which he wants to communicate. But it is not an incohate transmission of raw experience: it is shaped, as all art is, into a selection from experience; and the style and form, 'which carries its own independent feelings, which play against the feeling aroused by the subject', becomes the measure of its created life, its artistic quality. Raymond Williams has made the crucial distinction between a *source* and an *agent* in popular art:

Whatever the difficulty, a good speaker or writer will be conscious of his immediate responsibility to the matter being communicated. He cannot, indeed, feel otherwise, if he is conscious of himself as the source of a particular transmission. His task is the adequate expression of this source, whether it be of feeling, opinion or information. He will use for this expression the common language, to the limit of his particular skill. That this expression is then given multiple transmission is a next stage, of which he may well be conscious, but which cannot, of its nature, affect the source . . . the source cannot in any event be denied, or he denies himself.

Culture and Society

This is the difference between a Billie Holiday or John Ford and their myriad imitators. The struggle to produce work of such quality goes on continually—and this is true not only with the commercial system of communication but also within the more minority forms, and within every medium, the new as well as the traditional.

Finally, to return to Hannah Arendt's distinction, what has such popular art to do with 'art'? Has her gap between 'culture' and 'entertainment' been at all narrowed? The relationship of popular art to high art is not a direct one: when the popular arts aspire consciously to serious status we often get a compromised communication—an 'art' pretentiously serious, falsely complicated and sophisticated, or desperately seeking to be portentous and universal. It is a kind of mish-mash or *kitsch*. This compromise, which Dwight MacDonald calls Midcult,

> has the essential qualities of Masscult—the formula, the built-in reaction, the lack of any standard except popularity—but it decently covers them with a cultural figleaf. . . . Midcult has it both ways: it pretends to respect the standards of high culture while in fact it waters them down and vulgarizes them.
>
> *Against the American Grain*

Yet a connection does exist. It is salutary to remember that when, in 1758, James Ralph wrote (in *The Case of Authors*):

> As long as the Patient continues to swallow, he [the bookseller] continues to administer; and on the first Symptom of a Nausea, he changes the Dose. Hence the Cessation of all Political Carminatives, and the Introduction of Cantharides, in the shape of Tales, Novels, Romances, etc.

he was describing a commercial situation in a literary form which had already produced *Robinson Crusoe*, *Moll Flanders*, *Gulliver's Travels*, *Pamela*, *Clarissa* and *Joseph Andrews*, as well as a litany of trash. Or, to take another case, when, in a letter of 28 July 1597, the Lord Mayor of London wrote the following passage about the contemporary drama:

> nothing but profane fables, Lasciuious matters, cozoning devizes, & other vnseemly & scurrilous behaviours, which ar so sett forthe; as that they move wholy to imitacion & not to the avoyding of those vyces which they represent.
>
> Quoted by A. Harbage, *Shakespeare's Audience*.

such plays as *Tamburlaine*, *Doctor Faustus*, *Romeo and Juliet*, *Richard II* and *Henry IV* were among the many plays which had recently been performed.

Both Elizabethan drama and the novel were 'popular forms' (though not to the same extent, as Ian Watt points out in *The Rise of the Novel*). The outstanding Elizabethan and Jacobean dramatists produced plays within the same tradition, for the same stage and (being closer to an 'organic community') the same audience. It is not the existence of a drama 'of the streets', such as the plays of Dekker, which concerns us here, so much as the *substructure* of the popular in work of high seriousness: in Shakespeare, of course (see Miss Bradbrook's *Elizabethan Tragedy* and *Growth and Structure of Elizabethan Comedy*), but also more directly in Ben Jonson, Middleton, Massinger, Webster and Tourneur. In his outstanding work, *Drama and Society in the Age of Jonson*, L. C. Knights shows how the study of Ben Jonson's plays leads directly to 'the nerve centres of the social life of the time'. To get there, Jonson, in his great plays, made use of the popular psychology of his time—the interest in 'melancholie' and the 'humours'. He drew on the popular tradition of individual and social morality. He made use of the rhythms and idioms of colloquial speech, sermons and tracts, journalism, the traditions of caricature and abuse—work which embodied what Tawney called 'that living body of assumptions as to the right conduct of human affairs'. These popular idioms and images occur in Jonson's work, not simply as 'local effects' (usually a sign of decadence, or the wrong kind of contemporaneity) but as 'ways of thought and perception'. He had assimilated these popular forms which have since disappeared. Of course, Jonson was steeped in the classical tradition as well. The immediacy of his verse arose partly from the tension between these classical and popular elements—what Knights calls his 'tough equilibrium'. 'His classicism is an equanimity and assurance that springs—"here at home"—from the strength of a native tradition.' The popular element not only offered him his subject matter and his 'types', but also helped him to formulate an attitude towards them: 'the satire presupposes certain general attitudes in the audience, and . . . it builds on something that was already there'. The violent juxtapositions of death and life, the bitter irony, the immediacy of the physical world, the themes of lust and revenge which mark so much Elizabethan and Jacobean tragedy were made possible by the study of Seneca, but they were also an inheritance from a long line of popular work—revenge melo-dramas, miracle plays, the Dance of Death, even journalism (for example, Nashe's description of London under plague). To read the work of a popular dramatist like Jonson is to appreciate simultaneously the quality of a highly individual mind and style and the qualities of the popular traditions which helped to form it. In the revenge tragedies, from Kyd to Ford, we find a popular form, full of action and violence, which artists of varying talents used as a vehicle of dramatic expression. The closest approxima-tion to the revenge form we have in contemporary art is the western: the greatest revenge play, however, is *Hamlet*.

In this example from Elizabethan drama we see three possible connections between the popular and the serious in art. We find the substructure of the popular in the work of the greatest of the dramatists. We find great dramatists sustained in their work by popular attitudes which, though often in their own right ephemeral and inferior, give vigour, vitality and relevance to their work. And we find a body of the most outstanding drama drawing directly on a popular form to make popular work—the revenge tragedy of blood is one such example.

Perhaps the most significant connection between popular art and high art is to be seen in the way popular work helps the serious artist to focus the actual world, to draw upon common types, to sharpen his observation and to detect the large but hidden move-ments of society. New art forms frequently arise when profound modifications are taking place in social life and in the 'structure of feelinig' in the society. Often this change is first recorded in popular work, and new popular themes and conventions are devised to deal with them, or to express them. L. G. Salingar comments that 'The theme of revenge (the "wild justice" of Bacon's essay) was popular in Elizabethan tragedy because it touched important questions of the day: the social problems of personal honour and the survival of feudal lawlessness; the political problem of tyranny and resistance; and the supreme question of providence, with its provocative contrasts between human vengeance and divine.' Through its modes, the 'despair, or confusion' of that time of transition in English society was expressed—'the decay of the tudor aristocracy, and the disenchantment of Elizabethan men of letters. The Italian setting is used for social complaint and for a generalized satire, which includes minor comic figures from the court or the underworld resembling those in *Hamlet* and the comedy of "humours" ' ('Tourneur and the Tragedy of Revenge', *Penguin Guide*, Vol. 2). In the same way, at another point of transition in English social life, the novel emerges in its popular and its high forms. In Defoe—journalist and pamphleteer as well as novelist—is recorded the growth of commercial society, the rise of individualism, the collapse of the old order, the new philosophy, the beginnings of bourgeois society. In Richardson, the dissolving of older literary forms and classical formulae leads to the novel of sentiment and feeling, the instantaneous recording in prose of the details of experience and personal psychology, and the growth of a realism of the emotions. And these themes are common both to the outstanding novelists—Defoe, Richardson and Fielding—and to the more popular novelists. Indeed, the line goes back directly to Bunyan, and thus to Puritanism and the beginnings of capitalism (see Mrs Leavis's *Fiction and the Reading Public*, and Ian Watt's *The Rise of the Novel*). For nearly a century and a half the line between the popular and the serious in the novel is almost impossible to draw—we can tell the great novelists from the hacks and sentimentalists, but the medium of the novel is open to both: the substructure of the popular may account for some of the weaknesses of Dickens's art, but it is also closely bound up with his greatness.

The intention here has not been to argue by direct analogy. Clearly, one of the great—perhaps tragic—characteristics of the modern age has been the progressive alienation of high art from popular art. Few art forms are able to hold both elements together: and popular art has developed a history and a topography of its own, separate from high and experimental art. Nevertheless, the connection between the two cannot be denied. In some way difficult precisely to define, the vigour of popular art—whether communally or individually made—and the relevance of serious art are bound indissolubly together. So that when we look at the new media—especially those where the fragmentation between popular and serious is not yet complete (like the cinema)—we are showing a proper concern, not only for the moments of quality in the popular arts, but for the condition and quality of imaginative work of *any* level, and thus for the quality of the culture as a whole. It is this care for the quality of the culture—rather than the manufacture and manipulation of levels of taste—which is the ultimate *educational* responsibility we try to focus here. If for the word 'literature' we read 'imaginative work' the following passage from Ezra Pound could stand as an emblem of the whole study:

Has literature a function in the state, in the aggregate of humans? It has . . . to do with the clarity of 'any and every' thought and opinion. It has to do with maintaining the very cleanliness of the tools, the health of the very matter of thought itself. Save the rare and very limited instances of invention in the plastic arts, or in mathematics, the individual cannot think or communicate his thought, the governor or legislator cannot act effectively or frame his laws, without words, and the solidity and validity of these words is in the care of the damned and despised literati. When their work goes rotten . . . by that I do not mean when they express indecorous thoughts . . . but when their very medium, the very essence of their work, the application of word to thing, goes rotten, i.e. becomes slushy and inexact, or excessive or bloated, the whole machinery of social and of individual thought and order goes to pot.

The ABC of Reading

PART TWO

Topics for Studies

4

Popular Forms and Popular Artists

The blues is everybody's business.

THE BLUES

The blues are a popular form in almost every sense except the one which is most commonly applied to the new arts. True, the audience for the blues can never be measured in millions, like the fans for a pop song or a Mickey Spillane novel. Yet there is a most important sense in which the pop song or the Spillane novel is 'type-cast' for its audience, and therefore limited, whereas the blues 'is everybody's business'. This apparent paradox is important for an understanding of how the word 'popular' is applied to the various 'arts' discussed in this book.

The blues are one of the most original and authentic of popular forms. Within the limits of popular music, no form has managed to retain so much of its original force while being so rapidly and widely absorbed and adapted. The blues are both the heart of negro American folk music and the soul of commercial jazz. This is a double life which few popular forms can boast. To listen to Big Bill Broonzy or Memphis Slim today is to hear again the authentic voices of a 'folk' culture. Yet few musicians would deny Jimmy Rushing's claim that the blues are 'a foundation to the building of jazz'. Something closely resembling the blues existed long before the Civil War. Yet when Charlie Parker, one of the most complex and advanced jazz musicians, lay dying in 1955, he wondered aloud to Art Blakey 'when the young people would come back to playing the blues'. In spite of his highly sophisticated musical techniques, Parker blew the blues 'from the bottom', and many younger experimental jazz musicians have based their work on a return to the 'feeling', the 'soul'—if not the chord progressions—of the blues.

The blues are 'popular' in the sense in which most folk music is popular. Their origins cannot be traced back to any one outstanding or conscious creator. They have to be sought, rather, in the history of a whole people and a community—originally the slave minority of the Deep South. Almost certainly, the blues began with the use of the 'voice' among the field-hands on the plantations. The original 'cry' was a wordless field-holler, sometimes a single call of recognition between slaves, sometimes a warning of danger approaching. Later, these cries developed into work-songs, the verse sung by a leader, the chorus by the gangs of men working in unison. The original 'swing' of jazz was the swing of a pickaxe. The function of the work-song was to make intolerable work tolerable—to transform human suffering into a kind of art by the expressive gifts of music and rhythm. These songs became the distilled history of an exploited 'folk'.

But, as with other folk music, what started as a communal and anonymous art became an individual one with the gradual emergence of the skilled performer. This happened long before the classic blues singers made their appearance. In his *Romance of the Negro Folk Cry in America* Willis James says that the work-songs were 'the source for a series of startling variations, done in the freest manner imaginable, depending, of course, on the gifts of the crier'.

In the blues we find not only the experience of the negro folk, but a record of the influences to which the negro people were subject. When Christianity penetrated to the South, the negroes adapted the subject matter and songs of religion to half-remembered African rhythms and tones. The call of the Promised Land became a symbol of freedom here on earth. That connection is still made—indeed, the return of the younger jazz musicians after Parker to the blues and to 'soul' is directly connected with the new urgency with which negro minorities in America are seeking their identity and their freedom within the American community.

James Baldwin, the most outstanding creative talent in this new movement, has, in the titles as well as the language and texture of feeling of two of his books, made this connection explicit: *Go Tell It on the Mountain* and *The Fire Next Time*.

The connections are not only connections of content; they are also influences of form and style. The rich harmonies of the Sankey hymns were reshaped to the non-diatonic African musical scale. The Methodist choruses were 'jazzed' without the slightest loss of religious fervour. In one way the hymns, moulded to African patterns, kept something of the old continent alive in the new. But the reshaping of African notes to Christian words and symbols was also a means of adapting to the new life. Somewhere between these two processes, one of the classic blues forms was born—the 'gospel' blues, originating, perhaps, in the 'shouting' voice of the negro preacher, which is really a hell-fire and brimstone sermon becoming an African chant or a slave cry.

After the Civil War, when the negro began to travel, the blues as we know them emerged. The songs ceased to be the direct expression of the 'folk', and became instead the recorded story of 'folks'. It was a way of telling or talking about your troubles; a troubadour art before it was a professional one. Jelly Roll Morton, one of the original heroes of New Orleans jazz, 'told' his life to Alan Lomax at the piano (see *Mister Jelly Roll*).

The carriers of the blues were 'bar-room pianists, careless nomadic labourers, watchers of incoming trains and steam-boats, street-corner guitar players, strumpets and outcasts' (Nat Hentoff in 'The Blues', *Jazz World*, ed. Ceruli, Korall and Nasatir). Southern negroes sang about anything, 'trains, steam-boats, steam whistles, sledge hammers, fast women, mean bosses, stubborn mules—all became subjects for their songs' (W. C. Handy). Handy recalls a 'loose-jointed negro', in rags, with his toes coming through his shoes, singing songs familiar through the Southland since the mid-century. These songs, 'simple declarations expressed usually in three lines and set to a kind of earth-born music', already had the shape of the classic blues form (*Father of the Blues*):

> Boll Weevil, where you been so long?
> Boll Weevil, where you been so long?
> You stole my cotton, now you want my corn.

or,

> Oh, the Kate's up the river, Stack O'Lee's in the ben',
> Oh, the Kate's up the river, Stack O'Lee's in the ben',
> And I ain't seen my baby since I can't tell when.

In these terms the blues are a popular music, not because millions sang or knew them, but because they grew out of a common experience, an experience central to the life of a whole people, which they transposed into art.

But the blues are also a popular *form*. They allow for many variations, but these occur within the conventions of that form. The simplest form is the twelve-bar blues built around three basic chords. 'For each of these three four-bar sections, the blues singer strung a line. The first was usually repeated, and the third made the barbed point' (ed. N. Shapiro and N. Hentoff, *Hear Me Talkin' To Ya*):

> Sittin' in the house with everythin' on my mind,
> Sittin' in the house with everythin' on my mind,
> Lookin' at the clock and can't even tell the time.

The singer used up only half of each four-bar line, which 'affords the improviser, for one thing, a space in which his next idea can go through a period of gestation. . . . He can utilize his space, not as a hold, but as a *playground* in which his voice or his instrument may be allowed to wander in such fantastic musical paths as he pleases, returning (not necessarily, but usually) to the key-note, third or fifth, yet again before vacation is over' (Abbe Niles, preface to W. C. Handy's *The Blues*). This allows for invention and improvisation within a framework provided by the form itself. The other convention was the 'blue' notes, which arise partly, as Niles suggested, from the tendency of the untrained negro voice to worry or slur the note between the flat and the natural, but which are also a result of the attempt to adapt the tones and notes of a European musical scale to the non-diatonic scale of African music.

In the blues form, both convention and improvisation play their part. When the blues were adapted to musical instruments, the instruments were 'vocalized' and the 'breaks' became the place for instrumental improvisations. Leonard Bernstein has said that

the instrument imitating the voice . . . is the very soil in which jazz grows. Louis Armstrong improvising the breaks in a blues song by Bessie Smith is the essential sound in jazz.

The blues are not only a form—they are also a *feeling*. This core of feelings is what the younger musicians call 'soul', and it underlies a good deal of jazz that is no longer performed within the strict conventions of the classic blues. Blues singers have drawn upon this collective source of popular emotion in their art. The essence of the blues in this sense is that low-down, dragging feeling associated with personal 'troubles'—but never sentimentalized, as is common in so much folk music: sharp, bitter, with a strong edge of irony and a protest against misery. W. C. Handy says:

The blues came from the man farthest down. The blues came from nothingness, from want, from desire. And when a man sang or played the blues, a small part of the want was satisfied from the music.
ed. N. Shapiro and N. Hentoff, *Hear Me Talkin' to Ya*

The blues can also be songs of exaltation, as religious blues are, though even here it is exaltation over tribulation. Billie Holiday said: 'The blues to me is like being very sad, very sick, going to church, being very happy. The blues is sort of a mixed-up thing.

You just have to feel it. You sing the blues when you're sad, but you can also sing blues very well when you're feeling good, because you can tell another kind of story about the blues then. There's happy blues and there's sad blues.'

The blues grew originally from a particular place (the Deep South) and relate to a particular institution (slavery), but they are also a form of universal human expression. The feelings are simple enough, direct and frankly given, and the form well enough defined to be available as a mode of musical expression to many people in many places. The blues have to be lived and felt to be sung. They cannot be turned on and off according to some formula. They must represent deep and authentic human experiences and feelings, or they are nothing. Though Bessie Smith was one of the great entertainers, she sang the blues because 'she meant it. Blues were her life' (Frank Walker, *Hear Me Talkin' to Ya*). 'The blues? Man, I didn't start playing the blues ever. That was in me before I was born and I've been playing and living the blues ever since. . . . You gotta feel the blues to make them right' (T-Bone Walker, *Hear Me Talkin' To Ya*). 'The first blues that I heard, the ones my mother used to sing, were always homey things or things that were troubling her. She might sing about the dinner burning or anything like that' (T-Bone Walker, ibid.).

Though the root-feelings of the blues remain, they have been expressed in many ways (these are admirably discussed in greater detail in Francis Newton's book, *The Jazz Scene*, pp. 98–102). A form of the 'country' blues was—and still is—brought in from the backlands by travelling minstrels, mostly men. Later versions of this type have been recorded by Big Bill Broonzy, Brownie McGhee and Sonny Terry. The 'classic' blues were almost the exclusive art of the women professional entertainers, Ma Rainey, Bessie Smith, Clara Smith, Bertha Hill. In the 'city' blues the country blues were adapted to jazz and pop music of which the best exponents are Joe Turner and Jimmy Rushing. One form of the blues retained its connections with religious music—the 'gospel' blues, brought to a high pitch by women gospel singers, mingling the low-down feeling of the classic secular blues with the exaltation of the revivalist chorus. One of the finest performers of this kind is Mahalia Jackson. At the same time, the blues were adapted to musical instruments—the bar-room piano played with a honky-tonk 'drag' and the trumpet with its impure blues vibratos. Since then jazz has often gone back to the blues to be refreshed and replenished. The blues as an instrumental form were standard material for the New Orleans bands, and there is an unmistakable authentic blues feeling behind the best modern jazz players—Parker and Thelonius Monk, especially. Indeed, in spite of the immense variety in jazz since its origins, the blues have remained as a test of authenticity. They have also become a *lingua franca* between musicians. When jazz players from the different schools come together for a session, they often start off by 'just blowing the blues'.

The blues have also provided a source for pop music. The relationship between the 'country' blues and rock-'n'-roll is discussed in the chapter on 'The Young Audience', but it is useful to point out that a somewhat crude, but true, blues feeling lies behind the 'pop' recordings of Ray Charles. His 'shouting' voice recalls, at a very great distance, the immensely powerful range of Bessie Smith ('she was certainly recognized among blues singers— a shouter, they called her. They all respected her because she had a powerful pair of lungs'. Buster Bailey, *Hear Me Talkin' to Ya*), though there is nothing in Ray Charles of that deep reservoir of passion and feeling which welled up into her sonorous voice, and which 'just upset you'. Whereas Ray Charles is exploring the blues for more authentic (i.e. alive) and primitive material for the pops, Bessie Smith lived what she sang, and brought her great, intense musical gifts to express her life. She honoured the feelings in her self by her music. To that alone, even as a professional entertainer, she felt responsible. As Francis Newton recalls, 'She was alone all her life, and sang of the transitoriness of money, friends, liquor and men with the deep and wary bitterness of somebody who knows that "You can't trust nobody, you might as well be alone" ' (*The Jazz Scene*). But even the primitive crudeness of Ray Charles is closer to the real thing than most pop entertainers, and the clapping hands and hoarse choruses of his records recall something of the atmosphere of the prayer meeting.

To hear the blues is to respond to a range of powerful, simple feelings, sometimes exultant, often tragic, which grew out of personal and social distress, but which have been transformed by music into a truly enduring popular art.

Billie Holiday

It would be easy to write of Ma Rainey or Bessie Smith, two performers who brought the popular art of the blues to a pitch of classical perfection. It is more difficult to write of Billie Holiday, for she was not a classic blues singer. Though she sang blues often, she was a commercial entertainer in the 'cabaret' tradition. The best of the pops and the ballads were her standard material. Her voice lacked Bessie Smith's vibrant contralto and Ella Fitzgerald's lyrical flight and eloquence. Yet she matched her tragic life with a vocal tone which, at its best, remains one of the great and moving sounds in jazz.

All her life she worried about that tone. One of her few and faithful friends, Lester Young, had the same trouble matching other saxophone performers; though they could not equal the melody of his line or his phrasing, they were capable of a bigger sound on their horns. In her autobiography, Billie said:

> There ain't no rule saying everybody's got to deliver the same damn volume or tone.
> But anyway, this talk about a big tone messed with Lester for months. And me too. So I said, 'What the hell, Lester, don't let them make a fool of us. We'll get you a big horn with big fat reeds and things and no damn rubber bands around it holding you back. We'll get us a tone.'
>
> B. Holiday with W. Dufty, *Lady Sings the Blues*

By the end, when her voice had been stripped back to the bare elements by her hard life, loneliness and drugs, only her authoritative tone remained.

Music was in the family—her father played guitar with the Fletcher Henderson band—but Billie Holiday started singing, because she was hungry, at fifteen. Instinctively she turned to two truly original talents in jazz, Bessie Smith and Louis Armstrong.

I used to run errands for a madam on the corner. I wouldn't run errands for anybody, still won't carry a case across the street today, but I ran around for this woman because she's let me listen to all Bessie's records—and Pops Armstrong's record of *West End Blues.*

. . . I always wanted Bessie's big sound and Pops' feeling.

ibid.

From Bessie she learned how to 'say' the blues, even when she was singing pop material. From Louis she learned jazz improvisation. These were the elements of her art.

She never achieved Bessie Smith's 'big sound'. Her voice was harsh and gritty but haunting and sensuous, 'whose natural mood was an unresigned and voluptuous welcome for the pains of love' (Francis Newton, *New Statesman*, August 1959). By the time Billie started to sing, the blues and jazz had developed as instrumental arts. Billie gave something back to the music from which she drew. She 'instrumentalized' her voice. Teddy Wilson, with whom she made some of her finest recordings in the late thirties, said of her, 'You can feel her singing, like another instrument.' Billie said of herself: 'I don't feel like I'm singing. I feel like I'm playing a horn. I try to improvise like Les Young, like Louis Armstrong, or someone else I admire. What comes out is what I feel. I hate straight singing. I have to change a tune to my own way of doing it.'

She did not simply introduce jazz phrasing to the ballad song. She actually transformed her voice into a jazz instrument, 'playing' with the front line. She lacked range, but her elongated notes were like the cry of the high muted trumpet. In the best of her recordings (*I only have Eyes for You, This is my Last Affair, Miss Brown to You, What A Little Moonlight can do to You, I Cover the Waterfront, I Cried for You*) the group did not accompany her, she played with them. Frequently, they would play right through the whole song first, not worrying about an introduction for the singer. They did not alter the tempo to suit her but, on the faster numbers, maintained a strong, swinging jazz rhythm. Her voice would edge into the second chorus, picking up the beat, paraphrasing the melody as Armstrong does, working the words into a jazz phrase: like another trumpet taking first solo. Her last notes formed a perfect introduction or 'lead' for the next instrument. Bobby Tucker, who played for her for some time, said, 'She had the greatest conception of a beat I ever heard.' In the strict sense of the word, she had no melody at all. She didn't need it.

She phrased like a jazz soloist, twisting both the melodic line and the words to her improvisation (for a deliberate paraphrasing of rather hackneyed, sentimental tunes, see her rendering of *I'll Get By*, *Yesterdays* or *On the Sunny Side of the Street*). She dragged words and phrases out of their original shape, and stamped her sound and her tone upon them. Where she wanted a quicker beat, she slurred the words; when she wanted a wail, she flattened the vowels mercilessly and dragged the note (the word 'river' in *I Gotta Right to Sing the Blues*). Frequently she accentuated her lines across the rhythm of the accompanying group, so that the beat ceased to have the metre of the spoken phrase and assumed the rhythm and syncopation of the jazz solo. The best and worst of her material was transformed by her performance. The beautiful slow ballad *I Cover the Waterfront* became a 'blues'; the Porgy and Bess songs became jazz; the flapper tune *Miss Brown to You* became relaxed swing. As Francis Newton said in his moving tribute to her at her death:

Her unique achievement was to have twisted this [the pop song] into a genuine expression of the major passions by means of a total disregard for its sugary tunes, or indeed of any tune other than her own few delicately crying elongated notes, phrased like Bessie Smith or Louis Armstrong in sack-cloth.

New Statesman, August 1959

She was one of the few popular entertainers to make an original ballad into a popular nightclub song—the bitter anti-lynching *Strange Fruit*, based on a poem by Lewis Allen, which she arranged with her accompanist, Sonny White, and made into a masterpiece. 'It became my personal protest.' She did the same thing for that haunting song *Gloomy Sunday*. About *Strange Fruit* she wrote:

> When I came to the final phrase of the lyric I was in the angriest and strongest voice I had been in for months. My piano player was in the same form. When I said '. . . for the sun to rot', and then a piano punctuation, '. . . for the wind to suck', I pounced on those words like they had never been hit before.
>
> *Lady Sings the Blues*

When she sang *Strange Fruit*, she distilled so much of her terrible life into it that she was sometimes physically sick. She put the same feeling into every note she sang—the great recordings of the thirties and forties, and the tragic, agonizing recordings, based on the four or five notes her ravaged voice could manage, which she made at the end of her life. To listen to her at her peak, to recapture what Newton calls 'those coarse-textured, sinuous, sensual and unbearably sad noises', is to hear the blues reborn in another idiom, a folk music once again becoming a modern popular art.

THE WESTERN

Perhaps the most remarkable thing about the western film is its continued popularity. It is not only Hollywood's most original contribution but its most enduring; it is almost as old as the cinema itself. One of the earliest story films, *The Great Train Robbery*, made in 1905, was a primitive western. Today a new one reaches British cinemas at least once a month and the cowboy film has become a seemingly permanent part of television entertainment. The locale of the American West is the most universally recognized. The classic scenes—the stagecoach setting out on its lonely journey across the prairie, the line-up at the long bar, the poker game, the gunfighters facing each other in the empty street—these are familiar to audiences throughout the world.

The relatively fixed conventions of the western coupled with its popularity have encouraged critics to write about it in sociological and psychological terms; to explain its existence by reference to the needs and aspirations of the audience it caters for. The western, it has been said, is a modern morality tale. Good and Evil confront one another in the starkest terms, sometimes (as with *Shane*) in consciously symbolic images. The historical reality has been transformed into myth. An idealized world has been created in which conflicts are reduced to their most elementary forms: we are presented with moral choices shorn of the ambiguities and complications of modern life. By entering into this world, by submitting to it and identifying with its heroes, we are able to assume in fantasy the mastery over our lives we would wish to achieve in reality. But this submission also serves to clarify the desire for such mastery and perhaps therefore makes it a more active principle in our lives. The western has its own rituals, and these are never mere rituals of violence but imply a code, a certain way of life. When Henry Fonda initiates the young sheriff in *The Tin Star* into the skills of his craft, the emphasis is less on mechanical ability with the gun as on the need for certain qualities of mind and character; for control, for mental discipline. The bringing of law and order to the frontier townships, the wagon train setting out for the promised land—these persistent themes fulfil our need for community and utopia. (At the same time the heroic solutions satisfy our desire to act as free men.)

The appeal to Americans is, of course, quite specific. It matches both the longing for rural innocence and the ideals of rugged individualism, themes that appear in other kinds of American films, notably the early work of Frank Capra with its idyllic picture of small-town life and individualist solutions. Yet the western seems to offer something to urban peoples everywhere. In part the response is to the feeling of freedom evoked by the great beauties of the landscape, but primarily it is a response to the westerner as hero. In the cinema, and especially in the western, mere physical presence is important. For most of us, if we can leave aside what we have been taught by the books on film art and aesthetics, our memories of westerns are of the stars—Gary Cooper, Henry Fonda, Joel McCrea, Randolph Scott, James Stewart and so many others. They are all lean men and there is an expressiveness in the way they stand; and more—a quality of readiness, of inner tension, controlled by discipline born of experience. As these stars get older they seem the more effective in embodying elements of the myth. Their lined and weathered faces suggest a kind of weary resignation before the inadequacies of the world. Think, for example, of the face of John Wayne in *Rio Bravo* or *The Horse Soldiers* compared with the young Wayne of *Stagecoach*. Think of Cooper in *High Noon* or Gregory Peck in *The Gunfighter* (Plate 5). At least in the most distinguished examples the western offers us something like a tragic hero. He lives under some sort of moral compulsion, 'doing what he has to do' because of some deadly necessity. The western describes a man's world, but the hero honours women and in his relation with them exhibits a graciousness and reserve. It is this, alongside the moral element in the image of the lonely man pitted against injustice, that allows us to speak of this man as a latter-day knight, the only equivalent we have for the chivalrous hero in popular myth today.

Robert Warshow in his perceptive essay, 'The Westerner', has said:

What he defends at bottom is the purity of his own image—in fact his honour . . . the westerner is the last gentleman, and the movies which over and over again tell his story are probably the last art form in which the concept of honour retains its strength.

Of course, I do not mean to say that ideas of virtue and justice and courage have gone out of culture. Honour is more than these things; it is a style concerned with harmonious appearances as much as with desirable consequences, and tending therefore towards the denial of life in favour of art.

The Immediate Experience

The significance of the western hero is to be found in what he is, rather than in what he does. The plots remain the same but inside the rigid convention the film works like a ballet. There is an endless search for balance and harmony. The harmony extends outwards to his relationship with the natural world and inwards to his peace of mind which he either possesses or must achieve. 'The westerner', said Warshow, 'is a figure in repose.' His integrity is expressed in his style—in stance, movement and gesture.

> There is little cruelty in western movies, and little sentimentality; our eyes are not focussed on the suffering of the defeated but on the deportment of the hero. Really, it is not violence at all which is the 'point' of the western movie, but a certain image of man, a style, which expresses itself most clearly in violence. Watch a child with his toy guns and you will see: what most interests him is not (as we so much fear) the fantasy of hurting others but to work out how a man might look when he shoots or is shot.
>
> Warshow, ibid.

For all its stereotyping, the western is capable of presenting an image of the tragic life—the lonely, roaming hero destined to disappear as the reign of law settles over the West or as his scattered past catches up with him in some dingy bar-room.

But we must beware of too many generalizations which leave untouched the qualitative differences. Most westerns are too crude even to operate on the level of myth. Phrases like 'a certain image of man' and 'deportment of the hero' suggest a degree of refinement. We might reasonably use the term deportment in describing the physical presence of Henry Fonda in *The Tin Star* or even John Wayne in *Rio Bravo*, but it would hardly fit the lumbering gait of Burt Lancaster in *Gunfight at the OK Corral*. Henry King's austere and sombre film, *The Gunfighter*, could honestly be said to offer an 'image of the tragic life', but it would be pretentious to employ such language in describing the average western. It is at the point where it refuses to make critical judgements that the inadequacy of the social or psychological approach is revealed.

An obvious distinction is needed, for example, between the westerns of the cinema and those made for television. Both offer themselves for discussion in terms of myth but it is hard to imagine a subject more ill-suited to television presentation. Even when an interesting western, such as *High Noon*, is televised it loses more than half its significance because of the picture size and the poor quality of the image. The sense of relationship between the characters and their environment is lost and an undue weight is placed on dialogue. Although there are marginal differences between them, the TV series are very cheaply made, with an emphasis on dialogue scenes and library material. In the absence of any more subtle qualities they are even coming to rely, as bad films often do, on complicated plots. The demand for filmed westerns on TV is putting great pressure on the writers, who often produce scripts that have little to do with the form within which they are working and might just as well be made as crime stories or mystery thrillers. In one of the *Rawhide* episodes the central situation involved a Prussian count who had set up a miniature feudal state in the West. His German workers rebelled when he had some of them flogged, and the Count experienced a change of heart, suddenly seeing the benefits of the American way of life. An episode of *Tenderfoot* involved mysterious coffins, wreaths and freshly dug graves and might as well have been set in Victorian England.

In discussing westerns the TV series can, of course, be used as examples, particularly when talking about plot, character and motivation. But the strength of the best westerns is in their visual qualities, so conspicuously lacking on TV.

Even with the westerns of the cinema, distinctions must be made. It is all too easy to slip into the habit of talking about them as if all the films in the genre were of equal value and no changes of style had taken place over the years.

The first westerns were very simple and cheaply produced. They centred on the exploits of heroes like William S. Hart and Bronco Bill Anderson and from this tradition came the films of cowboy stars such as Tom Mix, Buck Jones and many others. More elaborate and carefully staged westerns developed after *The Covered Wagon* (1923), and these reached their height in the films of the middle and late thirties. These films, among them *The Plainsman* (1936), *Wells Fargo* (1937), and *Union Pacific* (1939), often consciously aimed at an epic re-creation of American history. Alongside them, and continuing after the war, were films less grand in aim but creating a romantic self-contained portrait of a past world. Of these the best examples are the films of John Ford.

In recent years the western has undergone a change. Its new form, variously called the adult, philosophic or psychological western, is more realistic. Characterization is more complex, the roots of behaviour are frequently treated in psychological terms and the moral distinctions have become ambiguous. There is often a conscious attempt to use the basic western formula to comment on some social problem or aspect of contemporary behaviour.

High Noon is a good example of this type. The story centres on the isolation of the Marshal from the rest of the community. A trio of bad men are about to enter the town and the Marshal (Gary Cooper) attempts to enlist the citizens as deputies. For various reasons they refuse. He also becomes alienated from his Quaker wife. The issue of violence is dramatized in the debate in the church, where the citizens argue with the Marshal about the rights and wrongs of the case, and in the conflict between the Marshal and his wife which springs up because of her religious faith. The film was also meant to be a comment, with references to McCarthyism, on how fear can undermine a community.

A similar situation, with one man being left in isolation by his fellows, is treated in *3.10 to Yuma*. Here most of the film is taken up with a psychological struggle between the tired, uneasy and rather inarticulate farmer hero (played by Van Heflin) and a bad man (played with immense charm by Glenn Ford). *The Big Country* reflects the preoccupation with the ethics of violence in its pacifist hero, and *Shane* is shaped quite deliberately as a morality tale balancing the purity of its mysterious hero against the menacing evil of its hired killer. All of these films have some quality. In *High Noon* we recognize the rightness of Gary Cooper's presence as we honour the intention of the film-maker. *3.10 to Yuma* beautifully captures the feeling of the isolation and loneliness of frontier life. In *Shane* the killer confronts one of the homesteaders, tempts him into drawing his gun and then shoots him.

The scene is superbly handled—the body falling into the mud and the sun glinting through watery clouds—and its implications are underlined in the carefully composed funeral scene that follows.

Yet these new-style westerns do not represent a simple gain over the previous kind. They are interesting but flawed. Some of them evade the very issues they pretend to deal with. In *High Noon* the Marshal's life is saved by his Quaker wife who forgets her principles at a crucial moment and shoots a man in the back.The hero's own brand of egotism is not examined. The pacifist hero of *The Big Country* resists the traditional challenge to his courage by refusing to ride the wild horse. However, once left alone, he does ride it. He is not quite alone, of course; the cinema audience remains. A good example of having it both ways.

More important, many of these films have a distinctly abstract quality. One senses that the real people and situations are not responded to but are manipulated rather mechanically to illustrate a thesis. Shane, the lone ex-gunfighter who comes into the settled community, is clearly meant to have some special significance as a rather mystical self-sacrificing figure. Perhaps it is largely the fault of the actor that this is never realized. But the other elements in the film—the heavily stylized, black and menacing figure of evil (played by Jack Palance) and the study of the working family in their homestead—seem too self-consciously symbolic. This is especially true of the scenes at the homestead where one becomes aware of the stream, for example, as a prop to help create an idyllic mood, a mood that finally seems thin and artificial.

In *High Noon* the total effect is similar. The scene in the church is handled like a debate with each contributor rising into the frame to present his point of view. Behind the children at play outside the church we can almost hear the voice of the assistant director. There is too much deliberation behind the shots of Cooper striding alone through the deserted streets, and the cross-cutting between this and the scene at the railway station, where we see the tracks stretching out to the horizon, may serve to build up tension but reveals little about the people involved. There is no genuine human feeling in these images and the film ultimately seems empty and cold. So too with *3.10 to Yuma*. As it proceeds we become increasingly aware of its mannered style—the trick of using crane shots, the contrived grouping of the figures. We may respect the aims of these films but eventually their purposes seem to be at war with the form itself. The western is a stylized form which works most effectively by handling external appearances. It is unsuited to the intimate treatment of character; its dominant image is of man in a landscape. Rather than analyse motive it presents behaviour. It states its values only implicitly by creating an image of a certain way of life. It is a limited form, but the work of John Ford remains as evidence of what can be achieved within its conventions.

John Ford

Ford has been making films for close on half a century. His experience stretches back to the early days of the silent film, and year in, year out, he has produced his quota of movies. Inevitably many of these have been routine productions in which he had no special interest. But when he has felt personally engaged he has produced work of distinction. Indeed he is one of the very few directors working in Hollywood who has managed, at least from time to time, to impose on his material the stamp of his own personality. What is more, he has done this not in defiance of the system but working within it. A professional film-maker since the age of twenty, he is completely a man of the cinema, and what he has to say has been said to the general audience and through the conventions of the popular film. His work covers a wide range of subjects but he is moved in particular by the stories of the pioneering days and has created some of the most memorable films of the old West. At one level these have been magnificent stories of action and adventure. We recall the flight over the salt flats in *Stagecoach* and, more recently, the long trek of the northern cavalry in *The Horse Soldiers*. But through these conventional stories Ford reveals to us his own ideals. He has a deep attachment to the established patterns of living and to the traditional loyalties. He has expressed this in terms of the frontier community (*Drums Along the Mohawk*), the army outpost (*Fort Apache*) and the cavalry (*She Wore a Yellow Ribbon*). In this last film Captain Brittle (John Wayne), now at the end of his career, prepares to inspect the regiment. He stiffens himself, sets his face and marches out into the cold morning light. The men stand in a motionless line as he awkwardly addresses them. Behind him the horses are restless; shafts of sunlight filter through the dust raised by their hooves. The quality of the handling, the unforced but authoritative way in which the mood and atmosphere is created, transforms a conventional situation. And of course this is more than technical mastery. Much has been written about Ford's visual sense; his gift for composing pictures and the beauty of the locations he chooses. But this beauty is not an abstract thing. Through these qualities he emphasizes what he feels to be valuable in life, and it is because of the authenticity of these feelings that we are entitled to call his work poetic. Ford's films are completely free from flashy devices. He rarely uses big close-ups, shooting most of his films from the middle distance. The dramatic tension springs from the characters and their situation and is not artifically created by the manipulations of editing. He allows his camera to rest on his players, revealing not only a respect for them but also a respect for his audience. He works with such assurance in putting his scenes together that one cannot imagine them being constructed in any other way. But the ease is deceptive. The films are consciously shaped. They move like musicals, so that it seems completely appropriate for the images to be supported every now and then by the singing of an old hymn or cavalry song.

Although he has directed some superb action sequences it is in the more subdued passages that he most fully reveals himself. *My Darling Clementine* is the best example of this. The hero, Wyatt Earp (Henry Fonda), decides to become Marshal of Tombstone when the younger of his three brothers is killed. He encounters Doc Holliday, a dissolute consumptive who rules the town, and Clementine, Holliday's former sweetheart, who has come to visit him from the East. The film reaches a climax with a gun battle at the OK Corral. Based partly on fact, the story is predictable. It is flawed by a sub-plot involving Doc Holliday's mistress (weakly played by Linda Darnell). Both these characters are familiar stereotypes, the one of the good/bad girl and the other of the drunken doctor who pulls himself together in time to perform the vital operation. In this case the operation has to fail, to allow Holliday's mistress to redeem herself in death while he is ensured salvation by being killed fighting alongside Wyatt Earp at the final gunfight. The heart of the film, however, is not in these plot devices, but in the evocation of mood, the creation of a sense of community, and, above all else, in the study of Wyatt Earp and his relationship with Clementine. Fonda plays with extraordinary delicacy, and we can sense behind every subtle movement and gesture the accord between director and actor. The portrait of Earp as a type of ideal man embodies all the virtues Ford most admires—courage, loyalty, dedication and gentleness. A long sequence towards the middle of the film is devoted to Sunday morning in a little township. It opens with Earp at the barber's shop. As he rises from his chair he peers anxiously at the mirror and gingerly touches his flat, brilliantined hair, which the barber assures him is the latest style from the East. He comes out to the verandah and stands in the half shade with his brothers, watching the farmers coming into town to dedicate their new church. At the end of this scene Earp takes Clementine to the dedication service. As they walk slowly along through the shadows of the wooden verandah and out into the sunlight the camera retreats gently with them. The voices singing the hymn drift down from the half-completed church. When the service has ended and dancing begins Earp and Clementine look on, but when she starts to keep time with her hands he finally masters his reserve and leads her in the dance with stiff high steps and a self-conscious dignity.

It is difficult to indicate in words the quality of such a sequence, but the stills convey something of the tenderness with which it has been put together (Plate 4). It is passages such as these which lead people to speak of Ford's direction as 'leisurely'. But this is a misleading word, suggesting a style that is slack and casual. The tempo here is slower than in an action sequence but the pacing is exact—the editing is no less precise.

Even Ford's best films are uneven. Like many popular artists he can easily slip into sentimentality. He is frequently careless, especially when dealing with unsympathetic actors or handling material he does not respond to; and equally he can be self-indulgent when, as in *The Quiet Man*, he gets the performers and subjects he likes. There is also a darker side to his work. His respect for physical courage and manliness can degenerate into a kind of callousness. In *The Searchers* the principal character, Ethan, is a man of brutish feelings with an irrational hatred of the Indians. Alongside this figure Ford tries to present a picture of family life. But there is no real sense that Ethan is presented to us critically, and indeed at the end of the film he is seen as a lonely, romantic figure in a shot that frames him in a doorway as he moves away from the homestead.

Nevertheless, Ford's achievement has been considerable. His films present a highly romantic picture strongly tinged with a yearning for the heroic past. But if it is objected that the West he has created never really existed, the answer is that he offers his myth not as an escape but as an ideal. His historical reconstructions are not so much an exercise in nostalgia as an affirmation. He is essentially a poet/craftsman rather than an intellectual and he does not bring to the cinema the cultural equipment of a Bergman or a Buñuel. It is partly this which prevents him from being a major director. But he is truly a popular artist. We can imagine many of the other outstanding directors making a career for themselves in some other sphere—as novelists, perhaps, or dramatists. It is impossible to imagine John Ford as anything other than a maker of movies. When he makes a western he is not self-consciously using the form; he has grown up with it. It is significant that when he has been persuaded (by himself as well as others) to make an art film the result has been a sad failure, as in the case of *The Informer*. Only once did he get a substantial subject that appealed to him, and *The Grapes of Wrath* remains a fine achievement by any standards. His career has been a remarkable one. Hollywood has exiled and broken some, and tamed many; few men have been able to continue over the years putting so much of themselves into their films.

5

Violence on the Screen

What is wrong with the violence of the mass media is not that it is
violent but that it is not art—that it is meaningless violence which
thrills but does not gratify.

NORMAN MUHLEN, *Commentary*, Vol. 1, 1944

The question of violence looms large in any discussion of the
mass media among educationists. When the Pilkington Report set
out to analyse the causes of public 'disquiet about television', it
was obliged to begin with violence (paras. 29–32 and 54–57 of the
Report, especially, repay close attention). The connection between
violence on the screen and juvenile delinquency was discussed by
a Commission set up by the National Council of Public Morals,
which reported in 1917, and again by the Wheare Committee on
Children and the Cinema in 1950. Yet this question of violence in
the media is more complex than appears at first sight. There may
certainly be some point in the complaint that there is too much
traffic in violent themes. But this complaint should be seen for
what it is: a criticism of the balance of content in the media
generally, and not a qualitative judgement on the particular *kinds*
of violence treated, nor an informed opinion on their various
effects. We must deal with the general question first. But since
violence, death and human suffering have always been the subject
matter of at least some great art, we must go on to draw the more
complex distinctions between different kinds of violence: between,
say, the violence of the BBC series of Shakespeare history plays on
television, *Age of Kings*, and that of *77 Sunset Strip*, *Wagon Train*,
Whiplash and *Gunsmoke*. Such distinctions are impossible without
some attention to questions of style and treatment: we shall have
to understand the different qualities expressed in these pro-

grammes, trying to decide how they work as dramatized experiences, and what their psychological impact is.

First, then, in general terms, so far as television is concerned, we are faced with problems of timing and volume. What is suitable for adults in the late evening may not be considered suitable for young children in the afternoon—always supposing that the television providers are alive to their educational responsibilities here, and that a time limit or boundary can be established. When, in a debate on the issue in Parliament in 1962, the Postmaster General said that the BBC assumed children were in bed by nine o'clock, a wise but unidentified backbench voice commented, 'They're wrong ' As for sheer volume, the Pilkington Report remarked simply that 'there was too much violence on television'. Few would disagree with this.

When an incorrect programme balance is combined with the general effects of repetition, the judgement is strengthened. Repetition is crucial. The steady networking of badly produced low-level dramatized series—many of them American in origin or feeling—is one aspect of this saturation process. The 'competition' between the BBC and ITV for the peak viewing figures is probably another. Both the Nuffield Report (1958) and the Pilkington Report (1962) present disturbing evidence on this score. And Dr Himmelweit, leader of the Nuffield team, in a more recent article on 'Television Revisited' (*New Society*, 1/11/62), adds the significant qualifying comment that

more recent westerns designed for adult audiences were of course a far cry from the *Cisco Kid* and *Lone Ranger* type of black-white children's western characteristic of British television when our first study was made.

Although it seems that only the child who is already emotionally disturbed will actually *learn* violence from a particular television programme (the evidence on this score seems fairly conclusive, in both *Television and the Child* and the comparable American study *Television in the Lives of our Children*), it is certainly true that we gradually become habituated to certain attitudes and situations *if they are repeated often enough*. The danger here is that we develop a permissive attitude towards the existence of violence in the world, come to regard it as a 'natural' solution to difficult social problems, or accept it as part of the background to life. This is what the Pilkington Report meant by the danger of a 'callous indifference'. The fear is strengthened when the whole balance is wrong, and when counter-images and attitudes, which enhance life or ennoble gentleness, kindness and love, are so difficult to evoke and often appear so trite and banal set beside the tension and vigour of the rougher scenes.

The effect of habituation on actual choice and preference has already been documented by Dr Himmelweit and her team, and is reported in a passage in the same article which deserves to be more widely known. Reporting in her second survey that 'four out of five in the secondary modern school [sample] and over half in the grammar school chose westerns' as their favourite programme, Dr Himmelweit went on:

However, the trend figures show how much of this fit is a function of supply. For example in 1956, especially on ITV, a spate of crime programmes were shown, e.g. *Dragnet, Inner Sanctum, Highway Patrol*, with BBC adding *Fabian of the Yard* and *Dixon of Dock Green*. Then it was crime programmes which received the top vote. In January 1960, both sides offered large numbers of westerns, so westerns attracted most votes with crime programmes taking fourth place among secondary modern and fifth place among grammar school pupils.

Undoubtedly the television industry creates taste: it does not just respond to it . . .

The image of the one-way traffic, with the public the master, the industry the servant, is a travesty of the situation and a negation of the industry's social responsibility. There is an interaction between viewer and industry, each influencing the other.

'Television Revisited', *New Society*, 1 November 1962

With something of this view informing their attitude—though perhaps without the precise references—the response of many teachers to the problem is simply to condemn and decry television violence wholesale, particularly when public attention is brought to focus on some flagrant example. But a more detailed look reveals the complexities involved as soon as we move away from the quantitative to the qualitative approach. (It is important to notice, however, that these two cannot be effectively separated: both Pilkington and the Nuffield Report use a quantitative-qualitative framework.)

A useful occasion was provided by the strikingly violent episode from the BBC serialized television version of Dickens's *Oliver Twist*. The episode portrayed the murder of Nancy by Bill Sikes. Philip Purser described it in the *Sunday Telegraph* (25/3/62):

Nancy pleaded, but Sikes shouted her down and then struck and struck again and kept on striking, violent, heavy blows. When he'd finished and gazed with despair on what he'd done, water from an overturned pitcher dripped down to mix with the blood on the floor, and somewhere his ugly little dog was howling.

This scene was greeted, as might be expected, with sustained public outcry. The BBC had warned viewers that the episode was a violent one; nevertheless, the Postmaster General, Mr Bevins, when questioned in Parliament, said he found it 'brutal and inexcusable'. There were phone-calls of protest to the BBC, letters in the press, a file presented to the Home Office and a government enquiry set in motion.

The reactions, however, now seem in retrospect surprisingly confused. Philip Purser himself found the episode acceptable, since the violence stemmed naturally from the story and was not gratuitously introduced. He commented that 'advocacy of the rough stuff' seemed more likely to reach young viewers via old movies on television, and he quoted the apposite example of *The Petrified Forest*, where the intellectual 'who doesn't believe in violence is finally driven to it because everything else fails'. The *Daily Express*, a paper which exploits verbal and visual aggressiveness in its editorial presentation, thought that Dickens 'would have witnessed this perversion of his motive with indignation.' *The Guardian*, one of the gentler papers, said that 'if Dickens is to be done at all . . . some unpleasant things are inescapable.' The *Police Review* asked, somewhat cynically (more in the tradition of *Z Cars* than *Dixon of Dock Green*), 'How many of the little perishers complained because there wasn't enough blood?' *Education*, countering the arguments from artistic integrity and fidelity to the spirit of Dickens's text, suggested that 'there are many scenes which convention allows to be graphically described in a novel which should take place off-stage in a play or a film'.

Any attempt to disentangle these conflicting attitudes shows how difficult it is to generalize. The murder of Nancy is, inescapably, a violent episode—matched only by the suicide of Sikes himself—and was intended by Dickens to be one of the climaxes of the book. The BBC claimed, with some justice, that it had respected this original emphasis. However, since transcription from one medium to another was involved, and since this implied a degree of foreshortening and compression which might have altered the total emphasis, the question still remains whether the BBC found the proper television correlative in their handling of the scene. There is a second consideration: the relation of the television episode to the structure of the serialization. The position is further complicated, since the programme was specially designed for children and appeared in Children's Hour; the timing emphasizes the special responsibility of television towards a young and inexperienced audience. A point to note here is that this Hour, which was usually in the hands of specialist producers, was, for the duration of the Dickens series, given over to the Drama Department, which could not be expected to be quite so sensitive to the educational implications of programme planning.

But a suspicion remains that public disquiet derived from the very success of the producer, Eric Taylor, and the actor who played Sikes, Peter Vaughan. Clearly the programme had impact —something which many television plays could not claim—and both production and acting were far above the average for Children's Television. Surely any programme which breaks with the grey monotony and blandness of routine television production deserves praise? Better the occasional blood-and-guts, one feels, than the perpetual aseptic wash.

One is forced back to the actual presentation and handling of the episode which is the only real evidence we have. When interviewed by Pearson Phillips, the BBC commented unofficially (*Daily Mail*, 30/3/62) that 'close-up camera shots make violent incidents inadmissible which would be all right in long-shot'. This is not a casual point. It recognizes the immense power which the television or cinema camera possesses to concentrate or fix our emotional attention on a particular aspect of a scene, simply by selecting it from a whole range of possible shots, and closing in on it until it fills the screen. This is not merely a technical point, as the BBC's comment implicitly recognizes. The choice of one emphasis over another reveals something of the producer's preoccupations or intentions at that particular moment, and he must ultimately carry the responsibility. If television is an 'art', those who make this claim for it must take responsibility for what they do with it, along with the compensating excitement of working in a new medium.

Pearson Phillips remarked that 'there was no other way of shooting the scene'. But there almost always is another way. Certainly the blows must rain on Nancy, and the dumb incomprehension and mental confusion of Sikes at this moment must come across, or the scene has no point. But the very distance of the camera from the blows themselves can reveal the producer's involvement with what is going on—his reticence, his tact, his honesty or his sensationalism. Viewing the episode itself, one could feel the force of the repeated blows and the senseless striking at the girl, as well as the terrible 'despair' on Sikes's face which Purser remarked on. This repetition is as significant a feature in the whole scene as the murder itself. But the overturned pitcher, the mingling of water and blood, the howling dog—these were surely much closer to the gratuitous clichés of television period drama or the horror film—an error of aesthetic tact and moral judgement, a crudity of feeling, as misplaced as the earlier passages had been successful. These visual clichés took the attention immediately away from the legitimate moment of violence and the man's despair—a proper human sequence of feeling—to far cruder sensational 'effects'. Another writer in the *Police Review* commented (without quite seeing the point) that 'three children' he knew 'were mainly concerned about whether the liquid on the studio floor was Nancy's blood or water spilled by Sikes'.

This illustration from *Oliver Twist* shows some of the complexities which arise when the question of violence is narrowed down to a particular instance, and especially when the general creative level of production is high. As *The Guardian* observed in an editorial, 'An isolated murder which strikes the viewer with horror is less corrupting than the incessant suggestion that murder is a bagatelle.' But the programmes in which this 'incessant suggestion' is made are those in which nothing seems to exist on the screen *except* the moment of violence—many of the television crime serials, for example, in which characters are, at most, two-dimensional stereotypes, the settings simply a procession of expensive penthouses, and the only visual moments of climax those when bodies slump to the floor. As the Pilkington Report commented:

Many submissions recorded the view that it [violence] was often used gratuitously, that it often did little or nothing to develop plot or characterization and that it was, presumably, thrown in 'for kicks'. Another common opinion was that it was often unnecessarily emphasized by being shown in close-up and by being lingered over. The damage was not necessarily repaired by ensuring that, in the end, the good were seen to win and the bad to lose, and that crime did not pay: conventional endings of this sort did not penetrate to the level at which the portrayal of violence had its emotional effect. What mattered was that violence provided the emotional energy, the dramatic content of the programme.

If the violence is to be responded to with 'fear', how does the fear arise? Partly, as Aristotle long ago suggested, because the characters are 'like ourselves', so that we fear when they are destroyed; partly because the act of violence reveals the human frailty of the agent; partly because it is a moment of revelation or self-discovery; sometimes 'from the contemplation of undeserved misfortune, considering his goodness'. In other words, the 'horror' is not the simple effect of the violent act, but a complex feeling arising from the total dramatic context. It arises from the whole play, and each production value established contributes to it. If the characters are like ourselves, then we must establish their dramatic probability in the play before the act is perpetrated. Human frailty is a delicate quality to evoke, for it is not the same thing as 'goodness'—the darkest villain when exposed as a human being can arouse our compassion at his 'fall'. The spectacle of human distress is an unnatural disorder in the human universe. If there is a moment of revelation, the action must develop and the characters change: the violence is then a 'sudden internal collapse', and the emotion is aroused as a contrast between what is happening now and what has gone before. We must feel the dramatic 'turn'—the reversal. 'Tragic characters are those involved essentially in the complexity' (*The Structure of Literature*, Paul Goodman—the whole book is worth reading in this context). Of course, most television drama and drama serials do not bear comparison with the serious tragedies of literature, but they are not different in the way they work as artistic experiences—they are examples of the same kind of literary truth. Granted that we do not expect to find on television the tragic complexities of a Shakespeare tragedy, or a Greek play, where the fall of the hero is contrasted against a whole human and moral order, nevertheless at a lower level the proper response to violence is fear, pity and a kind of compassion—'a steady will to remedy the distress'. Even in the simplest serial, the player must first 'live' for us if his 'death' is to be in any way remarkable.

Nor is this merely a question of making the moral explicit at the conclusion of the play. The most gratuitously violent pieces on television are precisely those which, with a guilty glance over their shoulders, establish in the final five minutes that 'crime does not pay'. But what 'pays' in television is what you *see*. If the characters are dull, flat and improbable, but the shooting is thrilling, lively and realistic, it will be the murder which pays off, whoever is handcuffed in the closing shot. When the violence is added for incidental excitement, to lift a sodden plot to life or restore a set of human stereotypes to the land of the living, then it stands away from its context, and cannot be related to the world which it violates. Time and again it is the butchery with the knife or the brawl among the furniture which alone seems to mean anything. The glamour of violence on television—which is what really ought to concern us—is often the glamour with which the camera invests the episode.

This should help us to see more clearly what is wrong with Dr L. Bender's argument that the casual violence of the comics or of television offers 'the same type of mental catharsis that Aristotle claimed was an attribute of the drama' (*Journal of Educational Psychology*). But where, in any comic story or television serial, is the tragic error, the human frailty, the contrasted human and social order, the self-discovery, the reversal, the pity and the compassion? Aristotle spoke of the 'purging' of emotions in the heart of the spectator because of the 'pity' and 'fear' aroused simultaneously at the spectacle of the hero's downfall. In this kind of play, emotions may be *aroused* but they are very rarely *purged* by any larger completeness in the drama: the killer may eventually be caught after a thrilling car-chase, but that is not what Aristotle had in mind. The emotion usually aroused is not 'fear'—because the characters are like ourselves, we fear when they are destroyed—but 'horror', a much cruder sentiment, the product not of tragedy but of spectacle—something we look on at but are never involved with. 'Pity' is almost wholly absent in Aristotle's sense—'pity . . . from the contemplation of undeserved misfortune, considering his goodness'. We can only feel pity for the human figure of the hero whom (in Elizabethan tragedy, for example) we respect as a man, or (in Greek tragedy) look up to as something of a god. It is difficult to be involved with the hero's fate in plays without heroes. You cannot feel much pity for a man who begins as a louse and ends up as a rat. Yet, for Aristotle, without pity and fear there was no tragic experience, and hence no catharsis.

Even in purely psychological terms, the defence by way of catharsis does not stand up. Both *Television and the Child* and *Television in the Lives of our Children* suggest that television has high 'user value'—that different children, with different emotional and social backgrounds and different levels of intelligence, may *use* television programmes in quite different ways. Unlike serious art and drama, where our response is largely controlled by what is being offered, television seems often to serve simply as a 'trigger' for fantasy experiences, a 'magic doorway' to some kind of substitute behaviour. It follows, then, that television violence may be, for some children, a way of vicariously working off aggression —social or personal—by means of fantasy experiences. One has still to ask whether, as in great art or serious literature, this substitute experience has compensating riches, intensities, values: whether, as in watching a Shakespeare play, it is an 'escape' to another order of life, or what Eleanor Maccoby calls a 'distractor', a 'wish-fulfilment' ('Why do Children watch Television?' *Public Opinion Quarterly*, 18. 1954, pp. 239–44). We cannot answer this question without a critical analysis of the various kinds of experiences offered. It is not simply a sociological or psychological question. Nor is there certain evidence that this low-level substitute experience—even if it justified the steady offering of violent episodes—really has such a function for all children. The Himmelweit Report says quite clearly:

> We have not proved any causal relationship between seeing these programmes and behaving undesirably; but what relationship exists we have shown more likely to be harmful than desirable. We find little evidence that these programmes are desirable as a means of discharging tension (they often increase it), but we do find evidence that they may retard children's awareness of the serious consequences of violence in real life and may teach a greater acceptance of aggression as the normal, manly solution of conflict. The main negative harmful effects of these programmes lie in preventing, by taking up so much time, the development of alternative, more worth-while programmes.
>
> *Television and the Child*

This view is supported by the American study:

> The outcome of their seeking behaviour is not always predictable in terms of the kind of material they reach. For most children, fantasy may help to drain off excess aggression, but for some it may actually build aggression and contribute to violent acts. This, we repeat, is not wholly predictable from the content; it is necessary to know the children.
>
> Furthermore, whether fantasy is, in the long view, 'good for them' is something we are not fully ready to discuss at this point. For some children, as Mrs Maccoby suggests, fantasy may make possible the testing of solutions to problems without the restrictions or the embarrassment of doing so in real life. For others it may merely result in postponing those problems or pretending that they do not exist.
>
>   Schramm, Lyle, Parker, *Television in the Lives of our Children*

Besides, as the Pilkington Report so aptly observed, replying to the defence that children were very resilient and would soon recover from any horror, 'It would be singularly insensitive to regard a child's resilience as giving one freedom to frighten it.'

A different sort of defence of television violence was offered by the Chairman of the ITA in his evidence to the Pilkington Committee: he argued that inevitably television was violent because the world is a violent place. Now although *International Detective* or *No Hiding Place* cannot be usefully compared with *King Lear* or *Oedipus Rex*, they do share one important thing in common. They differ from other kinds of television—documentaries, features, news bulletins and commentaries—because they are composed, dramatized. The psychological evidence suggests that the very act of dramatization heightens the child's response. Documentaries, news bulletins and commentaries, on the other hand, are designed to mirror the world. They cannot be edited for the susceptibilities of young viewers. Indeed, there is a strong argument that they ought not to be—that the line between fiction and reality ought to be, if anything, more clearly marked: particularly since the evidence suggests that 'one characteristic of mass-media art is its ability to dwell in both kingdoms ['pure fantasy' and 'pure reality'] at once' (*Television in the Lives of our*

Children). But actuality programmes establish their own relation to the 'real world' by their format and style. Children should be encouraged to know, when they see the news, that they are watching what is actually happening in the world around them. If they respond to much of what they see there with 'horror', so much, one feels, the better. But the drama serial is *not* life. It works upon the emotions, not with the direct challenge of reality, but as art. The relation to life is quite different. All the techniques of artistic composition are at work in even the poorest serial play—the author or producer bears the responsibility for composing his characters and his action, for making a selection from life, for heightening some aspects and compressing others, for giving his play human texture, and so on. It is no excuse to say that it is 'only a serial'. That phrase may define the conventions in which the producer is working, or it may suggest the level of the play, but it does not alter the kind of experience it is. (When Richard Sear, television critic of the *Daily Mirror*, compared the *Oliver Twist* episode with 'those grim newsreel scenes of dead and dying lying in the streets of Algeria', and asked 'Is there a difference between the two?' he made a serious point, but he was confusing two levels of reality, two kinds of communication.)

A far more perceptive comment on *Oliver Twist* was made in a letter to *The Guardian*, by a parent, Mrs Myrtle Pollard (31/3/62):

This was violence shown for what it is, in all its brutality and ugliness; there is even room for compassion, not only for the victim but for her murderer, trapped in the ugly circumstances of their lives.

I should have thought that the senseless, casual, meaningless violence, shootings, and killings which set no value on human life, which do not upset because they are not felt, were far more likely to be injurious in their influence. These, which are common occurrences on the television screen, apparently excite no comment in Parliament.

Mrs Pollard's comments go to the heart of the matter: the human emotions aroused and *felt* in the work, which place and contain the violence, and the general context of human values which the various kinds of television drama affirm. But if this approach is to have any particular force with a child, it will involve a real change in attitude among parents, who are responsible for the informal, as teachers are responsible for the formal, aspects of education. Her arguments imply that the whole field of emotional and imaginative experiences should be opened up for the child at an early age. There are far too few schools and homes in which this kind of free confrontation has actually been made.

Mrs Pollard made the distinction between plays where the violence is felt, and those in which there is simply 'senseless, casual, meaningless violence'. Yet even in this lower range there are important distinctions to be made. It may be thought, for example, that there is little to choose between the steady diet of westerns and the regular crime series offered more or less continually by both television channels. In terms of production quality, this is probably true. However, there are some significant differences. *Television and the Child* points out that the effects of the black-and-white westerns on view during the time of their first survey were quite different from that of the crime series.

The western has become a conventional art form. In the simpler versions, little variation occurs in the development of the plot from one to another. The appeal of the western, as we remarked in an earlier chapter, is almost a 'mythic' one—the myth has a certain force of its own, independent of the play in which it is particularized. The action involves a simple, stylized confrontation between good and evil. There is a comparable stylization in the delineation of character, and this even extends to their physical appearance which, from a very early point in the story, betrays their calling. The typical behaviour of the characters has been patterned, and this patterning also extends to the presentation of violence. The violent episodes regularly recur—the stagecoach attack, the bar-room brawl or gunfight, the hold-up, the chase with gun-fire, the final shoot-up. 'Menace, attack and injury are, like the characters, presented in a stylized manner.' There is a limited range of conventional ways of simulating injury or death, and a tendency for the camera not to linger on the wounded, but to

leap away in pursuit of the posse or the villain's lieutenant who is
lurking behind the rocks. The Nuffield Report noted that though
guns are symbols of power in the western it would be impossible
to learn from a western how they worked. Indeed, 'in one fairly
typical western we found that 149 shots were fired, yet no one was
killed . . .'

The simple western, in other words, does not offer itself as a
simulation of reality. Its fictional or fantasy life is dangerous and
exciting, but there is little temptation to confuse it with reality.
The violence ceases to be a function of the behaviour depicted,
and has passed into the art form itself. It has certainly been
distanced from the viewer—it is 'framed' twice, once by the very
fact that it is a play, and again because its conventions are so
obviously part of a pattern, and so easy to learn. Games based on
this kind of western are rarely imitations of the behaviour so
much as imitations of the form. They are not games of 'controlled
aggression', but 'versions of being chased and chasing'. In the
western, as in the game, there are unchanging 'sides' and un-
breakable 'rules'. There is even a sense of security about playing
the game, since the endings also are conventionalized, and the
hero is certain to come through the hail of bullets unscathed.

This is not offered by way of a total justification of the television western. One has to remember the point about the general
balance of programme material. We must also bear in mind that
the more adult and complex westerns, such as are increasingly
taking the place of the simple moralities of the West, deliberately
complicate the form or break the conventions. When the pattern
is disturbed, many of the elements which have been held in place
by the form are turned loose and gain once more something of
the impact of realism. But the average children's western does
have the advantage of conventional presentation, which, by
framing the violence, helps to redistribute the emphasis and
attention to other aspects.

The crime series, however, do not share even these negative
virtues with the western. The crime story has never properly
established its conventions. Certain stereotyped set-ups do recur,

but there is no clear pattern, and, above all, no conventional way of presenting the violence itself. So, in the crime play (going back to Miss Bradbrook's definition of a convention quoted in Chapter 2, page 57) there is no agreement between producer and audience on how violence should be presented, or of its place in the play. The violence is therefore made to look realistic and personal. The plots are also more complicated (though not necessarily more complex) and the characterization much less clear-cut. The western hero identifies himself by his conduct and bearing; the crime play usually offers more subjective and hidden psychological motives for crime. Villain and hero are often indistinguishable, since part of the trick of the crime thriller play is, first, to enlist sympathy for the villain, and then, later, to have him unmasked as a criminal. In the western, on the other hand, the villain is obvious from the moment he enters the saloon, and no sympathy is asked on his behalf. In the crime stories the settings are much closer to real life, and can be mistaken for it. In the western the landscape and the location is itself a distancing device. Simple westerns, it is suggested, 'are studies in black and white; crime and detective stories are studies in grey' (*Television and the Child*).

These distinctions may seem to be leading us to a preference for the conventional as against the more complex. In a sense, this is true. Neither the TV western nor the crime play is likely to enrich our imagination by the imitation of some deep and moving human spectacle. They are both fairly primitive kinds of drama— appealing by suspense and excitement. Given this, the form which has achieved some distinctive quality and a set of conventions of its own is preferable to the semi-naturalistic thriller. The very quality of the violence itself is different. In fact, the crime series only *seem* to be more complex. Their plot-line and motivations are more complicated, usually more confused, but there is no real complexity in characterization, and the psychology is skeletal. The human figures are just as two-dimensional as in the western, but they lack that extra dimension which the western mythology gives to its heroes. Given that both kinds of drama are stereotyped, and that many of each kind are pretty poor in quality, it nevertheless remains true that the western has achieved a kind of artistic clarity of shape which the crime play lacks. In the western the gun is clearly a symbol of power—crude but exact. In the crime thriller the gun is still an instrument of violence.

The whole world of the West, we have argued, has become a symbolic, mythical territory, with its own locations, its familiar names and events, its own values. These conventions help to support even the very poor-quality examples of the form which are regularly seen on television. Not only do they enable the presentation to be consciously simplified, but they create their own recognizable 'world' as well as a clearly defined 'code' of behaviour. This code, though rough and ready as befits the frontier, is not wholly without its moral points of reference. The physical and visual clarity with which the western hero is offered has overtones of a moral clarity, too.

At least the western hero has a code, which allows for the existence somewhere (at a great distance, no doubt) of a world where moral values are not wholly alien. He is usually on the side of some kind of rough justice. The crime series are, for the most part, rooted in far shallower soil. Shooting is what *happens* in the western: killing is what crime thrillers are *about*.

Of course the conventions of the western can themselves be criticized. Dramatic conventions are not, after all, part of the laws of nature: they arise and lose their power from one age to another (as Revenge tragedy did). It is always possible to stand outside the conventions themselves and ask what they mean, and why, at this particular point in history, conventions should grow up around particular experiences—in this case, experiences of violence. Where certain conventions of presentation have established themselves, however, it is important to understand how they do contain and qualify the violent episodes being offered.

Most of the crime, detective or police productions on television are regular series, many of them on film, many either American or mid-Atlantic in origin. Among those being offered on ITV at the time of writing are *Ghost Squad*, *Naked City*, *Route 66*, *Espionage*, *Casebook*, *The Avengers* and *No Hiding Place*, while the BBC are putting out *Maigret, Perry Mason, Z Cars* and *The Defenders*. It is worth looking at these in more detail.

The first thing to say is that most of them are of very poor quality. This is especially true of those on film which are churned out by a mass-production system. They must be made quickly, so there can be very few changes of camera position. The sets are usually small and reduced to the essentials, and in general there is little scope for technical refinement. This is the main reason why they have such a dead quality on the screen. Again and again we are looking at two people standing talking. Behind them a flat surface with perhaps a window and a picture. There may be a desk and telephone or perhaps a body on the floor, but one setting becomes indistinguishable from the rest. These short scenes are frequently linked by filmed sequences but as often as not these are stock shots of cars moving from one place to another. Everything is over-emphasized. At key moments (on ITV just before the commercial break) the camera plunges in for a close-up and the point is underlined by melodramatic music. The scripts as well as the production techniques are equally crude and, as most of the time nothing much is happening visually, the stories can become a tangled mass of irrelevant clues and false trails. The general effect is that the events portrayed seem to take place in a vacuum. The extensive use of library material serves as usual to emphasize this general air of unreality. Some of these series are made with the US market in mind, and in some of them the action is noticeably suspended every now and then to provide information about the strange customs and fascinating features of English life. One episode alone had shots of the Albert Memorial, dog-racing, Buckingham Palace, Westminster and the Cup Final.

No Hiding Place and *Maigret* are rather above this level. More attention is given to place (especially in *Maigret*) and to establishing some little degree of complexity in the characters. This, however, is fairly rudimentary; the characters are pretty well fixed at a series of mannerisms and the plots have all the tedious complications of the dated detective story. *The Defenders* has also been praised because of its more sober style and serious concern for the human issues it handles. But its moral statements tend to be made too explicitly. *The Avengers* is said to be popular with the 'educated' audience. It is designed in the 'kinky' style, complete with blonde in leather gear, but lacks the sophistication and wit which might make such elements palatable. The real exception is *Z Cars*, which happens also to be one of the programmes against which accusations of exploiting violence have been made.

For television, *Z Cars* is a series of quite remarkable quality. We must make the qualification because television suffers from obvious disadvantages when compared with the cinema. All the sets must be erected in the studio at the same time, and actors and cameras move between them during transmission. It is also impossible to have any degree of refinement in the lighting. The editing of the programme, the movement from shot to shot, which in film-making can take several weeks, must in TV production be conducted by the director as the drama is enacted. No doubt there are certain advantages—immediacy, for example, which can give both the actors and the director a certain edge to their work. It is possible to imagine a kind of improvised drama on TV which actually exploited its crudities. But this has not been done and in comparison with film it remains a relatively clumsy medium. It is therefore no small compliment to *Z Cars* to say that it compares favourably with many films, and in significant ways, allowing for its limited range, is better than most produced in this country. Part of its quality comes from production techniques. It uses six cameras with a great variety of set-up; there are many more shot changes than is usual in this type of production. It also has a high standard of design, and the well-constructed sets and good camera-work ensure that the picture on the screen has some richness. It is transmitted live every week, and the film sequences are beautifully edited into the studio playing.

The second important point is that it has been superbly cast—especially in the case of the quartet of policemen around whose lives the series revolves. The danger with this sort of basic plot device is that the actors would be picked as *well-contrasted types*. This is the kind of casting we have seen so often in dramas that put their characters into some artificially isolated position—an open boat, an aircraft about to crash and so on. In *Z Cars*, although the characters are contrasting they are not simply types, and the contrast is not sharp or obvious or more significant than the similarity. The acting itself is of a high standard and the players manage to suggest a complex set of qualities: a rough sense of duty, a kind of tired resignation verging at times on disgust and cynicism, and a feeling of belonging to the community yet set apart from it. These are experienced actors who can be left without dialogue, without plotted action for significant moments. There is an expressiveness in their movements, their way of approaching someone, or lowering their bodies into the seat of a car. It is acting of some weight. They have been blessed, of course, with scripts that at least most of the time allow for this.

Here we come to more fundamental matters. *Z Cars* is set in a New Town near Liverpool. It is a specific place—not the usual no-man's-land. What is more, there are recognizable attitudes, a certain pattern of values, which give the community a character and which spread over the divisions between public, criminals and police. The central figures of the drama are part of the landscape in a way quite different from other crime series. The stories themselves are comparatively free from the mechanical devices of clue-hunting and car chases, and there is a concentration on the development of character. The crimes involved are often petty and rather futile. When violent death occurs it seems unpleasant, as it is intended to be. In one episode a large brutish man was stabbed in a drunken brawl with his wife and son. There was no great mystery about what happened. The plot did not race on to the thrill of the hunt. Instead we were shown the expressions of shock and horror on the faces, not only of the neighbours, but of the policeman who bent over the body, and the stunned reactions of the wife and daughter. All this gains force because we know something about the policeman, his home and his wife. We are made to ponder on the way in which tragedy can suddenly overtake a family, arising unexpectedly out of a series of almost meaningless incidents.

The criticisms about the exploitation of violence derive from the fact that such scenes do make an impact. But they ought to. Unless we recognize this, unless we can see the intention and respond to the quality of human concern, we will be trapped into preferring the fantasies of *Dixon of Dock Green*. When *Z Cars* handles violence the treatment makes it seem squalid rather than exciting and glamorous. There is a vein of toughness running through the series, a sort of undercurrent that we feel even in moments of light-hearted jesting. But once more we must be careful in our judgement. This toughness exhibited both in the policemen and in some of the other characters is a reflection of their bleak environment. At its best it represents a spiritual strength, a hardness of character, which can resist the harsh pressures of life. True, it is dangerously poised on the edge of brutality. But this is merely to say that the policemen are not shown as simple manly heroes. They are held at a critical distance and an effort is clearly being made to prevent any easy identification with them. It is significant, for example, that senior members of the police force objected to the programme because it gave an unfavourable picture of the police. They preferred the father-figure of Jack Warner. There were complaints that one officer gave his wife a black eye and that policemen 'were shown eating disgustingly'.

Z Cars demands, therefore, a much more complicated response than its counterparts. Just because its qualities are rare on television it is dangerously easy to overpraise it. The intention of its prime originator, the writer Troy Kennedy Martin, was to examine the virtues represented by its leading characters: the sense of duty, the rough caring and stubborn honesty which he saw as representative of the northern community as a whole. He wanted to explore these qualities as they were put under the pressures of social change represented by the New Town. This aspect has not really emerged, but it does point to the way the series could develop. Yet it is doubtful if it can do so, and the reasons for this throw an interesting light on the way our contemporary media work. The programme has become very popular, the viewing figures rising from nine to fourteen million. The pressure therefore, even with the BBC, is to leave it where it is. At this point the idea of development is often rejected in favour of variations round a set theme. In the end the writing becomes mechanical, the actors, perhaps already tired, fall back on mannerisms, and what the critic Peter Lewis has called Sharples Disease ensues.

This is especially important in the case of Z Cars because of its potential. To fix it before its real purposes develop would be severely damaging. The criminals would become picturesque spivs and thugs, and the public would be presented as apathetic and sullen onlookers. More important, the critical distance (even now dangerously narrow) between the creators and their police-men characters would diminish. In the end the actors would begin to exploit their personalities, they would become TV stars and the whole programme would degenerate. It could easily remain crisply produced and *in tune with the times* while in fact subtly transformed into a dangerous glamorization of authority. By the time this book appears this may have happened or the series may have simply disappeared, or someone at the BBC may have decided to take the inevitable risk of being continually creative.

Because the images are more expressive, the editing techniques more subtle and the conditions of viewing more conducive to identification, the impact of violence in the cinema is even greater than on television. Also, because the cinema is free from the self-imposed restraints that still operate in TV, it has gone much further in the exploitation of violence, which occurs not only in the cheap crime films but also in the more expensive productions, particularly the spectaculars. Rather than nag at these familiar examples, however, more can be gained by considering a film which attempts honestly to engage with the problems of violence and places it in a recognizable social context.

The Angry Silence was made independently by the actor Richard Attenborough and the writer Bryan Forbes, and it is clear that they approached their subject very seriously. The story is about a factory worker, Tom Curtis, played by Attenborough, who gets caught up in a strike he believes to have been manipulated. When he refuses to strike he is 'sent to Coventry' and it is only when he is beaten up and loses an eye that his fellows realize how shame-fully they have behaved.

The film has many merits. There is, for example, an excellent feeling for the pattern of family life. Tom comes home and looks at television and does his pools and this is not meant, as it would be in many films, to be funny. Domestic irritation is part of this pattern as well as affection. You feel that Bryan Forbes has an ear for the way people actually speak and seldom degenerates into mere 'social observation'. Little incidents, the mother throwing the key of the door from the top window to her little daughter returned from school, Tom going off to play football with his son Bryan, and Bryan, after he should be asleep, pattering through in his pyjamas to announce 'me heart's stopped', all have the stamp of sympathetic observation. Against this the faults of the film are more disturbing. In the first place the treatment of the agitator (Communist? Trotskyist?) is handled in the fashion of the conven-tional thriller with strange appearances and mysterious phone-calls. Then it is never clear what the issues of the strike are. Even if manipulated from outside, strikes are usually the result of grievances which, if not real, are at least felt to be real. But this the film glosses over. Tom is shown to be reluctant to go on strike as he fears the loss of money and its effect on the family, but we are left wondering why the same considerations don't occur to all the others. Then the violence. Superficially this is seen as the logical outcome of the sending to Coventry and of the general callousness of the rest of the men. In fact, the violence is carried out by a group of young thugs who are quite outside the rest of the story. This importation is made worse by the fact that they are rather grotesque leather-jacketed stereotypes. We begin now to lose the feeling of conviction with which the film opened. The dice are too heavily loaded in favour of the hero. It would have been more to the point to have shown a strike in which both sides had strong and genuine grounds for believing in their stand, that would have forced a real moral issue. With this confusion, and because there was no real definition of intention, the violence gets out of control. Towards the end of a fight, blows are rained downwards into the upturned camera and faces are thrust upon us in looming close-ups. What is more, we are invited to approve because this time one of the young thugs is on the receiving end. The film even turns in upon itself and exploits its good points. Having treated the family quite nicely, it then enlists our sympathy by having the little boy tarred by his schoolmates because his father is a scab. A photo-graph of Curtis is pinned to a notice-board, the pin being pushed through his face—a quite unnecessary piece of unpleasantness. This is not only a matter of incident; the collapse also affects the style. Free from any firm controlling idea it degenerates into a series of flashy devices, vicious movements, sudden and violent cuts. The loss of control is strikingly illustrated by one particular shot—a close-up of a leather boot plunging down on a motor-cycle starter. But the boot belongs to Joe, a teenager living with Tom Curtis, who as a character quite contradicts the idea of him sug-gested by such a shot. He is, in fact, a lad who aims to avoid trouble, who feels little interest in the strike or anything else to do with the factory. In the end it is the basically good-hearted Joe who acts *for us* in beating up Eddie, the leader of the gang of toughs. We have been encouraged to wait for that moment and relish it.

One particular genre in which violence inevitably occurs, and which is peculiar to the cinema, not appearing on television largely for reasons of cost, is the war film. Although now showing signs of decline, war films have been, since the early fifties, most persistent box-office successes. Most of them have been accounts of famous actions—*The Dam Busters, The Battle of the River Plate, Dunkirk.* Others were escape stories (*The Wooden Horse*) and some have concentrated on individual heroes (*Reach for the Sky*). Parallel with this have been the considerable sales of paperback war stories. Many of the films were based on these books although in some cases it has worked the other way round.

Sink the Bismarck is fairly representative of the most character-istic kind of British war film. It opens in documentary style with newsreel material about German naval preparations, and continues this tone in the account of the action by employing the American commentator Ed Murrow. Clearly, however, the film-makers had no confidence in this approach and early in the film a variety of fictional elements is introduced. The officer who conducts the operation, Commander Shepherd (Kenneth More), is an invented character. He is presented to us as a cold authoritarian close to the ideal described by the Commander-in-Chief as *a man with no heart and an enormous brain*. This, of course, is only the superficial appearance and it is his Wren officer assistant who reveals to us the human being underneath. This is done in a scene where she talks about her boy friend who was killed at Dunkirk, and Shepherd describes how after he lost his wife in an air raid he vowed never to become emotionally involved again. The addition of these personal details which are intended to humanize Shepherd merely exchanges one stereotype for another.

The story is personalized in a variety of other ways. Shepherd's son serves on the aircraft carrier *Ark Royal*, one of the ships brought into the action. A message comes through that his son has been shot down, though towards the end of the film it is announced that he is safe. On a previous occasion it is said that Shepherd's ship was sunk by one operating under Lutyens, now commanding the *Bismarck*. Someone points out to him that he now has a personal interest in the engagement, and he himself says, 'I've fought these people before.'

These two elements, the documentary and the fictional, constantly conflict. For example, the introduction of Ed Murrow has the effect of making everything seem less rather than more real. Even to recite the plot of the film is to reveal its clichés of character and situation. A typical scene shows Shepherd moving ships about on a map and consulting the views of his Wren assistant as he does so. He has just decided to move support away from a troop convoy when the Commander-in-Chief approaches:

C.-in-C.: Are you willing to gamble with the lives of 20,000 men?
Shepherd: There is a difference between a gamble and a calculated risk.
C.-in-C.: Good man, Shepherd.
Shepherd: Of course, it's a difficult decision to take.
C.-in-C: The important ones always are.

All this conducted with pregnant pauses and grim, determined looks.

The other characters are equally caricatured. The German Fleet Commander is made to seem sinister by being introduced to us with his back to the camera. He talks about the war with a heavy accent in such terms as 'an interesting chess game—the important moves are the opening ones'. These clichés of characterization extend to the style. There is a scene where a spy is shot at the moment of sending a radio message. We are shown a close shot of his fingers still trembling on the key of his transmitter until another burst of firing stops them completely. This stands out as gratuitously unpleasant because it is a visual cliché we have become used to in gangster films. The way we respond to the violence is also affected by the context of the whole film. Towards the end the battleship *Hood* blows up, but because so much of the film is drained of reality we can watch this without feeling what it means in human terms.

The Bridge on the River Kwai is a more ambitious and complex film. As well as being an enormous box-office success and winning many international awards it was almost unanimously welcomed by critics. It is frequently regarded as a great anti-war film and compared to others such as *All Quiet on the Western Front*.

Kwai falls quite sharply into two parts. The first concerns British soldiers in a Japanese prisoner-of-war camp. Their leader, Colonel Nicholson, suffers torture at the hands of the Japanese Commandant when he refuses to allow his officers to work on a bridge the Japanese are building over the Kwai. Nicholson survives the torturing and, taking advantage of the problems the Japanese are having, offers to take over the bridge-building. He uses the expertise of the British soldiers and thus, by preventing his men from becoming bored, maintains discipline. The second half of the film shows the preparations of a British Commando party setting out to blow up the bridge. This group, led by a Major Warden, has in it an American, Shears, who had earlier escaped from the prison camp. The climax of the film comes when Nicholson celebrates the completion of the bridge and Warden's party wire it for destruction.

We are faced immediately with certain difficulties about the plot. We have to accept, for example, that the Japanese would not have the technical ability to design a satisfactory bridge, and that a British colonel would engage in a major act of collaboration without resistance from either his officers or the private soldiers. Aside from this problem it is difficult to see just what statement the film is making about war. Nicholson is the hero of the film. Certainly throughout the first part our sympathies are entirely enlisted on his side. When he has been released from his torture and the soldiers rush forward to chair and cheer him, the music swings into action and we are left in no doubt that he has achieved a moral victory. Our side has won. Even in the second half of the film, where the twists of the plot complicate matters, he is treated with more sympathy than any other character. However, most of the latter section is taken up by the story of the commando party and here our interest is sustained by the excitement of wondering whether or not the bridge will be destroyed. In the end it is, and while there are ambiguities, or more properly confusions, there is again the feeling that our side has won. The interesting thing about *River Kwai* is that its style invites us to identify with characters regardless of the purpose and meaning of their actions. Thus 'our side' wins when it builds a fine bridge and also when it blows it up. Towards the end of the film Nicholson is portrayed overlooking the bridge and reflecting on his stern but fulfilled life. The whole mood of the scene—the actor's gesture as he pats the bridge railings, the sunset, the calm of the evening—invites our sympathy. But then this is suddenly switched to 'our chaps' lurking behind the bushes above the bridge waiting to blow it up. This is just a confusion. The film is not held together by any central purpose. Of course the situation could have been an opportunity for irony as it is in the novel, but for that to work it would have had to be consciously explored. In fact, the style consists of the usual war-film clichés served up with more than the usual skill and padded out with unexplored bits of character-business.

There are, of course, many scenes that seem to make statements about the war. A Japanese soldier is killed and a picture of his girl falls from his wallet. In the jungle Shears makes a vigorous attack on Major Warden who is struggling on with a badly damaged foot. 'You have the stench of death about you,' he says, as he compares Warden with Nicholson. At the end of the film a British army doctor surveys the wreckage of the bridge and the bodies of both parties and cries 'Madness, madness, madness'.

The photograph of the girl is a self-conscious device. Shears's speech is important as it links both commando-hero and collaborator in a denunciation of military pride and folly, but to make this effective the part of Warden would have had to be presented to us critically. In fact Jack Hawkins plays him in the traditional soldiering-on manner. In any case Shears soon forgets these sentiments and, far from acting as a vehicle for a different set of values, becomes wholly identified with the action at the end of the film to the point of crying out, 'Knife him, knife him,' to a young commando struggling with a Japanese soldier, and then sacrificing his life in an effort to do the job himself. The doctor is such a peripheral character that his comment carries practically no weight, especially amidst the confusion of the end where, for example, it is difficult to know whether Nicholson blows the bridge up deliberately or falls on the plunger by accident.

The Bridge on the River Kwai was a very big and expensive production. With such vast sums of money involved the pressures to find commercial safeguards are enormous. The most obvious one here is in the role of Shears—tailored to fit the box-office star, William Holden. There is also the introduction of four attractive girl bearers who go along with the commando party. This allows for a bathing scene with Mr Holden. Such concessions, though obvious, are not always so important as the critics make out, but the defects here go deep into the heart of the picture's style. It is constructed in the skilful but academic manner typical of its director, David Lean. That is to say, atmosphere is well created (a silent sequence with Jack Hawkins stalking a Japanese soldier), tension is built up (the cross cutting of the final sequence) and shots are beautifully composed (high shots of the bridge in the jungle). In fact what happens is that the direction consistently blurs any of the positive comment that lies somewhere in the film. Vague textbook terms about atmosphere, tension and composition are of little use here. It may, in fact, be quite inappropriate to strive for beauty in composition. In one scene where Japanese soldiers are killed and fall in the water, the beauty of the composition makes the blood seem just another element in the colourful panorama. The photography has a glossy quality which produces a picturesque effect, frequently running counter to the implications of the plot. The opening sequence illustrates strikingly how this works. As the troops move into the prison camp they whistle *Colonel Bogey* in defiance of their condition. The camera views them from a low-angle past a graveyard. In theory, this striking composition symbolizes their situation. In fact, because of the slick style, it is an image which makes no impact whatsoever.

The film suffers mainly from divided intentions. No one seems to have decided whether it was to be an anti-war film, a study of the military mind or an adventure story. It is chiefly the last, but with the undigested pretensions of the others. Indeed, asked about the confusion of the ending, the director himself said that he had become totally preoccupied with the 'slow build-up of tension'.

In the novel by Pierre Boulle the bridge in fact is not blown up. In an exceptionally perceptive broadcast (reprinted in *The Listener*, 6/8/59) Ian Watt argued that Boulle's intention was to show the West's technological skill in contrast with its drive towards destruction. The bridge used in the film took eight months to build and cost $250,000. The producers, asked why they insisted on blowing it up against M. Boulle's wishes, said that they would not miss the chance for 'such a sensational bit of action'. On this Professor Watt commented:

On reflection the utter waste in building a fine bridge just to blow it up again to please a public avid for sensational realism seemed an ironically apt example of M. Boulle's point about the West's misuse of its technology; and so perhaps was the film as a whole.

It only remains to be said that at its first showing in London a recruiting booth was set up in the foyer.

Kwai immediately suggests a comparison with another film dealing with prisoners of war, *La Grande Illusion*, a film tragically made just before the outbreak of the Second World War by one of the great directors of the cinema, Jean Renoir. The action of the film takes place during the First World War. The main characters are three French prisoners-of-war—de Boeldieu, an aristocrat; Rosenthal, a well-to-do Jew; and Maréchal, who in civilian life is an engineer. There is also the commandant of the prison camp, Rauffenstein, a professional soldier. The film is a study of the characters of these men and of their relationships. Renoir had, in fact, served with the French Army during the war but his study is completely free from bitterness and the Germans are treated with extraordinary sympathy.

Maréchal is put in solitary confinement for leading a defiant singing of *La Marseillaise*. After days in the cell his spirit begins to break and he starts to shout and beat on the wall until an old German guard comes in to ask why he is making so much noise. The guard gives him a mouth organ and as Maréchal sits hunched on his bench quietly playing, outside, framed in the darkness of a doorway, the German soldier stands listening. A bond of sympathy also springs up between the two aristocrats, de Boeldieu and Rauffenstein. The human relationships continue despite the war. It would be too crude to call *La Grande Illusion* directly anti-war. Its treatment of the relationships simply makes war seem monstrously irrelevant. At the same time, the social distinctions of peace that bridge the nationalistic gulfs of war are not themselves treated uncritically. Rauffenstein asks de Boeldieu to give his word that he and his friends are not planning to escape. When de Boeldieu enquires why he does not ask the others, Rauffenstein replies, 'What, the word of a Maréchal or a Rosenthal against that of a de Boeldieu?' Again, when Rosenthal remarks that he owns a substantial part of France and that it is worth fighting for, de Boeldieu wryly says that he has never considered patriotism from that 'special point of view'.

To quote dialogue, however, gives the impression that the film makes its points directly. In fact, the images create a texture of subtly suggested meanings. There is, for example, a sequence where the French soldiers crowd round a basket containing theatrical costumes. Their hands stretch out to touch the delicate silks and other materials. A young soldier tries on a woman's costume. As he stumbles awkwardly forward in high-heeled shoes the camera holds back and the laughing voices on the sound track are stilled. Outside we can see young German soldiers being drilled and at the open gates a few women stand. Their black clothes make them seem like widows. The war itself is never handled directly but its implications are always breaking through in images like these.

One of the most striking things in the film is von Stroheim's portrait of Rauffenstein. After having seen him briefly at the beginning of the film as a virile soldier, we are re-introduced to him in the prison camp where he has been sent as commandant because he is no longer fit for active service. The camera first moves over his belongings, including his white gloves and scent spray, carefully and precisely laid out. In a beautiful scene with de Boeldieu, where they speak together of the war and their respective lives, he tells him that the war will see the end of the Rauffensteins and the de Boeldieus. In the latter half of the film when de Boeldieu lies dying, having been shot by Rauffenstein when he was assisting in an escape, Rauffenstein says: 'I must live on in a futile existence. To be killed in war is a tragedy for a commoner, but for us it is a way out.' Von Stroheim portrays a human being, but the figure of Rauffenstein, dignified, austere and slightly degenerate, his wounded and broken body held stiff and erect by a metal corset, is also a symbol of a passing age.

The film ends with images of peace and serenity. Maréchal and Rosenthal have escaped. High in the mountains they are cared for by a German war-widow. Maréchal busies himself with domestic routine about the house or stands at the doorway stretching himself. The valley below is still and quiet except for the sound of distant church bells. The spaciousness of the cottage with the light streaming through the windows makes a symbolic contrast with the dark fortress in which the men have been imprisoned. But it cannot last. The two prisoners must continue on their way and the final image is of both of them in the distance struggling through the snow.

La Grande Illusion is anti-war by implication only. It is not concerned with the relatively simple task of showing the horrors of war. It affirms the opposite qualities of humane and civilized relationships. The film is on the side of Marechal the artisan, but no one character is the simple vehicle of its director's view, and the ideals of the duty and honour of military life are given full weight in the characters of Rauffenstein and de Boeldieu. Part of the tragic irony of war is that it can call forth qualities of heroism and comradeship. The sincere portrayal of this must be sharply distinguished from phoney and glamorized heroics.

In his response to traditional loyalties and the duties of service John Ford is very much like Renoir. In a more recent Ford film, *The Horse Soldiers*, something of a genuine romantic feeling about war comes through. *The Horse Soldiers* is, of course, a film on an altogether different plane from *La Grande Illusion*. It is very much an ordinary entertainment film with box-office stars (John Wayne and William Holden) and a conventional Civil War script of standardized situations, characters and dialogue. Ford's own personal responses are, however, strong enough to break through. There is, for example, a striking passage where scenes of the destruction of a railroad are contrasted with shots of dead and dying soldiers. At one point the Southern army calls upon the young cadets at a Military Academy to help in the war. They prepare for battle assembling outside the Academy in a long line. As they march away their movements are the precise and careful ones of the school textbook. They look, in fact, like toy soldiers. The lawns of the college grounds are as neat and trim as the cadets and the red brick of the building glows in the bright sunlight. Cut against this in deliberately untidy compositions are the shots of the Northern soldiers—worn and tired veterans of war.

At the end of the film there is one final battle, from which the Northern colonel emerges on horseback out of the smoke. The bugles sound and behind him the banners flutter in the breeze. It is a very romantic image which looks like a nineteenth-century painting (Plate 6). But it is not glamorized. The romantic picture of war emphasizes the self-sacrificing heroism of soldiers; but in so doing it reveals that one of the major tragedies of war is its power to evoke such qualities. Because it is truly felt, the romantic presentation makes a criticism of war almost despite itself. The glamorized version does not, because it does not spring from a genuine response and because it makes cheap and coarse the qualities it handles. We can make such distinctions, once we study films and television programmes in detail; it is only through such study of actual examples that we can free ourselves from mis-leading generalizations.

Wholesale, uncritical condemnation of any violence on the screen is just as pointless as a simple-minded apology for it. The question of violence, as Kenneth Adam has said, may not be 'susceptible to dogmatic prescription' ('Improving Television', *Spectator*, 24/8/62), but between 'dogmatic prescription' and the free use of the ether there is a great deal of territory. It is difficult territory to cross, admittedly, for it demands detailed, particular judgements, again and again—judgements which are related to the growth of the imagination of the young, and which are sensitive to such questions as style and treatment; which hold the one continuously against the other, and which measure films and television, in all their manifestations, against some whole human standard.

6

The Avenging Angels

Respectability pays. Crime doesn't pay. That is the main difference between the two spheres. As for the arbitrary and precarious place one occupies in the respectable world or the gang world, that is a matter of calculated risks. But whereas the tycoon risks his money, the gangster risks his life.

MARSHALL MCLUHAN, *The Mechanical Bride*

The violence of the television or cinema screen seems tame when compared with what is offered in print for private reading. Who reads that colourful and bizarre collection of pulp fiction in the newsagent's window—the crime comics, the mysteries, the *Confidential*-style police exposés, the prisoner-of-war-camp tales, the private-eye thrillers with the luridly drawn heroines on the covers? It is difficult to tell, particularly after the paperback revolution. New outlets have been opened up—the high-street paperback bookshop, or the 'popular book marts', where old thrillers can be traded in for new on an exchange basis, have been added to the newsagent's rack and the railway station bookstalls. Many of the old distinctions are disappearing too. Often Zola, Balzac, Sartre or Defoe will appear, with a lurid cover, shuffled between the paperbacks and the girlie magazines.

No one seems to know how much of this kind of literature is sold and read, and few people have ever tried to find out what the books contain. In the action-and-violence category the authors are often unknown, in many cases pseudonyms, sometimes even a cover name for a syndicate of writers. Even many of the publishing firms are obscure. The covers vary widely, all the way from the flat, badly drawn sketches dating from Bulldog Drummond, with the detective in a mackintosh and hat holding a smoking revolver,

142

through to the American-style covers with tough heroes and their molls—good-bad girls disguised as striptease artists—where sex takes pride of place over mayhem. Teachers and librarians seem to agree that the most eager readership for this new literature are young men, particularly servicemen, and boys in their last days at school or first days at work. Apart from the thrillers and the war stories (these seem to be the favourites), many of these young men read little else. The older ones probably glance at *Weekend* or *Reveille*, or at the more specialized magazines (electronics, motorcycles, fishing, tape-recorders, etc.). The younger ones have graduated from Biggles in the school library but never made Hemingway or Steinbeck or even Eric Ambler at the local library. There are no general magazines catering specially for them (the girls, of course, have the women's magazines, and teenage equivalents like *Honey*, as well as the love-comics like *Marilyn* and *Valentine*). In many cases, the disappearance of the reading habit (as opposed to the scanning habit) follows a fairly intense period of reading in the early forms at school. The taste for fiction, for 'stories', has developed, but, with late adolescence, the interest has shifted over to adult life and sexual experience. The satisfaction of this desire for 'realism' appears to be offered in its most available form in the thriller or crime story.

The one author whom these young people will have heard of, and probably read, is Mickey Spillane. He is the pace setter in the field. The Corgi editions of his works (reprinted in 1961) claim a sale of seventy million. They cannot be far wrong.

The Spillane novels succeed because of their boldness. They contain all the elements of the thriller novel, each raised to its most advanced form. The style is tough and hard-boiled throughout. Murder, violence and sex are intertwined in each narrative, and each episode is graphically realistic in treatment. The novels also contain that other ingredient, the transcending of authority and accepted moral codes (represented here by the legitimate police force and what Velda, the good-bad girl friend of Mike Hammer, calls 'little people with little minds'). Finally the stories are set off against a background of the corruption and vice of the big city, a constant theme in the thriller novel. These are essentially urban fantasies.

The city background is never materially used in the novels, or explored. It is simply the setting or 'locale' for the violent episode, establishing the mood by means of a sort of pathetic fallacy. The city is inhabited by stick-figures who express in two dimensions the sensibility of the hero (usually but not always private investigator and Avenging Angel, Mike Hammer):

> If there was life behind the windows of the buildings on either side of me, I didn't notice it. The street was mine, all mine. They gave it to me gladly and wondered why I wanted it so nice and all alone.
>
> There were others like me, sharing the dark and the solitude, but they huddled in the recesses of the doorways not wanting to share the wet and the cold. I could feel their eyes follow me briefly before they turned inward to their thoughts again.
>
> So I followed the hard concrete footpaths of the city through the towering canyons of the buildings and never noticed when the sheer cliffs of brick and masonry diminished altogether, and the footpath led into a ramp. . . .
>
> *One Lonely Night*

It would be an understatement to say that Mike Hammer enjoys killing and violence. He is pathologically committed to it. It is not simply a question, as in some other novels in the same genre, of using the crime and pursuit of the killer as an excuse to indulge the reader in violent fantasies. Hammer in Spillane novels is himself the violent agent. His exploits range from murder (he has killed fifty-eight people in six novels, according to Geoffrey Wagner's calculation in *Parade of Pleasure*), the beating of a naked girl with a leather belt in *One Lonely Night*, to the shooting of a girl in the belly at the end of *I, The Jury*. He not only admits that he is a killer, he says again and again that killing gives him pleasure. 'Maybe I did have a taste for death', he says to himself in *One Lonely Night*.

He had to go back five years to a time he knew of only secondhand and tell me how it took a war to show me the power of the gun and the obscene pleasure that was brutality and force, the spicy sweetness of murder sanctified by law.

ibid.

The surcharge of emotion which comes through in a passage like that, in such phrases as 'the obscene pleasure' and 'spicy sweetness', is not incidental. They are deliberately placed and dwelt on throughout the novels.

Part of the pleasure is simply his love of violence. 'I shot them in cold blood and enjoyed every minute of it. I pumped slugs into the nastiest bunch of bastards you ever saw and here I am calmer than I've ever been and happy too. . . . God, but it was fun.' Another aspect of pleasure is the consciousness in the mind of the victim that he or she is about to be brutalized. 'I only gave him a second to realize what it was like to die, then I blew the expression clean off his face.' That pause is the essence of Hammer. Often he will take pleasure in the anticipation of violence

Maybe I'll see you stripped again. Soon. When I do I'm going to take my belt off and lash your butt like it should have been lashed when you first broke into this game.

In fact, I looked forward to doing it.

ibid.

Or, in the elaborate preparations for it, as when he cuts the nose off his bullets so that

they wouldn't make too much of a hole where they went in, but the hole on the other side would be a beaut. You could stick your head in and look around without getting blood on your ears.

ibid.

When he can't get directly to grips with his victims, he indulges in vicious reveries. Or vicarious pleasure at someone else's violence:

He was a good cop, that one. He didn't lift the night stick above his waist. He held it like a lance and when it hit it went in deep where it took all the sound out of your body.

ibid.

The episodes which evoke most pleasure for Hammer are those in which violence and sex come together. Of course, Hammer sleeps with several of the women quite casually throughout the novels—but never, interestingly enough, with his secretary and sweetheart. His women are always beautiful, voluptuous, sexually provocative and scarcely clad. They can't wait to climb into bed with him, and Hammer is never too busy to comply. In fact, he is always mentally stripping them as they climb out of his car or watching 'this vision in a low-cut dress who threw a challenge with every motion of her body'. But the greatest pleasure derives from those occasions when, having taken the 'vision' sexually, he can violate it physically. In *I, The Jury* he watches the girl strip before shooting her in the belly. In *One Lonely Night* he beats her naked body, which he has previously enjoyed, with his belt. In *The Long Wait*, the hero (not Hammer this time) reluctantly undresses a girl dying from a severe beating-up and finds incriminating evidence taped to her bare stomach. The novel ends with the hero forcing his former girl friend to strip, only to have her turn the tables on him, produce a gun, and force *him* to take off his clothes. The two stand, naked, briefly unravelling the violent crime.

The sex in Spillane novels is a form of pure, distilled, adolescent fantasy. The women are always drawn in cold, hard sensuality straight from the memory of pornographic pin-up sketches, naked or nearly so, palpitating with the desire to seduce Hammer. The sexual encounters are described verbally like the striptease. One of the most typical and developed of these is the close of *I, The Jury*. Here the novel counterpoints Hammer's long exposition of the way the crimes Charlotte has committed fit together, with passages describing the girl's strip in slow motion.

. . . 'I knew you were well versed in that angle, but I never caught on until yesterday.'

(She was standing in front of me now. I felt a hot glow go over me as I saw what she was about to do . . .)

. . . 'That was it, wasn't it? No, you don't have to answer me because there could be no other way.'

(Now there were no more buttons. Slowly, ever so slowly, she pulled the blouse out of her skirt . . .)

I, The Jury

These are powerful fantasies of seduction and mutilation, but that is not all. For Hammer has a 'code' and a 'cause' which dignify and are intended to justify his actions. He always takes on the great forms of corruption—city politics, dirty photographs and blackmail, police corruption, the Mafia and Communism. Thus his actions are to some extent explained because he is the Avenging Angel, the wielder of the flaming sword of justice in a land of crime. He has the advantage over the police, however, because he matches the villains and crooks in his methods. He is as brutal as they are. He gives as good as he gets. The whole machinery of justice is subverted by the efficient free-lance avenger who saves the law by working outside it. He has appropriated justice, relieving it of what he calls 'the tedious process of the law':

A jury is cold and impartial like they're supposed to be, while some snotty lawyer makes them pour tears as he tells how his client was insane at the moment or had to shoot in self-defence. Swell. The law is fine. But this time I'm the law and I'm not going to be cold and impartial.

ibid.

As another novel of his claims in its title, *Vengeance is Mine.* Here is Hammer's credo:

Want to hear that philosophy? It's simple enough. Go after the big boys. Oh, don't arrest them, don't treat them to the dignity of the democratic process of courts and law . . . do the same thing to them that they'd do to you! Treat them to the unglorious taste of sudden death . . . Death is funny, Judge, people are afraid of it. Kill 'em left and right, show 'em that we aren't so soft after all. Kill, kill, kill, kill!

One Lonely Night

When this philosophy is applied, as it is in the above-mentioned novel, to a Great Cause—in this case, the eradication of Communism on American soil—the novels seem to come very close indeed to the nightmare of Fascism. In one scene a policeman breaks up a public meeting by beating the speakers with a club and protecting the heckler (a 'soldier', whom Hammer spurs on with the cry, 'Attaboy, buddy'). Hammer not only revels in mob violence, but serves up from his imagination all the squalid stereotypes of the period:

The lump of vomit in the centre of each crowd was a Judas sheep, trying to lead the rest to the axe. Then they'd go back and get more. The sheep were asking for it too. They were a seedy bunch in shapeless clothes, heavy with the smell of the rot they had asked for and gotten. They had a jackal look of discontent and cowardice, a hungry look that said you kill while we loot, then all will be well with the world.

ibid.

Clearly, Commies. In this passage, as elsewhere, the plot-line is reinforced, at the deepest level, by masochistic emotions of violence which surge up and spill over into the descriptive phrases and adjectives. The 'moral' of the story is that in order to combat Communism from within, America must be 'strong', and that, to be strong, the politicians (even the 'good' ones like the weak Lee Deamer) need the protection of the private avenger. (Deamer, of course, turns out to be 'the biggest Communist of them all'.) Throughout the novel, however, this *thesis* is never presented in political terms—it is simply assumed as a self-evident proposition about democratic societies. It is woven into the texture of assumptions in the novel. Anyone who thinks otherwise is taken to be either treasonable or hopelessly naive. Hammer himself claims to know nothing about politics and seems to have as much regard for politicians as he does for the police (except for his friend, Pat Chambers, who admires Mike Hammer and respects his methods, but is forced by his job as a law officer to have regard for the 'tedious process of the law'). *One Lonely Night*, perhaps because of its theme, owes a great deal directly to the atmosphere of the McCarthy period and propounds a philosophy of politics which the Senator would have recognized. But the same assumptions govern all the Hammer novels.

The Spillane novels cannot be discussed in terms of their *effects*, since very little evidence exists on which such judgements could be based. They must be dealt with on their own account, as forms of popular fiction expressing certain attitudes or interests on the part of their author. They seem, in fact, in spite of their realistic treatment, to be closer to fantasies. In this kind of fantasy the wishes which are gratified form a distinct pattern, which can be traced in other novels of the same genre. The organizing principle is a general tough-mindedness, particularly in relation to sex and physical brutality. There is something compelling about this pattern, which is due, in part, to the fact that it is all of a piece. There are no saving devices in the novel by which the reader can distance himself from the action. They are all 'I' novels, so that identification between the reader, the hero and his acts is an easy process. Moreover, the first-person narrative makes the author seem to be closely caught up with what is going on as well. This may be the reason why a Spillane novel, whatever its faults, never seems to be coldly put together or manufactured out of stylistic spare-parts, like so many of its imitators (cf., for example, the Hank Jansen novels). The emotions are strong and direct, they thrust forward into the narrative and carry it along. In their own way, they are compellingly written and imagined. The questions which arise relate to the emotions and attitudes handled in this way; questions which are not, of course, separable from a response to the texture of the novels as a whole, and to their style.

No doubt it could be argued that these novels simply give back to their readers something from the night-life of the mind which was already present. Yet the act of composing stories which handle such submerged fantasies so directly is itself a conscious act. When the words form on the page, tenuous emotions are let loose in their primitive state, given a hard shape and feel and a dramatic context within which to work. Happily it is unlikely that many people respond to these images at precisely the level of crudity with which they are offered.

Some years ago, the American critic, Edmund Wilson, wrote an attack on the fad of the detective story and called it 'Who Cares Who Killed Roger Ackroyd?' (*Classics and Commercials*). But even at this stage the detective story proper had passed its peak. Its clientele today is more likely to be serious writers and readers seeking escape in what Wilson calls 'a kind of vice that, for silliness and minor harmfulness, ranks somewhere between smoking and crossword puzzles', than the casual reader who chooses books from the W. H. Smith bookstall. The detective story's place has been taken by the Spillane-type thriller, a faster-moving, tougher action-story, which owes more to the novel of violence in America than it does to Conan Doyle, Dorothy Sayers or Agatha Christie. The hero is more recognizably contemporary than Sherlock Holmes, Lord Peter Wimsey or Hercule Poirot. These novels reflect, to some extent, the stereotyped setting of the 'big city', particularly in the era of organized gangsterism and corrupt politics. This can be seen by a look at two classics by one of the originators of the form—Dashiell Hammett's *Glass Key* and *The Maltese Falcon*. The laconic, hard-bitten style of narration, fitted for the action novel, was first pioneered in such works.

One aspect of this shift in taste was commented upon by George Orwell in his essay, 'Raffles and Miss Blandish' (*Critical Essays*). In the newer-style thriller, any interest in clues and pure detection is purely incidental. The true interest now centres upon the deportment of the hero—especially his toughness in confronting both villains and women. The hero is rarely a police detective, since the police are presented as slow and rather stupid. He is more often the 'private eye'. Of course the hero who is part detective, part crook, has his antecedents in popular literature too—Richard Hannay (John Buchan), Raffles (E. W. Hornung) and The Saint (Leslie Charteris) all stood outside the law and in an ambiguous relation to it. But some restraining ethical framework was still maintained. In the later thrillers this has been thrown over altogether. It is the apparently incidental pleasure (what Bernard Bergonzi calls the 'affective superstructure' of the story) rather than the unmasking of the villain which carries us along. The quality of escapism here is quite different from the 'crossword puzzle' interest of the older detective story, with its maps and railway timetables. The escapism is to be found in the general atmosphere of the novel as a whole rather than in its strict plot-development. The difference may be summed up by saying that although both a Sayers and a Spillane novel begin with a murder, a Sayers novel ends with an *arrest*, a Spillane novel with a *shooting*.

In the Spillane novel, the hero, Mike Hammer, emerges as a metaphysical figure in pursuit of a Great Cause. This credo is worked out, beyond the long arm of the law, often in opposition to it. Yet both Hammer and the police are aiming at the same end —the retribution of justice for crimes committed. Both sorts of resolutions could be said to show that 'crime does not pay'. This only serves to show how crude this yardstick is as a measure of the attitudes implicit in works of this sort. The end may be the same, but the means are different—and, so far as reading-pleasure is concerned, it is the *means* which matter, which arouse our interest and hold our attention.

As one ploughs through a succession of novels in which the elements of the form are crudely welded together, with the drool of pleasure of the supposed reader already written into the novel, one begins to develop a perverse respect for Spillane himself. At least, in his novels, the incidents are given some pattern overall by Hammer's philosophy of life, repellent though it may be. Moreover, they are written with a certain cold-hearted gusto and drive. So many of the others wander rather forlornly from body to body, from girl to girl, with only a killing or a piece of strip-tease to relieve the drabness of the writing. Though the style is 'hotted-up' in the best imitation-American (American writers sometimes imitate the American manner too), the words are simply mental counters switched about to get the right glands working in the reader. The language is lifeless and repetitive:

'Can't you do something?' I panted . . .

'Yes,' she panted. 'Of course.' Her voice was almost a wail. 'Of course, I'll fix something . . . but please. Please!'

'I've gotta be sure. This is killing me,' I panted . . . The star streaked across the heavens, exploded mightily, and the glittering, burned-out fragments showered down and evaporated into nothingness.

Hank Jansen, Secret Session

But if one turns to the supposedly more sophisticated writers in the genre there is little relief to be gained. Ian Fleming, one of the best-known writers in this field, was himself a sophisticated man, a manager of the *Sunday Times* and regular reviewer on their book pages, a critic and clubman with literary tastes. His novels always appeared in hard covers first and were usually well and widely reviewed in the serious press. They have been serialized, in both strip cartoon and excerpt form (*Daily Express* and *Today*), and a series of James Bond films has been launched. Yet the main difference between Fleming and Spillane is the high gloss of social snobbery which gilds the Fleming stories. The characterization is often banal and crude. James Bond, the hero, is a typical 'tough', 'licensed to kill by the Secret Service'. In *Dr No*, one of his most popular novels (it was severely criticized by Paul Johnson in the *New Statesman* 5/4/58), some attempt is made to fill in the background, and yet most of the story is peopled by a fantastic race of Chinese negroes, and the attempt to capture local Jamaican dialect is represented by passages of dialogue from a native buddy of Bond's such as: 'We get nuthen out of dis gal, Cap'n. She plenty tough. You want fer me to break she's arm?' Fleming's range of information was wide, reflecting his experience as an international correspondent and a high official in Naval Intelligence during the war, but this air of professional know-how and expertise is made to serve a very shallow level of narrative and quite conventional effects. Dr. No himself is a typical thriller-fantasy figure. A giant with articulated pincers for hands, he creates atmosphere by tapping his metal claws on his contact lenses. The girl is first glimpsed nude except for a leather belt. She goes through torture by exposure to live crabs before finally winding up with Bond in a monster sleeping-bag.

It is the obsessive of social snobbery which appears to account for his popularity. The snobbery is not simply an irritating occasional habit indulged in by Bond. It is a controlling element in the whole novel. It occurs in countless occasional flashes and phrases, as well as in longer set-pieces. The narrative seems always to be dropping into this kind of casual aside: 'It was the sort of voice Bond's first expensive tailor used', or 'Bond noticed that the lift was made by Waygood Otis. Everything in the prison was *de luxe*' . . . or 'The air was fresh and cool and held a slight, expensive fragrance', or 'Colour lithograph reproductions of Degas ballet sketches were well hung in groups on the wall. . . .' What comes across here is not so much the relentless crudity of Bond's snobbery, but the hint of vulgarity on the part of the author. Each phrase seems to contain that tell-tale word which betrays the author's involvement with the trick which he is playing: 'Bond's *first* expensive tailor' . . . '*de luxe*' . . . 'a *slight*, expensive fragrance' . . . '*well hung* in groups' . . . (our italics).

Here is Bond surveying the menu in Dr No's island fortress:

> Propped among the bottles were two menus, huge double-folio pages covered with print. They might have been from the Savoy Grill, or the '21', or the Tour d'Argent. Bond ran his eye down one of them. It began with *Caviar double de Beluga* and ended with *Sorbet à la Champagne*. In between was every dish whose constituents would not be ruined by a deep freeze. Bond tossed it down . . .
>
> Ian Fleming, *Dr No*

> Without enthusiasm, Bond ordered caviar, grilled lamb cutlets and salad, and angels on horseback for himself. When Honeychile refused to make any suggestions, he chose melon, roast chicken à l'anglaise and vanilla ice-cream with hot chocolate sauce for her.
>
> ibid.

These deliberate status fantasies, one might think, are simply a joke. Yet they are often presented without much trace of a saving irony. Moreover, they serve an important function, for they seem to make palatable to well-off and well-educated readers those elements which they would be shocked to read (or embarrassed to be seen reading) in the more direct form in which, say, Spillane treats them. The particular unpleasantness of the Fleming novels is that they appeal, in such a vulgar way, to sophisticated readers, and the class snobbery is so compounded with the nastiest kind of sex and violence. For there is as much of both sex and violence in these novels as there is in Spillane at his 'best'. The heroines of *Diamonds are Forever* and *Dr No* have both suffered rape at an early age before falling into Bond's hands. Dr No himself perishes by suffocation in a heap of bird dung. In *Live and Let Die* the Communist agent is finally eaten alive by sharks. In *Diamonds are Forever* a man has his face disfigured by scalding mud. In *Casino Royale* Bond is beaten on the genitals with a carpet-sweeper. These sado-erotic episodes are retold with precisely the same pleasure that we find in a Spillane novel. But there is nothing in Spillane to match the vulgarity of this:

> It is not as aristocratic as it was, the redistribution of wealth has seen to that, but it is still the most exclusive club in London. The membership is restricted to two hundred and each candidate must have two qualifications for election: he must behave like a gentleman and he must be able to 'show' £100,000 in cash or gilt-edged securities.
> The amenities of Blades, apart from the gambling, are so desirable . . .
>
> *Moonraker*

and very little which is as cold and calculated as this:

> He wanted her cold and arrogant body. He wanted to see tears and desire in her remote blue eyes and to take the ropes of her black hair in his hands and bend her long body back under his. Bond's eyes narrowed and his face in the mirror looked back at him with hunger.
>
> *Casino Royale*

Perhaps, then, the genre is too corrupt and decadent—a popular form which has been swamped by the dangerous emotions and situations (dangerous in a psychological sense) it has handled and made useless by overwork and exaggeration. This seems almost true. Yet one or two writers have managed the thriller novel without being defeated by it, and of these Raymond Chandler is a supreme instance.

Chandler often wished that he had written a 'proper' novel. Yet he also recognized a truth with which all popular artists start:

> When a book, any sort of book, reaches a certain intensity or artistic performance, it becomes literature. That intensity may be a matter of style, situation, character, emotional tone, or idea, or half a dozen other things. It may also be perfection of control over the movement of a story similar to the control a great pitcher has over the ball.
>
> Gardiner and Walker, *Raymond Chandler Speaking*

The first thing which strikes one about Chandler is the quality of his intelligence. He possessed a serious, lively, precise mind and this can be seen at work not only in his novels but in his critical comments on the thriller novel, in his pieces on his Hollywood experiences and in his letters (a great deal of these are now collected in *Raymond Chandler Speaking*).

Chandler wrote eight full-length novels. In each the hero is the 'private eye', Philip Marlowe. Unlike either Mike Hammer or James Bond, however, Marlowe is not a 'private investigator with a licence to kill'. He rarely uses a gun, never with any pleasure. He possesses no superhuman physical prowess. When he finds himself in a tough spot he is scared. When a gang of toughs twists his arm, it twists. 'He bent me. I can be bent. I'm not the City Hall. He bent me' (*Farewell, My Lovely*). Face to face with a dangerous dame who produces a gun, Marlowe 'plays it tough', but he knows he's playing, and so do we:

> Her right hand came up from her coat pocket and she pointed it at me.
> I grinned. It may not have been the heartiest grin in the world, but it was a grin.
> 'I've never liked this scene,' I said.
>
> *The Lady in the Lake*

Marlowe lacks the pleasure of killing; he also lacks a meta-physical creed, a grand purpose. He is a professional, he makes a living—not a very good one—and respects the professional trust of his clients. He also demands that they respect him—they do not possess him simply by paying him a retainer, and they cannot buy his principles. This is especially true when his clients are very rich. (Chandler once wrote, in his usual ironic vein: 'P. Marlowe and I do not despise the upper classes because they take baths and have money; we despise them because they are phoney.') Here he is with the very wealthy Mrs Murdoch in *The High Window*:

> She laughed heartily. 'This is a delicate family matter, Mr Marlowe. And it must be handled with delicacy.'
>
> 'If you hire me, you'll get all the delicacy I have. If I don't have enough delicacy, maybe you'd better not hire me. For instance, I take it you don't want your daughter-in-law framed. I'm not delicate enough for that.'
>
> *The High Window*

This kind of gritty integrity, professional in tone but really more deeply based, lifts Marlowe as a dramatic creation, and Chandler's novels, out of the Fleming-Spillane-Jansen class. An ethical framework is present, as a point of reference, throughout Chandler's work. This has the effect of humanizing the 'private eye'. It also makes it possible for judgements, shadings and comparisons to be made within the body of each novel. Ruthlessly stylized though they may be, the novels remain images of human conduct. Chandler, in his usual manner, once said of Marlowe: 'P. Marlowe has as much social conscience as a horse. He has a personal conscience, which is an entirely different matter.' The same could not be said of Bond or Hammer, for in those novels the ethical framework is always eliminated, so that the private avenger can proceed about his business without restraint.

Marlowe has no social conscience, perhaps, but Chandler's novels handle the social background in a critical and satirical manner which is worth reading for itself. His novels are, almost incidentally, one of the most effective social critiques of Hollywood and the Californian life. This very often comes through in the cynical aside:

'I want to peddle a little dirt.'
She picked a cigarette out of a crystal box and lit it with a crystal lighter. 'Peddle? You mean for money—in Hollywood?'

The Little Sister

But there are also longer descriptive passages, and dramatized episodes only incidental to the plot, such as the hilarious exchange between Marlowe and a film magnate in a bizarre sunken garden about the peeing habits of dogs, or the scene on the film set with Mavis Weld, which accurately captures the deliberate bitchery of the film world. Both the zany unreality and the small-time nastiness of movieland come across sharp and true:

'That's a fair comment,' Ned Gammon said.
'Trouble is he only has two hundred and twelve feet of film, and that's my fault. If you could take the scene just a little faster . . .'
'Huh,' Torrance snorted. 'If *I* could take it a little faster. Perhaps Miss Weld could be prevailed upon to climb aboard this yacht in rather less time than it would take to build the damn boat.'
Mavis Weld gave him a quick, contemptuous look.
'Weld's timing is just right,' Gammon said. 'Her performance is just right too.'
Susan Crawley shrugged elegantly. 'I had the impression she could speed it up a trifle, Ned. It's good, but it *could* be better.'
'If it was any better, darling,' Mavis Weld told her smoothly, 'somebody might call it acting. You wouldn't want anything like that to happen in *your* picture, would you?'

ibid.

Here the scene is tightly created, dramatized—naturally, with deliberate exaggeration. But the skills at work here belong to the art of the novel rather than the art of the strip-tease. They immediately put in perspective those set-pieces of 'local colour' which one finds in Fleming, or the universal, anonymous 'city' through which Hammer is always striding, thinking his dark thoughts.

It is not surprising, then, that from his earliest novel, Chandler tried to capture an authentic social setting. *The Big Sleep*, Chandler's first and crudest novel, tries to picture a wealthy American family, a tough, remote father who is a General, and his degenerate but rich offspring. All this is not particularly memorable. But the opening of his next novel, *Farewell, My Lovely*, is quite different. The swiftness and deliberacy of the whole first chapter marks Chandler's narrative command and control. The pen-sketch of the negro speak-easy on Central Avenue and the colourful figure who picks Marlowe up and puts him down is swiftly mounted and sharply etched. As Chandler moves deeper into his natural territory, theme and social setting fill out and engage to a growing degree his real interests. *The Lady in the Lake* makes use of one of the standard themes of the thriller novel—the corrupt police—to paint a portrait of an evil and brutalized detective, but the portrait is a specific one, it is not generalized wildly as it would be in Spillane. *The Little Sister* lacks almost altogether the traditional element of suspense. The identity of the murderer becomes clear quite early on. It is the damning satire of Hollywood that stays in the mind. *The Long Good-bye* begins with a distinctive portrait of a weak but charming habitual drunk with whom Marlowe casually becomes involved. The novel explores, without ever sacrificing its genre, the mutual responsibilities which this relationship establishes, and the complex way in which Marlowe reacts to it—both fascinated and repelled by Terry Lennox's weakness. The novel is a third of the way through before the murder takes place. In this book Chandler extends his range, while still retaining the narrative pace of the thriller. The novel has many touches reminiscent of Scott Fitzgerald or Malcolm Lowry (Fitzgerald is directly invoked at more than one point). It is Chandler's most serious work and his most sustained. Throughout, his wit plays at its least forced. *Playback*, his last, is almost reflective, a recapitulatory novel. (It stands in relation to Chandler's work, if the comparison is permissible, as *Persuasion* stands to Jane Austen's.) All the themes are there—so is the wit, the speed of narration, the panache. But the pattern is breaking up. Marlowe falls in love. He discovers who disposed of the body, but doesn't turn him in (typically, however, he refuses to shake hands with him either: 'No. You hired a gun. That puts you out of the class of people I shake hands with.'). The novel closes with the telephone ringing. His girl is on her way back.

As Chandler's work develops, his themes emerge with greater clarity. When he died he was still at work on *The Poodle Springs Story*. This was to be only incidentally a thriller. Marlowe, married to the wealthy girl, is in danger of becoming her 'poodle', confined to the empty round of California cocktail parties. 'The contest between what she wants Marlowe to do and what he will insist on doing will make a good sub-plot. I don't know how it will turn out, but she'll never tame him. Perhaps the marriage won't last, or she might even learn to respect his integrity,' Chandler wrote, '. . . a struggle of personalities and ideas of life': the thriller becoming the novel of manners.

The thriller form was always, perhaps, too limited for Chandler's real gifts as a writer. Yet he never rejected it. He used it to write about the things which interested him and about which he knew. (He not only lived on the California coast but also had the deadly experience of a brief career in Hollywood, and wrote a devastating critique of it, 'Writers in Hollywood', for *Atlantic Monthly*.) Yet he worked within his form, commanded it, making it work for him, rather than, as Fleming does, exploiting it in a calculated way, or, as Spillane does, allowing it to exploit *him*. He was aware that the thriller is a form of illusion—'the private eye is admittedly an exaggeration—a fantasy. But at least he's an exaggeration of the possible.' He knew that it owed more to the melodrama and burlesque than it did to the novel of ideas or the novel of social significance. (In his Hollywood piece, he described 'those pictures of deep social import in which everybody is thoughtful and grown-up and sincere and the more difficult problems of life are wordily resolved into a unanimous vote of confidence in the inviolability of the Constitution, the sanctity of the home and the paramount importance of the streamlined kitchen' (*Raymond Chandler Speaking*). He knew that 'pace' in the thriller is not a question of how swiftly the private eye moves from body to body, but rather the apparent inevitability of the action, the stylized simplicity of the narrative line, the telescoping of space and time, the illusion of plausibility which, as he said, 'is a matter of effect, not of fact'. He was never tempted to treat the thriller as a species of wish-fulfilment. He dealt in a highly conventionalized art, and he handled the conventions deliberately and publicly. Though fascinated by character, and capable of the portrait in depth, he realized that in the thriller character had to be created 'by the objective or dramatic method as on the stage, that is, by appearance, behaviour, speech and actions'.

Chandler never disguised the conventions of his form. He exposed them. He is continually reminding the reader of them— a kind of insurance against their being mistaken for real life. From this stylistic audacity all his characteristic qualities flowed. His mode of seeing was a natural development of his way of working.

The essence of this art was irony. He mastered all the conventions related to the ironic vision: parody, satire, self-exposure, burlesque, sardonic comment, wit, melodrama. Irony is the natural mode of this kind of artist—the writer who sees continually the play of convention against realism, realism against convention.

This controlling irony works at many levels throughout Chandler's novels. Wit is the natural style in many of the narrative and descriptive passages. It is also his typical manner when painting the satiric portrait:

A fat man in sky-blue pants was closing the door with that beautiful leisure only fat men achieve. He wasn't alone, but I looked at him first. He was a large man and wide. Not young nor handsome, but he looked durable. Above the sky-blue gabardine slacks he wore a two-tone leisure jacket which would have been revolting on a zebra. The neck of his canary-yellow shirt was open wide, which it had to be if his neck was going to get out. He was hatless and his large head was decorated with a reasonable amount of pale salmon-coloured hair. His nose had been broken but well set, and it hadn't been a collector's item in the first place.

The creature with him was a weedy number with red eyes and sniffles. Age about twenty, five feet nine, thin as a broom straw. His nose twitched and his mouth twitched and his hands twitched and he looked unhappy.

The big man smiled genially. 'Mr Marlowe, no doubt?'

I said: 'Who else?'

The Little Sister

This is the satirist's gift, the art of the mock-heroic rather than the epic. It is Chandler's typical style of portraiture.

Another weapon of his ironic vision is Marlowe's speech. The typical trope used is the 'wisecrack'—the terse, brief, dry, witty epigram, chiselled down as far as he can get it. Not only is this Marlowe's natural manner of speaking, it sums up his whole *style*— the toughness which other thriller novelists create with fists and revolvers Marlowe creates by speech. What violence there is in a Chandler novel is always passing over into the language itself. It is the language which is tough and laconic. Chandler never allows us to forget that this is a stylistic effect, not a realistic one. People are always telling Marlowe to 'kill the wisecracking'. In one novel he irritates a detective who talks tough by nicknaming him 'Hemingway'. When someone else brings off a witticism Marlowe says, enviously: 'I ought to have said that one. Just my style.' This self-consciousness about language allows Chandler to hold his hero at some distance from himself as a *created* character, and it also permits Marlowe to distance himself from the *role* of the 'tough guy' which he is 'playing':

'One moment, please. Whom did you wish to see?'

Degarmo spun on his heel and looked at me wonderingly. 'Did he say "whom"?'

'Yeah, but don't hit him,' I said. 'There is such a word.'

The Lady in the Lake

Or:

'Just like Queen Victoria,' I said.
'I don't get it.'
'I don't expect miracles,' I said. The meaningless talk had a sort of cold bracing effect on me, making a mood with a hard, gritty edge.
                                                                    The High Window

Parallel with the witticisms and epigrams of the dialogue, there are the private, sardonic comments which Marlowe continually makes to himself, the disengaged, cynical observations which puncture illusions, take the wind out of the world he surveys with disenchanted eyes. By these means Chandler gradually creates a Marlowe 'point of view', almost a Marlowe philosophy of life. There is, too, the continual self-parody, by which Marlowe pokes fun at himself, destroying any pretensions he may have as a 'tough guy', making the reader aware of the stylization of the role which he is playing. At one point, in *The Little Sister*, he refers to 'all the tired clichéd mannerisms of my trade'. Later in the same novel he gives an instance of this:

I was psychic that night. I was a fellow who wanted company in a dark place and was willing to pay a high price for it. The Luger under my arm and the .32 in my hand made me tough. Two-gun Marlowe, the kid from Cyanide Gulch.

Sometimes, this style of self-parody extends into longer passages of self-mockery, in which Chandler assimilates the effects of the internal parody. Here is a reverie of Marlowe's, from *The Little Sister*, where the effect is most deliberately used:

Questioned at the University Heights Police Station, Marlowe declared he was taking the piano to the Maharajah of Coot-Berar. Asked why he was wearing spurs, Marlowe declared that a client's confidence was sacred. Marlowe is being held for investigation. Chief Hornside said police were not yet ready to say more. Asked if the piano was in tune, Chief Hornside declared that he had played the Minute

Waltz on it in thirty-five seconds and so far as he could tell there were no strings in the piano. He intimated that something else was. . . .

As these various satirical modes are more fully employed we begin to understand Chandler's real achievement. Like the true satirist, his gift lies in a disenchanted view of life, and depends upon a highly artificial style. Like the mock-heroic writers and poets, who made play with 'heroism', Chandler makes play with the notion of 'toughness'. He inverts the thriller conventions, draws attention to their artificiality. A hard, polished prose surface permits his wit to play freely. Where the lesser practitioners in the field break their necks to build up the arch-hero, the superman, at the centre of their work, Chandler sets out to portray the most practised of anti-heroes. Apart from Marlowe, who is keeper of both conscience and consciousness in the novel, and through whose elliptical eye every detail is observed and placed, few of the other characters have true 'depth'. They are consciously two-dimensional, like the characters in a Ben Jonson play or in Restoration comedy. Perhaps, like the latter, a Chandler novel is a decadent work of art, and there are signs of this in the language (for one thing the similes tend to be over-elaborate and ornate or bizarre). But his use of the witticism or the wisecrack has the same pointed 'surface' effect as the rhymed couplet or the epigram in Restoration comedy. There are countless effects of a literary kind which lesser novelists, practising in the more major literary genres, are able to achieve, but which escaped Chandler. But there are many compensating pleasures which are not to be found in their work. Few writers have used so compromised and over-worked a popular literary form with such skill, craftsmanship and tact.

7

Falling in Love

Let us get down to the realities and the origin of this deplorable book. It emanates from the warped mind of the author. The story he tells is pure invention: it never actually happened.

LORD TEVIOT speaking in the House of Lords about
Lady Chatterley's Lover

I count it a misfortune that serious books are exposed in the public market, like slaves exposed naked for sale. But there we are, since we live in an age of mistaken democracy, we must go through with it.

D. H. LAWRENCE

The gangster story or thriller is an interesting departure from similar types of action story in popular literature precisely because it brings together in a new form the two high themes of popular art: love and action. The theme that 'crime does not pay', the hunting down and punishment of the killer and the outlaw, the restoration of law and order in the land, the excitement of the chase and the unmasking of the villain—these are the common coin of popular literature of low life. They seem archetypal in their appeal to the popular imagination, and we can find them, in one form or another, in ballads, in highwaymen and outlaw stories, in picaresque novels and in Victorian melodrama. Placed in a modern setting, this action pattern is preserved in the modern thriller. Yet if we read these stories with some attention to their moral climate, to the distribution of stress and emphasis within the story, to particular passages which move and excite us in retrospect, we see the action is now merely a scaffolding which permits the working out of other tensions and experiences (particularly sexual fantasies) which are acceptable only when handled within a recognized set of conventions. This seems to be

164

a recurrent pattern. The same situations are worked through in each period in a contemporary setting, a similar type of hero or heroine is conjured into life, the story is supported by some collective myth (popular romance, for example, is full of variants on the Romeo-and-Juliet or Cinderella themes); the story moves to the same kind of resolution and points the same kind of moral. At this level (in her classic study, *Fiction and the Reading Public*, Mrs Leavis called it the 'anthropological' level) popular fantasy relies upon familiar themes and situations and follows a recognized pattern unchanged, except in incidentals, by place or period. Yet, within these acceptable patterns, in each new period we find the various elements assembled in new ways: in fact, quite new experiences and feelings are being dealt with. The writer responds, often without being aware of it, to a subterranean source within the collective subconscious of his society, and embodies these symbols within his story; and under pressure from this source the forms of the stories inevitably change.

Reduced to its anthropological elements, the modern thriller is almost as old as literature itself. Grendel, the monster in *Beowulf*, also threatened a whole way of life, she too left her 'clues'; the slaying of the monster was a testing of the hero, and, through him, of his society; in *Beowulf* there is even the final show-down, the 'unmasking' beneath the water. As Orwell showed in his comparison between *Raffles* and *Miss Blandish*, the modern thriller-hero can no longer afford to stand aside from the action in his story with that aristocratic detachment which was possible in his immediate predecessors. Unlike Sherlock Holmes or Lord Peter Wimsey or that meticulous *deus ex machina* Hercule Poirot, the thriller-hero must finally enter the action as the main protagonist. The omniscience of the earlier detective-heroes provided some distance between them and the mere mortals caught up in the drama and confusion of the crime. But now this hero, of all the figures in the novel, must be the *most* exposed to the play of passion and violence, the one most intimately caught up with the actual experience of punishment. And if we ask why this change has come about we are forced to give a complex set of reasons, all of which suggest how deeply rooted the literature is in the social imagination. Perhaps it is because we can no longer accept the figure who stands outside the action and yet knows all the answers: we demand greater verisimilitude today. Perhaps it is because these impersonal figures seem now too superhumanly remote: since the revolution in our thinking effected by Freud and psychoanalysis, we take a different view of crime, punishment and violence which the thriller reflects. We cannot believe in the hero who is himself wholly free from the inner compulsions of violence and lawlessness—we demand that he should stand closer to the villain, exposed to the very evils he is dedicated to remove: 'there, but for the grace of God . . .' Certainly, the philosopher would argue that the thriller also shows a collapse in the belief in an abstract and incorruptible Justice.

One of the reasons for the change in the moral climate of the thriller is, surely, that without a hero who is implicated in the action, the novels could not capture the blend of fantasy and realism they so effectively convey. The Mike Hammer or James Bond stories are, of course, fantasies—but fantasies which communicate a graphic and heightened realism. Characters may be overdrawn, situations stereotyped, resolutions predictable. But the fictional life of these stories is convincing at the very level at which the modern reader, especially the young reader, is likely to find himself most under pressure: at the level of the sensations. In a quite precise sense, the thriller novel is a novel of the sensations. Its power lies in its experiential quality, in the absence of relieving factors and the starkness of the action, and in the image of human behaviour which it offers. This is the image of a hero driven by inner necessities, to which he must directly and instantly react. If he has the urge to hit his victim, he does so. If he is attracted by a girl, he seduces her. Emotions, these stories suggest, are simple. Man, stripped of conventions and culture, is a creature of the instincts. At this subterranean level, these novels really live. The instincts are set free by the way the fantasy elements are manipulated in the plot. 'Emancipation', as Orwell said, 'is complete.' In some real way, the thriller *liberates*. Even when the actions take place in some bizarre setting, they are always urban fantasies. The proper location of the thriller is the City—the anonymous City—where men are both crowded and alone, tied to one another by few remaining links; the setting for what Durkheim called the anomic experience in modern life. The City is not a real place—it is a location in the mind, where everything *adult* is supposed to take place, only hotted-up, heightened, at a faster pace, thrilling, compulsive. In thriller literature today, this treatment is almost synonymous with what we have come to identity as *realism*.

Thrillers, then, offer one mode in which contemporary experiences are set to work within the frame of fantasy, and they provide one kind of compensation. But another, equally urgent, need seems only to be fulfilled when situations are handled with the opposite emphasis—where realism yields to romance, situations are enveloped in a sentimental glow, where the heroine mopes when things go badly, and then, at the end, is 'swept off her feet'.

There are many kinds of fiction with love and romance as their main preoccupation—the list would include, at one end, those 'searing' novels in paperback about a passionate sexual affair, 'frankly told' (which we might call the thriller-romance; then the 'hospital' romances, the fiction stories in the women's magazines, the conventional book-of-the-month romances and the love comics for teenagers. Like the thrillers, the sexy novelettes are experimental—they serve, in C. S. Lewis's phrase, as 'channels to the Event' (*An Experiment in Criticism*). The other types of romance provide the reverse side of the coin. They enable the reader vicariously to participate in pleasure or reverie.

They may be love stories, and these may be either sensual and pornographic or sentimental and edifying. They may be success stories. They may be stories about high life, or simply about wealthy and luxurious life . . . I distinguish the kinds thus for clarity. Actual books for the most part belong not wholly, but predominantly, to one or other of them. The story of excitement or mystery usually has a 'love interest' tacked on to it, often perfunctorily. The love story or the

Idyll of High Life has to have some suspense and anxiety in it, however
trivial these may be.

C. S. Lewis, *An Experiment in Criticism*

Contrary to the usual concern expressed about this kind of
fiction by educationists, the contemporary significance of these
stories is not that they deal with sex (often outside marriage or
adulterous), or falling in love. Many of the situations in the
modern romance can be found in earlier types of fiction and indeed
in every kind of novel. The girl in the diaphanous négligée
threatened by the monster with glaring eyes has her prototype in
Gothic melodrama. The defensive virgin of the woman's magazine story springs from the same stock as the heroines of Richardson's novels, and the countless imitators of Richardson who
contributed to the didactic novel of the eighteenth century (see
J. M. S. Tompkins, *The Popular Novel in England*). Romantic
fantasies of high life and love in fashionable but decadent circles
preoccupied that indefatigable popular novelist Reynolds in the
mid-nineteenth century in all eight volumes of the *Mysteries of the
Court of London*. The prostitute with the heart of gold enters the
history of the novel at least as early as the heroines of Defoe's
novels: and although she has a hard time of it in the moralistic
climate of Victorian literature, she can be found in some of the
Salisbury Square novels of the mid-century, with their 'scenes of
robbery and seduction' (see Margaret Dalziel, *Popular Fiction
100 Years Ago*). The young girl in the love comics beset by the
problems of the heart and bent on marriage can be seen as a reworking of the sentimental heroine of Victorian literature, who
survives Jane Austen's critique in *Sense and Sensibility* and lives on
into the era of the 'literature of the rail' and the penny magazines
for women. In his book, *Passion and Society*, Denis de Rougemont
argues that ever since the chivalrous romances of courtly love (he
takes the *Tristan and Iseult* story as his paradigm) fiction has
exalted the adulterous relationship at the expense of the relationship in marriage. This conflict, he believes, runs right through
western European fiction. It is the tension around which a great

deal of Victorian literature is built, but it is also the tension
expressed in almost every drawing in the latter-day love comics.
And perhaps, because of Puritanism, marriage and the middle-
class ethic in which it is embedded have had a longer innings in
English fiction than in most others; popular novelists working
within the safe conventions of the woman's magazine story are
handling not a new problem but an ancient theme:

> On the one hand, we have today a morality concerned for the species
> and the general well-being of society, though none the less bearing
> some impress of religion—what we call middle-class morals. On the
> other hand, there is a morality spread among us through our literary
> and artistic atmosphere and general culture—and this produces
> passionate or romantic morals. The whole of middle-class youth in
> Europe was brought up to regard marriage with respect; and yet at the
> same time all young people breathe in from books and periodicals, from
> stage and screen, and from a thousand daily allusions, a romantic
> atmosphere in the haze of which passion seems to be the supreme test
> that one day or other awaits every true man or woman, and it is
> accepted that nobody has really lived till he or she 'has been through
> it'.   Denis de Rougemont, *Passion and Society*

We do not need to accept de Rougemont's interpretation of or
attitude towards this tension to recognize it as the central one in a
great deal of contemporary romantic fiction.

It is not, then, the simple presence of these themes, tensions
and experiences which deserves attention, it is the way in which,
in each period, they are being handled. If a tension is maintained
between conventional and romantic morals, how precisely can it
be resolved? Morally, what other attitudes and values coexist with
the values governing romantic and sexual behaviour? Artistically,
with what force and intensity is the dilemma presented? What
aspects of human nature are brought selectively to the fore in the
several ideal types of heroes and heroines offered to the reader?
Art is a way of giving meaning to experience: what meanings are
associated with love in popular fiction now? Orwell noted that,
although Raffles 'has no real moral code, no religion, certainly no

social consciousness', yet, in respect of violence, he has 'a set of reflexes—the nervous system, as it were, of a gentleman':

snobbishness, like hypocrisy, is a check upon behaviour whose value from a social point of view has been underrated.

George Orwell, Critical Essays

What 'nervous system', which 'checks upon behaviour', do we find active within the romance fiction? What valued aspirations, other than the aspiration to 'fall in love', to be 'swept off one's feet', to marry, are called into play?

In English fiction, both popular and serious, the most prominent recurring theme is the theme of 'heroic virtue'—stories which centre upon the rigorous defence of her chastity by the young and vulnerable virgin. This theme is almost synonymous with the rise of the novel as a popular form. But it does not loom with any real force until, through Puritanism, we get the idealization of marriage itself, and, with the development of bourgeois society, marriage becomes a commercial social contract. The code of values assumed by Richardson and the didactic novelists is the middle-class ethic, and here 'strictness in sexual relations tends to coincide with the increasing importance of private property—the bride must be chaste so that her husband can be sure that it is his son who will inherit' (Ian Watt, *The Rise of the Novel*). The woman, through marriage, enters more fully into the household of the husband: and part of Richardson's purpose is to provide a sustaining ethical code for the woman in her new role. The men in Richardson's novels are still the rakes of Restoration comedy— attackers, serpents in the garden. But the woman has been strengthened in her dealings with this enemy—in the courtship her sexual instincts are held in check by a rigorous ethic of behaviour, and the prospects of marriage. In *Pamela* the tension rests upon 'an unprecedented disparity between the conventional roles of the sexes and the actual tenor of the oracles of the heart'. (This analysis draws widely upon Ian Watt's perceptive chapter, 'Love and the Novel', and his study of Richardson in *The Rise of the Novel*.) Pamela's cry offers to the young heroine a motto which rings through the novel for a century and a half: 'to rob a person of her virtue is worse than cutting her throat'. As Ian Watt points out, 'Words such as virtue, propriety, decency, modesty, delicacy, purity came to have the almost exclusively sexual connotation which they have since very largely retained.' The preoccupation with romance colours the moral notions which are active in the novels as a whole. The romantic and sexual themes do not only relate to relationships between the sexes (in which, incidentally, Richardson assumes the viewpoint of the woman), but encompass larger social questions as well—'conflicts between social classes and their different outlooks, for example, and conflicts between the sexual instinct and the moral code'. When the code is successfully attacked, the heroine is morally and socially 'undone', and the novel ends with death and defeat (*Clarissa*). When the code is heroically defended, the heroine reaps her reward, which, in the case of *Pamela*, is not only marriage, but union with one who is economically and socially well above her station—'an unprecedented victory for her sex'.

Richardson, then, was providing a new model of conduct for the relations between men and women—he used the romantic theme as a focus for major moral and social changes in attitude. He gives us a subjective understanding of these changes but at the same time manipulates the plot in such a way as to flatter or warn the majority of his readers, who were, of course, women. His novels, therefore, have a representative significance. They bring into literature, adjacent to the romantic theme, a whole area of middle-class experience. They provide a model for the didactic novelists, his imitators, who stereotype the situations, characters and ethical code, but at the same time popularize and disseminate it. Richardson adopts the point of view and the moral interests of the woman. But he is followed by the women novelists themselves, who take up the romantic theme where he laid it down, and view the experiences recorded in their novels wholly from this one point of view. The centre of these novels is the home, the arena of action, the domestic scene. The home is 'dependent on an obscure male world of action and business, which its occupants can seldom envisage, but of which they feel the reverberations' (J. M. S. Tompkins, *The Popular Novel in England*). Theme dictates both setting and point of view. It also governs moral tone. Delicacy and prudence are the watchwords, ethical pointers to the readers, but providing a whole encompassing body of assumptions about life and the emotions, a tone, a style. Delicacy, as Miss Tompkins remarks, becomes 'spontaneous moral taste'. It also makes possible a subtle adjustment by the woman to her social role. 'As from our birth', wrote Miss C. Palmer, 'we are but secondary objects in creation, subordination is the natural sphere in which we are intended to move. This subordinate state does not degrade us. The degradation is when we attempt to step out of that state.' In the didactic romance the regulation of social position and the regulation of the feelings go hand in hand.

This manner of handling the romantic theme, with the domestic scene as its centre and marriage as its triumphant culmination, with its subtle adjustments of social role and its dependence upon the decorum of emotions and the validity of accepted conventions, seems to carry the novel unchanged up to and through the work of Jane Austen. Yet if we attend to the way in which these themes and patterns are linked with new experiences and attitudes in Jane Austen's novels we can see the changing structure of feeling. Richardson struggled to command a new morality in the novel. Jane Austen accepts this as the natural scaffold of her action. It has become 'a truth universally acknowledged' that 'a single man in possession of a good fortune must be in want of a wife' (the opening of *Pride and Prejudice*). Her novels never stray outside the confines of domestic life. Each novel ends with the marriage of the heroine—sometimes, as in *Pride and Prejudice* or *Mansfield Park*, a match above her station, but often, as in *Emma*, on the level to which she is accustomed (and Harriet, whom Emma 'mistakenly' encouraged to have notions above her social position, makes a fitting match in the end too).

And yet the heroine is no longer the embodiment of conventional wisdom—she has a moral sensibility altogether more subtle, more individual and intense. Jane Austen's novels deal with the 'education of the heroine'—but it is an education, not into the conventions of chastity, but into personally realized moral values and an understanding of the self. 'To understand, thoroughly understand her own heart, was the first endeavour.' This is the end of *Emma*, but it is also the *real* theme of all her novels, and the romantic twists and turns of the plot provide the opportunity for this deeper growth to self-hood to be worked through. Where the didactic novelists force their heroines to acknowledge a social ethic, Jane Austen brings her heroines to a pitch of self-awareness which leaves the conventional standards of society far behind. Indeed, those who are 'right' simply by conventional standards provoke her irony and satire: her villains are men who, civilized in their behaviour, are nevertheless villains of the mind and the heart: and by means of her controlled irony (or, as D. W. Harding has called it, 'regulated hatred') these distinctions are subtly but clearly drawn. Far from accepting uncritically the conventions about love and marriage laid down in her social milieu, the suffering of the heroine springs from the fact that she is thinking and feeling too conventionally; in *Emma, Pride and Prejudice* and *Persuasion* the heroine learns—it is this moral knowledge which brings social rewards. Jane Austen's heroines, capable of being seen as moral stereotypes and yet so richly and individually realized, are certainly not rebels against the marriage ethic; but they are not 'subordinates' either. They are no longer the etherealized virgins of the didactic novel. Limited though they are by the home and domestic routine, they have achieved within this something of the freedom and self-consciousness of the fully human character.

Romances of sexual restraint last deep into the nineteenth century. Yet, around this manner of handling love and marriage, changes of taste, sensibility and attitude are rapidly taking place. It is as if the novelists, unable to free the romantic theme itself from the conventional ethical code in which it is embedded, compensate for this by plunging the sentimental story into wilder and stranger settings. At the same time, the emotions which are still on the surface transfixed by the code are steadily undermined from below—they become wilder, more extreme, more rapturous and 'sublime'. This is the 'romantic revolution' in the novel—the process by which, without ever seeming to yield a single ethical victory to the passions, the novel of delicacy and decorum becomes the novel of feeling and sensibility. The revolt begins early. In the middle of the eighteenth century Horace Walpole, who regarded Richardson's novels as 'deplorably tedious lamentations', unlocks the door to Gothic Romance, and through it—preserving her chastity all the while to the very end—the heroine escapes to a setting, and to adventures, more in keeping with her suppressed nature. The *Castle of Otranto* is a 'literary witches' sabbath', replete with 'darkness and the howling of the wind; hidden trapdoors and subterranean passages; unnatural passions and unacknowledged guilt; a portrait that steps out of its frame; a statue that drops blood . . .'. The hero and the heroine are, of course, recognizable figures from the sentimental romance of the period. But the atmosphere is wholly different. Manfred, Prince of Otranto, is as anxious, in his own bizarre way, to marry off his son Conrad as Mrs Bennett is to be rid of her daughters in *Pride and Prejudice*. There is something all the more symbolic, then, when Manfred's wish is thwarted and Conrad is struck down by a gigantic supernatural helmet. This comes as a blow to the didactic romance from outer space, but it is also a thrust from the subconscious. Sir Walter Scott, who wrote an appreciative introduction to one of the editions of *Otranto*, took Walpole at his face value, and interpreted the novel as an attempt to 'draw such a picture of domestic life and manners, during the feudal times, as might actually have existed'. But a better key to what is actually happening may be found in the ambiguity of Walpole's own introduction to the novel: 'I have not written the book for the present age, which will endure nothing but *cold common sense* . . . I have given reins to my imagination till I became on fire with the visions and feelings which it excited . . . I told you from the beginning you would not like the book—your visions are all in a different style.'

Gothic melodrama might not have succeeded in modifying in any substantial way the objective moral code governing love and sex in popular fiction and the novel. Yet it did, subconsciously, unhinge many of the conventional conceptions underlying what Walpole ironically called 'cold common sense'; it coloured the atmosphere in which this code was worked out and it intensified the passions, offering fantasy 'in a different style'. Without some such break in ethos—such as the Gothic achieves by resurrecting a fantasy version of feudal times and the trappings of the 'Italian' style, and which the later historical romances achieve by altering costumes and manners—the transition from the novel of prudence to the novel of sentiment would never have been made. That it provides a bridge of this sort can best be seen from the work of Mrs Radcliffe, whose tone and ethics were those of the didactic period. She was so committed to 'cold common sense' that, in the final chapters of her novels, she always attributed the horrors and supernatural torments to natural causes, thereby restoring the story to the limits of the everyday world and placating the agitated reader. Her heroes are the refined men with insinuating manners common to the period—Miss Tomkins links them with Richardson and Fanny Burney. She subscribed to the eighteenth-century code, saying that delicacy 'included beneath its modest shade every grace which ought to adorn the female character' (Tomkins, ibid.). Yet in her work the romance story is no longer at the service of moral instruction. The sensibility of the young woman, held in delicate postponement in Richardson, yields to the romantic atmosphere, to the picturesque settings, is intensified and enriched by the fear and trepidation which accompany the Gothic plot, and reaches out more audaciously towards the extremes of feeling hitherto denied it, attuning itself to the more pronounced pitch of the sublime and the tremulous. One can see how the ethical pattern of the didactic treatment of love and marriage is maintained, and yet by its treatment is transmuted to allow for a major change in feeling. Speaking of Mrs Radcliffe's Gothic, Miss Tomkins writes:

In all of them a beautiful and solitary girl is persecuted in picturesque surroundings, and after many fluctuations of fortune, during which she seems again and again on the point of reaching safety, only to be thrust back again into the midst of perils, is restored to her friends and marries the man of her choice.

These heroines 'have no enemy within; they are sure that innocence will be divinely shielded'—yet they are pursued and menaced from without, beset by images of guilt and punishment, threatened by exorbitant passions and perverse sexual appetites. Guilt is projected into the supernatural forces; repentance and expiation for breaking the ethical code are replaced by a much deeper interest in 'the passionate excesses that precede them, and presently repentance ceases to be the most popular sequel to crime, and yields to a picturesque defiance'. Like the thriller—though for quite different attitudes—the Gothic melodrama provides a sort of liberation of the popular imagination. In terms of a whole culture, it prepares the way for the Romantic movement and the age of revolution; in social terms, it leads into Mary Wollstonecraft's appeal on behalf of an adulteress; in literary terms it makes possible Peacock, Collins, much of the atmosphere which we now call Dickensian, and that apparently 'freak' novel, *Wuthering Heights*.

In the nineteenth century, as Mrs Leavis and others have documented, the reading public was more sharply differentiated and, with the coming of the penny press and of serial and magazine fiction, the types of romance were much more varied—changing more directly in relation to social class and ethical outlook of the readership. Stories in the improving magazines were more selfconsciously upright, instructive and 'approved'—they are intended to win converts, and had about them all the narrowness and earnestness of missionary work done in unfavourable circumstances. This did not mean, however, that the romantic fiction against which, of course, they were directed, had altogether abandoned the pattern of didactic romance. The connection between sin and suffering was still made quite clear. In the Salisbury Square periodical fiction of the mid-century, 'there is little gloating over or relish of any kind of vice . . . virtue is universally triumphant, and wrong-doing is punished by obloquy and ruin in this world, by threats also of eternal torment in the next' (Dalziel, *Popular Fiction 100 Years Ago*). The code, one could assume, was still fully intact. Yet the betrayed heroine—martyr though she was—was now placed, in Lloyd's penny press fiction, amidst 'theft, seduction, violence, adultery and murder'. The romantic theme was engrossing new kinds of experience in its Victorian setting. There is also a striking difference in moral tone, typified in the contrast between Pamela's comment that 'to rob a person of her virtue is worse than cutting her throat' and the cry of a heroine of Salisbury Square, 'The being who has once strayed from the path of virtue, alas, can never again be permanently happy.' It is a telling contrast. Pamela's comment comes with the terse force of a moral comment, a plain and rational ethical judgement, and the rhythm of the statement has a typicality, a pithiness, about it. Pamela's position may be more idealized than her Victorian counterpart, but her attitude is more realistic and unsentimental. 'To rob a person of her virtue' has a recognizable eighteenth-century weight about it: the act of betrayal is faced, and so is the consequence. The Victorian lady may have a wider experience of the ways of the world, but the important thing about her observation is the manner in which the code has been sentimentalized. Compare Pamela's succinct phrase with her Victorian counterpart's euphemisms—'The being that has once strayed from the path of virtue'. As if this circumlocution is not enough, the sentimentality is reinforced by the apostrophe of self-pity—'alas'. 'Worse than cutting her throat,' Pamela says. 'Can never again be permanently happy,' says the Victorian heroine. What a wealth of longing is contained by that ambiguous qualification—'permanently'.

This is one of the crucial distinctions between the popular romantic fiction of the eighteenth and the mid-nineteenth centuries. Victorian periodical fiction and railway literature preserved the chaste heroine as an essential type, 'marriage as the most important event and the happiest state of life . . .':

Neither the occasional suggestion that, like most human institutions' it has its ups and downs, nor the descriptions of marital unhappiness . . . make much impression compared with the fact that story after story ends up with the bad characters punished and the good ones rewarded, that the best reward is marriage, and that the people so paired off live happily ever after. This same fact that nine-tenths of the stories *end* in a wedding, to which most of the events described have been preliminary, gives the impression that marriage is of unrivalled importance.

Margaret Dalziel, Popular Fiction 100 Years Ago

The heroine, the ethical code, the suspense and the rewards—all these have remained unchanged. Yet the whole emotional climate is different, for the heroine is now governed not by reason but by emotion, guided by the feeling heart, given over to the sway of sentiment and sensibility. Of course, the heroine who is totally dependent upon husband and home needs some additional support, some personal compensation, and in Victorian fiction she gets it through the intensification of personal feeling. Yet more than intensification is implied by the term most appropriate to Victorian romance, 'sentimentality'. Sentimentality occurs when the emotions cannot find legitimate expression, spill over and invade every sphere. It is emotion *in excess of* that which seems to be appropriate to the object of devotion or the situation described. In Victorian fiction, sentimental excess of feeling seems to indicate an imbalance between feeling and subject, points to an unresolved dilemma. But it also makes possible many evasions, for the whole problem is suffused in the general display of sensibility. Strict though the code may be in the didactic romance, the threat to the heroine from outside, in the person of the lover, and the threat within from sexual passion is clearly recognized; and, by recognizing it, the heroine is able to hold 'disaster' at arm's length. But a great deal of popular Victorian romantic literature is written as if no conflict of any kind exists:

The writers are determined not to allow that there can ever be a true conflict between love and virtue, or between virtue and happiness.

When there seems to be a conflict, the love is not true love, and the happiness vanishes before it can be enjoyed.

Dalziel, ibid.

The conflict is not posed or dealt with again in the popular novel, which assumes that the old ethical code is still intact, but it does become a compelling theme in the serious novel—in two such apparently dissimilar romantic novels as *Wuthering Heights* and *Middlemarch*, and, later, Shaw's plays, the lesser Edwardian social novelists at the turn of the century, and, of course, pre-eminently in Lawrence. Popular fiction reflects in various ways the conflicts between 'the conventional roles of the sexes and the actual tenor of the oracles of the heart', but it is left to the serious work of fiction to pose the conflict with any intensity or to suggest imaginative resolutions to it.

So far, we have made no artistic distinction between the different novels in their treatment of romantic themes. Literary merit matters enormously. To say that Richardson defends a certain ethical code governing romantic behaviour or that in *Mansfield Park* Jane Austen manipulates the Cinderella theme is to say very little about the quality of these novels. But a look at the way the novel has developed shows that many of the same themes which capture our attention in contemporary romantic literature have been dealt with before; and that by looking at the context in which these themes are embedded we can gain some insight into the changing moral, social and literary attitudes towards them. This has the advantage of giving us a proper perspective on the contemporary debate about the romance story and the thriller-romance, for each of these genres stands at the end of a long and complex tradition which embraces both popular and serious work. We can see now that it is not the presence of rape and seduction as events in the novel which should interest us, nor are these inventions of the twentieth century. They are there in *Clarissa*. The question is, how are they treated, where does the emotional stress fall? In *Clarissa*, as Mrs Leavis remarks, the stress is not on the seduction, rape, and similar events, where the modern reader would naturally expect it, but on the long-drawn-out dying of the heroine who, like the Man of Feeling, is a martyr to an exquisite code of *mœurs*.

Fiction and the Reading Public

But the sacrifice of the heroine to a code of honour can only be dramatic if the code is an active and living one. What we see in the modern thriller is the unacknowledged collapse of such a code— either the strict one which governs the disposition of stress in the didactic romance or the sentimental version of it which governs the action in its Victorian counterpart. Not only has the code collapsed, but no other has come to replace it. The absence of any such ordering framework leaves the reader totally exposed to the events in the modern thriller-romance, and gives them their full sensational impact.

The fiction in the women's magazines, the hospital romances and the love comics for teenagers all conform to a quite recognizable pattern. They are all simple *resolution* or *wish-fulfilment* stories. Here, too, the ultimate reward is 'marriage' and it is towards this resolu- tion that all the events in the plot, the complications, surprises and disappointments, are directed. The hospital stories are especially interesting, since they portray the heroine outside the home in an accepted profession. But the stress is not upon work or career or skill. These are enveloped in the romantic theme, and the conflict which inevitably arises between love and career is resolved in favour of love. Women's magazine fiction, on the other hand, retains the home as the centre of interest. Magazine stories are basically of two kinds—stories which lead through the romantic episode to marriage prospects, and those which deal with marital problems. The first type of story is a *fulfilment* story: the second type is an *adjustment* story.

An emotional situation is described from a feminine point of view. It is then complicated in some way—the beloved hero falls for someone else, or is already engaged to be married, or turns out to be no good. The heroine is thrust into the depths of despair.

Then, magically, the situation is resolved—the boy friend proves his fidelity, gives up his betrothed for the heroine or is seen not to be so attractive as first thought. Occasionally, the situation is resolved in the reverse way: if the boy friend is not available, the heroine discovers that she wasn't in love with him after all, and turns her attention to the neglected, less attractive but more steadfast 'boy next door'. Sometimes, in the stories for adult readers, the resolutions are *therapeutic* (cf. Raymond Williams, *Communications*)—the thwarted love is sublimated and the heroine adjusts to her new role with regret but without serious emotional disturbance. In the love comics, which are simple premarital stories, the plot has to be less complicated and the reversal of the heroine's fortunes or the recognition of her 'true' feelings takes place more swiftly. In some of these stories, the complication in the path of true love is provided by a conflict of social status. In one typical story in a woman's magazine the girl falls in love with a plumber, but is embarrassed when she takes him out to dinner with her friends. This problem is resolved magically, too. The plumber turns out to have a bank account and a bit of money stashed away 'for a rainy day', and the social embarrassment vanishes overnight. In contrast to the romance-thriller, which deliberately sets out to associate love and sex with violence, and thus to arouse and disturb emotionally, the romance proper soothes, reassures and adjusts. Yet in both types of story the basic pattern is the same. Certain associations of a romantic or sexual kind are evoked: the situation is complicated or elaborated for the sake of suspense: then resolved and fulfilled.

The love comics deserve a special place in the study of contemporary romance, since they not only replace an earlier type of fiction-story or picture magazine for girls, but have also grown up side by side with the teenage pops and the culture-hero of the generation, the pop singer. Indeed, without him, *Mirabelle*, *Marty*, *Valentine*, *Roxy*, *Boyfriend* and the rest would hardly exist. The make-up of these papers is very simple. The cover attracts because of a romantic drawing or a photograph of a pop singer. The reading matter follows the model of the woman's magazine, and is divided between fiction and features. The stories consist of drawn pictures. Sometimes they are 'full-length' (three pages), sometimes serialized. The features are more varied: a 'postbag' with replies to questions—again, mostly about pop singers; an interview or article about pop music and the stars (sometimes a centre-spread feature on a singer); a page on fashion or beauty hints, usually presented with a romantic twist; a horoscope. There is comparatively little advertising. In the features the tone is up-beat and contemporary—'If you're the sort of girl who likes dating boys, jiving and going to coffee bars, then these are the picture stories for you.' The stories, however, are uniformly about teenage love— 'the paper that brings you romantic reading'. The presence of the pop singer not only commands the allegiance of readers but provides a visual and romantic model for the drawings, though his image is generalized or stylized for the purpose of the story. In an issue of *Mirabelle* selected at random (February, 1962) Jess Conrad appears on the cover, trapped within a Valentine heart; p. 3 has a picture of Bobby Vee and eight queries, all about pop singers; on p. 7 there is an article about pop singers and Valentine's Day, illustrated with photos of Cliff Richard and Shane Fenton; pp. 14–15, the centre spread, is an illustrated interview with Jess Conrad; on p. 18 an intrepid fan is shown with Billy Fury; on p. 22 Adam Faith gives a 'boy's eye view of a girl's world'. Sixteen of the other pages are drawn stories and serials. To add to this, the triplets who appear in the girl's dream in the story entitled 'The Gift of Love' bear a striking resemblance to the Everley brothers; the hero of the serial, 'Johnny Bluenote', is a song-writer; and the father of the heroine is a 'big-time music agent'. The pop singer is, therefore, more than merely a gimmick to attract readers. He is *the* romantic prototype for these stories. The magazines assume— how accurately it is difficult to tell—that the typical reader is also a fan; an interesting fact, particularly when one remembers that many of the readers are not unmarried teenagers but middle-aged housewives, and some of the readers are in fact boys. According to the Institute of Practitioners in Advertising, in 1960 47 per cent were over 45 and 23 per cent were male, though this was the readership for the rather older-styled 'Feminine Five' published by Thomson of Dundee—*Red Letter*, *Red Star Weekly*, *Secrets*, *Family Star* and *My Weekly* (see Flann and Mary Campbell, 'Comic Love', *New Society*, 3/1/63).

We said that the climax to the modern romance is still marriage, but this is not strictly true. The real climax to the story in the love comic is the 'clinch'—the kiss and embrace. In the issue of *Mirabelle* referred to above, there is a story—'A Kiss to Haunt Me'—in which the whole plot turns on the magical power of the kiss. A love affair is resolved by the fact that an embrace, which begins as a joke, is proved, by the intensity communicated in the act of kissing, to be the beginning of 'the real thing'. 'Haunted's too strong a word to use, honey, but . . . well, that kiss has never been out of my mind. . . .'

In the serial which comes next—'Afraid to Love'—the heroine falls in love with her boss, an attractive young doctor, around whom, however, sinister rumours have gathered in the town. They kiss, but something the doctor says brings back to the heroine's mind the warning voice of the postmistress: 'I'm warning ye. She [the doctor's former wife] came to a bad end.' The final frame is drawn in a highly cinematic way, with the girl's startled face in 'close-up', her frightened eyes spotlighted, and the remembered image of the postmistress, wagging a warning forefinger, 'super-imposed' or 'back-projected' behind her. 'More' is promised 'next week'—but the story can have only one possible conclusion. The mystery about the doctor's wife will be explained, and Miss Wayne and the doctor will be united. This conclusion is so plainly pointed that the interest of the story cannot possibly be in any way related to suspense as to what is going to happen. One must suppose, then, either that what the reader gets is some sort of satisfaction at having her expectations firmly satisfied, the known pattern reassuringly affirmed; or that the satisfaction arises from the images of romantic love and anxiety in the individual drawings— in which case the drawings do not point forwards to any satis-faction postponed, but are their own justification.

In three of the four other stories, different interests are engaged

by the love-theme, especially the question of career. In two of
them the apparent conflict is resolved in favour of romance. In
'My Bride Book' the girl reporter is asked to cover the wedding
of a celebrity with whom she is in love. She cannot face the ordeal
and hands in a fake story instead. But the boy doesn't go through
with the wedding and returns to find her. She loses her job, but
wins the boy. 'Well, sweetie, isn't a honeymoon in the South of
France better than reporting?' The second story, 'Escape to
Happiness', shows the operation of magic in a particularly heightened form. The heroine, a fabulous movie star, goes on a holiday
to 'get away from it all'. She falls in love with a blue-jeaned boy,
who doesn't know how famous she is. 'That night I realized how
different our lives were.' 'Of course I love you,' she says, 'but
we're from different worlds.' But the youth turns out to be a
famous writer, on his way to Rome to write a script for the girl.
Since they *are* from the same world, the story implies, they are free
to fall in love. They do.

In 'The Gift of Love', however, things do not turn out so well.
The heroine, who is in love with a young executive director, is
heaped with gifts—chocolates, jewels, furs—but she cannot hold
his love. When she confronts him in his office he is too busy to
listen, has to hurry away to a directors' meeting. This situation is
closer to those in the fiction for more adult readers, and here a
therapeutic solution is offered. The girl chooses love rather than
riches. 'But for me there will be no consolation until I find true
love. . . . So I'll go on waiting and hoping till I find my happiness.'

The pattern in these stories is so stereotyped that a reader, given
the opening situation and the climax, can work out with the
exactness of a formula what has happened in between. If the
starlet falls in love with an 'unknown' at the beginning, but the
final frame shows them in a romantic embrace, then only a limited
number of things can have happened in between. For example, it
will rarely be the case that they are pictured at the end meeting for
the last time, for this would be to admit that love can be both
intense and brief. Certain sacrifices *are* permissible—for example,
the girl could have decided to renounce her career for him. This

solution is acceptable because it leaves the romantic sentiment at the heart of the story untouched and unqualified. But it is much more in keeping with the magical tenor of the story that their careers or social roles should be 'reconciled' so that the romance can proceed. If love and career conflict, career often yields. Love never.

Even within the sketchy limits of the three-page comic story, every situation is so worked out that it flatters the romantic ethic. The women's magazine stories are longer, so that some development is possible in the story, and the mood can be enriched by poetic phrases and romantic descriptions. Yet even here, the power of romance is virtually unlimited. It can resolve any dilemma. Both kinds of story provide fairly precise definitions of the kind of love involved. It is a *glamorous experience*—in the love comics associated with dating, chance meetings and a gay round of coffee-bar evenings and parties—but it is not a particularly strong emotion. Love in these stories is tamed, domesticated, and relationships which fall outside the conventional limits are rarely permitted to last through to the end unchanged or to achieve a happy resolution. If the hero is a beatnik or delinquent type (in the love comics), or charming but unsteady (in the women's magazines), either he will change his ways and 'steady down' or the heroine will see through him and give him up. The stories do not show unconventional romances in a favourable light. If the heroine in the women's magazine story risks social disapproval for a time, this is because she is sure that time will prove her right. Love never sways the heroine beyond a judgement which, in the long run, can be approved within social conventions. A situation such as is described in *Wuthering Heights*, where passion develops in direct conflict with the middle-class code, where the relationship between Catherine and Linton is devalued in favour of that between Catherine and the outsider, Heathcliff, and where the hero is both lover and villian is impossible within contemporary definitions of romance. For here love *is* a passion, and the passionate experience carries the characters beyond the conventional limits. If we use the word *romance* to describe these types of stories it is in the glamorous sense—all fadeouts and sunsets and stringed music—not in the passionate sense. They are not even romantic in the manner of the Victorian melodrama, where love stirs up deep emotions elsewhere in the story, such as jealousy and hate. This has altogether too much vigour and gusto about it for the domesticated mood of these stories. The fiction for adult readers sometimes deals with marriage problems, and here a second woman may be involved: but the pattern is never disturbed by the hint of sexual infidelity and the 'other woman' is a rival, not a seducer or adulteress. Besides, she is usually routed by the faithful wife to whom the hero eventually returns. Love is not a passion here—it is a preoccupation. There may be romances, but they lack romanticism.

It is also a version of romance which consistently evades sex. This is especially true of the love comics, which betray a striking moral dualism in their attitude towards this component of the romance, though in general they show a rigorous and unquestioned allegiance to the conventional moral code. The Campbells describe the moral code in the love comic as a 'curious mixture of titillation and suburban gentility'. Sexual feeling is immanent everywhere, but it is never directly discussed. It is evoked in the drawings, referred to in the monologue of the heroine, but somehow transmuted by the mood of the story or held in check by the prevailing ethic. 'Then suddenly I saw . . . all six foot of him . . . it took my breath away. I could hardly believe it! And my eyes started to ache with just looking at this hunk of handsomeness.' This sentiment, associated in one story with a forceful 'close-up' of the young man in question, modelled after the dark-haired Cliff Richard stereotype, is quite common in these stories. A good deal of flirtation, kissing and embracing usually follows, but these never lead to seduction or love-making or unprepared pregnancies. The code intervenes to safeguard the decent feelings of the young reader. Yet this code is never directly invoked: it has been completely internalized. It is simply a part of the total structure of feeling of the story. The love comics and the women's magazine stories lack a moral language of any sort—either conventional, unconventional, social or religious. Thus the system of rewards and punishments dictated by the more rigorous and explicit moral code of the didactic or sentimental romance is absent. The heroines pine—not for an emotional experience or as martyrs to society, but simply for a state of mind: they pine because they are 'not in love'.

Being 'in love' does not represent, as Denis de Rougemont would have us believe, a secret desire for passionate experience. It represents, on the part of the heroine, a desire to fulfil an approved social role—that of being a girl friend. This condition has two requirements: the girl must capture a boy, but she must also feel the feelings which are accepted by her age group as appropriate to her role as 'a girl friend. . . .' The romantic feelings in the story are those which are expected of the adolescent girl. What the love comics 'teach' is how one is expected to feel in the typical teenage situation—the boy-and-girl situation. Not to be in this situation is —so the stories imply—not to be properly adolescent, not to belong to the teenage code, to be emotionally, and hence socially, deprived. As Margaret Mead observed of the dating pattern of American adolescents, the teenage romances define 'the relationship between a male and a female as situational'. To adapt her description of the attitude of the boy in *Male and Female* to the attitude of the heroine of the love comics: 'The girl who longs for a date is not longing for a boy. She is longing to be in a situation mainly public, where she will be seen by others to have a boy, and the right kind of boy, who dresses well, gives her an exciting time and pays attention.' There is never any question in these stories of the girl who might legitimately not become interested in love and sex until a much later stage in life. Without the boy friend—himself attractive, and therefore desirable—the heroine cannot feel who she is, does not know how to be a teenager. The route to the establishment of a successful identity in these terms is, of course, by way of the physical attractions of the girl and the possession of a boy friend who is himself physically handsome and attractive to her peer-group. But the game played with these powerful counters has its enforced limits, since it cannot result in sexual experience, and cannot therefore be played through to the end. In teenage literature we find this contradictory situation:

> A picture of a people, especially a youth group, who are tremendously preoccupied with sex, whose only interest in life is love, and whose definition of love is purely physical. Yet this seems to me an enormous mis-statement. Rather, this continuous emphasis on the sexually relevant physical appearance is an outcome of using a heterosexual game as the prototype for success and popularity in adolescence.
>
> Margaret Mead, *Male and Female*

The main point about the love comic is not that it traffics in disguised sex but that it romanticizes the role of the adolescent girl at a time when being a teenager has become a powerful and disturbing experience for many young people in our society.

The contemporary romance engages attitudes which are at one and the same time deeply personal and yet essentially social; it poses two kinds of questions: How do men and women today feel their maleness and femaleness? How does society today think about the relationship between men and women? Each generation, each society, offers different answers to these questions, and the literature of romantic fantasy has always to some measure reflected changes in sensibility about them. Thus in the thriller-romance we find a type of story which would have been virtually impossible before the sexual emancipation of women had become a common theme in public discussion and in fiction. In these novels it is not the frequency of rape, seduction and sexual intercourse which is most illuminating—it is the quality of the relationship between men and women sketched in them. For the woman has achieved the 'freedom' customarily accorded to men, at considerable cost —they portray her as almost entirely a sexual object, still the subordinate in the relationship. Her escape becomes a trap, since she is a valued object only in so far as she is willing to gratify man's desire, and yet this does not bring with it the kind of fulfilled and sustaining relationship in whose name freedom was originally demanded. Between the premarital tales for adolescents and the marriage-problem stories for older readers there is another kind of contradiction. The young girl plays a dangerous game which, according to the code, she must always win—she has both to be attractive to the opposite sex and yet never to yield. This presents problems of its own, but these problems are either absorbed into the romantic glow generated in the stories and drawings, or magically manipulated out of existence. But, once married, the young wife must fulfil another, quite opposite, set of expectations, for now her marriage depends upon her having a happy and fulfilled sex life. 'We actually place our young people in a virtually intolerable situation, giving them the entire setting for behaviour for which we punish them whenever it occurs', Margaret Mead observes. But we also devise an intolerable dilemma for adult women, since we expect them to succeed in a relationship for which their whole adolescent experience—if they have satisfied the code—has unfitted them.

It is impossible to say what the young or adult reader takes away from these stories. Perhaps they are neither compelling nor intensely enough realized, in the artistic sense, to have much force. Indeed, they can be dealt with in 'anthropological' terms, without reference to their literary quality, only because they are so impoverished. These stories are 'symptomatic', revealing latent tensions, but they cannot, as serious art can, deal imaginatively or creatively with such tensions. They can be reduced, in discussion, to their fantasy source precisely because they express this source so directly, and manipulate their fantasy content with such abandon.

Most young readers of the love comics seem to recover from their addiction without any apparent emotional damage, though there is no evidence either way—it is difficult to know what kind of evidence would count. Women readers who skip through the magazine fiction may live happy and fulfilled lives. Yet, in the total picture of a culture, the regular and widely circulated description offered of the relationship between men and women is in itself a crucial fact. The expressive symbolism of popular and mass art carries with it particular meanings which occur over and over again in a culture only because they feed on certain real social experiences, only because, by reading and responding and assenting to these symbols, even in their fantasy form, we give them a kind of legitimacy. It is not necessary to establish a crude relationship between the number of thriller-romances and the rate of pre-marital pregnancies or between the number of love comics and the divorce rate to admit that their existence matters.

It matters especially because these powerful stereotypings of love and sex are widely disseminated at the time when these same problems have come to preoccupy young people. The onset of puberty with its growth of sexual feeling is always a difficult and confusing stage in development. At a superficial level the rules of the game have been made quite explicit, within 'teenage culture'. Adolescence is no longer a transition: in modern societies it is a stage of growth in its own right. But this social experience has brought its own dilemmas as to how young people should behave towards one another, and to adults, and of what the adult role in society consists; all this in addition to the emotional and psychological problems which already exist. Even when they do not directly follow in their own lives the models offered n the stories, or accept the magical twists of the plot except as pure fantasy, young people are especially vulnerable to those cultural forms which stereotype their dilemmas and experiences. The form, context and content of the romantic tales may be fantasy constructions, like dreams. But what we know of the workings of the mind suggests that fantasies and reveries provide an important way of coming to terms with emotional problems not resolved in our waking lives. Love-comic fiction is fantasy fiction, it deals with a certain kind of experience by recurring romantic symbols and it manipulates these symbols by magic. Yet, as in a dream, the very displacements and distortions are interesting in themselves: the absence of the sexual problem in the conventional romance is as significant as the reduction, in the thriller-romance, of every experience to the sexual level.

The 'substitute gratification' produced by the dreamwork, mainly by displacements, helps the dreamer continue sleeping. However, one

major function of art is precisely to undo this dreamwork, to see
through disguises, to reveal to our consciousness the true nature of our
wishes and fears. The dreamwork covers, to protect sleep. Art discovers
and attempts to awaken the sleeper. Whereas the dreamwork tries to
aid repression, the work of art intensifies and deepens perception and
experience of the world and of the self. . . . Though dreams and art may
disregard literal reality, they do so to answer opposite needs. The dream
may ignore reality to keep the sleeper's eyes closed. Art transcends
immediate reality to encompass wider views, penetrate into deeper
experiences and lead to a fuller confrontation of man's predicament.

E. van der Haag, 'Of Happiness and Despair', *Mass Culture*

Such substitute gratifications are widely available in romance
today, and the likelihood is that some young people find in them,
at least for a time, what education is still so unwilling to offer—a
rudimentary education of the feelings. 'We are hopelessly un-
educated in ourselves', D. H. Lawrence once wrote. 'We have no
language for the feelings, because our feelings do not exist for
us. . . . Educated? We are not even *born*, as far as our feelings are
concerned' (*The Phoenix*).

It is still current in educational practice to regard this area as
lying beyond the boundaries of the school, and a common
educational strategy tries to deal with the problem, when it arises,
by a series of brusque and cumbersome devices and, as the name
of Lawrence reminds us, by the dubious tactic of censorship.
Censorship is the one tactic which is bound to fail. By its prohibi-
tions it draws attention to and highlights the very subject which
has been made taboo. It adds to any dish the spice of secret
pleasure. The determined teenager will undoubtedly find his or
her way to the forbidden material. And the school which relies on
censorship cuts itself off from the crucial problems of adolescence.
It believes it is drawing a *cordon sanitaire* around the imagination
of the young reader, but is only in fact circumscribing and
isolating itself. It is true, for example, that in *Lady Chatterley's
Lover* Lawrence deals at length and in detail with sexual experience, whereas the typical love novelette, strictly obeying the code,
only hints and nudges, whipping a veil of restraint over the

proceedings at the last possible moment, when the temperature begins to rise. Yet it did not seem to strike some teachers as extraordinary to prefer the teasing substitution-thrill of the novelette, available in every bookstall, to the frankness of Lawrence. It was Lawrence himself who wrote, in *A Propos Lady Chatterley's Lover*, that the real obscenity 'only comes in when the mind despises the body, and the body hates and resists the mind'. This is as precise a description as one could want of the most debased of the sexy thrillers, where sexual feeling is offered as a monosyllabic emotion, arising as a blind biological urge which must be 'satisfied', untouched by love, feeling or value of any other kind, and most thrilling in our culture when it exists in the context of sadism or when it feeds into violence.

Surely no greater disservice could be perpetrated in education than that, by default, this notion of love and sexual feeling should pass into general currency among young people? Yet disabled notions of love will stand as compelling interpretations until they are confronted by richer and more varied concepts. It is not the role of the school to prescribe moral attitudes, especially at a time when they are undergoing some profound revaluation, and when conventional attitudes are under attack, not least from young people themselves (see, *inter alia*, Professor Carstairs' 1962 Reith Lectures, *This Island Now*; the whole 'new morality' debate; also the recent discussion in *New Society* and *Towards a Quaker View of Sex*). But it is the task of education to provide a range of experiences and concepts on which to base a mature judgement. Education is the transmission of cultural values, and cultural values have to do with 'the slow reach again for control'. But the controls in each period will be different—they have to be lived through in each generation, made valid in personal experience, examined critically. And those which were valid for one era may no longer be serviceable to a new generation. This question—which is the central social issue in the education of young people today—the school evades at its peril.

There is a great deal, then, to be said for bringing this area of experience directly into play in the school, through the use of art and literature in which the problems can be most imaginatively highlighted. It is an 'education of the feelings' to turn from the enfeebled romance of the contemporary mass arts to the enormous resources of romantic feeling which lend such power to a novel like *Wuthering Heights*, where the clash and conflict between two opposing ways of feeling is realized with such intensity:

> I cannot express it; but surely you and everybody have a notion that there is or should be an existence of your own beyond you. What were the use of my creation, if I were entirely contained here? My great miseries in this world have been Heathcliff's miseries, and I watched and felt each from the beginning: my great thought in living is himself. If all else perished and *he* remained, I should still continue to be; and if all else remained, and he were annihilated, the universe would turn to a mighty stranger: I should not seem part of it. My love for Linton is like the foliage in the woods: time will change it, I'm well aware, as winter changes the trees. My love for Heathcliff resembles the eternal rocks beneath: a source of little visible delight but necessary. Nelly, I *am* Heathcliff! He's always, always in my mind: not as a pleasure, any more than I am always a pleasure to myself, but as my own being. So don't talk of our separate lives again: it is impracticable.

Here romance and passion are fully engaged—drawn in and fixed by the rhythm of language in the passage. It makes the contemporary romance of mass art seem undernourished.

Or one might seek to create the kind of dialogue with young people which would make it possible for a work like the controversial *Lady Chatterley's Lover* to be used as a serious text in the school. The novel has many faults, compared with Lawrence's richer work: it is prophetic in the bad sense of the term. It is coloured by the argumentative side of his nature rather than by the poetic. It is seriously weakened by the manner in which Lawrence manipulates Sir Clifford as a symbol, and seems to take advantage of his predicament. Yet the book may, as Lawrence intended, have the effect of crashing the 'sound barrier', not because of its use of obscene terms but because of the levels of feeling at which it is directed. The core of the novel, as Lawrence wrote of fiction in

general, is to 'reveal the most secret places of life, above all, that
the tide of sensitive awareness needs to ebb and flow, cleansing
and freshening'.

This ebb and flow, between the 'mechanical consciousness',
which is the 'death' represented by Sir Clifford, and the 'flow of
sympathy which ought to determine our lives', which grows
between Connie and Mellors, is the central movement of the
novel. And it is within this dialectic that Lawrence places his
passages of sexual encounter. What seem at first sight to be set-
pieces of pornography are, unlike their counterparts in the sexy
novelette, meaningless except in relation to this movement and
flow through the novel. Thus the emptiness which Connie
experiences at the opening of the novel springs not from her
casual sexual encounters but from the damage done to her whole
emotional being by the habit of 'yielding to a man without
yielding her inner self'. And when she comes alive to Mellors in
their love-making it is not her sexual instincts, isolated from
everything else, which are satisfied but the whole balance of her
emotional life which is restored. Each episode, then, becomes a
paradigm for her difficult descent into love. From the first time,
when she no longer has to 'strive for herself', to the moment when
'she was giving way, she was giving up. She was flowing and
alive now and vulnerable'; through the last resistance, when 'her
queer female mind stood apart' and she wrings from herself the
despairing cry, 'I . . . I can't love you', to the final episode where
she is all 'disclosed, unprotected, open to his mercy and his
tenderness'.

And oh, if he were not tender to her now, how cruel, for she was all
open to him and helpless!

How often, in a context infinitely weaker and more banal, have
those words 'I . . . I can't love you' been uttered in adolescent
literature. How difficult today to use the word 'tender' with any
emotional force or resonance. Think, by contrast, of the multitude
of 'helpless' women we have seen or read about, collapsing weakly

into the arms of their lovers, with nothing sacred of themselves left to give.

It may be thought that the emotions handled by Lawrence are too dangerous for education, his frankness too heavy-handed. Yet on every side, the literature of romance—whether safe and conventional or thrilling, nervous and disabling—is trying, as well as to 'entertain', to *educate*.

Our education from the start has *taught* us a certain range of emotions, what to feel and what not to feel, and how to feel the feelings we allow ourselves to feel.

D. H. Lawrence, 'A Propos Lady Chatterley's Lover',
Sex, Literature and Censorship

The danger which contemporary romances bring with them is not that they make us feel too strongly and deeply, but that they confine our very notions of love within their conventional framework, and thus prevent us feeling strongly and deeply enough.

People allow themselves to feel a certain number of finished feelings. . . . This feeling only what you allow yourselves to feel at last kills all capacity for feeling, and in the higher emotional range you feel nothing at all. This has come to pass in our present century. The higher emotions are strictly dead. They have to be faked.

D. H. Lawrence, ibid

8

Fantasy and Romance

Brahmin boy meets untouchable girl.

poster for an Indian film

I cannot myself see what harm a Bardot film ever did; it is only
what goes on in ordinary heads and beds anyway.

KATHERINE WHITEHORN, *Spectator*, 26 August 1960

By contrast with contemporary romance fiction, the cinema, a
powerful erotic medium, is rich and varied. Pornographic art has
always been of a *visual* kind, even when created in words, because
response to an image is more direct than the response to
descriptions of it. (Erotic feeling does not, as is sometimes supposed, belong only to impure art: Sir Kenneth Clark observes in
his book on *The Nude*, 'no nude, however abstract, should fail to
arouse in the spectator some vestige of erotic feeling, even
although it be only the faintest shadow—and if it does not do so,
it is bad art and false morals.')

The cinema can compel with a single image. One has only to
compare the typical pin-up photograph on the front page of the
Mirror, *The People*, *Tit-bits*, *Reveille* or *Weekend*, with a still from an
early movie by Pabst, von Stroheim or Fritz Lang to feel the
qualitative difference. The pin-up is buxom and full-breasted, but
in an anodyne way, thrusting herself at the reader with a fixed
photographer's smile. She is never really sensuous, but she is
always trying to 'act sexy'. She is a show-off. She relates to nothing
in our experience. In real life the girl looks quite different: in the
photograph she is 'processed'—she conforms to a stereotyped
dream. She cannot suggest or invoke anything, since there is
nothing behind her but a trumped-up beach scene or the bric-à-

196

brac of a studio. The artificial lights have robbed her eyes of any message. If we were to pull, we feel, she would come away from the page like a cardboard replica. She has very little to do with human emotions of any order, and men who exclaim at the sight of her are often faking their feelings: they feel nothing, but they know that in our culture they are expected to. She is a space-filler, a layout-man's device, a printer's devil.

Compare these with, say, a frame from von Sternberg's film, *The Blue Angel* (Plate 10). Marlene Dietrich's very posture and costume reverberate with subliminal sexual intimations. She is richly evocative. The hat and skirt belong to the world of the inter-war Berlin *cabaret*, their quality gives her a place in time and a space in the imagination: they connect her, as an image, with everything else in the room—with the baroque interior, the costumed figures posed around her, the encrusted objects and the paraphernalia. Her legs are exposed, but the sensuality of the impression arises, not from these conventional signs, but from the particular way in which her whole body is a gesture—as well as from the total context. Deliberately, she has been made part of the décor, as Siegfried Kracauer remarks in his fascinating study, *From Caligari to Hitler*. It is as an object that the bourgeois professor worships her, and to debase himself before this powerful sign he must fight his way through the other objects in the room. Even then, she will be somewhere else, smiling at his puny efforts. Her sexuality is an immanent thing: it suffuses the whole room.

In his article on 'the highbrow cinema' (*Encounter*, January 1963) Nicola Chiaromonte attacks the cinema generally for 'attempting to distort the nature of the cinematic image by forcing it to express ideological or lyrical meaning'. Yet this is precisely how the complexity of the image in *The Blue Angel* works. It is powerful, not only because of its sexual connotations but because it connects these with the social and psychological life of the whole society at a particular moment in history. The collapse of the professor prefigures the collapse of a class in pre-Hitler Germany. The techniques of expressionism were admirably suited to probing at these subterranean levels; the imagery of sexual disorder becomes, in the film, the language through which the director's total view of the society is most effectively expressed.

It is perhaps in its handling of sexual themes that each national cinema most sharply reveals characteristic national attitudes. Although its treatment is quite different from the tortured and perverse symbolism of the early German film, the traditional British cinema, behind its conventional disguises—the farce, the costume fantasy, the romantic melodrama—has long shown a preoccupation with sex. British actors (at least until the advent of young stars like Albert Finney and Richard Harris) may have seemed to lack the sexual expressiveness of their Hollywood counterparts. One of the few British actors with the capacity to express sensual feelings—James Mason—went to Hollywood. Perhaps the British star has been on the whole too conventional and respectable. The British cinema has in the past fed upon the actors and actresses of the middle-class stage and the drama 'finishing schools'. Yet in fact the British cinema has been only marginally less concerned with sex than Hollywood. From the early Aldwych farces with Ralph Lynn permanently trapped in the bedroom, or films with that superbly representative actress Enid Stamp Taylor perpetually condemned to black underwear, to the *Doctor* films and the recent *Carry On . . .* series—the British stage and screen have always been able to offer as the staple basis of farce the perplexing problem of who goes to bed with whom. Unlike their American equivalents, however, the British sex-farces are always comedies of 'missed opportunities'. *Doctor at Sea, Doctor in the House*, the *Carry On* series, *The Amorous Prawn, Watch It, Sailor, Operation Bullshine, Petticoat Pirates*—these are films about what is sometimes called 'good, clean fun' but might be more correctly described as 'clean smut'. The pattern is familiar. An attractive young lady, preferably 'continental' to get the right air of naughtiness (Bardot in one of the *Doctor* films), turns up in some extraordinary male situation—on board a battleship, perhaps, or in a barrack-room. She is rapidly drawn into the 'high jinks'. No sexual encounters are shown, of course, for this is what the farcical element consists of—arbitrary events always intervene just at the right moment. Usually, pandemonium disrupts the smooth functioning of the 'unit'. There is sure to be a scene where the general or admiral comes into the room through one door just as the girl slips into the shower through another. Eventually, but with many mishaps, the whole thing is carried off without 'loss of face'. This kind of treatment is not limited to the British farce—it invades other kinds of comedy too, often throwing them off balance. In the film version of *Only Two Can Play*, for example, a serious domestic situation is established with a nice mixture of comedy and naturalism; but the sexual adventures of the husband are treated with heavy-handed farce (at one point a scene of premeditated adultery is interrupted by a wandering cow) and the film more or less collapses.

With their ogling and sniggering and relentless display of male embarrassment, coupled with high spirits, these British films unwittingly depend for their appeal upon one of the most perplexing of British attitudes: that which both despises and is titillated by sex. They are male fantasies about 'naughty' sex. The Hollywood equivalents are not only more sophisticated—they deal, in fact, with a different aspect of the same situation. The American sex comedies are 'bedroom farces' based on the joke about the professional virgin. The heroines of the British films are curvaceous continental girls. The heroines of the American comedies are healthy little homebodies. This fantasy is well established in the Hollywood repertoire and in recent years has had a new lease of life. The heroes are now wealthy executives or millionaire playboys and the comedy provides the occasion for the ritual display of plush penthouse apartments or swanky holiday resorts: they show what de Rougemont calls 'a vague yearning after affluent surroundings and exotic adventures'. Doris Day has incarnated this theme in several films—*The Thrill of it All*, *Lover Come Back*, *That Touch of Mink*. But the list is apparently unending —*Let's Make Love*, in which Marilyn Monroe, as a chorus girl, successfully resists the millionaire; *Boy's Night Out*, in which Kim Novak resists the syndicate which installs her in an expensive apartment, *All in a Night's Work*, in which Shirley MacLaine emerges unscathed in a towel from an aged millionaire's bedroom . . . These are typical of the American sex comedy, though every now and then, just to prove that they can do it, Hollywood directors produce a naval comedy in the Best British Manner, with continental starlets and (as Alan Eyles observes in *Films and Filming*, April 1963) 'panties fluttering in the breeze to inspire the fleet'. (*Don't Go Near the Water* and *Operation Petticoat* are two such examples.) In *That Touch of Mink*, the rich company director comes into collision with a healthy blonde American working girl. She is propositioned and refuses. The hotel room is booked, the bed prepared, the director at the ready. His prey, however, eludes him. First she refuses on principle. This defence successfully negotiated, she breaks out in spots. Finally, in desperation, he marries her. This makes it 'all right'. The defence of American virginity has once again been triumphantly secured.

The weakness of these films is that the sex-situation is the only evident source of comedy, which consequently becomes coarse. (In *Lover Come Back*, for example, a woman displays an ornament around her neck which provides the members of the Advertising Council with an excuse to ogle her bust.) Compared with Hollywood comedies of an earlier era the dialogue limps feebly along, the jokes fall on shallow ground. Richard Whitehall, in his review of the Marx Brothers film, *Duck Soup*, reminds us of a line of dialogue based on the same kind of situation which contains more wit than all the lines in *That Touch of Mink*. It is the moment when the Marx Brothers and Margaret Dumont are beseiged by a troop of soldiers. Groucho urges his companions on with the words, 'Remember, you're fighting for this woman's honour', and then adds, after one of his searching looks at Margaret Dumont, and an expressive raising of an eyebrow, 'which is more than she ever did'. Comedy is an art form, which calls upon skill, wit, and invention. It does not inevitably flow from the simple presentation of the female, endlessly pursued, endlessly evading her suitor around some technicolor set, nor troops averting their straying eyes with a courageous show of good form. Lacking a style, these films function as propaganda for 'the American way of life'. In *That Touch of Mink*, Alan Eyles observes:

how gently treated is Cary Grant, the business man who doesn't take to marriage. Doris Day may be on the dole but you wouldn't know it to look at her or her apartment. New York automats were never so cosy in my experience, nor did they look so clinically clean behind the service hatches. Against this backcloth of happy, humming hyper-active commerce, only little matters of romantic misunderstandings cause concern. Millionaires, oil-kings, advertising executives, magazine publishers, as well as lesser 'organization men' may have their temptations and aberrations but come back to the system (and its morality) in the end.

'Uncle Sam's Funny Bone', *Films and Filming*, April 1963

Cary Grant pursues his quarry with a mixture of the casual and the calculating while Doris Day—yielding inch by inch to his charms—maintains to the end a bogus simplicity. It is this compound of sophistication and naivety which allows us to view the whole story with sophisticated eyes until, just before the climax, naivety comes to the rescue and saves the code.

In contrast to the British cinema, however, the Americans can still handle sexual themes with some degree of stylishness. In Billy Wilder's *The Apartment*, for example, farce, wit and satire are held together by the director. Jack Lemmon plays a young man in an insurance office who makes his way up the ladder of executive success by the unorthodox method of lending the key of his bachelor flat to various married executives who are having casual affairs on the side. The nature of the game is exposed when the girl he is serious about turns up as one of the partners. The story of the love affair between Lemmon and Shirley MacLaine is sometimes mawkishly treated. But there are some very funny situations. There is also room for a good deal of witty observation, viewed with the detached, cynical eye of Billy Wilder: the classic set-piece of the office party, for example. And, as Lemmon becomes more and more entangled by the situation, as the gag takes over, the film is able to edge over into a more deeply-laid satire about the intrigues of executive life. *The Apartment*, unlike *Let's Make Love* or *That Touch of Mink*, is never taken in by the confused attitudes which it satirizes, nor is it seduced by its own gloss. The comedy is sufficiently independent to allow for oblique comment on the world which it presents.

An earlier example is Minnelli's *Born Yesterday*. This film makes use of the archetype of the dumb blonde, played by Judy Holliday, the girl friend of a crude but wealthy racketeer who is trying to make use of Senatorial and government influence to clinch a number of shady deals. The blonde falls for a disenchanted intellectual whom her boy friend (Broderick Crawford) hires to educate her: in the process she learns the meaning of her lover's clandestine activities and decides to expose them. In her efforts to attract the intellectual (William Holden's) attention, she takes up such unlikely pastimes as reading and visiting famous Washington monuments. 'Say, are you one of them intellectuals?' she asks over the tops of her bejewelled glasses, 'or would you be interested in a little action?' The triumph of the film, however, lies in the way in which Judy Holliday turns the convention of the dumb blonde inside out. The little-girl innocence, which she plays for all the sex it is worth at the beginning, is precisely the quality which enables her, at the end, to act on what she has been taught with a sort of simple honesty, a moral literalness. It is this naivety which finally undermines the shady sophisticates around her, who simply can't believe that a girl whose horizons have been limited to diamonds, bed and furs can ever grow up sufficiently to take the American Constitution seriously. The humour in *Born Yesterday*, therefore, takes on a serious moral force without ever losing its comic hilarity. Both *Born Yesterday* and *The Apartment* take their sex with less embarrassment, and phoney restraint, than *That Touch of Mink*. Yet their comic range is in fact much wider; they are richer, funnier films in a popular convention. Via the sex theme (and in *Born Yesterday*, the sex stereotype) they bring within reach of comedy a more extensive set of references to contemporary life. They do not depend, as *That Touch of Mink* does, upon the joke, maintained for an hour and a half, of how the heroine can both have her fun *and* evade it successfully.

The comparison we are making between the genuine sex comedy, a legitimate popular conventional form, and the stereo-typed version can be most neatly pointed in two films which have Marilyn Monroe as their heroine: *Some Like It Hot* (Billy Wilder) and *Let's Make Love* (George Cukor). In the former, the humour is maintained by excellent team playing between Jack Lemmon, Tony Curtis, Marilyn Monroe and Joe E. Brown. Lemmon and Curtis, musicians on the run from a gang of Chicago crooks, take refuge in an all-girl orchestra on their way to Florida for an engagement. The basic joke is, therefore, a very old one—men in female disguise. However, the two men, Lemmon and Curtis, bring to this stagey situation a wealth of invention and comic nuance. They enter with enormous gusto into the spirit of the farce. No Billy Wilder film is without its moments of tastelessness —there is an immensely vulgar seduction scene and some crude satire on gang warfare—but most of the time he controls the comedy with a dominant rhythm, and is constantly searching for revealing contrasts which parody the conventional situations and add another level to the humour. Thus the sight of Lemmon in high heels, clutching a double bass and fending off the approaches of Joe E. Brown in the hotel lobby, is made far more piquant by the evocative femininity of Marilyn Monroe juxtaposed neatly beside him. Marilyn Monroe's performance is particularly well judged from this point of view. Wildly attractive sexually, she is utterly unconscious of her femininity (Lemmon and Curtis, of course, are hyper-conscious about their lack of it). She is gay, open, light-hearted and simple. Her sexual grace is used deliber-ately to accentuate the awkwardness of the men. In one memorable scene, when she sings *Running Wild*, Lemmon is to be seen, immediately behind her, in heavy matronly disguise, giving her every support on the bass fiddle. The whole scene develops with enormous physical swing, but at the same time it touches the high points of parody.

In *Some Like It Hot* a creative use is made of Marilyn Monroe's

capacity to suggest innocent sexuality. In *Let's Make Love*, however, her well-known prowess is simply exploited for a hackneyed
version of the chorus-girl-and-the-millionaire theme. Her
physical radiance lightens Wilder's touch: but in Cukor's film her
role as the innocent home-spun girl beset by the Don Juan
millionaire makes her seem simply vulgar. (The comedy scenes
with Yves Montand being instructed by a procession of famous
comics are also utterly without invention.)

Let's Make Love does possess five minutes of real entertainment
pleasure. These are also the most sexually evocative moments in
the film—Marilyn Monroe's singing of *My Heart Belongs To Daddy*
in the opening sequence. This song is the classic tease of the dumb
blonde. Marilyn Monroe, however, makes it a much richer offering
by the exercise of a delicate style. In this scene she raises innocence
to the level of self-caricature. She is not a professional dancer or
singer. (Maurice Zolotow, in his biography, *Marilyn Monroe*,
describes how the scene had to be shot in many very short takes:
she followed the steps which were performed by her choreo-
graphers, Cole and Banks, just out of camera range.) Her performance has the quality of a 'take-off'—she mimes the typical Hollywood chorus girl song-and-dance act, she does an 'imitation' of
herself. This stylization works against the line of meaning in
the words of the song, and provides an oblique comment upon
them.

What counts in our evaluation of films of this kind is not the
mere presence of the erotic element but the production values of
the film *as a whole*.

The romantic comedy is, of course, a film convention, a form
of escape entertainment. Nevertheless, within this form we are
offered distinct feminine types and certain typed attitudes towards
the roles of men and women in the romantic situation. That a
stereotyping process is going on in these films can be seen, firstly
from the fact that a number of films within the same period
portray the same kind of situation, and, secondly, that this version
differs markedly from other types of romantic comedies in
previous periods. In the current examples of the genre the girl is a

simple, homely but attractive type. She subscribes to the morality of 'fun'—love is a gay adventure, undemanding except in one respect, that of resistance to sexual conquest. She is attracted by all the good things which the man offers—money and status, (though they never appear in this crude form, but are present simply as part of the hero's whole ambience, his plush office, his penthouse apartment, his swanky limousine, his experienced good looks). These he offers on a lavish scale: the one thing he never offers, without prodding, is the rather humdrum, routine permanence of marriage. These the heroine takes—but at a price: marriage. In the end, but well after the final sequence, they settle for one another. These films have all the attraction of the expensive affair, but save their face at the end with the most conventional kind of resolution.

The mood of these comedies is far less demanding that that of the romantic comedies which they have almost completely replaced—the wise-cracking farces, often about marriage, which were so common in the thirties. In the earlier versions, the woman was too tough-minded and intelligent to play the simple All-American girl: she was much more the man's equal, trading joke for joke. Here, within the conventions, a surface equality at least was being established between the sexes—the films had a social, as well as a sexual, point. They were brittle but unsentimental in their treatment. One thinks of the stars in these films in terms of the team rather than the heroine: Myrna Loy and William Powell, Rosalind Russell and Melvyn Douglas, Katharine Hepburn and Spencer Tracey. The heroine assumed a masculine toughness in her attitude to the romance, and yielded to the charms of the man only when he accepted her in her own right. She was not to be bought off too lightly—with the promise of a vacation in Rio or the marriage ring. In comparison with the more recent style, these films seem in retrospect much more adult fantasies. They were able to make an audience believe in the heroine outside of the romance situation. In *The Bells are Ringing* Judy Holliday's job at a telephone-answering service is only a flimsy excuse for putting her on the line to Dean Martin's flat. In Howard Hawks's *His Girl*

Friday Rosalind Russell's job as a newspaper reporter is quite solidly established, and has a bearing on how she behaves towards the caddish hero, on her independence and her drive. A film like *His Girl Friday* depended, for its pace and vigour, not only on script-writers like Ben Hecht with an ear for dialogue or on actresses like Rosalind Russell and Katharine Hepburn with the capacity to deliver it: it depended on the whole climate surrounding the changing relations between men and women. It was this climate to which Hawks was responding when, reading again the dialogue from Milestone's film, *Front Page* (on which *His Girl Friday* was based), he exclaimed, 'Hell, it's better between a girl and a man than between two men.'

The older comedies, when they were good, also treated the theme of *mariage à la mode* with a certain spirit. The more recent versions do not possess a style of any particular kind. Their appeal is the appeal of their décor—they are essentially films of interior decoration, of fashion and *haute couture*. They are like high-grade advertisements, the credit titles being often the best things about them. They remind one of the ritzier magazines—like *Vogue* or *Town* or *Queen*—all layout and no content. The really distinctive quality which they possess is *glamour*.

It is interesting to see that the more unsentimental heroine has not altogether disappeared from romantic comedy, but has been absorbed into the sub-plot. She makes her appearance as the All-American's heroine's buddy—the friend who provides light relief with her barbed commentary on the rose-tinted affair and her soured views on the wicked ways of the male world. If she lacks the confidence of her prototype (Myrna Loy, Rosalind Russell?) she retains a feminine cunning and wit of which the fluffy heroine stands in some need. Her loss of status is, however, cruelly revealed in that she fails in the two criteria which define the heroine—she is not glamorously attractive and she is not very successful with men of the right sort. Occasionally she is allowed to pair off with her opposite number—the hero's buddy. A number of intelligent supporting actresses have been consigned to this role —Eve Arden and Betty Garrett are two examples—and they often bring to the comedy a vigour which the main plot lacks (see especially *My Sister Eileen*).

Apart from the marriage comedies of the thirties and the unsentimental friend with minor status in the romantic comedies more recently, the only place where the heroine of a conventional film genre achieved anything like equality with the hero was in the black thrillers of the forties. In Howard Hawks's *To Have and Have Not* and *The Big Sleep*, Lauren Bacall managed to fight Humphrey Bogart, line by line, to a standstill. In addition to their strikingly economical style and their sombre mood of violence, these dour black-and-white films offered a real, if disguised, interest in the relationship between hero and heroine. Bogart, whom Hawks recognized as the most insolent man on the screen, is matched in every scene by the laconic Bacall. This caricatured by-play between the two central figures relieves these thrillers of their more violent compulsions, and turns what would have been simple melodramas into witty parodies, based on the antagonism between the sexes. The plot of *To Have and Have Not*, too melodramatic to be credible or to sustain interest for long, is now admitted by Hawks to have been 'an excuse for some scenes' between Bogart and Bacall (interview in *Movie*, December 1962). And *The Big Sleep* had a plot whose intricacies neither the director of the film, Hawks, nor the author of the novel, Chandler, were able to follow. In the film, however, the real climax is not the resolution of the mystery, but the point at which Bogart is forced to recognize that in Lauren Bacall he has met his match. In a different way from Chandler, but with the same effect, this tension is allowed to dominate the plot, and provides a kind of entertainment in itself which is richer than the conventional thrills which one expects from the private-eye film. They are not serious films on commanding human themes, or even convincing images of human behaviour. But their style rescues them from banality.

A study of the varying treatments of romantic themes and heroines can provide us with some insight into changing attitudes to love and sex. In particular we can learn a great deal by following the trends in heroines through different periods: at one time the voluptuous curves of Betty Grable seem to predominate, at another the cool languor of Grace Kelly, the *gamin* simplicity of Audrey Hepburn or the pouting provocativeness of Bardot. These swings in fashion offer us certain clues to the emotional climate of each period.

Every society has its myths and legends. All sorts of stories of past and current events, of heroes, and of institutions enter into our beliefs, convictions and ideas. Social myths are imaginative interpretations of past, present, or future events. However, they are not created out of nothing, but have, as their basis, some crisis. They deal with economic needs, with warfare, adventure, success or failure in life, with birth, puberty, marriage, death and the future life. They may arise as a wish fulfilment in some difficult situation, yet they serve to stabilize us in the presence of our own distresses.

K. Young, 'Stereotypes, Myths and Ideologies',
Handbook of Social Psychology

We call the screen heroines *legitimate* fantasy figures—because the audience accepts them as the agents of the fantasy. They provide a pivot for the film—scenes are enlivened by their presence, plots develop around them, their very appearance can make one film seem immediately contemporary in feeling, while a different kind of heroine against whom fashion has moved seems immediately dated. The audience may not approve of who they are or what they do in any conscious moral sense. Yet to find them entertaining is to recognize and to give some degree of assent to the stereotype, to admit that they connect with our everyday experience, even when it is difficult to trace exactly how this relationship arises.

This gallery of types is closely related to that remarkable phenomenon of the cinema industry—the star system. To some extent, the star system was the product of the economics of the industry. But it was also the creation of the medium itself. The cinema restored the human face and body to a place in popular culture which it had not had for many years. It made a visual culture available to a wide section of the population. Particularly in the silent cinema, gesture, movement and expression were the essentials of the art of acting. The techniques of film-making—the selection of details in close-up, the blocking and composition made possible by the camera, the use of angle and lighting—only heightened the symbolic meaning of the figures set in motion on the screen. The coming of sound modified, but did not alter fundamentally, the *charismatic* appeal of the human image. The effect of this new art seems to have been paradoxical. On the one hand, the film image made the human figure more vivid, real, immediate in its appeal to the senses. At the same time, the cinema seemed to transpose these figures into a sort of symbolic imagery. The stars were both familiar and strange:

> Photographs have the kind of authority over the imagination today, which the printed word had yesterday, and the spoken word before that. They seem utterly real. They come, we imagine, directly to us without human meddling, and they are the most effortless food for the mind conceivable. Any description in words, or even any inert picture, requires an effort of memory before a picture exists in the mind. But on the screen the whole process of observing, describing, reporting, and then imagining has been accomplished for you. Without more trouble than is needed to stay awake, the result which your imagination is always aiming at is reeled off on the screen.
>
> Walter Lippmann, 'Stereotypes', in *Reader in Public Opinion*

The stars quickly passed beyond the limits of the screen. They carried over into real life qualities which the camera had bestowed upon them. They *became*, to some extent, the roles which they played. But also, because film plots were constantly being re-written for the stars who played in them, their roles became *them*. This interaction between life and the illusion of the screen goes some way to explaining the compulsive power of the stars. Often, when audiences watched them perform, they were watching the stars rather than the characters in the story. The stars therefore carry with them an accumulated power, composed of all the many parts they have played, into the playing of any particular role. There is a continuity from role to role. These roles take on a life of their own, independent of the films. And this has given the stars an extra dimension. They seem, Edgar Morin remarks in his book on *The Stars*, part-human, part-divine.

This extra-dimension is not directly related to their acting ability. Some, of course, are fine actors in their own right. Many of them lack great histrionic force—Garbo, for example, or Valentino. Yet they were superb stars, projecting back to the audience images which possessed powerful associations. To some extent star quality is always a *physical* attribute, inherent in the face, the gestures and movements of the body. But it is also an emotional quality, with moral implications. Bela Balazs wrote of Greta Garbo, in his *Theory of the Film*, that she possessed 'a physiognomy expressing a very definite state of mind':

> Like the face of all other actors, Greta Garbo's face changes expression during a scene. She, too, laughs and is sad, is surprised or angry, as prescribed by her part. . . . But behind this variety of facial expression we can always see that unchanged Garbo face, the fixed unchanged expression of which has conquered the world. . . . Greta Garbo's beauty is a beauty of suffering; she suffers life and all the surrounding world. And this sadness, this sorrow, is a very definite one: the sadness of loneliness, of an estrangement which feels no common tie with other human beings.
>
> *Theory of the Film*

It was the *unchanging* quality of her face, as much as the variety of her acting parts, which constituted Greta Garbo's magic in the cinema. Men and women responded to her idealized portrait of this type, and of the ideals and aspirations latent within it.

The outstanding male and female stars of the cinema were all in their different ways idealized types. They became identified, through frequent appearance in the same kind of role, with distinct attitudes and romantic situations. They were stereotyped, and younger stars who emerged in the same period were drawn to the same kinds of roles and developed similar characteristics.

For a long time Rosalind Russell, then an unknown starlet, spent her time replacing Myrna Loy in roles which that actress, for one reason or another, gave up, and then stepping aside when Miss Loy returned to the set. Eventually, of course, Rosalind Russell became more adept at playing 'Myrna Loy' than Myrna Loy herself. At different periods, different types have dominated the screen, so that it is possible to establish a rough evolution or typology of the stars (see Plate 8). A favourite figure in the silent cinema was the 'innocent or roguish virgin', associated with the names of Mary Pickford and Lilian Gish, the little 'American Sweethearts'. Early in the history of the cinema the 'vamp' appeared—a striking image of carnal passion, which we can recapture in watching the films of, say, Theda Bara. The vamp recently returned to the screen in Joseph Losey's *The Servant*, a curiosity reminiscent of the early Theda Bara film *A Fool There Was*. At a later stage, passion was etherealized, and the stars became divine and mysterious romantics, objects of inspiring passion, yet distant, remote, inaccessible. This is the quality we find in Garbo, in Pola Negri and in some of the earlier films of Marlene Dietrich. In the cinema of the thirties and forties, various strands in the feminine role seem to be disentangled, and associated with separate kinds of actresses. Some screen heroines become gayer good-time girls, like Mae West, Jean Harlow and Joan Blondell. The more sentimental romance is reserved for the 'girl next-door', a type which looks back as far as the little Clara Bow and forward to June Allyson and Doris Day. There is a special place for the experienced middle-class woman of the world, whether in comedy (Rosalind Russell, Myrna Loy, Katharine Hepburn, Claudette Colbert) or in romantic melodrama (Bette Davis, Joan Crawford, Susan Hayward). This is also the period of that most interesting psychological stereotype—the 'good-bad' girl, an attempt to fuse together the sexual impulses awakened by the 'vamp' and the pure and affectionate love aroused by the 'girl next-door'. The 'good-bad' heroine is a safety-device in the American film—she appears to be bad throughout most of the film, with the vamp's sex appeal, promiscuous, involved with shady acquaintances, even perhaps caught up in crime and vice. In the end, however, she reveals that she has been hiding all her virginal virtues, 'purity of soul, natural goodness, and a generous heart' (Edgar Morin, *The Stars*). She is a fusion in fantasy of two apparently irreconcilable feminine ideals. The hero 'has a girl who has attracted him by an appearance of wickedness, and whom in the end he can take home and introduce to Mother' (Wolfenstein & Leites, *Movies: A Psychological Study*). Many stars have inhabited this stereotype—Lana Turner, Susan Hayward, Rita Hayworth, Ava Gardner—and others have played it occasionally—Lauren Bacall, Elizabeth Taylor, Marilyn Monroe. One familiar type—dominant in the cinema throughout several periods—is the 'big blonde' with the elongated legs and the pneumatic bosom: Betty Grable, Lana Turner, Jayne Mansfield, Sabrina, and their brunette counterparts, Jane Russell and Gina Lollobrigida. Generally, there seems to have been a progression in the typology of the stars, from the remote, generous-hearted prostitutes and the great divines, to a more realistic, middle-class type of heroine, and, recently, a regression to the neurotic and the childish. Susan Hayward and Elizabeth Taylor may be taken as types for the neurotic heroine, Marilyn Monroe, Audrey Hepburn, Brigitte Bardot and Natalie Wood as sexy innocents, 'little creatures on the frontier of childhood, of rape, of nymphomania'. It is not that the star has become more 'realistic' in her roles, but rather that she plays roles closer to *her own* psychological experience. The contemporary heroine often seems to use her role in the film as a way of living out the tensions of her life: at any rate, there is now an awkward confusion between the role being played and real life. Where in the past the screen personality enriched and helped to mythologize the life of the star, the star's personal problems are now being brought to the screen personality to give it life. We can see something of this in Elizabeth Taylor's films, *Butterfield 8* (with Eddie Fisher) and *The VIP's* (with Richard Burton), in Judy Garland's *I Could Go On Singing*, and Marilyn Monroe's *The Misfits*—but the most poignant instance is to be found in the tragic story of Marilyn Monroe's whole career and death (and, of course, in James Dean).

The rise of the star system and the stereotyping of the romantic heroine and situation provide an interesting example of a cultural process. In one dimension the star's personality is highly individualized—it belongs to her, and she carries its resonances with her from one role to the next. In another dimension this continuity from role to role helps to fix an identity between the star and a particular definition of the romantic heroine—she comes to embody one kind of romantic personality and her parts in the films take on a social character and meaning. The response of the cinema audience to the star contains both elements—it is a response to the subliminal power of the star herself, and it is also a recognition of the type she embodies. But this consideration of the star as symptom must be qualified by critical judgements about quality of performance. Brigitte Bardot and Marilyn Monroe both seem superficially to play the same type of heroine —the sexually precocious nymphette, with the combined qualities of 'extreme innocence and extreme eroticism': what Simone de Beauvoir calls 'The Lolita Syndrome'. Yet it is clear from watching the two actresses at work that each feels her sexuality in a different way. Both radiate erotic power; in both sensuality is strongly blended with a certain childishness. Yet in Bardot, especially when she is playing to the direction of Roger Vadim, childishness is incapable of suggesting the complementary quality of innocence. The kitten face, the pouting lips, the uncombed rope of hair, the 'proffered nudity'—key elements in the Bardot screen personality —seem prototypes of a certain kind of male dream, and she conforms to this dream-image totally: she holds nothing *of herself* back, she is wholly at the disposal, as an image, of the men in her audience. It is not fortuitous that the central sequence in her films is a version of the strip-tease—her naked swim in *Light Across the Street*, her bath in mare's milk in *The Week-ends of Nero*, the strip contest in *Mademoiselle Strip-tease*, the strip-tease mambo in *And God Created Woman*—for the strip-tease is the climax of the male erotic fantasy and, as we saw from the thriller novel, the fantasy in which the woman is cast entirely as an *object* of the man's desire. Marilyn Monroe also revelled in her physical beauty—indeed, she was obsessed by it. Yet in her screen performances the quality of innocence was real—there was a certain protective honesty about it which contrasts with Bardot's 'indifference', a way of saving something of herself from the total publicity of the sexy roles she played. In most of her films this was the hint of an underlying melancholy, the touch of pathos that made the very perfection of her beauty seem vulnerable rather than crudely available. Gavin Lambert, in an early review of *Niagara*, described her acting as 'reluctant':

> She is too passive to be a vamp; she is no menace because she is so easily frightened; and she is certainly no bombshell because she never bursts. . . . For all the wolf calls that she gets and deserves, there is something oddly mournful about Miss Monroe. She doesn't look happy. She lacks the pin-up's cheerful grin. She seems to have lost something, or to be waking up from a bad dream.
>
> quoted in *Town*, 'M.M.: The Last Pictures', November 1962

It was this quality of 'reluctance' which gave her comedy its special flavour, made more complex her riotous or provocative performances, and which forced from her audiences not only the expected physical response but also a tempered sympathy, a desire to protect her from herself, and themselves. The same point is made by two contrasting films: *The Girl Rosemarie* and *Love Now, Pay Later* (see Plate 9). Although both are based on the same real-life story of a German call-girl, the whole mood of *Love Now, Pay Later* works against the moral statement it pretends to make, while *The Girl Rosemarie*, through its stylization, achieves an ironic effect.

One could take two films based on a similar and familiar romantic situation: in the first, the husband has an affair with a girl who, later, meets with an accident. The husband returns to his wife, promising to try to make up to her for his failure. In the second, the wife has an affair with a doctor, but decides in the end to return to her home and husband. Described in this way the films have a superficial similarity—yet they could hardly be more different. The bizarre but intriguing comparison between

Butterfield 8 and *Brief Encounter* is a contrast in moral tone. Yet both films could be said to point the same moral.

From the very opening moments of each film, however, we can tell at once that we have entered two totally different worlds. Every word, image, location in *Brief Encounter* reveals delicate British middle-class checks and restraints. It is there in the fashions of Celia Johnson, in the insistent underplaying in the final scene between the lovers in the railway station tea-room, in the romantic mood of the walks in the country. In *Brief Encounter* hesitancies count as much as climaxes. When the lovers are interrupted by the friend whose flat they have taken over, the emphasis is on the wife's self-disgust and guilt. And in the final meeting, which is interrupted by Dolly, an insensitive friend, the emotional commitment of the film is summed up by the wife's comment: 'Alec behaved splendidly'. In *Brief Encounter* the episode is recorded in flashback. This device helps to establish a consistent tone—the whole affair is seen in the perspective of a regretful nostalgia. This nostalgia distances us from the events, it foretells—not so much in words as in its tone and balance—the rejection of the love affair, the return to respectability, home and reassuring, understanding husband. It lends to the respectability of the story an emotional support, which is, throughout the film, always a stronger presence than the adulterous affair. It is, in its clichéd way, a triumph of middle-class sensibility. Every image contains its own regrets.

Compare this with the opening of *Butterfield 8*. The seduction is already complete. Elizabeth Taylor rises languorously from the bed, clad only in a towel, pours herself a gin, and sensually strokes the fur coat which belongs to the wife of the man she has just seduced. Regret of any kind is as alien to this as seduction was to *Brief Encounter*. Both films contain their clichés, but they express two different levels of reality. In *Butterfield 8* the husband has left some money in the flat of his mistress. This annoys her, and when next they meet she drives her stiletto heel into his foot—slowly. In response he twists her arm. 'At last,' she says, 'we can be honest.' But when the lovers in *Brief Encounter* meet, the voice in the flashback says, 'It was our last day together—our very last.'

Most of the images in *Brief Encounter* reinforce the feeling that the whole episode is slipping into the past, that it will soon become a faded and pleasantly romantic memory. Every image in *Butterfield 8* has the impact, the seductive glamour, of advertising. In *Butterfield 8* the adulteress is seen, and relished, as a destroyer. And the wife, standing by until her husband returns to her, is deeply involved in the illicit experience too, and dramatizes her suffering: 'Someday Wes will find himself and when he does I want to be there.' In *Brief Encounter* the woman is seen as a guilt-ridden suburban housewife. And the husband, sitting watching the changing expressions on her face by the fireside, has been spared all the pain of the experience, and plays his final line with unnerving understatement: 'I don't know where you've been, but you've been far away: thank you for coming back.'

Contemporary romantic comedy has interesting affinities with Restoration drama:

> The preoccupation with love (in both tragedy and comedy), the stress on sex-antagonism, the common conventions that marriage is a bore and love primarily or exclusively a physical appetite—all these are as typically immature attitudes as is the complementary love-idealism of Restoration tragedy. Here, perhaps, may be suggested a critical approach to the 'immorality' of Restoration comedy. Henry James, in a famous passage, asserted 'the perfect dependence of the "moral" sense of a work of art on the amount of felt life concerned in producing it'. The amount of life *felt* by Restoration dramatists was severely limited, and the feelings too often at the level of cliché.
>
> P. A. W. Collins, *Pelican Guide, 5*

The same terms could be applied with equal force to the romances of the cinema. Yet perhaps it is true that we never go to such films with the expectation of seeing an adult experience treated in a mature manner.

A film like *Butterfield 8*, however, must stand here as an example of a film which passes for an 'adult' one on a 'serious' romantic theme. The word adult implies that it deals with a grown-up theme—adultery—in a serious manner, and that the way the characters talk and behave to one another is what we expect of experienced men and women of the world. Gloria Wandrous(!) the good-bad woman, admits evil to the story in the shape of a female destroyer. By allowing adultery to intervene the film acknowledges that all might not be perfect in the garden of marriage, and seems closer in this way to real life, to 'reality'. Yet the sophistication of treatment is not matched by a greater maturity in the attitudes. The female destroyer is an adolescent image, and her presentation is adolescent too—the confused yearning for evil together with the underlying subservience to what is conventionally regarded as good. She is dramatized in a fantasy way—glamorized in contrast with the prosaic wife, set off by lavish settings and surrounded by objects of wealth and luxury. Yet in the end she is whisked away by the arbitrary intervention of death, which solves everything. There is nothing within either the characters or the plot which demands her death: it is demanded from outside, by the 'code' which governs this kind of film as surely as it throws out of balance the romantic comedy and the sentimental fiction story. No moral values are at work within the film itself. The man takes no decisions either about his own life, his family and marriage, or his feelings for the girl. He simply waits around for the script-writers to solve the equation of the eternal triangle and restore the *status quo*. It is a film in which no consequences flow from the actions which men perform or the decisions they make. Its scheme is an arbitrary and manipulated one. In this context the good-bad girl is easily detached from the film's total meaning, and her sexuality is a separate element standing on its own, licensed as an excuse for our vicarious erotic feelings by the unconvincing resolution: a pornographic image, in fact. Elizabeth Taylor may have intended a more conventional attitude when she described Gloria Wandrous as 'the slut of all times' and the script as 'the most pornographic I have ever read', but the judgement is nevertheless accurate. (Miss Taylor must be given credit for wanting to reject the part: she was forced to take it by her studio to whom she was under contract, and who are said to have threatened to keep her off the screen for two years if she refused. She also described MGM's decision to cast her husband Eddie Fisher in one of the supporting roles as 'icing on the cake'. (See Alan Levy, *The Elizabeth Taylor Story*.)

The judgement depends neither on the fact that the images are erotic ones nor that the film deals with an adulterous situation. One can think, for example, of a film of Renoir's, *Partie de Campagne*, in which the whole force depends upon the unfolding sensuality of the young heroine. In this unfinished sketch, a typical French *petit-bourgeois* family spend a day in the country. They meet a pair of young *roués*, and, while the father snoozes or fishes, one of the young men flirts with the mother, while the other pursues the daughter. The second relationship, however, casually entered on, develops into the girl's first adult experience. The film is rich with contrasts: the exuberant sexuality of the middle-aged mother, expanding under the scheming attentions and flatteries of one of the boys, the intense romanticism of the young girl who falls in love with the other young man. Both women are set off against the rest of the family—the portly father who snores, the idiotic young man who fishes and the aged grandmother. Every image in the film speaks of sensual emotions —the mother, chased by the mocking boy, who feigns escape but plays an elaborate game, the breaking of the calm river and the plunge into the woods by the young girl and her friend. The seduction is both tender and violent, the camera moving from the images of nature around them to the experienced face of the man, and coming finally to rest on the troubled, tragic innocence of the girl in her first moments of passion. In an earlier passage Renoir beautifully captures the ripening feelings of the girl as the men watch her in a swing. The higher she goes, the more her emotions soar. At the apex of her swing she is merged with the budding blossoms of the tree and the flowering of nature around her. Yet there hangs about her face even then a touch, a foretaste, of sadness. Here is a film in which the morality is transmuted into the felt life of the images—an intensely moving, physically and sensually full, portrait of the emotions in youth. With *Butterfield 8* or *Splendour in the Grass* or *Peyton Place* or *And God Created Woman* on the circuits, one might call *Partie de Campagne* a film for a courageous school.

If, on the other hand, we try to find examples of the triangle situation dealt with in any other manner than with stress upon its adolescent intensities, we will have to go outside the limits of popular cinema. Truffaut's *Jules et Jim* provides us with some standard against which to measure 'adult' films like *Butterfield 8*. This film is composed of a series of sketches about a woman who falls in love with two men—both friends. They meet when the men are still students, and form a team, the girl very often dressing up or acting the part of a third man. Both men are caught by the liveliness and the strangeness of the girl. They both fall in love with her, but—and here the real complexities of the film begin—their friendship is also enriched by her. The stock figures of the adulterous situation—aggrieved husband, ardent lover, wayward wife—are totally absent. Instead, the film explores the three people's need for one another, the delicacy of the balance between love and friendship, the different ways in which the two men care for the woman who, whatever she does, whatever her caprices, is the centre of their lives. The quality of the film, then, lies precisely in this evocation of life, and in the enormous respect which Truffaut shows towards the distinctiveness of the three characters, his willingness to allow them to exist in their own right and on their own terms. He abandons any moral scheme, and for this reason is also forced to restrain himself from imposing a firm structure on the film. The structure, therefore, seems episodic, the qualities momentary and fragmentary, rather than unfolding to some preordered resolution. Even the final episode, when, in full sight of Jules (holding them all together to the end), Catherine drives herself and Jim over the bridge, does not have its conventional weight and solemnity. It has a piquancy of its own, even an edge of farce—it is one of Catherine's many 'acts', another of her quick touches, a *finale* rather than a conclusion. It is the last, and almost unconsciously tragic, of her epiphanies. The death of Catherine is consistent with the undertone of seriousness in Jeanne Moreau's most exuberant scenes.

If we look for British films which take us beyond the almost unbearable inhibitions of *Brief Encounter* and create a fuller and more complex image of love, we shall have to turn to the group of films which constitute the British 'new wave'—films like *Room at the Top, Saturday Night and Sunday Morning, A Kind of Loving, This Sporting Life*. Though these films contain weaknesses of their own, they come to their emotional problems with less faked histrionics and less reservation than we find in the *Brief Encounter* melodramas of the heart. *Room at the Top* is particularly interesting in this context. The film seemed at the time to represent a break-through in the British cinema—its theme, the young man striving to get to 'the top', seemed peculiarly contemporary, and the provincial setting strikingly new. But we find, in retrospect, that the most important advance lay in the quality of the emotional life in the film. And this was not due to anything offered directly by the British cinema—the playing of Laurence Harvey and Heather Sears was wooden and clichéd—but to the triumphant appearance of Simone Signoret. Here was the full and rounded image of an experienced married woman of feeling—Signoret suggests this in the very way she looks at Laurence Harvey over her drink in the pub, in her gesture of farewell to him after she has been humiliated by her husband before her friends, in the way she walks. Her playing has the weight and gravity which set Harvey off—in spite of all the sympathy which naturally moves to this declassed working-class boy—as an immature and jumped-up young man, incapable of matching her in any terms except the physical. And thus the end, which is rather sketchy in John Braine's novel, and could well have seemed arbitrary in the film without Signoret's support, is made inevitable: throughout she has managed to suggest that the hero's betrayal is implicit in his actions—it is dramatically placed.

In both *Saturday Night and Sunday Morning* and *This Sporting Life*, however, the interplay between characters on the emotional level is richer and more substantial. Rachel Roberts gives to the role of the married woman in *Saturday Night*, and of the widow in *Sporting Life* a tense realism, all the more remarkable because its power does not depend upon glamour or conventional good looks. It is not only that *Saturday Night*, in Albert Finney's portrayal of Arthur Seaton, brings a heightened dramatic sense to ordinary scenes of working-class life and suggests complexity in apparently inarticulate people. The emotional relationships, too, though secondary to the study of manners in the film, emerge from the deceptive camera-tilts and faded glows of *Brief Encounter* into the clear, cold light of day. It is Rachel Roberts's screwed-up face, when she reveals to Arthur that she is pregnant, which makes the half-teasing, half-unfeeling seduction credible and moving. It is the moment when Doreen complains to Arthur that 'you treat me like a bit of muck', and Arthur for the first time softens to her, that gives the film a depth which *Brief Encounter* misses. In *Saturday Night* it is the quality of the experience which counts—the kind of response it aims for, the fuller grasp which it seems to have on the emotions of the characters involved, and hence the richer quality of thought and feeling which it stirs in the viewer. In *This Sporting Life* it is the destructive nature of the love between Mrs Hammond and Frank Machin which is the central experience of the film (as it was of David Storey's excellent novel). In the conventional sense there is no moral problem here—no attractive girls for Frank, no older men offering security and a home to Mrs Hammond. They are free to marry (the stock drama of the 'adult' problem film) if only they can make a life together. In fact, they cannot, for all the attraction they have for each other. In one of the tenderest scenes, Frank does come some way to breaking down Mrs Hammond's resistance to him—the lyrical scene with the children in the park. But that addiction to death which is felt in Mrs Hammond's memory of her dead husband, her stubbornness, an inner lifelessness or withdrawal, is precisely the quality which drives Frank to destroy what remains of love between them, for it is a denial of the deep, brutal but mastering energy which is the core of his character. Just as he drives and hectors her to recognize him for what he is, so she is always holding some part of herself separate from him, keeping him in check, and making him feel fettered and unfree. It is a Lawrentian theme—a conflict of temperament, of spirit. Lindsay Anderson, in his efforts to establish Machin's compulsiveness, is at times too entranced by simple images of massiveness and close-ups of Frank Machin intended to carry more weight than they do. One or two scenes—the quite superficial satire in the restaurant, which suddenly declines into broad parody, or the stagey posturing at the end—are badly judged, and out of tune with the more subjective camera-work of the earlier scenes. Yet the film has a demanding emotional force which makes it painful to watch, as a destructive emotional relationship ought to be.

Whatever the individual merits of these films, we find that in them the relationships between men and women, the experience of love and physical passion, are lifted out of fantasy and established with some real grasp of a human setting, with respect for the complexities of life. For the more profound treatment of love, and the erotic feelings as elemental forces capable of disturbing the lives of characters below the level of the conscious, we would have to turn to the work of Vigo or Buñuel. Set against *L'Atalante* or *Viridiana* or *Los Olvidados*, *Saturday Night and Sunday Morning* or *This Sporting Life* are likely to seem, in their turn, too straightforward. In comparison with the states of feeling explored in Antonioni's *L'Avventura* or *La Notte*, *Room at the Top* is a simple, relatively crude and exterior handling of personal emotions. The remarkable fact is the range actually available within one art form—a form which contains, at one end, the crude, up-beat high spirits of *Operation Petticoat*, and, at the other extreme, the slowly unfolding pessimism, the evocative images of emotional emptiness and sterility, in the final scene between Mastroianni and Jeanne Moreau at the close of *La Notte*.

Many of these films are too difficult for young adults. Antonioni's slow interior realism, his depiction of inner restlessness, of the indeterminacy of feelings which, as he has said, we 'regard as having a kind of definite weight and absolute duration' but which are in fact 'fragile, vulnerable, subject to change', his determination to 'look pitilessly right to the bottom' and to 'follow my characters beyond the moments conventionally considered important for the spectator'—these require a kind of patience and an experience of life which we can expect very few young people to possess. The states of mind they express are too complex, and the images too charged with meaning, the texture of the film too impacted, to appeal to the more open and generous sensibilities of a young audience. There are a few films, standing between the 'art film' and the cliché genres, which deal with love, sex and the emotions in a way which makes them both valuable and accessible to a young audience. Among these we would mention *Innocent Sorcerers*, in which Wajda presents two young Poles who discover the serious feelings within themselves in the act of playing at love, and Olmi's excellent *Il Posto*, about a young man and his first job in the big city. The boy is superbly played by Sandro Panzeri, and perhaps the film's most effective passage is his first meeting with a girl applying to work at the same vast and impersonal organization. They have coffee together, the boy slightly uncertain of how to behave, responding to the warmth of the girl and relishing the whole simple experience of his first day in the city. The camera observes them unobtrusively, allowing us to share something of that experience as well.

Of the British 'new wave', the most useful for discussion is probably *A Kind of Loving*, John Schlesinger's adaptation from a novel by Stan Barstow. The hero and heroine, Vic (Alan Bates) and Ingrid (June Ritchie), are young people whose lives and ambitions are a problem to them because on either side the conventional forms of behaviour and feeling are undergoing change or have collapsed. On Vic's side the closeness of the working-class home no longer offers the kind of security of place and environment it did to a young man a generation before: on Ingrid's side, the banality and petty-mindedness of the lower-middle-class mother offers to the young couple nothing rich or sustaining as an image of married life. They are trapped into marriage, by Ingrid's unprepared pregnancy, by Vic's false sense of duty, but the actual inexperience of the couple, in the face of a long life together, is sensitively portrayed. One feels a sympathy with the couple as they strive to lay hold on some kind of meaningful life, as they try to give shape to their feelings for one another, and fumble towards some deeper understanding. It is a film in which we feel a real growth in the characters, though, like so many of the more recent British films, outside the central relationship, there are some striking errors of judgement (the mother, for example, is a totally stock figure, and Schlesinger weaves into his film certain stereotyped provincial objects of satire which conflict with the more sober mood). What is even more unfortunate, the final images of the film suggest a quality of defeat—as if the characters have been diminished by their experience—which is disturbing. This is a fault which *A Kind of Loving* shares with other 'new wave' British films—an unrelieved drabness, a kind of meanness of spirit and imagination, which seems unintentional, but which is too characteristic to escape comment. When Vic and Ingrid drag themselves up the road from the cramped little house they intend to make a home at the end of *A Kind of Loving*, we rebel against a view of life which holds out so little possibility of growth, characters whose ideas and feelings seem to have so little space in which to flower, whose ambitions are so limited.

The best of the recent British films have handled new social experiences, while at a higher level of achievement some of the European films have penetrated more deeply into personal relationships. Important gains have been made for a cinema that exposes and explores. Yet alongside this kind of cinema there will always be a need for films that merely affirm, which offer a fantasy of delight and a genuine release in a celebration, rather than a criticism, of life.

9

Friends and Neighbours

It's the perfect medium. I mean, it's real, you see people, you can figure them out.

ROY THOMSON (on TV)

Lord Thomson's claim that television portrays the 'real' world is also made for other media in so far as they handle documentary material. Not only—it is argued—are these media 'popular' in the sense of reaching large audiences, but also because they deal with people and with the situations of real life, they 'present the people to the people'. This is not a comment simply about the *material* transmitted by the media—it is also a comment on the *relationship* between these media and their audiences. The mass media are accessible to ordinary people in a way which would not be true for the more traditional high arts and the older entertainments. There is, it is suggested, a real community of interests and feeling between the popular means of communication and ordinary folk.

It is true that a good deal of media material is of this kind. The journalistic arts, reporting on people and the 'real' world, have extended through these media from the press to the general magazines to the various kinds of documentary film and television. In television alone we could include within this category the news report, the specially prepared documentary or journalistic essay, the many kinds of interviews and live discussion programmes in which, as Lord Thomson suggests, we 'see people' and try to 'figure them out', the use of the brief survey of popular opinion on any topic by means of the posed question (the so-called 'vox pop') as well as the many programmes where our interest is centred not only on the entertainment act but also on the reactions of the ordinary people in the audience—*Juke Box Jury*, for example, or *Sunday Night at the London Palladium*. There is also the naturalistic play or serial with a heavy documentary emphasis which is closely related to this particular trend–for example, *Coronation Street*.

The trend is not a surprising one. Journalism has always depended on the 'human interest' story, and this has been taken over into the newer media—radio as well as television. Media with a large cross-section of the general public among their regular audiences respond to this pressure by extending the scope of their material to include the life-situations and interests of their audiences. In the 'popular' media, the hero is, naturally, the common man. This is a condition of their continued popularity.

We can also account for this trend towards 'popular naturalism' and documentary in terms of the *nature* of the media themselves. To a far greater extent than previously, the new media are adapted to documentary because of their visual character. Here the development of the art of photography and the rise of the cinema have played an important part. In 'popular' journalism we have seen the growth of the picture-paper and the tabloid with their emphasis on design. The photo-magazine has evolved, with *Picture Post* standing at an important point in the line of development. Even in the ordinary daily or Sunday newspaper, far more attention is given now to news pictures and to visual layout. In a later chapter we note the shift of emphasis in display advertising from word to picture. Taken together, this amounts to a revolution in the sphere of visual communication: Daniel Boorstin calls it 'the graphic revolution'. We can see this revolution simply in terms of means or techniques—here the photograph, still or moving, is the significant element, since photography is really the art of 'composing nature'. But we can also consider it as a change in the character of communication itself, as a shift in sensibility. For instance, it is only in the age of the graphic revolution that the word 'image' could take on its current significance. In the early stages 'image' meant, simply, pictorial representation, with the implied suggestion that what we saw was a visualization of actuality, 'what was *really* there'. But now that pictorial techniques have become so widely used in communication for persuasive purposes, particularly in advertising, promotion and public relations, the word has taken on a different shade of meaning. It refers to the designed public impression created with the help of visual techniques: the 'image of the firm', the 'Party image', 'brand image'. It now carries the implied meaning, 'presenting to the public only that part . . . which we wish them to see'. There is even the hint that, by means of the *image*, we can present 'what is not really there at all'. This is an important shift in meaning and language, and shows the extent to which the visual emphases of modern communication have altered social habits. The *image* in this sense, Daniel Boorstin remarks, 'is a value-caricature'.

. . . we plainly confess a distinction between what we see and what is really there, and we express our preferred interest in what is to be seen. Thus an image is a visible public 'personality' as distinguished from an inward private 'character'. . . . The overshadowing image, we readily admit, covers up whatever may really be there. By our very use of the term we imply that something can be done to it: the image can always be more or less successfully synthesized, doctored, repaired, refurbished, and improved, quite apart from (though not entirely independent of) the spontaneous original of which the image is a public portrait.

The Image

We shall see when we come to discuss particular examples how, within this field of 'popular naturalism', the primacy of the visual element has contributed both to growth in our ability to document and visualize accurately, and to a persuasive or false presentation of ordinary people and 'real' life.

The conditions of reception are also important. Here television provides the key. The activity of viewing fits snugly into a domestic routine. The gossip of the screen mingles with the gossip of the home and family. We have to take into account, also, the expectations of the audience—the sense which television gives of an immediate and actual transmission of events taking place at, or close to, the very time of viewing. We are watching the election returns being made in Stratford, or the astronaut climbing out of his capsule in the Pacific. This contributes to the illusion of *actuality*—those people are really there, now, this is happening there, the medium is 'live'. We expect from television not only this illusion of immediacy, but a range of ordinary, real-life situations. There is a naturalistic continuity between medium and audience. We are geared up for successive glimpses of 'real' people: the Minister being interviewed, snippets of people with points of view not much more informed or thought-out than our own, the quick comment from the 'man in the street', groupings around what one television critic described as 'some "occasional" table that never knew an occasion in its life', panels of teenagers asking questions on *Sunday Break*, or tapping their feet in *Juke Box Jury* or screwing up their faces in an agony of concentration in *University Challenge*, 'young married' couples being jollied through 'Beat the Clock' on *Sunday Night at the London Palladium*, housewives aiming at the big bonanza on *Abracadabra* or playing a panel game on *What's My Line*, a workman caught unawares in *Candid Camera*. . . . If we take all these occasions together, it is true that, for a significant proportion of television time, the faces of ordinary people and real-life situations dominate the screen.

The same thing is true, to a lesser degree, of the popular press. Here we have in mind not simply the habit of treating events and items of news by way of a discussion of the personalities involved —the 'men behind the news'—though both television and the press do a great deal of this. There is also the continuous presentation of brief items which are simply stuff and stories drawn from the margin of other people's lives—'human interest stories'. Lowenthal calls this 'a kind of mass gossip' (*Literature, Popular Culture and Society*)—a gossip not confined to the gossip-column, but covering, in a highly selective way, situations which the producer of the paper or the journalist takes to be representative of the lives of his readers. A glance at the pages of the *Mirror*, the *Sketch*, the *People* or the *News of the World* will confirm the trend. This is what was implied in the advertising slogan adopted by the *News of the World*: 'All human life is there'.

This trend raises certain crucial questions about the processes of 'mass communication' and the relationship between the media and their audiences. It is in terms of this relationship that we can best understand why these media try so hard to build up a 'friendly' atmosphere and to secure an intimacy with readers and audiences. We can also understand why the providers claim, on the basis of this intimacy, that these are 'democratic' media—they 'present the people to the people'—although the more we examine this claim, the more it falsifies what the relationship actually is between a provided communication and a receptive but relatively inactive set of publics.

The relationship between communicator and audience has changed as the systems of national communication have developed and become more concentrated. It might be useful to contrast here the type of relationship common to this period with three writer-audience relationships which were significantly different. Some local newspapers were—and are—deeply embedded in a network of local life and interests. While carrying news of the 'outside world', the heart of the paper was bound up with the local community. Often these ties transcended the paper's loyalty to sectional opinion within the town or locality. There was a genuine reflection, if somewhat selective, of the variety of interests, events and experiences of a community bound, primarily, by place or *locality*. The weakness of such papers was often that they were too provincial, and that the prevailing tone of the editorial writing did, more often than not, bear heavily against anyone who deviated from the accepted norms of the community. Nevertheless, the relationship between the paper and its audience was not a fabricated one. (An interesting documentary film was made about such a paper—*Wakefield Express* by Lindsay Anderson.)

A quite different relationship existed between journalist and publisher and readership in the radical press of the late eighteenth and the first half of the nineteenth century. This heroic struggle to create and maintain a press independent of the commercial organs —a story which stretches from Wilkes's *North Briton* and Cobbett's *Political Register* to the Chartist *Northern Star*, and which is central to the whole history of the British press—was built around a quite different principle. This was a journalism 'of the people' as well as 'for' them. Journalists and publishers like Cobbett, Hetherington, Carlile, Wooler, Hone and O'Connor were united with their readership through a common political cause. The 'Great Unstamped' press which grew out of the radical agitation depended not on local ties or even upon its 'felt sense for the texture of life in the group' but on its expression of the discontents, the struggles and the aspirations of the people. Press and public were held together by the form of a common agitation, by a political tradition, by shared *opinions*, a policy, an *interest*. The readers formed something of an organized reading public, part of a conscious, dissenting, radical culture.

Given this quite different organizing principle, we can see how radical journalists developed a distinctive tone towards their audience. In an excellent study of Cobbett in 'Radical Culture' in *The Making of the English Working Class*, E. P. Thompson comments on this 'tone' in relation to passages from the *Political Register*:

Cobbett's relationship to his audience in such passages as this . . . is so palpable that one might reach out one's hand and touch it. It is an argument. There is a proposition. Cobbett writes 'metaphysical', looks up at his audience and wonders whether the word communicates. He explains the relevance of the term. He repeats his explanation in the plainest language. He repeats it again, but this time he enlarges the definition to carry wider social and political implications Then, ·these short sentences finished with, he commences exposition once more. In the word 'Now' we feel is implied: 'if all of you have taken my point, let us proceed together . . .'
. . . Cobbett, for thirty years, talked to his audience like this, until men were talking and arguing like Cobbett all over the land. He assumed, as a matter scarcely in need of demonstration, that every citizen whatsoever had the power of reason, and that it was by argument addressed to the common understanding that matters should be settled.

(The passage commented on is from
The Political Register, 27 January 1820)

Yet another relationship of writer-to-audience is discussed by Richard Hoggart in his description of the older-styled weekly working-class papers (in the *Peg's Paper* tradition) in his chapter on 'The "Real" World of People' in *The Uses of Literacy*. Hoggart singles out as the main element in these papers their 'overriding interest in the close detail of the human condition', their 'assumption that ordinary life is intrinsically interesting'. This is the passage in which he comments on the 'felt sense of the texture of life in the group they cater for' which we quoted earlier. These papers were not local papers, embedded in the life of a community. Nor were they speaking, as the radical journalists did, to articulate values and demands in their readership. They were nationally produced in the commercial market for a national working-class public. Yet, again, the relationship between paper and readership seems to have been a close and authentic one—Hoggart sees the link here as running through attitudes within the culture of the audience: he relates the paper's 'interest in the close detail of the human condition' with the characteristic sense for the 'personal, the immediate and the concrete' in much of working-class culture.

In each of these examples, we have to judge the relationship between writer, medium and audience in terms of its *tone*. Tone is manner and matter moving together: it is the stance or attitude of the writer in relation to his audience, his *mode of address*. It tells us what assumptions lie behind the communication—what assumptions the writer is making about his audience. It also embodies, as a concrete nuance or inflection in the communication made, the writer's ideal relationship with his public—how he himself would like to be told, if he were in his audience's place. Tone tells us whether he is distant or close, patronizing, hectoring, flattering or offensive. It shows us what the character of the communication is —whether it is dominative, persuasive or democratic. As E. P. Thompson said of Cobbett:

It is a matter of tone; and yet, in tone, will be found at least one half of Cobbett's political meaning. . . . It is not difficult to show that Cobbett had some very stupid and contradictory ideas, and sometimes

bludgeoned his readers with specious arguments. But such demonstrations are beside the point unless the profound, the truly profound, democratic influence of Cobbett's attitude to his audience is understood.
Making of the English Working Class

We have seen why, in media which are directed to a wide public and dependent on large audiences, the pressure to 'connect' with the audience, to establish a 'family-feeling', to build a community of interests, is exceedingly strong. The more organized the modern systems of communication become and the more communication is defined in terms of transmission alone, the more the relationship between communicator and audience narrows down into the single, unsatisfactory relationship of the uncertain speaker trying to penetrate the mind of the unknown listener—the formula based on the 'mass audience'. We say 'uncertain' because, in the absence of much organized come-back from the audience, the modern communicator seems often incapable of believing that 'active reception and a living response' are there, and lacks any inner sense or standards for judging the tone and attitude of his own communication, short of consulting external sources such as readership figures or the TAM rating. Of course, the loss of variety in communication and in the available means has hastened the process. To take only the three examples which we have already discussed, weeklies like *Peg's Paper* have been absorbed and then gradually given way to the glossier metropolitan magazine substitutes; the local and provincial press is losing its distinctive local voice, and is subject to take-over by the syndicated chain or absorption by the national commercial publishing giants; after the success of Chartist journalism, the independent dissenting press of the radical agitation fell back in relation to the established commercial press of the middle classes, and, later, the penny daily and the tabloid produced in London on the great presses. In each case several publics and several types of communication have been forced within the national and commercial systems:

This is the recurring tendency in the history of journalism: the absorption of material formerly communicated in widely varying ways

into one cheaply-produced and easily-distributed general-purpose sheet. The economics of the newspaper business had, from the beginning, set this course, and it is clear how appropriate these factors of concentration and cheapness were, in a continually expanding culture.
Raymond Williams, *The Long Revolution*

Of course (the point of view is central to the thesis of this whole study) the variety of tones and of relationships between speakers or writers and their audiences did not represent simply forms of communication: they were also forms of social life, part of the complex cultural fabric of any period. These forms and their respective tones of voice did not disappear with the expansion of the more organized national communication-systems. They were absorbed, but they then reappeared *within* the national systems themselves. Even today, when media communication appears so one-way, the variety of tones of address struggle and conflict with one another within the media—radicalism and dissent versus the accents of established opinion in the press, information versus the siren voices of persuasion in advertising, the democratic versus the contrived-egalitarian approach in television. The struggle for quality in the media, and for the democratic uses of communication, is directly related to this conflict, and at many points in this book we have been concerned to show precisely how, within the so-called 'mass media', this contention is being fought through.

In this chapter we are particularly concerned with the attempt of the modern media to discover a genuine relationship, or to fabricate a phoney relationship, with the 'people'. We shall examine a variety of such tones as they appear in the press, television and naturalistic drama:

Public taste is forever changing, and the secret of the *Mirror* in cartoons as well as in other editorial activities is that it marches 'Forward with the people'. No newspaper can succeed without men in charge who *instinctively know* what is right, who can assess the temper of public opinion without moving from their desks. Fleet Street calls it FLAIR.
Hugh Cudlipp, *Publish and Be Damned*

If we use circulation as a rough guide, the *Mirror* and the *Express* are the two most popular daily papers. The *Mirror* has held the circulation lead among the dailies for some time—it claims the highest circulation in the world (not counting *Pravda*)—but the *Express* is also on a confident rising curve. Yet these two papers differ radically in the ways in which they address, or strike up a relationship with, their publics. The distinction is between the aggressive frontal journalism of the *Express* and the *Mirror*'s 'popular touch'.

One important clue is to be found in the distinctive social-class breakdown in the readership of the respective papers. If we take the readership of the *Mirror*, the *Express*, the *Telegraph* and *The Times* by social class we find the following distribution:

By 'Social Class'	AB	C1	C2	DE
	(5,580,000)	(6,570,000)	(11,692,000)	(13,783,000)
Mirror	16%	28%	44%	39%
Express	36%	36%	32%	28%
Telegraph	25%	11%	3%	2%
Times	10%	2%	1%	1%

Raymond Williams, *The Long Revolution*

This table not only reveals some startling facts about the social character of the press readership—such as, for example, 'that the leading daily paper of the rich and well-to-do is not *The Times* (which is in fact exceeded by the *Daily Mirror*) nor the *Telegraph* . . . it is the *Express*'. It also shows quite clearly that the *Mirror* is very firmly rooted in a working-class readership, whereas the *Express* has the evenest spread of all daily papers across all social groups. This strong class allegiance is clearly reflected in the *Mirror*'s journalistic style, its tone and approach, as well as its design and format. Hence it is in the pages of the *Mirror* that one finds the counterpart in journalism for Bruce Forsyth and Wilfred Pickles, for *Family Favourites* and *Coronation Street*. But how, in journalistic terms, has this popular touch been achieved?

In his first book, *Publish and Be Damned*, Hugh Cudlipp described the tabloid revolution led by Guy Bartholomew:

> One Monday morning in 1935 the readers were informed, just as they had been in 1934, 1933, 1932 and 1931, that the swans on the lower reaches of the Thames were mating. Three weeks later they picked up their *Mirror* to learn that Queen Ena of Spain had shocked the guests at a dinner at the Savoy by using a toothpick after the succulent savoury and before the dreary orations; furthermore, that an actress had found it absolute hell to dance at the Dorchester Charity Ball because of her screaming corns. Her husband, a famous actor, threatened to horsewhip the columnist.
>
> From Bath and Bournemouth came letters of protest; from Cardiff and Newcastle guffaws of delight.

The subject-matter of the new *Mirror* was unchanged—queens and duchesses, famous actors and actresses, the Savoy and the Dorchester. What had changed was the *slant*, the angle of presentation. Even today, the content of the *Mirror* is much the same—Rex North's regular reports on the 'gay goings-on of the champagne and grey-topper season' belong to exactly the same strip of territory. But the social trivia of Ascot week is made acceptable to the readership of the paper through a popular formula of presentation. The secret of the *Mirror*'s success is the skill and effectiveness with which this formula is used. It is a formula which places itself firmly in tone with the guffaws of Cardiff and Newcastle, though in content much of the paper is still Bath and Bournemouth. The recipe for identification has paid off.

We can break the *Mirror* style down into a number of elements. First of all there is the paper's abiding interest in 'life'—in human-interest stories drawn from the marginalia of human existence. Whatever else is happening in the paper, the hum of human gossip is an unmistakable sound in the background. All 'events' in the *Mirror* take place against this backdrop. No deep pre-occupation with human nature is reflected here—the technique of the 'human-interest story' is essentially fragmentary, and consistently works against depth of treatment. The style reflects its earlier antecedents—the 'tit-bit' journalism pioneered by Newnes, Northcliffe and Pearson, the magic ingredient of *Tit-Bits, Answers* and *Pearson's Weekly*. Cudlipp has described those papers as consisting of

> ... the same formula; short paragraphs, half a dozen lines instead of half a column, scraps of jumbled news and information of the 'Fancy That' variety, competitions with prizes, answers to readers' queries, coloured cover, free railway insurance.
>
> *Publish and Be Damned*

This is a style designed to mirror life's incessant surface flow. 'In the hurrying years', Cudlipp writes, 'the *Mirror* began to reach out and take up strange handfuls from the brantub of life.' The 'handfuls from the brantub of life' are still being scooped up in the *Mirror* of 1964: short paragraphs, scraps of news and stories, competitions with prizes, strip cartoons, answers to readers' letters—everything except the coloured cover and the free railway insurance. The jumbled montage of a *Mirror* page derives directly from this tradition in journalism; it is here that the paper staked out its professional interest in that area of working-class culture which Richard Hoggart described as ' "the dense and concrete life", a life whose main stress is on the intimate, the sensory, the detailed and the personal' (*The Uses of Literacy*).

To the brantub of life was added those other 'human interests' —sex and crime—which have lived in very close proximity to the 'human-interest' story in popular journalism. The third element was the typographic—a revolution in newspaper layout which the *Mirror* pioneered:

> First eye-opener was the transformation of the news pages. Sledge-hammer headlines appeared on the front page in black type one inch deep, a signal that all could see of the excitements to come. Human interest was at a premium, and that meant sex and crime.
>
> *Publish and Be Damned*

The particular style of presentation which the *Mirror* devised for its human-interest stories can best be described as a determined *intimacy* of tone. Like the music hall or the variety comedian, the *Mirror* is on christian-name terms with everyone: Princess Margaret is always 'Margaret', Lord Snowdon always 'Tony' or 'the Jones boy', President Kennedy's wife, inevitably, 'Jackie', the Soviet astronauts 'Pop and Andy', Khrushchev 'Mr K' and so on. This relentless personalization is central to the paper's technique, a method which tends to reduce all kinds of news to the level of the 'human-interest' story, and to familiarize all world figures, whatever may be their true interests, spheres of work or achievement. This has the effect of creating a peculiarly unshaded human world in the paper's pages, where the significant distinctions of kind and the differences of powers and meaning disappear. The *Mirror* often seems to report on a single, continuous, homogenized world of 'people'—BOY BITES DOG IN SCUNTHORPE here, MAN EATS SUPPER ON VENUS there. 'It was a cheeky pup of a paper', Cudlipp remarks of the *Mirror* in its formative years. 'In a popular paper we are bound to write of politics in terms of persons not of principles', he once wrote in a letter to Churchill. It is not a distinction which Cobbett, say, would have easily understood.

The art of being intimate and audacious—this is the very heart of the paper, its emotional centre. The *Mirror* relishes its own cheek more than anyone. It is irrepressibly upstart, bubbling over with life and gay impertinence.

Thus the *Mirror* reaffirmed the tenets of the 1935 Tabloid Revolution and regained the gaiety, originality and effervescence which had been dimmed or doused during the war years.

Publish and Be Damned

In the mind of the *Mirror*, this liveliness is closely related to the paper's reputation as 'provocative and controversial'. 'Controversy and the *Mirror* were inseparable. . . . That was its secret.'

A popular paper has to be more than merely interesting; it must be alarmingly provocative in every issue and abundantly confident of its own prowess and importance.

Ibid.

The *Mirror* is both. But what is it 'alarmingly provocative' *about*? It has developed the art of 'speaking-out' to a high degree. Sometimes this is simply a matter of giving rather jaunty advice to people in high places. This is designed to register with a mild shock upon its readers because of the perky familiarity with which the advice is offered, and the determined 'plain-spoken common sense' of the views contained within it. But this shock must not be confused with the taking of a really strong and unpopular editorial line. Rather, what the paper does is to make legitimate as a public utterance what every ordinary bloke is assumed to be thinking in private: the shock lies not in what is said, but in the fact that, with the weight of the *Mirror* behind it, it can be said at all. An excellent example of this calculated shock was the headline written by Cudlipp himself at the time of the Captain Townsend affair:

COME ON MARGARET, PLEASE MAKE UP YOUR MIND!

The jauntiness here lay in the direct invitation to Margaret to put the *Mirror* and the public out of their agony: but the really provocative action on that occasion would have been for the *Mirror* to voice the opinion that if Princess Margaret wanted to marry Group Captain Townsend that was her business. The shock-effect, nevertheless, was achieved: the headline became 'the centre of an acrimonious controversy', though it was 'intended to be a genial shout from the genial crowd' (Cudlipp, *At Your Peril*). The *Mirror* is much given to genial shouting from the crowd. It is skilled at expressing a conventional judgement in an unorthodox and provocative manner.

On occasion, certainly, the radicalism of the paper has passed beyond this safe point—but far less frequently than the *Mirror*'s own claims would lead us to imagine. When the *Mirror* challenged the Establishment because of its manœuvrings at the time of Edward's abdication, or when it excoriated the Chamberlain government during the 'phoney war', or attacked Eden at Suez, the paper was offering, in popular terms, real controversy and a genuine challenge. On other occasions it has come close to simply 'nagging at authority' through habit. And it is often difficult to tell whether the *Mirror* is mounting a real or a phoney controversy.

The paper's controversial reputation stems directly from its much publicized social conscience:

> It remained and still remains a popular sensational newspaper, but its sense of purpose became highly developed; it regarded itself as a paper with a mission and it was accepted as such.
>
> *Publish and Be Damned*

Before the war, 'it exposed commercial rackets, avaricious house agents, promoters of snowball schemes . . . police methods of obtaining evidence . . .' During the war, apart from its criticisms of Chamberlain, its prodding of Churchill and its preparation for the Labour victory of 1945, it identified with 'the man at the receiving end' and 'settled down to fight his fight and air his grouse'. In the late fifties, however, when it became clear to the *Mirror* 'that, for a period, party politics were not going to be a live issue . . . I devised a new technique—The Shock Issues', wrote Cudlipp. These included death on the roads, the youth service, child neglect, housing. 'The technique, always, was the *Daily Mirror* hammerblow: the arresting headline above the dynamic picture' (Cudlipp, *At Your Peril*).

Here again it is difficult to disentangle manner from matter. The *Mirror* inherited, as did so much of the popular press, some of the radical inclinations of the earlier press, albeit in an attenuated form. 'Radicalism' stands here for one strand in the tradition of popular journalism, rather than a view of society, just as 'human interest' stands for the 'titbits' style of editing a working-class paper, rather than for anything deeper by way of an abiding interest in the substance and complexities of experience in its readership. In one way, as Raymond Williams commented in a piece on the *Mirror* in the *Observer* (29/4/62):

> When the *Mirror* speaks out plain, as it sometimes does, and as it

knows as well as anyone how to do, it is genuinely articulating one of the new voices of Britain, straightforward, self-respecting, informed, ordinary.

Yet radicalism is not a matter of journalistic technique alone. It has to be measured in terms of attitudes and opinions voiced by the thorough-going quality of the attack, the depth to which the subject is probed, the point at which the probe encounters the resistance of established opinion and power, vested interest or prejudice, and the paper's performance when it is so confronted. It is a matter of the paper's social convictions. Radicalism in its weaker forms has been inherited elsewhere without making any difference at all to the overall quality of attack, and one brand of 'radicalism'—the exposure-every-issue-plus-sensational-techniques—has been a staple ingredient of the popular and Sunday press for over a century.

In many cases, the *Mirror*'s radicalism seems to be a compound of journalistic technique and popular identifications. Were Cudlipp's 'Shock Issues', for example, the result of a real desire to highlight the shoddy aspects of Britain's 'affluent society', or were they a replacement for that controversial element in the paper's tone which had been previously supplied by party politics? Or an ambivalent mixture of both?

We might take another example. Cudlipp records that when 'in desperation at dwindling sales' of the *People*, 'Grant Morden induced Hannen Swaffer to become its editor . . . Swaffer started a policy of "a crusade on every page" and Fleet Street began to sit up and take notice'. When, in 1946, Campbell moved over from the *Pictorial* (until 1963, Sunday's *Mirror*) to the *People*, 'anybody who had anything to confess confessed to Campbell of the *People*'. Cudlipp's own comment on this piece of journalistic history is that 'What the *Pictorial* did by daring, the *People* countered by exposing.' Can a distinction, then, be drawn between the *Mirror*'s claim—'alarmingly provocative in every issue'—and Swaffer's 'crusade on every page' in the *People*? Or, again, between the *Mirror*'s 'social conscience', the *Pictorial*'s 'daring' and the *People*'s 'exposing'? Are they different names for the same thing—variants of a popular formula in journalism, belonging not to the radical tradition of the early popular press, but rather to the 'exposure' reflex from which Sunday journalism has suffered since the early years of the last century?

Another clue to the essential neutrality of *Mirror* journalism can be deduced from the very existence of a paper like the *Sketch*. True, the *Sketch* has never come anywhere near the *Mirror*'s circulation. As a paper the *Mirror* has far greater skill than its parasitic rival. The *Mirror* seems to have some feel for how its readers think, whereas the *Sketch* only has a feel for how the *Mirror* feels. The *Mirror*'s 'independent left-ism' has always been related to something larger altogether, in social terms, than the working-class conservatism of the *Sketch*. Yet some uneasiness must remain when the *Mirror* techniques can be parodied quite so easily, when they are being used to precisely the reverse effect, and supporting quite opposing social philosophies. When pushed, the *Sketch* can expose and be controversial right alongside its rival. Indeed the papers are often indistinguishable (at any rate until recently, when the *Sketch* modified slightly its front-page format). They often have exactly the same headlines—word for word. They seem to choose, unerringly, the same trivial human-interest story to exalt to the front page to soften the 'hard news'. Their layout, use of sensational tones of voice, hammerblow headlines, are absolutely identical. Compare, for example, the two on the day of the Pilkington Report (see page 428). This similarity is not mere coincidence. A style which is simply a style—hard-hitting and controversial as it may be—governs, to some extent, the selection of material as well as the angle of presentation. With skill and application, a paper can learn to hit hard—in any direction.

It is not only the political view and opinions of the paper which have been transformed by the typography and format. It is also social attitudes. In his chapter on 'The Last of the Taboos', in *At Your Peril*, Mr Cudlipp gives an interesting example of performance in this field—in this case from the *Pictorial* over the question of homosexuality. This is a subject about which there is a great deal of double-talk and deceitful euphemism, as well as a powerful substratum of public prejudice. A radical and controversial paper with a purpose, one imagines, is one that would set out, against the prevailing current of public opinion, to establish a more humane view of this problem among its readers, preparing the way for some such social reform as was adumbrated in the Wolfenden Report.

But the crusade which Mr Cudlipp describes is of quite a different order—one which the *Pictorial* (in the more permissive atmosphere of Sunday journalism) waged in 1952. The crusade began with a series on 'Evil Men', devoted to the 'worst aspect of the problem', which the paper judged to be 'the protection of children from the perverts'. The campaign was personalized in the shape of a certain Father Ingram, head of the London Choir School at Bexley. The campaign is described by Cudlipp as if it were a striking challenge to social conventions. It is much more likely that if the crusade had any effect at all it was to confirm prejudice, or even to mobilize such feelings and to strengthen them. And this effect was achieved partly because of the language and techniques of exposure which were so ruthlessly brought to bear on the episode. This language has spilled over into Mr Cudlipp's own narrative: the schools, he says, contain 'pockets of corruption'; Father Ingram is, of course, described as 'chubby-cheeked and dog-collared', he extends a 'soft, moist hand in welcome', sits the investigator down in the expected 'chaste Victorian drawing-room' and replies to questions in 'a lilting Irish brogue'. Every stereotype of Sunday journalism seems to be there.

This leads on to a consideration of two other aspects of the *Mirror* style common to its techniques when the formula is working at full throttle. The first is sensationalism in the presentation of news and information. There is no need to qualify this element, since the *Mirror* has always acknowledged its sensationalism with that saucy bravado which is so common in its pages. Its addiction to sensationalism as a technique was enshrined in Sylvester Bolam's famous statement: 'Sensationalism does not mean distorting the truth. It means the vivid and dramatic presentation of events so as to give them a forceful impact on the mind of the reader. It means big headlines, vigorous writing, simplification into familiar, everyday language, and the wide use of illustration by cartoon and photograph'. . . . This seems at first the classic formula for a journalistic style which is aimed at popular identification with a wide readership: impact, vigour, simplification, illustration. In fact, sensationalism is really something more—it is these elements *pushed to that limit* where they begin to distort the essential truth of what is being said. The argument should not be confused at this point by the familiar contrast between the *Mirror* and, say, *The Times*: the answer to bad popular journalism is not high-brow mandarin, but good popular journalism. Simplification, illustration, directness of approach and vigour—these are, properly, the province of a responsible popular journalism. But the element of sensationalism enters when the exaggeration is designed simply for maximum impact; for the purpose of heightened and continuous impact is not to open a dialogue between writer and reader, but simply to shock and stun, and thus overbear the reader, to close off communication by the brute weight of techniques. This kind of exaggeration is the besetting sin of popular journalism—it is really an unfair advantage taken of the reader in a dialogue which begins on unequal terms—and the *Mirror* has contributed as much as any popular paper to its refinements. Hence the restless search for a mode of presentation more exciting and vigorous than the last, even when the item reported demands to be taken more slowly, calls for thought and argument, is not 'exciting', cannot be reduced to a drawing, cartoon or diagram, or even limited to paragraphs of three sentences with words of one syllable. The *Mirror* can certainly be lively and vigorous and when it is it deserves credit. But it can also be crudely sensational, and many of its techniques properly belong to this category. The distinction is sometimes difficult to make, but it is, in the field of journalism, one of the most crucial distinctions to hold in mind. The point at which directness and true simplicity of style pass over into exaggeration and sensationalism is the point when communication ends and one-way transmission begins. It is where the formula takes over from reported experience or opinion, honestly stated. It is one thing to call a spade a spade: it is quite another thing to call a spade a bull-dozer.

The other element in the *Mirror* style is its contrived insolence —the temptation to call every spade a bloody shovel. This, too, is part of the *Mirror*'s 'popular touch'—the exaggeration of common, plain-spoken man into professional, aggressive philistine. This is the 'Gilbert Harding' end of the paper, and the master of the art is, of course, Cassandra. Cudlipp himself says that Cassandra has made a career out of 'big-scale, incessant rudeness (skilfully written)'. He is the perpetual belly-acher, the blunt-spoken individualist, the anti-intellectual iconoclast. Once again, the shock of this style of journalism lies, not so much in what is said, as in the attitude which goes behind the column (a thorough-going philistinism) and the simple fact that it is being said. Like the rest of the *Mirror* staff, Cassandra has penned some brilliantly scathing columns in his time, but he is also capable of turning on the techniques of rudeness even when he has nothing much to say. Yet it should not be thought that this is the style of this columnist alone; it belongs to the whole *Mirror* approach—it represents that distrust of ideas, intellectuals, deviant opinions, dissent and difficulties which the *Mirror* imagines its readers want to hear from their paper. It is part of the paper's attempt to devise a tone which matches its estimate of the reading public: a popularity formula, as well as a consciously held attitude.

Finally, there is the attempt of the paper not just to report the world to its readers in popular terms but to *connect* its readership with the world, to take the side of its audience. We can find the best examples of this approach in the manner in which the *Mirror* writes to its readers about royalty and the aristocratic rich. The *Mirror* has quite a reputation as a critic of royalty, but, as Mr Cudlipp freely admits in his chapter 'The Royal Revolution', in *At Your Peril*, this has been something of an 'insider's' campaign. The paper is in no sense a republican organ: rather, it has worked hard to make the monarchy *more* popular—its real complaint is that the

Royal Family have been, on occasion, out of touch with the people and the times, that 'this should be the age when kings mixed with commoners, when the paraphernalia of protocol surrounding royalty was swept aside, when pomp shaved off its whiskers and came down to the people'. To bring about this 'palace revolution' the *Mirror*, it is true, has used all its unorthodox techniques, breaking conventions of address, using the intimate headline, calling on 'Philip' and 'Margaret' to do things, criticizing unnecessary bits of pomp and circumstance, etc. But the attitudes were, basically, only too conventional. The approach raised eyebrows in Fleet Street, but it only warmed hearts at the news-stands. One can tell this by Mr Cudlipp's good-natured proposals as to how Malcolm Muggeridge, who really *did* affront public opinion on this score, and paid for it with abuse—some of it from the popular press itself—should be rewarded for his efforts: 'his elevation as a life-long peer'.

One might imagine that the *Mirror* would experience some difficulty, when reporting on the lives of the rich and the powerful, in maintaining its 'popular' tone, since the gap between the lives led by Rex North's set and the average *Mirror* reader is so wide. The paper has managed this task by a skilful mixture of genial shouting from the populace and an attitude of deference. The tone here might be described as that which the *Mirror* imagines is appropriate to the people who throng the railings of Buckingham Palace at the time of a royal event, or the onlookers at a celebrity film première. Thus the *Mirror*'s idea of an attack on the system of debutantes was to organize a rival show for its own readers. 'A hundred girls who are working for their living at typewriters, or in factories, or standing behind counters' were there: the winning deb's dress, however, was designed by the Queen's dressmaker, Norman Hartnell; and Tommy Kinsman, 'the society Deb's pet bandleader', played, and the Reverend Simon Phipps, 'Princess Margaret's friend', and Captain Ronald Bowes-Lyon, 'a cousin of the Queen Mother', and 'genial Lord (Bob) Boothby', and 'a few handful of viscountesses and ambassadors and statesmen' and 'Anthony Armstrong-Jones' were there as well. When a twenty-seven-year-old charlady beat the panel on the TV show, *What's My Line*, the *Mirror* threw a Charladies Ball at the Savoy. This is all jolly good fun, and the paper regards it as testimony to its own high spirits and egalitarianism, but it is a good deal less than the attack on social conventions and institutions which the paper's self-advertisement leads us to expect. One cannot break down the institutions of deference and social snobbery merely by recapitulating them, in a proletarian form, at the other end of society. This simply *maintains* the institutions intact, legitimizes social differences, and yet reconciles those who would not in ordinary circumstances enjoy such privileges to their continued existence.

None of this suggests that the *Mirror* tone is a simple affair. It is a skilfully organized and orchestrated one, and, within its own terms, remarkably successful. The blunt, no-nonsense, plain-speaking of Cassandra and the editorial columns is close to the heart of this formula. So is the pub-cameraderie which suffuses its presentation of society high-life, its Debs' Balls and Charladies' Dinners. So is Andy Capp, that archetypal proletarian slob, the stylized working-class drone, a humorous montage composed of cap, beer, fags, football and the occasional punch-up with the 'old lady'. So is the constructed personality who reigns over the Letters column—the Old Codgers—where a most suspicious uniformity of style is somehow achieved. Can *Mirror* readers really write letters which sound as if they are *all* veterans of question time on a Wilfred Pickles show? Into this amalgam of styles the *Mirror*'s social iconoclasm fits quite neatly. This, as we have tried to show, is less a matter of opinion or conviction than a set of egalitarian prejudices, aggressively presented. The *Mirror* is a Labour paper—though when Party fortunes were low, it was so with a good deal of heart-searching. But it is not a paper with a political view, in the sense that, though independent of the Party organization, it tries to link the policies of the Party with the aspirations of potential supporters among its readers. It is Labour by tradition rather than by belief. Its politics have largely been absorbed into its general tone and style. Something of the same is

true of its handling of the news itself; for even the news is to some
extent packaged by the paper's format. If the news is serious, a
naughty pin-up will be there close at hand to lighten the mood and
rally the troops. The assumption here is that working-class
readers don't take things too seriously—they want a bit of this and
a bit of that. The *Mirror*'s approach to the headline news is that of
the slogan, the banner or poster: if it's important, then they must
hit them over the head with it. To the rest of the news, the *Mirror*
adopts the 'spotlight' approach, picking the items out as snippets
which are then arranged—on pages often dominated by the
advertisements—as brief digests. For the rest, the paper adopts the
principle of the inspired jumble. Its format *is* its world—familiar,
bitty, popular, low-brow, jumpy, a kaleidoscope of sensational
impressions. The defence of this style by people intimately
associated with its refinement is that it simply reflects what
Mirror readers are like. But the format is much more creative than
such a defence allows. The *Mirror* takes an essentially static view
of its readership. There is very little to challenge or extend the
expectations of the reader. Readers grow into its style. They find
in its pages not only a view of what they are, but also, by implication, a view of what they should be. The paper's style creates
tomorrow's readership. That is why the *Mirror* is so utterly
convinced by itself.

Yet, in spite of its self-assurance, the world of the *Mirror* seems
a little outdated. And this ironically is just because its format is so
static and rigid. The *Mirror* clock stopped at the end of the war.
Its hey-day was the days of Churchill—for whom the paper has
feelings this side of idolatry—when *Jane* stiffened the morale of
servicemen abroad, when the paper stood, with the rest, against
Hitler's bombers, and Labour prepared the silent social revolution. Now that changes have begun to overtake British life, as a
result of those very experiences, the *Mirror* remains confident and
buoyant, but seems slightly puzzled about where the country is
going next. It has tried to bring within its ambience those highly
prized 'young readers', but does not quite belong to their world.
As Cudlipp commented with some real puzzlement, it dropped its

slogan, *Forward With the People*, 'because the people have gone forward. The problem now is how to *keep them there*.'

It is interesting to compare the tone of the *Mirror* with that of its closest rival, the *Express*. Here again we can use format and style to discover the emotional centre, the 'world' of the paper. Where the *Mirror* looks back to *Tit-Bits*, the *Express* looks forward to the picture magazines and the glossies. Its layout is far more stylish, its use of photographs streets ahead of the *Mirror*'s rather crude-quality reproductions. It is not difficult to locate the working-class elements in the *Mirror* make-up, but the essence of the *Express* is harder to place in social terms because it is not so closely identified with any one social group. The quality which comes across most strikingly is its snobbery. Whereas the Rex North column in the *Mirror* filters gossip about the rich and well-to-do through to its readers, the William Hickey column in the *Express* is about the goings-on of people, some of whom, it confidently assumes, will themselves be among its readers. This snobbery, or status-consciousness, gives the paper an *arriviste*, a *nouveau-riche*, tone. It is the paper of the social climber at any level of society. It speaks across the frontiers of class to the status instinct. As Clive Irving has written of Arthur Christiansen, one of the foremost architects of the modern *Express*:

His technique was altogether more subtle, realising not only the embryonic affluence of *Express* readers in their bijou houses on the Watford bypass, but also the need for a pop culture.

Spectator, 4 October 1963

Both papers package the news for their readers: the *Mirror* uses the spotlight and the digest, the *Express* personalizes—*Express-men* are always first on the spot, a fact which has been known to take precedence over the event being reported (a pseudo-event). The *Express* also exalted the rule of the sub-editors, who were responsible for fashioning out of a variety of reporting styles a composite *Express* prose. Irving calls this 'New Brunswick staccato'. And it is true that, whereas the *Mirror*'s politics grow naturally out of a core of feelings which are part of that slice of society which it 'mirrors', the *Express*, under Beaverbrook's direct influence, speaks out on behalf of a firmer set of idiosyncratic prejudices, an evangelizing 'Little Englandism'. This is not the politics of any particular social group, it is the voice of a certain distinctive mood in British life. The *Express* has tried hard to capitalize that mood.

Both these papers have perfected techniques for maintaining a foothold in the lives of their readers. To some extent, they do inhabit that world—they are *of* it, though they are not *all* of it. They reflect what they think they see, though they do this in their own 'mirrors'. But the differences and distinctions which make for real interest in the human world which they report, the complexities and dilemmas and aspirations which make up the individual lives of their readers—these the popular press finds it difficult to deal with, and the solution seems to be to adopt a formula which masses readers together in such a crude manner that awkward individualities of experience find little place. Hence the controlling format of the paper—format being journalistic device, composed of style, tone, design, a set of selective principles, for coming to terms with the real world. It is an orchestration of stereotypes and simplifications. When discussing the popular touch of the press, we are too inclined to take the format as a true representation of the readership, to interpret the audience from it, whereas what we should really pay attention to is the formula itself. It is a simple point, but one which is too frequently overlooked—the *Mirror* is not written by its readers, it is composed for them. To put the same point another way, a newspaper format is not a form of life: it is a mode of communication and transmission, and has to be examined in terms of the intentions of those who compose it, not of those who receive it. The point can best be illustrated by an exchange between Mr Cecil King, director of the Mirror-Pictorial and Amalgamated Press Group, and Mr Laurie Stenhouse. The argument concerned the use of the pin-up in the *Mirror*, and is reported in the National Union of Teachers' Report of a Conference on *Popular Culture and Personal Responsibility*

Stenhouse: The example I want to take is the pin-up . . . in what way
the public demand for the pin-up exerted itself before the pin-up was
introduced. A professional photographer friend of mine explained to
me that he thought pin-ups were going to be taken from the back—
they had discovered how to get more salacious content from that angle.
Pin-ups are going to turn round—and they did. It does not seem to me
that this is a response to public demand. I doubt whether it is a creative
feeling. I am being naive about this, and I would like to ask how this
demand exerts itself?

Cecil King: An inspired editor knows what his public wants. An un-
inspired editor sends out little people to enquire of their readers what
they would like most. I think that is true of the editors in history and
other producers of popular entertainment, which popular journalism is.
They just know.

So far we have been examining the demotic tendencies of mass
communication in terms of the popular press. But the techniques
of intimacy, mateyness, the family atmosphere and the popular
touch are just as common in the field of television. Indeed, this is
one of the most powerful claims which Independent Television
levelled against the BBC in the days before Pilkington and the
post-Pilkington revolution within the Corporation—the claim
that the commercial companies had a greater rapport with 'the
people' and spoke in their genuine accents. We can find this as a
constant theme in publicity for commercial television, such as the
following item from the *TV Times* which was designed to draw
the audience into the 'family of the small screen':

We like to feel that the *TV Times* is part of the family—*your* family.
Overall, *TV Times* is read by more than 13,500,000 people every week.
This is the latest figure given in a national survey by the Institute of
Practitioners in Advertising.

It is indeed proof that *TV Times* is more than a programme journal—
it is a friend in the house for the *whole* family.

TV Times, June 1962

There are many examples of the way in which this glad-handed intimacy of the studio can be exploited or devalued. In an article on television in *Twentieth Century* (November 1959) Marghanita Laski wrote about the artificial atmosphere of intimacy which tends to dominate television:

> The question of friendship and of what constitutes a friend is something that being a TV personality forces one to examine. I would not accept any definition of a friend that would not include the concept of a personal relationship in which affection annihilated all considerations of status and prestige. In the TV-personality-world, friendship stands for something quite different. In the first place, all the trappings of friendship—first-names, expressions of affection, embraces, hospitality —are exchanged as a matter of course between two people whose relationship to each other is solely that of business acquaintances. Secondly, efforts are deliberately made to create illusions of surrogate friendship between TV personalities and the viewing public, and it is far from unusual to meet TV personalities who say that they look on the public as their friends or to meet members of the public who behave as if friendship between themselves and the TV personality was mutual and established.

In the permissive atmosphere of television, this approach has been projected into the medium itself, and can be identified in certain styles of interviewing and compèring popular shows and programmes. In the area of light entertainment, for example, where television reaches its audience at widest stretch, two styles at least can be distinguished. On the one hand, there is the persuasive charm of the record men and disc jockeys, groomed specially for the younger viewers, and distinguished by a certain cool and sophisticated detachment. A master of this tone is David Jacobs, presiding over a difficult session of *Juke Box Jury*. He has to maintain an atmosphere of buoyancy and optimism on the programme, the 'hit' mood rather than the 'miss': yet he cannot control what the panel are going to say about a record, except by way of an indirect command over the whole mood. He is wholly identified with his audience, and yet he must be prepared for the (unlikely) possibility that the week's crop of pop records will all be turned down by the panel. The programme is immensely confused in its intentions, since the panel of judges is inclined to make comments on the record's quality, whereas the main purpose is to predict its commercial success: Jacobs frequently has to steer them back to their proper function. He manages throughout all this to generate a studiously relaxed air of familiarity and ease, even on the not infrequent occasions when the singer whose record has just been turned down emerges in the flesh as that week's guest artist. It is an object-lesson in the art of television intimacy.

On the other hand, there is the approach to light entertainment which is derived from a style previously established in the music hall and the variety shows. The apogee of television 'show business' is *Sunday Night at the London Palladium*, and the master of this style is the show's most successful compère, Bruce Forsyth. Forsyth is more adapted to television than *Sunday Night*'s original, Tommy Trinder, though he is less wholly absorbed in the medium than his successor, Norman Vaughan. Indeed, through these three and the evolution of the *Sunday Night at the London Palladium* style we can follow the process by which Val Parnell has transformed his stable of variety artists from the declining medium of the music hall to the boom market of weekend light-entertainment television (ATV). Forsyth is the master of nudge-and-wink television: a sophisticated version of the guess-what-happened-on-the-way-to-the-music-hall comedian. He uses the slightly 'blue' approach of the 'entertainer'. He is quick at repartee, like the pub comic, and endlessly cheery. He drops into Cockney asides without hesitation—almost as fast as another past-master of this mode, Pickles, could broaden out into a fruity Yorkshire with his working-class 'mums'. His catch-phrase, 'I'm in charge', caught on overnight—an assertive 'proletarian' expression—to be quickly imitated by Norman Vaughan, with 'swinging' and 'dodgy'. Forsyth sentimentalizes and flatters his audience. He is at his best when he feels the pulse of his public by way of a perpetual flow of chatter, advice and assistance to the competitors in the 'Beat the Clock' game on the programme. At one moment he can be cheekily familiar: at another he seems surprised to find himself at the centre of the biggest spotlight in the business. His success lies almost entirely in his ability to project a mood of mateyness to his audience. Like the *Mirror*, he seems never to have been on anything but christian-name terms with them.

Sunday Night at the London Palladium and *Juke Box Jury* are relatively crude attempts in television to maintain the popular tone. A much subtler and more complex approach is offered in *Tonight*, particularly earlier phases of the programme with the renowned team of Michelmore, Whicker, Hart, Robertson and Allsop under the editorship of Alasdair Milne. Both Baverstock, *Tonight*'s creator, and Milne were highly conscious of the programme's wide appeal, and of the need to devise a format which would enable them to maintain this breadth. The approach was described by Milne himself in a passage quoted by Derek Hill in his article in *Contrast*:

> ... I would say that entertainment is to *Tonight* what discipline is to the schoolmaster. No matter how fascinating the subject the instructor is trying to put across, he must have discipline in the classroom before he can hope to achieve results. With us it's much the same thing. Unless you entertain the audience sufficiently you can't begin to inform them.
>
> Autumn 1961

This accounts for the consistency of tone in the programme. Length of items, balance of serious and trivial subjects, may vary, but the *Tonight* tone, based on the 'discipline of entertainment' as the team interprets this, is always maintained. With very few exceptions, *Tonight* is resolutely light-hearted. This makes the programme a good hardy perennial of television journalism, which perhaps a daily programme with a viewing audience of rarely less than seven million needs to be. But it has the disadvantage of robbing the programme of any variety in the weighting of items, tends to reduce all the subjects which it treats, whether serious or ephemeral, to the level of the magazine digest—all the more regrettable since it is clearly well within the capability of the

Tonight team to provide something more demanding, while still retaining an overall consistency. Many of *Tonight*'s items deal with serious subjects which cannot be reduced, without distortion, to the entertainment, throw-away formula: the programme would be more compelling to watch if the formula were more adaptive to the range of subjects covered.

In fact, the 'entertainment' quality of the programme depends not so much upon what is intrinsic to the subject as upon the manner in which it is handled. And the most important element in this style is what Milne called the 'shared attitude to life' among the team, and the balance between the informal and relaxed Michelmore and the professional attack of his roving commentators. 'The first essential in any *Tonight* reporter', Derek Hill observed, 'seems to be . . . a total conviction that he represents the absolute norm.' The programme itself identifies with its audience. Within this identification, the functions are skilfully balanced. On the one side there is Michelmore, 'amiable foil, professional moron', everybody's *homme moyen sensuel*:

His function is to be beautifully surprised at what the clever lads have brought back to the studio. 'Fancy that,' says his slightly rueful smile. 'It's a rum world, eh? Whatever next?' The trick is that Michelmore is the puzzled, uninformed plain man with no contacts. He doesn't understand the songs (who does?). He's on our side, in fact, he's one of us.

Peter Lewis, 'The Tempo And The Place',
Contrast, Spring 1962

On the other side are the expert probers, the team:

Whicker, aggressive but amused; Robertson gruff and canny; Hart, charming but persistent; Allsop, alert and hawklike. All cool shrewd boys. Life doesn't put one over on them.

ibid.

The programme develops a dialogue between these two centres of interest. This suggests that the *Tonight* format, like that of the popular press, is simply a contrived affair. And this would be to miss the really relaxed expertise of Michelmore, confident before the cameras, unperturbed by temporary breakdowns in transmission, or the professional bite of the reporters. On the other hand, there is a certain open-ended neutrality in the programme's form as a whole which is left intact despite the hard-boiled, tough-minded aggressiveness of some of the interviews, or by the pervasive irony into which the team too often relaxes. In the context of what Derek Hill calls the programme's 'easy popularity', *Tonight* has settled too easily for a popular formula.

One example of the weaknesses of the *Tonight* approach, which also provides us with an opportunity to look more closely at that favourite technique of television reporting, the interviews with a cross-section of the public, can be found in the extract, *Vox Pop*, from an early *Tonight*. In this item Alan Whicker interviewed a number of people about Parliament: he was trying to discover how closely people follow Parliamentary affairs. Among those interviewed were two teenage girls who didn't know the name of the Prime Minister, a business man who claimed to follow Parliament closely, but who couldn't name the last important Bill passed there, an elderly man interested in the reform of the currency and the calendar, and a building labourer who said that all MPs were 'layabouts'.

The item tells us practically nothing about the state of public opinion on political affairs. The sample is too small, too random, the situation is unreal—Whicker popped the question to people in their lunch-hour in a park. Clearly we are not intended to take it too seriously, for the detached irony with which Whicker handles his subjects is dominant throughout. This is one of *Tonight*'s throw-away items. Yet the approach is not consistent. Immediately after the currency reformer has been interviewed by Whicker (who obviously regarded him as a screwball, a curio), this attitude is underlined by a quick cut of the cameras away to a gaggle of ducks swimming about in a pond. A slick piece of editing, but it confuses both the tone (generally good-natured and relaxed) and the conventions (a fast piece of editorial comment thrust into an occasional documentary item). It looks a little like taking advantage of the man interviewed, and the smartness of the editing strengthens this impression. We have the feeling that Whicker or the *Tonight* editors can take this liberty only because of their supreme assumption that they represent the norm of public opinion, whereas the crank is a deviant who does not need to be taken seriously. On another occasion, we see the interviewing techniques of the team used in inappropriate circumstances. The business man who claims to follow Parliament in *The Times* is decidedly embarrassed when he is caught out. The camera, however, holds relentlessly to his face; Whicker ignores his plea for help, and leaves him to flounder. This is the manner of the pursuer or interrogator—a Robin Day, for example—who is smoking out the skilful ambiguities in a political statement by a practised public figure. It isn't at all the technique to be used on a rather innocent, if pretentious, man stopped in his lunch-hour by the camera crew in St James's Park. It is a thoughtless capitulation to production values and to techniques, a rather slack absence of discrimination in the matching of manner to subject.

There is, therefore, a lack of definition in our response to the item. How are we meant to take it? If it is of 'magazine' interest only, should the techniques of interviewing and presentation be so sharp? If the subject is of real significance, should the shape be so casual? If Whicker is simply reporting, isn't the commentary too direct? If he is editorializing, then this should be justified by a more open comment, somewhere in the programme, of the significant gap between the importance of politics and the lack of interest in the general public. The objection here is *not* to the fact that Whicker's personal view has intruded: the problem with television journalism is not that it is biassed and personal, but that it is not personally committed enough. The objection is to the rather confused blend of commitment and nonchalance which *Tonight* so frequently achieves. Is the programme concerned with an issue of public importance, or is this a rather indulgent attempt to show people in a somewhat ridiculous light? The problem with television journalism like *Tonight* is that it does not put these questions seriously enough to itself: it often seems to be satisfied with putting itself on the side of 'the common viewer' who, we are slowly coming to recognize, doesn't exist. For a programme which holds so crucial a section of the viewing public in television, the discipline of entertainment is not enough.

Against the 'vox pop' habits of television journalism, one needs to set a series of programmes, still within the documentary genre, which makes use of the lives and comments of ordinary people without falsifying the producer's relationship with his audience or sacrificing the authenticity of his material. The short television documentaries of Denis Mitchell reject the easy identification with a popular audience for the sake of something else—a more fundamental respect for ordinary life. Here is an interesting example of a man who has been able to grow within the limits of a popular medium with his own special art. Against the frenzied pace of television production, Denis Mitchell has been content with a slender body of work. He has picked up, in television, a tradition of previous work in the documentary film, though the influence of such masters as Jennings and Grierson, of whom his work reminds us, seems almost unconscious. What is even more interesting, Mitchell's art begins where a good deal of television journalism and documentary also began—with the short interview and the occasional 'vox pop' of the local news and sports programmes on radio. Mitchell, like the teams of more high-powered reporters, began by taking tape recorders to the spot. But where journalistic instincts have pushed television more and more towards moulding such interviews into an already established format, Mitchell allowed the rhythms of speech and experience to dictate their own form. His edited tapes in his radio feature, *People Talking*, Philip Purser observed in his *Contrast* article (Winter 1961), 'lent a flavour and spontaneity to the spoken word undreamed of by Lord Reith'.

It is this respect for the discovered complexities of experience, this fidelity to actuality as it unfolds, which distinguishes Mitchell's work in television. His programme about young people in

Britain, *On The Threshold*, is still the most authentic treatment of this theme in television, in spite of the exaggerated publicity which the subject has received since it was made (1955). The same combined use of wild-track voices with counterpointing visual images was used in his feature on prison life and his recreation of the life of Mac the Busker, *In Prison* and *A Soho Story*. The marriage of sound and image realized in the accomplished style of his two impressionistic pieces, *Night in the City* and *Morning in the Streets*. One is more aware in these two of the skilful balance which Mitchell has maintained between actuality and composition. The material speaks for itself, and Mitchell never dominates it or forces it out of its natural shape. Yet the natural line is strengthened by the editing, by the counterpointing, by the organization of the material which makes its own comment on the themes. *Morning in the Streets* 'took a hard look at the precarious good times of the fifties and weighed them against the backlog of two world wars, depression and unemployment'. This was the context and these the comparisons in depth which Mitchell discovered in his material. But one is aware of something else—Mitchell's own deep human commitment to the voices and faces he uses, his care for other people's experiences, the patience and tact of his observation. These are not 'production values' imposed upon the material—Mitchell almost never uses the direct commentary: they are human values embedded in the techniques, in the communication itself. In his later work—the brilliant evocations of American civilization, *Chicago*, *Ed and Frank*, *Grass Roots*—and in his immensely striking series about Africa—*The Wind of Change*—we see Mitchell beginning to compose and create more directly, to shape and to impress connections upon his material, with greater freedom. But even here, where the strict terms of documentary begin to fall away before a kind of art which is closer to poetic naturalism, we have the impression of a man *discovering* in the rhythms of ordinary life and speech the 'organic form' of his work.

But Mitchell is no longer working for the BBC, nor indeed has any significant movement of 'poetic' documentary grown out of his work. The film-makers still employed by the Corporation seem

TWO VIEWS OF TEENAGE DANCE, *see Chapter 1, page 32. A scene from Karel Reisz's* We Are the Lambeth Boys *and a scene from Basil Dearden's* Violent Playground.

1

2 & 3

A SEQUENCE FROM ANDREJ WAJDA'S *A Generation, see Chapter 1, page 42.
The final image above (page 44)*

SUNDAY MORNING IN TOMBSTONE CITY, *see Chapter 4, page 108. A sequence from* My Darling Clementine, *directed by John Ford*

4

John Wayne Rio Bravo

Gregory Peck The Gunfighter
Henry Fonda Warlock
James Stewart Winchester 73

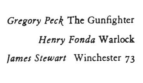

Sink the Bismarck

IMAGES OF WAR, *Chapter 5*

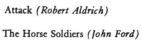

Attack *(Robert Aldrich)*

The Horse Soldiers *(John Ford)*

6

ADMOVIES. Lover Come Back—*A scene from the movie starring Rock Hudson and Doris Day (top) and* Funny Face, *starring Fred Astaire and Audrey Hepburn*

Virgin—*Mary Pickford*   Vamp—*Theda Bara*

Goddess—*Greta Garbo*   Go-getter—*Jean Harlow*

Buddy—*Betty Grable*   Innocent—*Marilyn Monroe*

THE STARS, *see Chapter 8, page 211*

8

The Girl Rosemarie

Love Now—Pay Later

TWO VERSIONS OF THE SAME STORY, *see Chapter 8, page 214*

10

Love Me Tender

G. I. Blues

CLEANING UP THE IMAGE—*Elvis Presley,*
see Chapter 10, page 287

MARLENE DIETRICH *in a scene from*
The Blue Angel *(page 197)*

11

VINCENTE MINNELLI'S Lust for Life, *see Portrait of the Artist, page 423*

12

13 SOURCES OF A STYLE, *see Chapter 10, page 276. Adam Faith (top, left)*

Take
a girl
like
YOU...

in BRI*
NYLON

WHY
BRI*
NYLON?

IT'S BRI BEFORE NYLON—
FOR RIGHT NYLON . RIGHTLY USED . RIGHT IN FASHION

ONE PRODUCT: TWO APPEALS,
see Chapter 11, page 315

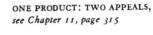

14

How Long

SINCE

THIS

HAPPENED

TO

You

?

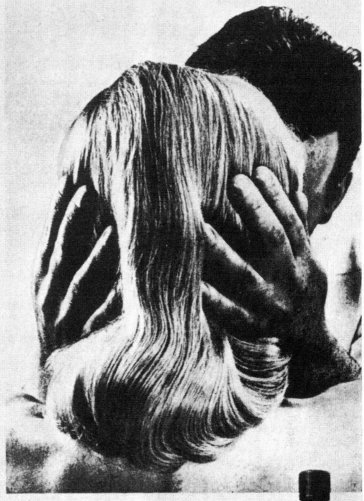

Too long? Then look to your hair. Does it invite his touch? It will when you use Vaseline*Brand Liquid Shampoo! At once your hair takes on new interest. Becomes lustrous. Soft. Exciting. Adorable. Vaseline Liquid Shampoo is good for hair, leaves it so easy to set and style. Let Vaseline Liquid Shampoo do fascinating things for your hair. Then your hair will do things for you!

Everyone knows the high standard of purity and quality represented by the famous trade mark VASELINE. Care for your hair with the shampoo that maintains hair health and gives irresistible glamour.

FOR THE LOOK THAT GOES STRAIGHT TO HIS HEART!

*REGD. TRADE MARK   BOTTLES 3 3 & 1 6. SACHETS 7d.

15

ANALYSIS *see Chapter 11, page 322*

"resists creasing, travels well"

Madonna of the Rocks

a touch of sadism?

from advertiser to manufacturer

FANTASIES OF SALESMANSHIP, *see Chapter 11, page 329*

16

pretty well confined to producing mere illustrations for TV reporting. Unhappily this does not appear to be an accident, but part of a plan. The 'New Men' who have emerged at the BBC to do battle with commercial TV are dominated by the limited approach of *Tonight*. The trend is to journalism, to the hard-hitting, down-to-earth didactic approach. Anything that deals with its subject more obliquely, or attempts to explore it in poetic terms, is suspect. The same thinking seems to have infected sound radio, and the Radio Ballads team of Charles Parker, Ewan MacColl and Peggy Seeger has been disbanded.

Apart from the Goons at a quite different level, and one or two isolated experiments, the Radio Ballads represented the only truly imaginative attempt to use sound broadcasting creatively. Radio, of course, has given us many worthwhile things, particularly in the sphere of serious music, but it is important to distinguish here between the use of the medium merely as a means of reproducing already existing work and its development as a distinctive art form in its own right. The achievement of the Radio Ballads group was, in fact, to create a new art form out of the tape recorder.

The first programme, *The Ballad of John Axon*, was broadcast on the Home Service in the summer of 1958. Axon was an engine driver who was killed in a goods train crash in 1957. The programme used field recordings of Axon's family and workmates, the sounds of work, industrial folk songs of the railway, some original songs in this traditional mode and jazz improvisation. No commentary was used. This basic method has since been applied to civil engineering workers, herring fishermen, miners, polio sufferers, teenagers and boxers.

The core of the method is the relating of actuality material to song, and indeed the old name for these programmes was the more apt one—*Actuality Ballads*. The field recordings are edited down from about eighty minutes to about twenty-five, being woven in with the music and song. It would be wrong to think of this as a compilation job—the whole material is creatively worked, seeking an organic rather than mechanical relationship. The aim is to give dramatic form to a whole way of life. It should be clear that this is quite different from what we have come to think of as 'documentary'. It is not a report on an experience but an imaginative re-creation of it. Nor should anyone who has not heard these programmes imagine that they are in any way folksy—bank clerks in bells seeking Merrie England. Most of the ballads have been about work and the folk elements are there to put us all in touch with a real and rich tradition in the same way that the field recordings, which are nearly always in the vernacular, put us in touch once again with the poetry of the oral tradition which has been submerged in the age of print, but which Charles Parker in particular believes can be made to live again through radio. The ballads are therefore about the way we live now and attempt to give this life the quality of epic. 'To make,' as John Grierson once said, 'the everyday significant.' Just because these programmes are so unique to radio, it is almost impossible to convey in print what they are really like. The following quotations merely hint at some of their qualities. The first is from a herring fisherman in *Singing the Fishing*:

There's no feeling like coming into harbour with a good catch of fish. There's no feeling like it, especially if you're in a boat like we used to be, with a good crew. . . . You'd come up to the quay, tie up; now there's everyone come you see. . . . Hundred cran!! cor, lovely shot! Get your sample out, let's be selling 'em see, and you, you just lean back in the wheelhouse and you look. All I can think of is you know if you was one of the old hunters in the old tribal days. Now you's brought home . . . the meat! You see share it out, do what you like with it you see. I've done my bit! . . .

Then an Irish tractor-driver in *Song of a Road*, a programme about the building of the M1:

I still prefer the muck and the dirt and the grease and everything to being inside in a factory, ah I don't think I could work in a factory— No, I like the rough and go, y'know, plenty of rough and go. Dig it! dig like blazes . . . get into the machine and go like hell and get the job done ye know!

The Radio Ballads team was broken up, as a previous and some-what similar BBC TV experimental team, the Langham Group, was, because it was troublesome. The team took too long to produce its programmes and was too expensive. Thus one of the few attempts to make a genuine popular art out of new media was abandoned. The work of Denis Mitchell and the Radio Ballads team occupies the borderland between documentary and drama. The naturalistic documentary drama of television is, of course, written and acted, but its connections with everyday life, with 'actuality', are very close and it is this which provides the main interest of a series like *Coronation Street*. It is the selection of one area of everyday experience, and the treatment of the stories and episodes in a naturalistic manner, which make these, in tele-vision terms, 'popular' drama.

Within the naturalistic convention, good work *has* been done, especially by playwrights such as Paddy Chayefsky, who, in the Preface to his *Television Plays*, offered a kind of Apologia for plays of this type:

In television you can dig into the most humble, ordinary relation-ships: the relationships of bourgeois children to their mother, of middle-class husband to wife, of white-collar father to his secretary—in short, the relationships of the people.

The Granada series *Coronation Street* has claims to be just such a dramatic genre. It is based on characters living in a working-class neighbourhood in the north of England. It began as a local serial without stars, but achieved such remarkable popularity that it has become a national programme, and virtually created its own stars.

Violet Carson, who plays Ena Sharples, the best-known character in *Coronation Street*, described Ena in these terms:

Of course she's a bit Dickensian in the play, a bit larger than life, but she's very true to that kind of woman. In the old days there was always a local busybody—a bossy, managing woman to whom everyone turned in time of trouble, like the rock of ages.

Contrast, No. 4, Summer 1962

The style of the programme, then, depends upon verisimilitude. The emphasis within the programme is on character and on the naturalness of the playing. In contrast to many other plays and serials of a similar type, *Coronation Street* tries to extend this naturalism into the reflection of a way of life, and the qualities of humour, honesty and grit associated with working-class life are presented sympathetically. From this point of view, it is far more ambitious than its BBC counterpart, *Compact*, which is simply a televised women's magazine story set (just to confirm the association) in the office of a women's magazine.

The real weakness of *Coronation Street*—as with a good deal of drama in this style—is that, by concentrating so much on capturing the surface accuracy of life, it remains, essentially, a drama of surfaces. As Mitchell's documentaries suggest, plays which simply mirror life accurately will inevitably lack that inner reality, that level of meaning and complexity, which lies *behind* the external appearances, and which constitutes the real drama of life. The achievement of Mitchell is that he is willing to wait and to observe until the meaning of that inner experience begins to register through the spoken words and speech rhythms. And he is willing to select from his material and to compose in a creative sense so that this inner reality emerges. It is only his self-effacing technique which allows such moments of genuine human revelation to 'emerge', as if naturally, from the flow of life. It is his eye and ear for the telling or significant detail which in *Chicago* enables him to select, from his wild-track, precisely the phrase of dialogue which sums up the whole point of the film:

Well I would like my children to live in a world where if I had shortcomings and I couldn't quite keep up the world would come and take me by the hand and say, 'All right, you're going to slow us up a little bit but you've got to come along too, you're a human being, you're a human being.

quoted by Philip Purser, 'Think Tape',
Contrast, Winter 1961

Dialogue in *Coronation Street*, however, is very rarely able to suggest this kind of complexity. It is closer to the description which Chayefsky offers in his Preface:

> I tried to write the dialogue as if it had been wire-taped. I tried to envision the scenes as if a camera had been focussed upon the unsuspecting characters and had caught them in an untouched moment of life. The sort of meticulous literalness is something that can be done in no other medium.
>
> *Television Plays*

This is a method of observation, it is not a method of dramatic creation; and Denis Mitchell's work suggests that even in the strictly documentary field, such 'meticulous literalness' by itself is not enough. Often, then, in *Coronation Street*, the writers have an acute ear highly tuned to the qualities of everyday speech. Yet, time and again, phrases and comments which would have a kind of representative truth about them in a documentary seem, in the mouths of the *Coronation Street* actors, stilted aphorisms. Their very surface accuracy makes them unreal. For what is really convincing in a play is not the rightness of speech to life outside the play, but the rightness of the speech in relation to character and situation presented. It is this level of realism which *Coronation Street* lacks.

Coronation Street lacks conviction on another level—one which is closely related to the very reasons why plays in such a naturalistic mode are generally popular. *Coronation Street* episodes stand out from the general run of drama in that they depend upon the pleasure which the audience experiences as a result of recognizing something true and familiar in their own lives. The contrast here is with *Compact*, where the interest—such as it is—lies in the wish-fulfilment of becoming absorbed in something which is wholly alien from popular experience. Nevertheless, it is possible within the framework of *Coronation Street* to offer escapist qualities of a different kind. The characters of the Street are rooted in life and recognizable, but they are a little exaggerated, a little stereotyped, and they lead cosier and less complicated lives than people in real life. What Mitchell does is to suggest the complexity within an apparently simple and inarticulate character, as in *Ed and Frank*.

In *Coronation Street* this complexity is deliberately evaded as not being 'true to life'. But the constant parade before us of a series of trivial incidents responded to in a trivial way may, in the end, add up to an experience which we only enjoy because the challenges have been extracted. From this point of view, *Coronation Street* is often simply dull and flat—not because the lives it depicts are dull, but because the eye which observes those lives is unconvinced. The distinction in the end between *Morning in the Streets*, which has no 'plot' to sustain it, and *Coronation Street* is a difference between two 'ways of seeing', two kinds of commitment.

It may seem odd to call *Coronation Street* escapist, for escapism is normally associated with the portrayal of desired freedom offered to the characters by the possession of riches and high social position. But for the working-class audience the depiction of a life similar to their own yet lacking the intensity and the complications of experience can itself be a form of relaxation—a playing-through of experience at precisely that speed which is calculated not to disturb. And for the middle-class audience, plays and films about working-class life may also play an escapist role. For someone who feels acutely the pressure of 'getting on' and of 'success', the images of neighbourliness and co-operation may be exactly the wrong sort of compensation and consolation. It may be an important function of art and entertainment to console us, and to encourage us by showing us new qualities and new possibilities in life. But if the viewer has no actual experience of the world portrayed, and if it is presented to us with all its unpleasant features glossed over, the attraction could be both strong and misleading.

It may well be that the *Coronation Street* producers believe that, as Chayefsky wrote:

There is far more exciting drama in the reasons why a man gets married than in why he murders someone.

This is true: and yet, in a series which deals with a 'whole way of life', there is the real danger that an over-commitment to 'the ordinary, the everyday' will ignore precisely what constitutes so much of drama—the unexpected, the exceptional. Such a drama has to begin from a different point—with the recognition that, in terms of our emotional experiences, no one is 'ordinary'. At this point, however, we encounter a still more fundamental problem: can a drama which is committed to the 'slice-of-life' approach handle deep or profound emotions without making the characters articulate about them in a way which inevitably disturbs the conventions of naturalism?

This is a point which has not been sufficiently grasped, and the natural affinities of television as a medium for this sort of everyday drama—its wide audience, its domestic setting, its success with the small, intimate group on the screen—have perhaps dangerously strengthened the trend towards an unthinking and slack variety of popular naturalism. The error here arises in a confusion between naturalism as a 'way of seeing' and as a 'convention of presentation'. In his chapter on 'The Dramatic Tradition' in *Preface to Film*, Raymond Williams draws the crucial distinction between

the film which is using naturalistic conventions to express an 'inner, hidden psychological movement', and, on the other hand, the film in which a relatively crude, 'routine' conception of experience is given *apparent* actuality by the convincing representation of *external* details ... we are offered what I would call a 'false actuality', in which the convincingness of the external detail is operating as a substitute for a convincing actuality of considered and genuine feeling.

The naturalistic play remains a *play*, and all the evident visual accuracy cannot take the place of a reworking of the experience presented in dramatic terms. Life here is not a substitute for art, and nothing is gained by a fuzzing over of the line between them. The 'false actuality' may make it easier for the audience to identify with the play, but in the end the identification leads nowhere.

The point may be strengthened by comparing the literally accurate, naturalistic *Coronation Street* with the deliberate stylizations of *Steptoe and Son*. *Steptoe*, too, has one foot firmly in 'reality'.

But the style of the series is, in fact, based upon the conscious *exaggeration* of reality. At first sight the settings seem naturalistic enough, but when we look again we see that the living room is impossibly overcrowded with junk. Somewhere in the background is a continuity with a 'realistic' past—Harold's start on the cart at twelve, his father's First World War experience, the old days with their poverty, illness and disease. Yet every time this background is conjured up we are distanced from it by Harold's comment, 'Here we go again.' The talk of the 'good old times' is invariably accompanied by Harold on an imaginary violin. The Steptoes are working-class—but the class myths are treated with deliberate exaggeration. The old man is dirty—but even 'coals in the bath' receives a wild twist when he actually eats supper in the bath, solemnly putting the pickled onions he has dropped in the bath-water one by one back into the jar.

The relationship between father and son provides a welcome relief from the great good pub-heart of the folk in *Coronation Street*. Harold and Albert live in permanent antagonism with one another—yet it is precisely this which makes it impossible for them to separate. They are always, like most families, about to break up. Harold is convinced that, but for the old man, he would have bettered himself long before this. But Harold is now thirty-seven, and the chances of his making it on his own are, in fact, quite remote. It doesn't stop him trying, however, thus precipitating endless bust-ups with Albert and a mutual suspicion. Whenever Harold sets off on a date the father insists on knowing where he is going. 'I'm thirty-seven, Dad, not a sixteen-year-old girl. I'm a bloke not a judy. No one is going to get me drunk on a half-pint of cider, take me up a back alley and do me.' Yet Albert always manages to sabotage Harold's romances, and when Albert thinks of getting married again himself, Harold does the same. Behind the gags and the laughter which this love-hate relationship generates, we can feel something indestructible between them.

The jokes develop out of this relationship. They are generated by the abrupt contrasts between illusion and reality. They centre on class and status, not, as we might imagine, through a resolute affirmation of working-class attitudes, but rather through the conflict between the real culture and attitudes which are there, set off against Harold's illusions of grandeur.

Coronation Street is a series in which working-class life is continually being affirmed in an unreal way by characters like Ena Sharples. *Steptoe and Son* is a working-class comedy where the incidental aspects of the way of life emerge with a kind of conviction because the characters are at such pains to escape it. Harold, at least, devotes much of his time to this pursuit. He tries to build up a wine cellar by storing the dregs from discarded bottles. Refusing to tell Albert where he is going, he suggests he 'try the Silver Grill at the Savoy'. 'Dinner at six,' he tells the old man, 'that's dead working-class, that is.' He is a constant critic of his father's lack of culture: 'Fancy you confusing a Ming dynasty with a Tang dynasty—and what about that antique cocktail cabinet you bought, they didn't have cocktail cabinets in antique days. And then there was that Georgian record-player . . .' On his father's birthday, he insists on taking the old man to a Shakespeare play and a meal in a Chinese restaurant. The father would have preferred darts and a pint of beer, but he makes an effort and puts on his best suit. 'Shall I wear my medals?' he asks. 'Don't bother, Dad,' Harold replies. 'Where we're going most of the people you fought against.'

The concern with class, the jokes based on social and cultural pretensions—these are typical of a good deal of television comedy material. In the end it is the quality of pathos in the relationship which lifts *Steptoe* out of the ordinary. The series sets out to create comic characters and situations, but its strength lies in the almost incidental moments at which it is genuinely moving. In these terms *Steptoe* is more ambitious than the script-writers' (Galton and Simpson) other success, Hancock. Hancock has the same pretensions, but failure leaves him always defiant, with a stream of rationalizations to buoy him up and carry him to the next episode. Harold Steptoe in contrast is vulnerable in a wholly human way, always being made to face up to his own inadequacies. Those inadequacies are deliberately exaggerated and caricatured by the script-writers and actors; but within this stylization the emotions have the touch of reality about them. In the same way the junk-world of the Steptoes is pure fantasy, but the logic of the situations carries conviction. Even the overt aggressiveness of the relationship between father and son seems to be based on an absolute acceptance on either side, a kind of love. In *Steptoe and Son* fantasy and realism, comedy and pathos work in a dialectic—they reinforce one another. This is the clue to its richness: our response is more complex than we expect. Of course the episodes do not always succeed, but the success of some in the way described is remarkable. This is due in large measure to the actors, particularly Harry Corbett (Harold) with his marvellous sense of timing and wonderful control over his voice. There is also the contribution of the script-writers, the gags and jokes, both verbal and visual. But the humour of *Steptoe* is essentially a humour of character, and this is where the producers score, for they allow the camera to dwell on the faces of the men. It would be impossible to translate *Steptoe* directly in terms of working-class life; yet the series contains more emotional truth than episode after episode of the more strictly accurate *Coronation Street*.

Life is more complex than the media imagine; people are harder to 'figure out' than Lord Thomson or Cecil King assume. They cannot often be fully 'caught' simply by 'holding the mirror up to nature'. Realism and naturalism are two legitimate modes in art, but they are not the only ones. The problem is, in part, that media which visualize or establish with such speed fall too easily for the trap of naturalism, and their simplifications become distortions and misreadings of experience. But the most worrying aspect of all is when popular naturalism and documentary effects are used, not as modes of communication with their own strengths and limitations but as ways of giving the communicators an easier passage into the mind of an audience, and of 'making friends' on the cheap.

10

The Young Audience

We have no delinquent generation of young people; we have a
most selfish generation of young people. We have a materialistic
generation of young people. We have a greedy generation of young
people; having been given so much on a plate they expect the lot for
the taking.

Teachers' World editorial, 8 December 1961

Go for the youngsters, go for as much sex as you can, go for as
much violence as you can—and we are going to succeed.

MR J. GOODLATTE, Managing Director of ABC
(Reported in the *Daily Cinema*, 26/4/63)

The main emphasis in this book is on the content and forms of
mass communication and the popular arts, rather than the
sociology of audiences. But when we come to deal with 'teenage'
entertainments and culture, the distinction between media and
audience is difficult to maintain. For one thing, the post-war spurt
in the growth of the media and the change in adolescent attitudes
have gone hand in hand—apparently two aspects of the same
social trend. Secondly, we are dealing with a whole culture from
one specialized point of view: in our study particular weight is
given to the nature and quality of popular entertainment for young
people, whereas a full account of the culture would place more
emphasis on other aspects of life—such as work, politics, the
relation to the family, social and moral beliefs and so on. Thirdly,
we are dealing with the complex interaction between the attitudes
of the young and what is provided for their consumption by the
world of commercial entertainments. The picture of young people
as innocents exploited by the sharp merchants of Denmark Street
has some truth in it, but is over-simplified. We have a situation in
some ways more similar to that of television, where the use

intended by the provider and the use actually made by the audience of the particular style never wholly coincide, and frequently conflict. This conflict is particularly marked in the field of teenage entertainments, though it is to some extent common to the whole area of mass entertainment in a commercial setting. Our main purpose here is to show how these two aspects of the culture interact, and then to attempt an evaluation of the quality of the culture itself. Thus, in looking at the field of pop music, we shall have to consider the boom in teenage music, but also the role of the performers, their social biographies, the quality of their popular appeal, the music industry which promotes them to stardom, the publications, depending on the teenage reader, which support them, and the attitudes and feelings which are caught up and transposed by the beat of the music, the words of the lyrics and the vocal texture of the performers.

It is impossible to give any full account here of the sociology of the changes in tastes and attitudes among young people generally which have been so marked in the last decade. But anyone dealing with this subject will have to try to piece together a picture for himself, since the problem of teenage culture cannot be dealt with in isolation from this changing landscape. The literature on the subject is voluminous, but not always helpful. Some aspects we still know next to nothing about—e.g. the impact of work and the work situation. This is only just beginning to be studied. Some of the evidence seems contradictory: for example, although in adolescence the working-class teenager may adopt the current style, older patterns seem to persist and reassert themselves very strongly as soon as marriage and family life begin. But is the change-over really so smooth? A great deal of the evidence has been exaggerated: for example, the vexed question of teenage earnings. This is rarely set in the context of the overall rise in living standards which has occurred since the early fifties—it is usually abstracted from the total picture and made an occasion for carping moralizing. (There is a great deal of social envy concealed somewhere here, and also a good deal of confused social thinking. Very few critics, if challenged, can say precisely why it is a bad thing for teenagers to have more money to spend at eighteen than their grandfathers did.) In both the economic and the moral sphere the discussion among adults about the 'teenage problem' tells us, ultimately, more about adult society than it does about young people themselves.

Briefly, then, anyone trying to understand this cultural trend has to bear the following sketch in mind. First, there is the sheer impact of numbers—the growth, proportionately, in our population structure, of the very young (and the very old) at the expense of those in middle age. Coupled with this is the lowering of the age at which physical maturity is attained. When this factor is seen against the trend towards longer periods in school for a significant minority and the continuation of further education for some young people even after they have gone out to work, we confront the first major social conflict: the clash between sexual maturity at fourteen and the postponement of full adult status until twenty-one. For the best of reasons, we have extended the no-man's-land period between childhood and adulthood. And this creates a climate of rebellion even for the large majority who are not actually in any kind of education after the age of fifteen. This process of early maturation—which is not simply a matter of sexual capability, but also a familiarity with adult situations and experiences—is greatly exaggerated by the mass media, which do so much to present the world to the young person, and 'put him in the picture' at a very early stage of adolescence.

Then there is the question of schooling. Education now plays a major role in determining the job-opportunities and hence the life-chances of the young person. The present structure still maintains something like a class distinction between the 20 per cent in grammar schools and the 80 per cent in secondary moderns. The 80 per cent are those earliest to work, and hence most fully exposed to the full force of the media: and, given our social structure, they are predominantly working-class. Hence there is a rough correlation between education, class and cultural attitudes. In a broadcast, Basil Bernstein, Senior Lecturer in Social Studies at the London Institute of Education, remarked that the more rigorously we select, the more we increase the sense of social failure among those whom we do *not* select. This sense of social failure lies somewhere behind the teenage revolution, though it is hard to pin down exactly. It also accounts for certain marked attitudes towards culture generally—that dissociation from 'high' culture which we discussed in the opening chapter, and the general drift of attention away from school to the more attractive world of work and leisure which many teachers have noticed half-way through the secondary modern school career.

Thirdly, there is the wider social context. A great deal of nonsense has been talked about the 'welfare state' and the 'affluent society', but even when much of this is discounted there is some obvious connection between the pace of social change since the end of the war and the changes in attitudes among the young. Throughout this period the physical, social and cultural landscape of Britain has been undergoing a transformation. Living standards have improved, there has been a marked drift away from some of the older industrial areas—and the kinds of community life for which they were so well known—to newer areas, different kinds of work, new social environments and, inevitably, new kinds of communities. Nowhere has this settled into anything like a stable pattern, and social change of this kind is always slower and less uniform than the sociologist would like (some of the best work done to document this change is to be found in the work of the Institute of Community Studies). But it has undoubtedly led to a great deal of shifting about and some social uncertainty. Many of the familiar landmarks of the earlier industrial culture are slowly disappearing, though many still remain. The social structure of society may not have altered essentially, but the actual relations between the social classes has been changing. And the whole adjustment of society to these changes and to the post-war world has involved a break with many traditional beliefs and assumptions, without as yet any clear set of alternatives. This process cannot be discussed in British terms alone, since it is connected with Britain's changing role in the world and with the climate of the Cold War and international relations which have so dominated life since 1945. Some of the most interesting social criticism written in the past decade has been the attempt to describe this process of adaptation and change more accurately, and to relate the various aspects to one another. There is once again a 'condition of England' question, and the 'teenage problem' is very much at the heart of it.

For many young people, Britain in the fifties and sixties has been a society in transition, a society throwing out a number of confusing signals. Teenage culture is, in part, an authentic response to this situation, an area of common symbols and meanings, shared in part or in whole by a generation, in which they can work out or work through not only the natural tensions of adolescence, but the special tensions of being an adolescent in our kind of society. Sometimes this response can be seen in direct terms— kinds of radical political energy with certain clear-cut symbolic targets (the threat of nuclear weapons, political apathy, the bureaucratic quality of political life, all that is summed up in the phrase 'the Establishment'). Sometimes, the response takes the form of a radical shift in social habits—for example, the slow but certain revolution in sexual morality among young people, which Professor Carstairs described in his Reith Lecture on 'The Vicissitudes of Adolescence' (*Listener* 29/11/62, and *This Island Now*):

> In their place a new concept is emerging, of sexual relationships as a source of pleasure, but also as a mutual encountering of personalities in which each explores the other and at the same time discovers new depths in himself or herself.

In these and other ways the younger generation have acted as a creative minority, pioneering ahead of the puritan restraints so deeply built into English bourgeois morality, towards a code of behaviour in our view more humane and civilized. Much of the active participation of the younger generation in their own sub-culture has this flavour about it—a spontaneous and generative response to a frequently bewildering and confused social situation. In these conditions the problems of the young seem important largely because they are symptomatic of the society as a whole. The shift in sexual attitudes, for example, draws attention to itself, not only because it contrasts sharply with the code of behaviour subscribed to by adult society (though rarely lived up to), but also because it illuminates in a striking way the confusion about these questions among people of all ages and all backgrounds. There is no common consensus any longer among adults about sexual attitudes or about the role of authority in society, or even about our expectations of how young people should behave. The young sense the absence of this consensus. And this stimulates the trend towards independence, self-reliance and spontaneity, as well as exposing them to powerfully suggestive alternative models such as the media put forward. One has only to read the extra-ordinarily conflicting views expressed at the time of the publication of *Lady Chatterley's Lover* to appreciate the level of confusion in the public mind. (The record of the trial, written up for Penguin by C. H. Rolph, is a useful social document in this context.)

Of course, there is always a gap between the generations and it is difficult to judge whether the gap is now wider than it has been in the past. The conflict between generations is really one form of the maturing process in adolescence, and should trouble us only when it is so wide that the maturing process itself is disrupted. But it does seem likely that when we have, on the one hand, parents occupied with making the adjustment to a new tempo of life, and, on the other, a young generation which is itself the product of those changes to which adults are adjusting, the gap in social experience and feeling between the generations can become dangerously wide. Parents are always one generation behind their children: today they seem to be two generations behind. Naturally, there are many young people who don't experience these tensions at all, and one must be constantly aware of how varied the pattern is. But there is something like a majority feeling, even if the trends are really set by a small minority, and in the age of the mass media these tensions communicate themselves much more rapidly from place to place, group to group. One of the special features of this is the role of the media in speeding-up the fashion-cycle among the young.

This helps to isolate teenagers as a distinct grouping from the rest of society. Paul Goodman suggests that youth is the only sub-culture which behaves as if it were a class. And this isolation is often stressed and validated by the media themselves. Some teenagers are genuinely 'misunderstood': Dr Winnicott has suggested that at this stage of adolescence they don't really want to be understood. But many more learn to feel misunderstood because they are told so often that they are. One could cite a host of articles, features and reports which, without trying to probe to the heart of the problem, loosely glamorize this feeling of group isolation. As an example of the trend in journalism, one selects almost at random an early edition of the magazine *Today*, still during this period in search of a new audience and format (12/3/62; *Today* used to be *John Bull*). A rather jazzed-up 'Teenage Report to the Nation' ends with a familiar warning to adult squares: 'We're interesting people when you get to know us. Only you never will.' Earlier in the same article, in the section on teenage slang, we find the same emphasis: 'I'm giving all this knowledge away, but it will do you no good.' (Incidentally, judging from the jiving couple on the cover, this whole issue of *Today* was angled at the younger generation, but the list of contents provides a very strange glimpse of the composite editorial image of its audience: Today's Post—'Anybody Want a Dream Home?': 'How to Play the Stock Market'—'Hitch your wagon to the big-money boys, the take-over bid specialists, who know where the profits are to be found'; 'The Snobs Who Come to My Parties'—by the Duke of Bedford; the Teenage Report; a feature entitled 'Look at the Accidents Pedestrians Cause'; 'Of Course I Believe in Luck'—by Gilbert Harding; a colour spread on the film *Can-Can*; 'When the Killer Strikes . . .'; and a story by Nevil Shute entitled 'Departure into Danger'. James Bond was promised for the following issue.)

The isolation of the sub-culture also becomes a major emphasis in the songs, lyrics, interviews with pop stars, teenage films, comics

and stories. The culture provided by the commercial entertainment market therefore plays a crucial role. It mirrors attitudes and
sentiments which are already there, and at the same time provides
an expressive field and a set of symbols through which these
attitudes can be projected. But it also gives those attitudes a
certain stress and shape, particularizing a background of feelings
by the choice of a certain style of dress, a particular 'look', by the
way a typical emotion is rendered in a song or depicted in a
drawing or photograph (see Plate 13).

Teenage entertainments, therefore, play a cultural and educative
role which commercial providers seem little aware of. Their
symbols and fantasies have a strong hold upon the emotional
commitment of the young at this stage in their development, and
operate more powerfully in a situation where young people are
tending to learn less from established institutions, such as the
family, the school, the church and the immediate adult community,
and more from one another. They rely more on themselves and
their own culture, and they are picking up signals all the time,
especially from the generation just ahead.

Teenage culture is a contradictory mixture of the authentic and
the manufactured: it is an area of self-expression for the young
and a lush grazing pasture for the commercial providers. One
might use the cult figure of the pop singer as an illustration. He is
usually a teenager, springing from the familiar adolescent world,
and sharing a whole set of common feelings with his audience.
But once he is successful, he is transformed into a commercial
entertainer by the pop-music business. Yet in style, presentation
and the material he performs, he must maintain his close involvement with the teenage world, or he will lose his popularity. The
record companies see him as a means of marketing their products
—he is a living, animated, commercial image. The audience will
buy his records if they like his performances, and thus satisfy the
provider's need to keep sales high: but they will also regard the
pop singer as a kind of model, an idealized image of success, a
glamorized version of themselves.

The economic base for this revolution in cultural tastes is the increased spending power of unmarried young people. This, as we noticed above, has been much exaggerated—it is part of the current myth that teenagers all over the country have money to burn. In fact, consistently high earnings are limited to a minority of jobs and to certain parts of the country. There is now some evidence that the contribution made to home and upkeep has been underestimated. Thousands of young people are in badly paid dead-end jobs, and the employment situation has noticeably worsened in recent years. Their prospects are not good. However, Mark Abrams estimated in his early study, *The Teenage Consumer* (since supported by further studies), a growth in the real earnings of unmarried teenagers of 50 per cent as compared with 1938. This is double the rate for adult earnings in the same period. In 1958 he estimated that Britain's 5,000,000 unmarried teenagers were grossing about £1,480,000,000 annually. More significant was the proportion of uncommitted or 'discretionary' spending money they had available—about £900,000,000. This is a rise in discretionary spending of 100 per cent as compared with 1938. The significant point is the high concentration of spending in certain limited fields. Nearly a quarter of that sum went on clothing and footwear (£210,000,000), another 14 per cent on drink and tobacco (£125,000,000), 12 per cent on sweets, soft drinks and snacks (£105,000,000), £40,000,000 on records, record players, papers and magazines, £25,000,000 on bicycles and motorcycles. These sums are decisive in the chosen fields of purchase: 25 per cent of all consumer-spending on bicycles and motorbikes, records and record players, cinema and other entertainments, and between 15 per cent and 25 per cent of all expenditure on sweets, soft drinks, footwear, women's clothing and cosmetics. On the other hand, in the main consumer range (household purchases and fuel, furniture and consumer durables, insurance) their contribution is negligible—less than 3 per cent of the total.

These large sums reflect the rise in living standards generally as well as the trend towards personal consumption in Britain in recent years. But the teenage contribution is most significant because it is concentrated in the whole range of goods and services which reflect cultural tastes, social life, gregariousness of the group or gang or clique, leisure and entertainment and the consumption of provided teenage culture. It is in these fields that the most noticeable increases are to be found.

Commercial providers have been quick to cash in on this volatile market—one which is easily stimulated because turnover is high and the market is highly fashion-conscious. The providers know that fashion and style play a key role in governing the flow of teenage purchase. As Mark Abrams remarked, 'Teenagers more than any other section of the community are looking for goods and services which are highly charged emotionally.' In a contribution to a BBC symposium on *The Young Affluents* a social worker described the teenage propensity to consume in this way: the woman who wants a sweater primarily to keep warm will buy a single one; but the teenager who wants a pink sweater in order to feel bright and gay and extrovert on one day, and a purple sweater to feel dark and intense and introspective the next will feel she needs two, and perhaps many more, if she can afford them. We are all subject to the play of fashion, but teenagers seem to be particularly so. The search for a 'style' among young people is really part of a deeper search for a meaning and identifiable pattern in life. It is one aspect of the search for identity which is an essential part of the whole process of maturing. As D. W. Winnicott expressed it (in his article, 'Struggling Through The Doldrums', in *New Society*, 25/4/63, part of a *New Society* series on adolescence):

Is it not a prime characteristic of adolescents that they do not accept false solutions? They have a fierce morality which accepts only that which feels real, and this is a morality that also characterises infancy. It is a morality that goes much deeper than wickedness, and has as its motto, 'to thine own self be true'. The adolescent is engaged in trying to find the self to be true to.

When commercial providers become involved in creating new fashions and setting styles, they are inevitably caught up in the psychological processes of adolescence, in the crisis of identity which many experience at this age. They provide one set of answers to the search for more meaningful and satisfying adult roles. And the danger is that they will short-circuit this difficult process by offering too limited a range of social models for young people to conform to, a kind of consumer identity, which could be dangerous even when ultimately rejected by them. There seems to be a clear conflict between commercial and cultural considerations here, for which commercial providers take no responsibility.

The commercial images sometimes work in this way because they invoke such powerful elements in the teenage culture. They play upon the self-enclosed, introspective intensity of the teenage world. One aspect of this tribalism which the media exaggerate can be seen lying behind the remarks of a young girl interviewed in a series on adolescents on BBC Schools Television. 'You see a woman who is well dressed,' she said, 'in the latest fashion, made-up and all that . . . Well, you wouldn't say she's "modern"—she's "smart", but "modern" is more for young people.' This innocent comment catches a feeling which is stressed again and again in advertising for the teenage market. In a different mode, the song *Teenage Dream*, sung by Terry Dene, carried precisely the same message:

> Mum says we're too young to love
> And Dad agrees it's so,
> But the joy and bliss I find in your kiss
> Is a thrill they'll never know.

This inward-turning, self-pitying quality of many of the slower teenage ballads, the community-of-lost-souls feeling invoked in words and rhythms, is both an authentic rendering of an adolescent mood and a stylized exaggeration of it.

This apparent self-sufficiency in teenage culture is not simply a matter of keeping adult experience at arm's length; it is also a by-product of the limited subject-matter and emotions dealt with in commercial entertainments. A study of the lyrics of teenage songs and the situations dramatized in them shows the recurrence of certain set patterns. These all deal with romantic love and sexual feeling. The emotion is intensely depicted, but the set-ups recur with monotonous regularity and the rendered style stereotypes the emotion. They deal exclusively with falling in love, falling out of love, longing for the fulfilment of love, the magic of love fulfilled. Of course, this has been the typical subject matter of popular song throughout the ages. But one has then to compare the actual quality of the statement in pop music with, say, the folk song or the blues or even the pointed Johnny Mercer lyric of the twenties to appreciate the particular flavour, the generalized loneliness and yearning—a yearning of 'no-body in particular for anyone-at-all' as Philip Oakes once wrote.

> Johnny An-gel
> He doesn't even know I exist
> . . . I pray someday he'll love me
> And together we will see
> How lovely Heaven will be.

These songs, and the romantic stories with which they have so much in common, portray what Francis Newton calls 'the condition, the anxieties, the bragging and uncertainty of school-age love and increasingly school-age sex'. They reflect adolescent difficulties in dealing with a tangle of emotional and sexual problems. They invoke the need to experience life directly and intensely. They express the drive for security in an uncertain and changeable emotional world. The fact that they are produced for a commercial market means that the songs and settings lack a certain authenticity. Yet they also dramatize authentic feelings. They express vividly the adolescent emotional dilemma. And since they are often written on behalf of the adult providers of the entertainment world by teenage stars and songwriters, who share the cultural ethos of their audiences, there is a good deal of interaction and feed-back going on all the time.

These emotions, symbols and situations drawn off from the

provided teenage culture contain elements both of emotional realism and of fantasy fulfilment. There is a strong impulse at this age to identify with these collective representations and to use them as guiding fictions. Such symbolic fictions are the folklore by means of which the teenager, in part, shapes and composes his mental picture of the world. It is in this identification that we find an explanation for the behaviour of the teenage 'fan', the contrived absurdities of the fan-club, with its sacred relics, ritual strippings of the 'hero' and personally autographed images. Fan-club behaviour has now extended to younger teenagers, as can be seen on any public occasion such as the personal appearance of pop groups like The Beatles. At the same time the teenage magazines have to some extent institutionalized fan-club behaviour in their pages. Roy Shaw remarked that the tone of some of these magazines for young girls is so intimate that 'the readers feel, and are intended to feel, that they are members of a vast teenage club, where no do-good youth leader obtrudes his presence'. The same contrived intimacy is characteristic of teenage films—the Cliff Richard films, *The Young Ones* and *Summer Holiday*, are good examples of the deliberate manufacturing of this mood. These films are composed to catch the more superficial values in the culture, but to anyone outside the cult circle they irritate by their gloss, their forced light-heartedness and their embarrassing 'tenderness' (one remembers the moon-struck Richard delivering a love-sick ballad amidst the Acropolis ruins). They derive in style straight from the colour advertising travelogues—the continuity is between *Summer Holiday* and the more inane *Look at Life* short features. Again, compare *Summer Holiday* with the imaginatively shot and delicately treated Clive Donner film, *Some People*. As in the Richard films, the colour was rather crude (deliberately so?), but the sensitive playing of the group of young people, their witty and brittle high spirits, their tough independence and self-reliance, captured in a far more authentic fashion the positive elements in the teenage world. Contrasted with the playing of the three boys, it was the ham-fisted imposition of adult solutions (the Duke of Edinburgh Award Scheme) and adult situations (Kenneth More in his best brusque RAF manner) which seemed false and forced.

Because of its high emotional content, teenage culture is essentially non-verbal. It is more naturally expressed in music, in dancing, in dress, in certain habits of walking and standing, in certain facial expressions and 'looks' or in idiomatic slang. Though there is much to be learned from the lyrics of pop songs, there is more in the *beat* (loud, simple, insistent), the *backing* (strong, guitar-dominated), the *presentation* (larger-than-life, mechanically etherealized), the *inflections* of voice (sometimes the self-pitying, plaintive cry, and later the yeah-saying, affirmative shouting) or the *intonations* (at one stage mid-Atlantic in speech and pronunciation, but more recently rebelliously northern and provincial).[1] One can trace a whole line of development in popular music by listening to intonations—Louis Armstrong's gravelly rasp on the last word in *I Can't Give You Anything But Love, Baby* becomes Elvis Presley's breathy, sensual invocation, 'Bab-eh', is then anglicized into Adam Faith's 'Boi-by', with a marked Cockney twist (in *What Do You Want If You Don't Want Money?*) and provincialized by groups like The Beatles.

Certain attitudes seem not only to recur with emphasis in the provided culture, but to have found some specially appropriate physical image or presence among teenagers themselves. This teenage 'look' can be partly attributed to the designers of mass-produced fashions and off-the-peg clothes and to the cosmetic advice syndicated in girls' and women's magazines. C & A's and Marks and Spencers, by marketing fashionable styles at reasonable prices, have played a significant role here. But these styles have a deeper social basis. The very preoccupation with the image of the self is important—pleasing, though often taken to extremes. Dress has become, for the teenager, a kind of minor popular art, and is used to express certain contemporary attitudes. There is, for example, a strong current of social nonconformity and rebelliousness among teenagers. At an early stage these anti-social feelings were quite active--the rejection of authority in all its forms, and a

1. See later reference to the extrovert approach of The Beatles.

hostility towards adult institutions and conventional moral and social customs. During this period, adult commentators often misread this generalized nonconformism as a type of juvenile delinquency, though it had little to do with organized crime and violence. The 'Teddy Boy' style, fashionable some years ago, with its tumbling waterfall hair-style, fetishistic clothes, long jackets, velvet collars, thick-soled shoes, and the accoutrements which went along with them—string ties with silver medallions, lengthy key-chains, studded ornamental belts—was a perfect physical expression of this spirit. Contrary to expectations, this style did not disappear, but persisted in the dress of motorcycle addicts and 'ton-up' kids, and reappeared with the 'rockers'. A variant of this non-conformity could be found among 'ravers' or beat-niks, with the trend to long hair, heavy sweaters, drain-piped jeans and boots or black stockings and high heels. The Teddy Boy look, an historical throw-back, with its recall of Edwardian times, matched exactly the primitivism of the attitudes it expressed.

Sometimes this attitude is more inward and internalized, relating to real failures in the relationships between children and parents, and the sense of being misunderstood. For two teenage generations at least, James Dean did much to embody and project this image and to give it a style—his films *Rebel Without a Cause* and *East of Eden* are classics which, despite their exaggerations (e.g. the chicken-run scene in *Rebel*) and emotional falsity (the relationship between Dean and his parents in the same film), have a compulsive and hidden quality, due largely to Dean's true dramatic gifts. *Rebel Without a Cause*, directed with disturbing indulgence by Nicholas Ray, who seemed incapable of placing any distance between his dramatization of the teenage world and his own point of view, is really a cult film, and its most impressive moments are ritualized scenes from the teenage fantasy viewed from within the culture itself. In all his films, James Dean portrayed the ideal of blue-jean innocence, tough and vulnerable in the same moment, a scowl of disbelief struggling with frankness for mastery in his face and eyes, continual changes of mood and expression on his features, still, as Edgar Morin describes him, 'hesitating between childhood's melancholy and the mask of the adult', and with a studied inarticulateness in his gestures and walk. The Dean films have never left the circuit, playing continuously since his death to teenage audiences at the local cinema.

Related to the same set of attitudes, but more recent in origin, is that style of 'cool' indifference—a kind of bland knowingness about the ways of the world, even, at times, a disenchantment, an assumed world-weariness. This detachment can be either cynical or sad. It is best described by that evocative word 'beat'—but *not* beatnik. It lies behind the mask-like, pasty-faced, heavily mascara'd look which became fashionable among teenage girls—originally a copy of a Paris style, but when assumed by teenagers suggestive of so much else. There is something of it, too, in the variations of the 'continental' or 'Italian' style which became required wear for teenage boys when dressed up (elsewhere, jeans are ubiquitous), with its modern, lazy elegance, its smooth, tapered lines, light materials, pointed shoes or boots, and the flat, rather dead 'college' haircut which often accompanies it. A model of innovation in this field was the drained face and the whole casual ensemble of Adam Faith. This style, with certain bizarre innovations, is that of the 'mods'. Something of the conflicting pressures, internal and external, which have created these physical images can be seen at work in the case of Adam Faith himself. Here are two passages from his autobiography:

Ricky saw how depressed I was. And I can tell you that this bout of depression was worse than anything I'd been through before.

Physical pain I was well acquainted with. I'd suffered from migraine between the age of nine and sixteen, and anyone who has migraine will tell you that it can drive you out of your mind.

. . . But this depression was a thing of the mind, a sort of mental growing pain.

                                                                Poor Me

And a few pages later:

Jack was pleased with the results. Not long afterwards I met him strolling in Wardour Street.

'Why don't you come and do more TV for me?' he asked. 'Come on my next programme as a solo artist. I've got an idea' (Jack always did have ideas). 'I'll build you up as Britain's singing James Dean. You know. The black leather jacket lark . . .'

Black leather jackets were 'in' at that moment. So was the James Dean cult of moody rebellion. The two sort of went together.

James Dean had been killed in a sports car crash in California, and his fans were making almost a religion of his tragic death.

This idea of Jack's suited me fine.

                                                                    ibid.

The Adam Faith look contrasts sharply with the more moody, insolently sensual appeal of, say, the early Elvis Presley or his transatlantic mirror-image, Cliff Richard (both Faith and Presley became the type-base for illustrations in the girls' romantic comics) or the 'poppett' appeal of The Beatles.

Against the somewhat limited range offered in the provided culture, we have to set the real access of independence and the genuine charm—the naivety as well as the assuredness—which allow teenagers to play, mould or conjure with their experiences and derive pleasure from them. This life and spontaneity is never far from the surface, however powerful is the pull of fashion towards conformity. A light-footed, free-wheeling quality comes through, both in the elegance of casual dress and the grace of movement in dancing, walking or animated conversation—a real growth of sophistication which has taken place since the 'teenage thing' first began. The sullen Teddy Boy style was a copy of an already exaggerated upper-class fashion; now the balance has shifted, and the fashion trends move the other way—the wool shirt and the slim Italian line penetrated to the West End and Chelsea from the outer working-class suburbs. As Colin MacInnes pointed out in his chapter on 'Sharp Schmutter' in *England, Half English*, this is the first real casual style developed in England for many decades, contrasting favourably with the sporty floral elaborations of 'county' or the downright dowdiness of 'men's wear'. The lightness and freeness of girl's fashions also capture this element of playfulness and sophistication. This whole shift in sensibility was first recorded in MacInnes's novel, *Absolute Beginners*, which is not a social documentary but a poetic 'evocation of a human situation, with undertones of social criticism in it'.

The Melody Maker reported (August 1959) that when the jazz critic, Bob Dawbarn, asked Larry Parnes, the pop-music impresario, whether he thought teenage tastes had changed much over the past couple of years, Parnes replied, 'They have not so much changed as had their tastes changed for them.' One of the main controls which the record and promotion companies exercise over the teenage taste in the pops is the pop singer himself, around whom in recent years there has developed something of a youthful religion of the celebrity. We have seen this search for popular heroes elsewhere—in the careers of the cinema idols. Even in the field of popular music, many will recall the affection with which some of the female singers in war-time were held by radio audiences and the apparently universal appeal of a crooner like Bing Crosby. There was always something domestic and comfortable about Crosby, however, which discouraged wild extravagances among his fans. Something quite new entered this field with Sinatra and Frankie Laine. One can still recall the screaming teenage fans whose cries drowned the final phrases of every Sinatra song on the American programme *Hit Parade* in the forties.

Sinatra, however, provides a useful contrast, where musical ability is concerned, with the younger denizens of the pop-music jungle. Like many of them, his voice is not in itself a powerful or rich musical instrument. Unlike Bessie Smith, who naturally produced a tumultuous sound, Sinatra's is closer to a speaking voice. His material is almost entirely 'commercial'. Like the teenage stars, he has had to struggle to maintain his place at the top, and this has involved a change in personality and style. Yet his success has depended on two things: a genuine growth in his musical command, and a determination to mature as an artist. Musical command he shows now in several respects: he has developed an incomparable jazz phrasing, and his emotional range is quite striking. Compare, for example, the genuine nostalgia of his *Moonlight in Vermont*, the sophisticated edge of *The Lady is a Tramp* and the dramatic performance he gives to *One More for the Road*. His diction is impeccable—clear, hard, articulating the lyrical notes at the ends of lines or in the bridges on songs. The voice is now deeper, rougher, more sophisticated and dry than in the days when he was 'momma's little boy' on the *Hit Parade*— but it is also much more interesting. This is because of a depth of personal feeling as well as a certain maturity. He has achieved an effortless ability to swing without the support of elaborate sets on stage, dazzling costumes, echo chambers or physical contortions of the pelvis. Indeed, to judge from his last concert tour, his act is drastically simplified, relaxed and unencumbered. He commands the full stage by his musical intensity—not an 'effect', but related to the final product and therefore much more organic. Sometimes he closes his eyes, but the purpose seems to be to 'focus' more clearly a difficult note. His throat muscles contract to give the phrase either its soft, off-colour pitch or a particular bite. Both musically and by force of personality—the image of the experienced man who has seen a good deal of life and wants to record it through the medium of popular song—he transforms weak or trite material.

How much of this capacity to grow and deepen as a performer is potentially there among the galaxy of pop singers who have flashed on and off the teenage screen in the last decade? Perhaps it is too early to tell. One can see some awareness of the problem in a performer like Tommy Steele, who has put in a great deal of effort to extend his range now that his brief spell in the teenage charts is over, but this has meant not a growth in his quality as a singer but a shift to new fields of entertainment—to pantomime, compèring and straight drama. The same is true of Elvis Presley, who has managed to stay at the top by dint of superb commercial management and judicious modification of his image (compare the Elvis of *Jailhouse Rock* and *King Creole* with the 'All-American' Elvis of the Army films like *G.I. Blues* and the pudgier, softer, more sentimental star of *Girls, Girls, Girls*. Plate 11). Others, like Adam Faith, Cliff Richard and Billy Fury, have 'gone into films' as an extension of their singing careers, but this is simply a transfer of the same talents to another location, often (in the case of Faith) with quite disastrous results. One thinks again of Sinatra's film career in comparison—not films like *Ocean's Eleven*, which is a pleasant but inconsequential indulgence of the cult of the Sinatra clan, but of outstanding roles, such as that of the Private in *From Here to Eternity*, where really new and exciting dramatic talents were revealed. By contrast, the pop singers in film remain the teenage innocents of *Easy Beat* and *Saturday Club*.

Yet these groups have achieved in a short spell a degree of popular magic which even seasoned stars like Sinatra might envy. The intensity of rapport between audience and singer cannot be explained wholly in terms of the contrived engineering which makes the singer an idol. As Edgar Morin said, in relation to cinema idols, 'In the last analysis it is neither talent nor lack of talent, neither the cinematic industry nor its advertising, but the need for her which creates the star' (*The Stars*).

Something in this primitive force depends upon the representative character of the idol's biography. These singers are not remote stars, like Garbo, but tangible idealizations of the life of the average teenager—boys next door, of humble beginnings, almost certainly of working-class family, who have like the Greek gods done their 'labours' as van boy, messenger, truck-driver, film-cutter or clerk in a routine occupation (that is if they have not come straight from the 'labours' of the classroom). What makes the difference between himself and his fellows is that he has been touched by success—picked out by a talent scout from Denmark Street or given a break in some provincial beat club or created a stir in the columns of a provincial paper. He is marked out, not so much by his musical talents (which more than one recording manager has said can be a distinct handicap in the business) as by his personality. He's got 'something' and luck—in the shape of John Kennedy or Larry Parnes, say—has come his way.

But from this point on he is made over in the image of the entertainment celebrity—he can afford to buy every week the clothes many teenagers can only afford once a year, he drives the fast sports car, goes on the much publicized foreign tours, and will finally seal his achievement with a Royal Command performance. The material essence of this rise to success is frankly but disarmingly stated in Adam Faith's preface to his autobiography:

> All I need is a title to get the story rolling. Maybe I could pinch one from one of my discs. How about POOR ME?
> Come to think of it, that's a giggle. POOR ME—only got £50,000 a year to manage on! HOW ABOUT THAT!
>
> *Poor Me*

Rags to riches—the myth of the teenage star draws together both the familiar and the fabulous; he joins the teenage reality to the dream of success. We saw the same process at work in the recasting of names which became part of the legendary translation from the council estate to the Palladium stage: Tommy Hicks to Tommy Steele, Reginald Smith to Marty Wilde, Terrence Williams to Terry Dene, Roy Taylor to Vince Eager, Ray Howard to Duffy Power, Dicky Knellar to Dicky Pride, Terry Nelhams to Adam Faith, John Askew to Johnny Gentle, Ronald Wycherley to Billy Fury—each one powerfully suggestive, each one at that stage slightly Americanized.

In the pop-music business, 'personality' as well as names is manufactured and marketed. What the audience sees (or saw: stars now seem more real and audiences less naive) as a magical process is very Big Business in the pop world. A whole industry has gone into the 'production' of the star. Few promoters take this as far as John Kennedy did in his handling of Tommy Steele (recorded in his book *Tommy Steele*) in the early days before the craze was properly under way. Kennedy believed that somebody had to lift the 'teenage thing' out of 'its Teddy boy rut, give it class, and get society as well as the thousands of ordinary decent kids singing and dancing it'. He was convinced that 'kids in this country . . . need someone like Tommy to fall in love with. They need the boy next door, who comes from the same kind of street, went to the same kind of school, and talks in the same kind of way.' He admits to faking a debutantes' party in order to secure a 'Now the Debs Are Doing It' headline, and a picture of the Duke of Kent leaving the theatre which was sold to the press as 'the Duke just coming out of the Stork' where Tommy had just performed, though it was in fact a quite different occasion.

> . . . and I added that I had got a short interview with him.
> 'To quote his own words,' I said solemnly, 'he described Tommy as being "Great . . . great . . . great".'
>
> *Tommy Steele*

These are examples of what an American critic Daniel Boorstin, in his book *The Image*, called 'pseudo-events'—events which do not happen but are created by and for publicity.

Nor do many managers of pop singers go to the lengths recorded in the February 1960 issue of *Photoplay*, where two American promoters, Joe Mulhall and Paul Neff, describe how they created a pop star from nothing. They conducted a questionnaire among 3,000 teenagers, and evolved a summary of their ideal performer:

> A boy who sings well . . . not too polished but well. About 5 ft. 7 in. tall, of Italian descent (because they look so romantic). Fine build and nice smile; sharp sports clothes; intelligent, considerate of others, sincere, honest and quiet.

Then they started looking for a boy who fitted the description. Finally they hit on a photograph in a physical culture magazine, and tracked down a young, fifteen-year-old Johnny Restivo who (they must have been pleased to discover) also *sang*. After he had been trained he was booked at various shows, each time accompanied by a second questionnaire which asked the audience, 'Would you like to get to know Johnny Restivo better?' Surprisingly, 88 per cent of the boys and 95 per cent of the girls said, 'Yes'. He was finally recorded and became a well-known pop singer of the second rank.

Still, most managers have their work cut out for them—arduous, chancy but lucrative. In the production of the pop-singing idol the manager comes first. He takes the risks on which there is no certain return, backing unknown singers whom he believes to have 'star quality'—though most managers today hedge their bets by running a whole 'stable' of singers so that losses on the swings can be made up on the roundabouts. Bunny Lewis, one of the successful managers, says that he looks first of all for the boy who is physically attractive, vocally individual, easily recognizable. Then, he advises, the embryo star has to be groomed—'style their hair, fix their teeth, dress them properly, coach them vocally. Instil a little sanity into them—they are going from a few pounds a week to a lot of money, and they must remain sound about it all' (from a BBC Schools Television series about teenagers entitled *Your World*). The manager not only grooms the star but often chooses the appropriate look for his personality, for this is the point of real connection with the audience. Larry Parnes, who, with John Kennedy, first broke into the business behind Tommy Steele, is typical of the newer pop-music manager, with a stable of stars and his own publishing house for teenage composers which by-passes the older, more established publishers of sheet music. In fact this group of new men with the teenage 'touch' were often bitterly resented by the older organizers of Tin Pan Alley.

The next important link in the promotion chain is the Artistes and Repertoire man (A-and-R), who is either employed by a record company or free-lance. He is really the record producer, who puts the singer and his manager in touch with the media through the disc company. He selects the artist and the song, decides the style, length and accompanying group as well as the place for recording. His role is vital, for he exercises a real power of choice over what material gets recorded. He is also closely in touch with composers of teenage ballads—very often themselves teenagers.

The recording engineers will be almost as responsible as the singer, in many cases, for the final quality of the record. A song can be recorded many times until it sounds just right to the A-and-R man's ear, and, if necessary, a good first chorus can be spliced with a good second chorus from a different take to make the perfect record. Depth, resonance, volume and pitch can all be 'created' in the modern recording studio. The voice can be made to resound from the heavens by the skilful use of an echo chamber. A heavy hand on the guitar can be softened, or a beat of the bass accentuated, by the turn of switches.

Only some records ever get played sufficiently to build up a mass following; and only some of those played reach the zenith of popularity—a place in the Top Twenty charts. Success here, too, depends on other things than musical quality. For example, a record by an unknown singer released in the same week as a new Cliff Richard or The Shadows or The Beatles has much less chance of making it to the top. On the other hand, a place in the charts—even a lowly one—is a guarantee of some measure of success, since teenagers often ask in the shops for 'No. 1 in the Top Twenty' without being quite sure what it is. This is an easy habit to form, as can be seen from the occasion when, in a television interview with Billy Fury, Kingsley Amis, referring to a new Fury record which had only just been released, said, 'Now let's hear your forthcoming hit.'

Radio is now considered a relatively declining mass medium, but it still has an immense influence on the pop-music business—a more direct impact than that of television. A crucial part in the history of any 'golden disc' is played by that famous élite of radio and television 'disc jockeys' (D-J's) who compère teenage music shows, interview the singers and introduce discs, especially on BBC Radio and Radio Luxembourg. A good deal of the magic of the pop-music world seems to have rubbed off on them, for they are almost as well known as teenage idols themselves—David Jacobs, Pete Murray, Alan Freeman, Jimmy Saville, Brian Matthew, Sam Costa, Keith Fordyce. Others, like Jack Good, have moved over from compèring or directing television shows (e.g. the famous *Six-Five Special*, now considered the Original Paramount Teenage Show) to free-lance A-and-R work. The

Daily Herald once made a guess that Jacobs, once a £7-a-week BBC announcer, now earns something like £35,000 a year.

Once the record has been made, the most important factor is the amount of 'air-time' which it gets, for it is this kind of plugging which will build up a demand for it in the shops. Recognizing this link between repetition on the air and commercial advantage, the BBC has made the ruling that compères should not choose their own records on popular radio programmes. In spite of the many opportunities there must be for putting pressure on disc jockeys to get particular records played, there has never been any suggestion of malpractice in this field in Britain, though there has in the US (elsewhere in the trade no doubt what Francis Newton calls 'the universal *schmier* or sweetening of useful contacts' is not unknown). However, by the very nature of their job, disc jockeys must to some extent prejudge taste. The process is much more clearly seen on what might be called Britain's first commercial radio, Radio Luxembourg, where programmes are directly sponsored by the record companies and plugging is legitimate. Of thirty-six hours of broadcasting in one week of the summer of 1962, EMI ran sponsored record programmes for eight hours, Decca for five. On average in the first three months of the same year there were 6,290,000 listeners to Radio Lux in Britain. Here repetition and plugging is taken to absurd lengths. *The Guardian* quite fairly commented (7/8/62):

> An evening of Radio Luxembourg consists of pops and pops and pops. The material defeats the most determined effort to give it serious attention. There are none of the mind-provoking diversions of ITV . . . The records provide no relief from the disc jockeys, nor the disc jockeys from the records. The whole is similar in effect to the uninterrupted ringing of a telephone bell. First it makes you jump, then it makes you forgetful, and finally it gets on your nerves and you put a stop to it.

Roughly forty singles are issued each week—eighty sides. Of these, two or three at most will reach the Top Twenty. These will have an average life of six to eight weeks. Staying power does not count for much in so uncertain a trade. But making records is only one aspect of the pop singer's career. There is the whole business of keeping the star fixed in the teenage firmament. This is partly a matter of sheer hard grind on the part of the star and his agent or manager—one-night stands in different towns, the summer season in a seaside town, a good deal of travelling and rehearsals. It is also a matter of highly organized and sustained publicity—radio and television appearances and interviews, feature articles, gossip news, original or ghosted columns in the teenage papers. For example, as well as the photographs of the stars which are found in the illustrated love comics for teenage girls, each one of these papers has a pop singer or two as resident columnist, plus large colour photo insets, details about their tastes and love-life, letters requesting information about them from fans, their horoscopes, etc. (The content of the fiction in these papers is discussed in the chapter on *Falling in Love*.) One of these papers, *Valentine*, bases each little story on the title of a current pop song, giving the recording company and the number of the record at the bottom of the page. These papers are, in fact, wholly parasitic on the pop-singer industry, and would fold up overnight without its support. Perhaps they are mutually inter-dependent. It would be difficult to guess, for example, whether an aspiring singer like Jess Conrad pays *Mirabelle* to interview him, or *Mirabelle* pays Jess Conrad, or they both thrive on mutual admiration and goodwill.

In what terms is it possible to establish even rough standards of judgement about this kind of music? There are many forces at work which inhibit any judgement whatsoever: pop music is regarded as the exclusive property of the teenager, admission to outsiders reserved. In these terms, disqualification is by age limit. But, of course, this is nonsense. Like any other popular commercial music, teenage pop is light entertainment music, intended for dancing, singing, leisure and enjoyment. It differs in character, but not in *kind*, from other sorts of popular music which have provided a base for commercial entertainment since the advent of jazz, and before. If we are unable to comment on its quality and to make meaningful distinctions, it is largely because we lack a vocabulary of criticism for dealing with the lighter and more transient qualities which are part of a culture of leisure. We need that vocabulary very much indeed now, since this is the area in which the new media are at play.

On the other hand, there are counter-forces at work which dismiss *all* pop music simply because of its teenage connections and its cult qualities. This reaction is just as dangerous since it is based upon prejudice. It springs in part from the inability of adults to establish their own points of reference in relation to popular culture—even though, lying behind the rejection of Elvis Presley, there is often a secret addiction to Gracie Fields or Vera Lynn or the Charleston or Al Jolson or Nelson Eddy. (One needs to listen carefully to the older Tin Pan Alley tunes which survive in the repertoire of any pub sing-song to detect the connections.) There must also remain the suspicion that pop music provides a sitting target for those who have, for some unaccountable reason, to work off social envy or aggression against the younger generation. From this point of view, contemporary pops could not be better designed, since they are basically loud, raucous, always played at full volume, an obvious affront to good taste. They are frankly sensual in appeal, with persistent themes of youth, love and sex (but then, look again at the lyrics in Reeves' *Idiom of the People*): and these themes are given a physical image in the pop singer himself, whose behaviour on and off stage is a challenge to British modesty and reserve. Worst of all, the music itself is an affirmation of a spirit of adolescent rebelliousness and independence, and therefore, it is supposed, symbolizes some sort of deep undermining of adult authority and tastes.

Pop music may well be all of these things, but that does not help us much at the end of the day. For it is more difficult to judge, keeping one's respect both for the lively qualities embodied and the standards of light entertainment generally, the quality of a music which is so entwined with the cult of its own presentation, so mixed in with the mystic rites of the pop singer and his mythology and so shot through with commercialism. It might be said, then, that the pops cannot be judged at all—but have rather to be seen as part of a whole sub-culture, and handled as one would the chants and ceremonies of a primitive tribe. Are the only standards anthropological?

This method, too, has its pitfalls. It invites a slack relativism, whereby pop music of any kind is excused because it plays a functional role in the teenage world. Functional it is—but the relationship between what is authentically part of teenage culture and what is provided for that culture by an adult and organized industry is not a simple one. If we add the evidence of the first part of this chapter, which deals with authentic features of the culture, to the second part, which describes the organization of the industry, we see how necessary it is to view this phenomenon both from within and without teenage culture itself. And this consideration brings us back to one of the basic problems in popular culture—does the audience get what it likes (in which case, are those likes enough?) and needs (in which case, are the needs healthy ones?), or is it getting to like what it is given (in which case, perhaps tastes can be extended)? Nowhere in this whole field is it so true that the real answer lies in an understanding of how these two factors interact in contemporary popular culture.

This can best be illustrated by looking at the history of the growth and changes in the main styles in teenage music since the recent phase began. The most authentic music—in the sense of being least commercially induced—was 'Skiffle'—an almost wholly British development, though with American roots. The skiffle 'movement' was born in the early fifties and disappeared in any major form almost as quickly as it had come before the advancing tide of rock-'n'-roll by 1958. Yet it has not entirely disappeared, as the astonishing growth in the number of young people who have mastered the guitar, and the recent eruption of provincial groups like The Beatles and the Pacemakers, reveals. But it has lived a somewhat subterranean life since its early boom. Skiffle marked the first real break-through of one of the many forms of jazz to a British teenage audience. It was a resolutely uncommercial, do-it-yourself kind of music, which took root in schools, youth clubs and places of work. It was played by amateurs, often on improvised instruments—a bass constructed out of a broom handle and box and a washboard. It led to the startling rise to a position of dominance in the pop-music scene of two elements which still keep the wheels of teenage music turning: the guitar and the male singer. Skiffle had to be a music you made for yourself in your own groups. The attempt to convert it into a commercial music was the kiss of death.

In musical form, skiffle was a highly simplified, almost rudimentary, form of jazz. Its roots were authentic enough. In the early decades of the century the 'spasm bands' played a kind of home-made jazz on improvised instruments—kazoos, combs-and-paper, harmonicas, washboards, bottles and jugs, etc. In his book on *Skiffle* Brian Bird records the existence of a spasm band in New Orleans as early as 1896, with such instruments as a zither, harmonica, guitar built from a cigar-box, a string bass made out of a half-barrel, and a banjo constructed from a cheese-box. The spasm bands played the old blues, jazzed work songs, ballads, Gospel hymns and many of the 'country' ballads from the backlands (what we now call 'country-and-western', some of which are based on transported English, Irish and Scottish folk-songs). 'In the old days of Mississippi folk-music a free-and-easy party with dancing was known as a "skiffle".' Later the skiffle bands played at home parties and informal negro gatherings.

In 1948 some of this type of music was at last recorded, and, shortly after, skiffle groups began to be formed in this country, including groups within both the Ken Colyer band and the Chris Barber jazz band, whose basic music was revival Trad. The skiffle movement then gained ground in unexpected places, taken up by many young people who had never heard either live performances or recordings of this kind of music.

The amateur skiffle craze nevertheless prepared the way for the advent of rock-'n'-roll—itself a 'folk' music in origin, but rapidly transformed by the emergence of the commercial managers and the record companies. Groups and singers who were later to make their names as 'rock' stars first learned the basic guitar chords and something of the vocal wail from early skiffle groups. Tommy Steele was only the first and best known of a whole crop of entertainers who came into rock and the pops via the skiffle group.

Rock-'n'-roll also has its authentic jazz antecedents. Kenneth Allsop once described it (*Twentieth Century*, December 1960) as a 'shotgun wedding of two traditional forms given a deliberately manufactured crudity and amplification'. One of these forms was the hill-billy songs and the tunes of the white South known as 'country-and-western'—music heard at 'hoedowns', barndances, church socials, country fairs, rodeos and cattle sales'. C-and-W is a generic term itself—it can be 'a blues-yodel, a square dance, a waltz, a guitar blues, a work-song, a gospel-shout, a Civil War narrative ballad, a reel or one of those Victorian tear-jerkers'. This was the music of the rural Protestant South, with which Elvis Presley first made his name on local Tennessee radio stations. The other tradition was, naturally, the blues. By the time the shotgun match was made between these two folk-musics, the blues had grown up and dispersed. The particular form which was integrated with country-and-western was that version which had been developed by negro jazz far from the New Orleans cradle and played by the 'rhythm-and-blues' bands popular in Harlem and elsewhere. In the forties, bands like Louis Jordan's were playing a form of 'jump' or negro rock-'n'-roll—music with a heavy, accentuated beat, a raucous honking tenor saxophone behind, heavily nasalized and 'shouting' (Chick Webb and Lionel Hampton played a version of 'Harlem' music in the thirties, and Earl Bostick in the forties). One can still trace the line back through some of the popular records of the forties—for instance, Louis Jordan's *There Ain't Nobody Here But us Chickens* or *The Honeydripper*, an instrumental version with a regular rock-style beat.

Johnnie Ray, Bill Haley and Elvis Presley are the three names most prominently associated with the beginnings of American rock-'n'-roll. Tommy Steele and Lonnie Donegan, who were perhaps first in the field·with a British version of this music, had both been skiffle men before (Donegan, of course, was also an accomplished traditional jazz man). Donegan's famous record, *Rock Island Line*, marked a turning point in the British scene. From that point forward rock music was heavily commercialized and exploited, with a continual boost from America. Unknown groups and artists were recorded, singers discovered by the musical entrepreneurs in coffee bars, and the market was infiltrated by films with rock stars (e.g. the trend-setting *Rock Around the Clock*). The promotion business moved in on teenage music for the first time. Skiffle resisted commercial exploitation almost to the end. But the second wave, rock-'n'-roll, stormed and captured the citadels of commercial music and the record companies, urged on by the fans. The amateur quality of skiffle had made it difficult to commercialize—the skiffle sound was neither smooth nor sophisticated enough for the many young people who hadn't the patience to master an instrument for themselves. Recorded rock was in a much more favourable position to meet the demand. Since this period, rock has broadened out to include several styles— including an adaptation to the romantic lyric in the form of the teenage ballad—all of which are usually referred to now as 'beat' music. And, with many variations, this has remained the basis of commercial teenage music.

In one sense Denmark Street (the British equivalent of Tin Pan Alley) collapsed before the new beat music because the combined influence of skiffle, American films and records and the promotion of the pop stars had built up a demand among teenagers. The established world of light-entertainment music did not give in easily, but it was driven along by popular demand. Since then, however, as teenage tastes have come to depend more and more upon what is supplied, tastes tend to be led from in front rather than propelled from behind. The audience has been saturated with the dominant style by the record companies. On one or two occasions, when the demand seemed to be falling off, the companies have attempted to pre-empt and manipulate taste directly— never in the direction of other forms of jazz (with the dubious exception of Acker Bilk), but always in the direction of some commercialized version of the same basic formula, which it would be possible to record and produce with ease. Occasionally the air is filled with rumour and prophecies of recession (at regular intervals, the musical press runs panic-stricken headlines enquiring 'Are Teenagers Deserting Beat?'—but up to now the answer has been a resounding 'No!'). At one such moment, an attempt was made to create a market for a Europeanized version of the calypso, but the fans simply refused to wear it—an interesting piece of consumer resistance.

With the twist, however, a new pattern of engineered tastes emerged. The attempt to promote commercial pop music via the dance is not new—it was quite common in the twenties and thirties (the charleston, the shimmy, the big apple, etc). During the mid-fifties, teenagers danced a sort of patterned jitterbug to rock-'n'-roll music. With the coming of the twist the commercial providers, recognizing rather late the essential connection between dancing and pop music for young people, reverted to the older pattern, and began to tie up the style of the music with the novelty of the dance steps.

Musically, the twist was not new. It was a kind of faked rock-'n'-roll, a variant of a variant. It differed only slightly from beat music in style, tempo, delivery or instrumentation. It was the mixture as before—but newly packaged. The twist was the invention of a young negro American, Chubby Checker. When Checker's first record, *The Twist*, was introduced, no one took much notice. But, as the *Sunday Times* put it, 'the twist was not, like rock-'n'-roll, to wait for spontaneous enthusiasm. After Christmas the highly pressurized boom was on.' In 1961 the twist became popular in the Parisian night-clubs, and, shorn of its American antecedents, and freed from the taint of the 'palais', 'it became worthy of acceptance as a status symbol by the West End smart set' ('Inside the Twist', Graham Turner, *Encounter*, June 1962). When Checker's *Let's Twist Again* was released, in August 1961, very few people did. Then Philip Nathan, editor of Mecca Ballroom's publicity journal, *Dance News*, with a readership of over 100,000, ran a series of articles. Rank, owners of a chain of twenty-four ballrooms, sent Peppi and his New York Twisters round the circuit popularizing the dance. The twist was explained on Mecca's Radio Luxembourg programme, and the companies began to push out twist records, which had been lying in cold storage, together with instructions for the dance. Just before Christmas, Columbia pictures produced *Twist Around The Clock*, a title designed to awaken reminiscent echoes among teenagers. The picture was made in two months ('We needed it fast if we were going to cash in', publicity manager Pat Williamson is reported to have said). Brigitte Bardot and 700 other teenagers were summoned to the preview. But Columbia hadn't been fast enough. Paramount sneaked in a counter-film, *Hey, Let's Twist*. Press, television and radio picked up the signals of an important turn in the fashion cycle, and the campaign began in earnest. The twist, as they say, was 'becoming popular'.

Still the teenage audience seemed reluctant to adopt the twist as 'their' music. A gigantic publicity push was made, jointly sponsored by film companies, record dealers, managers of local cinemas and dance halls, local dress shops. The film softened up the market: then the ancillary organizations moved in. Manufacturers produced 'twist' skirts, specially flared for dancing, 'twist' necklaces, 'twist' shoes called 'twisties', which was in fact a new name for a slow-selling old model (though whether these were designed to withstand the wear and tear on the soles which the dance makes the manufacturers did not say). The book, *Dance the Twist*, appeared in January, sold out in a couple of weeks. Radio Luxembourg played nothing but twist records for months. Surprisingly, by March 1962, teenagers were twisting. The twist had arrived.

In a feature on 4 March 1962 the *Sunday Times* tried to calculate what had been the value, the golden payoff, of this piece of commercial engineering. The list included the following items:

EMI RECORDS (issuing under eight labels, including Capitol, Columbia, Parlophone and MGM) spent £5,000 on the campaign, netted a sale of 1,500,000 records, at a retail price of 6s. 9d. each.

DECCA RECORDS 800,000 records sold at 6s. 9d. each.

MECCA DANCEHALLS recorded 10 per cent higher attendances in their dance halls (i.e. 40,000 more). Average price of entry—3s. 6d. each.

RANK BALLROOMS 10 per cent higher attendances in half their twenty-four ballrooms. Average price—4s. each.

BRITANNIA BOOKS first edition of *Dance the Twist* sold in ten days—25,000 at 2s. 6d. each. Reprint half sold. Estimated profit—5d. per copy.

MARTHA HILL, a Leicester store, produced the first twist dresses. Sold 2,000 a week at three to ten guineas each. Estimated percentage profit—between 5 and 15 per cent.

WYLES SHOES in Derby. Produced the first twist shoes. 15,000 pairs sold in two weeks. Estimated profit—10 per cent.

WEST END FASHION STORE 3,500 dresses sold—£5-£10 each. 1,000 skirts, 3,000 necklaces sold. Estimated profit—27 per cent average.

When an audience can be induced to go crazy for a dance or a particular kind of music, as happened in the history of the twist, what we are observing is not, strictly speaking, the movement of popular taste so much as the creation of artificial wants in the field of commercial culture. Yet, such artificial selection and stimulation of a particular style, fashion or craze operates within a broad field of popular taste or behaviour which makes selective promotion possible. The taste for simple dance music of a popular, inexacting kind certainly exists: the twist campaign was lucky in its timing, and expertly packaged. The connection between the twist craze and the audience is not the simple one which the commercial promoters often seem to claim, but the link is not merely an exploitative one. In some way, the music and the dance do connect with the audience. The twist appeals to them through the natural entertainment channels, it offers a pattern of popular activity closely linked with their interests in going out, dancing, parties and social occasions of many kinds. It was personalized through the medium of young singers and entertainers. But it has also been made to connect. The study of the twist is, therefore, interesting, both as an example of the sociology of teenage tastes and as an aspect of the sociology of the entertainments business.

But even this kind of music can still be judged—not so much for its classical stature, its folk roots, its authenticity, but more simply

as commercial entertainment music, and according to standards
set by the best and most inventive music which has been produced
in the past under similar conditions. The similarity between the
twist and the Charleston, or between the teenage ballad and the
earlier romantic ballad, gives us some rough-and-ready comparisons, and indicates a useful time-scale. Are the contemporary
versions of pop music good even within these limits?

Pop music does have many genuine entertainment qualities.
Its beat is simple and repetitive, but it is easily adapted to dancing,
especially for audiences who are not particularly sophisticated
rhythmically, and therefore find it difficult to adapt physical
movement to the subtler rhythms of jazz, especially modern jazz.
But it is the pulse which marks off beat from other kinds of
commercial dance music, and this is where its primary appeal lies.
The beat is strong and insistent. It gives to most pop music more
vigour and drive than we find in, say, the big dance-band music,
popular until fairly recently. It is crude in its simplicity, but lively
and compulsive. And this compulsive quality, pushing the
audience into an induced excitement, is the element which connects the music with the culture. The instrumentation has been
skilfully adapted to this beat. Thus the guitar holds the highlight;
the only other prominent instruments are the 'rhythm' or percus-
sive ones—bass, or bass guitar, drums, and piano used as a
rhythm, rather than a solo instrument. The accompanying guitars,
supporting the lead instrument (or more frequently, of course, the
singer's voice), can strike one chord on each beat: the drummer,
too, taps one stroke for each beat in the bar. In this way, the beat is
reinforced by several instruments. This gives the music a 'rolling-
on' rhythm, a 'ratchet' effect. In the faster numbers there is no
pause at the end of four or eight bars, but the basic pulse drives
the rhythm forward to the next bar. All the flowing 'line' instruments typical of jazz, such as the trumpet and the saxophone, have
been eliminated altogether, or play a subordinate role.

When critics or commentators of pop music are at a loss for
words to describe the music (as they frequently are on *Juke Box
Jury*) they often fall back on the word 'swing': 'This one really

swings.' This is a careless use of a word which has some precise meaning in jazz, but which hardly applies at all to pop music. Swing is a difficult element to isolate even in jazz (see, for example, André Hodier's brave attempt to analyse its meaning in musical terms in his book, *Jazz: Its Evolution and Essence*), but it is certainly the product of rhythmic subtlety, phrasing and accent. These are precisely the qualities which most pop music lacks. The quality which distinguishes the best beat music—in both instrumental and sung versions—is the quality of *drive*. Drive is a combination of heavily accented beat, punch in delivery and sheer physical thrust. It was this thrust which marked out the earlier Elvis Presley records from all his imitators. Presley added to this a crude sensuality of gesture, but also a resonant voice capable of all the notes in both registers, with occasional evocations of the negro blues and folk country-and-western, both of which are indigenous to the Bible belt around Nashville where he first made his name. Presley sang from the loins (his later work is much more sentimental and *schmaltzy* and lacks any true individuality or excitement). The most memorable notes in an early Elvis record were sensual musical gestures in themselves.

No British singer has ever been able to match Presley's musical energy. They have all tended to equate this with sheer volume, whereas with Presley's voice, the most suggestive notes were always slurred and breathy, the sensuality suggested rather than fully given. Until recently British singers have made more of the slower type of beat music, particularly the teenage ballad. These are often praised for their 'lyrical quality', but they seem to lack the true lyrical or soaring qualities. In the popular song, lyricism has always depended upon a sweetness of tone and a mellowness of voice which few teenage performers possess. Commentators on pop music use the word 'lyrical' to refer to the sweetness of the sentiments expressed in the song: an emotive judgement, not a musical one. Adam Faith's songs, for example, have this teenage 'tenderness', but the voice itself is without much melody. Cliff Richard's voice is also 'soft' in the accepted style, but it is without colour or tone. Less popular singers, such as Danny

Williams or Kenny Lynch, do possess something of the soaring quality we associate with the lyrical (in Williams's *Moon River*, for instance), but these are not strictly teenage ballads at all, and Williams (a coloured South African by origin) is closer in tone to Johnny Mathis or Nat King Cole than to Cliff Richard. Musically, one of the most interesting recent developments was the rare—and apparently brief—appearance of a young female singer of some quality. Helen Shapiro, a young Cockney East Ender, sings with a deep, prematurely mature, almost masculine, contralto. Jonathan Miller (*New Statesman*, October 1961) remarked that her songs were 'uncannily orthodox invocations of the teenage creed', but they were delivered with a detached seriousness, a directness and confidence, which distinguish her in this male-dominated world. She was best known for rather typical ballads such as *You Don't Know*, but her range was wider, and included the lively *Walking Back to Happiness* as well as more traditional blues songs. Her voice is true, but the pitch of the voice is perhaps too rigid for real development in terms of musical quality: in any event she has had little success in the teenage charts recently. She was certainly not helped to mature as an artist by her meteoric rise to fame, and the exaggerated claims made for her talent (even by usually so excellent a commentator in this field, Colin MacInnes, in 'Socialist Impresarios', *New Statesman*, June 1962). Her talent was genuine when compared with so many of her competitors, but she could certainly not be compared with the finest of female jazz singers, as MacInnes suggested. She lacked the melody, taste and pitch of Ella Fitzgerald, the 'torch' quality of Sarah Vaughan, the rhythmic ingenuity of Anita O'Day or the incomparable phrasing of Billie Holiday. There is always a disquieting sugges-tion of nasal monotony in her pitch.

For the most part, American trends and tastes have dominated the pop-music scene ever since the advent of rock-'n'-roll. But there has been a continuous and vigorous effort to impose an authentic British style on the music, and thus to give it a more solid foundation in British teenage culture. We can trace this in the essentially native, Bermondsey charm and innocence of the early Tommy Steele (eloquently written about by MacInnes in *England, Half English*), in the scatter-brained Cockney voice of Joe Brown, in the Cockney take-offs of Mike Sarne (*Come Outside*) and even in the popularity of some familiar London songs given a beat treatment. This trend has now emerged with considerable force with the discovery of very large numbers of pop-music groups, singers and instrumentalists, in the provincial centres of the North. Groups like The Beatles, Gerry and the Pacemakers, Freddie and the Dreamers, etc., have, apparently, continued to produce a kind of native beat music, closer in feel and tempo to skiffle and early rock-'n-'roll than the typical songs familiar in recent years in London; these groups have been singing and playing locally without much impact on the national scene, at weekend dances, beat clubs, local concerts and coffee bars. A city like Liverpool has recently yielded up nearly 400 such groups. The Beatles, for example, sing in aggressively flat Liverpudlian accents, and the *Melody Maker* has recorded the fact that many young groups have travelled north to Liverpool and Manchester in order to pick up an authentic provincial accent. This phenomenon is perhaps simply a sign that the mid-Atlantic affectations adopted by most of the earlier pop singers are beginning to wear off and that the music now has an autonomous life in British teenage culture. But it also seems to mark a return to the older beat style, and suggests that some of the traditions of skiffle groups were maintained, as a kind of local folk music, long after the skiffle craze itself has passed in the south, and, strengthened by its native roots, has now begun to re-emerge within the limits of commercial beat music. The pops are often fed and sustained by infusions of vigour from such sources.

Pop music has a certain vigour, but its lack of variety is staggering. Most of the ballads tend to sound the same even to a sympathetic ear: they are often variations on a basic set of chords and chord sequences. Where old favourites have been reshaped to the beat style, they have lost everything and gained very little in the transposition—except an occasional yodel. Musical formulae have been applied here mercilessly. Variety of tempo, theme, instrumentation or effect are rare. Occasionally, variety is added in the shape of the musical gimmick: castanets or bongoes are introduced for 'effect', but which effect is hard to determine, since the music is not a whit more Latin in rhythm. (When in jazz Dizzy Gillespie uses Afro-Cuban rhythmic phrases, or Miles Davis interprets a Latin idiom in his *Sketches for Spain*, the whole cast of the music is changed without the jazz base being abandoned.) The very repetitiveness of the beat in beat music means that special care ought to be taken to compensate for rhythmic monotony. Yet drummers appear, on the whole, content to tap out the same tempo on disc after disc. One can legitimately add a note of distress on the debasement of certain instruments—the saxophone, for example, which, if used at all in beat music, is reduced to honking and snorting in the background to add to the 'effects' (in early rock-'n'-roll concerts, the saxophonist was often required to perform lying flat on his back).

The conditions of production in pop music so nearly resemble those of assembly line that it would be unfair to compare this music with folk music or early jazz. A more revealing comparison is with commercial jazz. Certainly, there is nothing even in the most raucous versions of the pops—rock-'n'-roll—which equals the insipid formula music produced by so many of the commercial dance bands—the strict metronome-accuracy of Victor Silvester, for example, with its total divorce from swing of any kind. BBC general record programmes provide regular feast-days of music of this sort. In contrast with Silvester, beat music is loud and vulgar, but it is at least music for the living A good deal of commercial jazz has been produced by groups as keen as the teenage performers to become popular and to make money. (Nat Hentoff reminds us in his book, *The Jazz Life*, that much jazz 'is a constant battle between raw feeling and what it takes to buy a Cadillac'.)

The difference between commercial pops and commercial jazz lies, not in the fact that the music is produced in a commercial environment, since this would be true for both types, but rather in the fact that commercial jazz seems capable of inner growth and change. By inner growth we do not mean changes in the style of the music, for pop music is more subject than perhaps any other to a fashion cycle. But we do mean that commercial jazz has provided for the slow maturing of individual musical talent, and has shown itself as responsive to the demands placed on it by those who play it as it is to those who buy or produce it. It has internal, as well as external, standards by which to measure its success.

A comparison might be made here with one of the very successful commercial jazz bands—the Count Basie band. Basie is noted for his musical caution. His band, formed from the remnants of Bennie Moten's band after Moten's death in 1935, became a classic big band of the swing era in jazz, and has remained so ever since. He has held to the mainstream path of standard numbers and familiar arrangements. The elements of the Basie sound—its bouncing pulse provided by the rhythm section, the organized strength of the brass section, riffing in unison, and the solo instrumental work of the tenor-men—are still the same, although the composition of the band has changed. The Basie sound, like the essence of beat music, has been standardized—yet it has never become simply a formula. This is due, in part, to the quality of Basie himself, who has a clear conception of the sound he wants though he never theorizes about it, and whose restrained and occasional intervention on the piano—'contributing the missing things', as Freddie Green once said—in fact ties the tumultuous big-band sound together into a single style, pushes the whole band ahead together and feeds the soloists. The band as a whole has therefore been able to develop one of the most distinctive and exciting 'big' sounds in jazz. Its effect is that of a unity—a *whole* sound, rather than an accretion of separate parts.

But the other, and more important, factor is that the Basie sound has provided a climate and a form within which a host of brilliant musicians have been able to harvest their talents. The original rhythm section of the thirties and early forties was one of the greatest ever assembled (Basie himself, Freddie Green, Walter Page and Jo Jones). In his essay on Basie in *The Jazzmakers* Nat Shapiro reminds us that the list of Basie tenor men includes Lester Young, Herschel Evans, Chu Berry, Buddy Tate, Don Byas,

Illinois Jacquet, Paul Gonsalves, Lucky Thompson, Wardell Gray and Ben Webster, and his list of trombonists Dickie Wells, Benny Morton, Vic Dickenson, Don Minor, J. J. Johnson and Ed Cuffie. To some extent, Basie's insistence on the primacy of the pulsing beat has made it easy for these men, so varying in style, to find a place in the band as parts of a unit: but Basie was also able to blend contrasting talents into his band—the dry, aphoristic tone of Lester Young, for example, against the tidal wave of riffs in unison laid down by the brass section. That an innovator so elegant, restrained and sophisticated as Lester Young should have done some of his best work in a band organized around such a sound is itself a tribute to Basie's triumph over his own formula for success. It is not simply that musicians in the Basie band have maintained a high standard of musical proficiency. The dominant saxophone style at the time when Lester Young joined the Basie band was that established by the genius of Coleman Hawkins. To this tradition belonged the majority of Basie's tenor men. Yet, within this climate, Lester Young evolved a style of saxophone playing that was radically different, an economic, spare phrasing, a cool, deliberate tone, and a gift for harmonic paraphrase. If one listens to the Young solo in *Lady Be Good* one is hearing a musician who, in the midst of the tumultuous big-band sound generated by the Basie orchestra, is still able to have his inner ear attuned to his own personal sound. Musicians like Young, and other soloists who brought their gifts to maturity with Basie, have managed to use a standard approach and even a commercial setting to advance their own styles and gifts, to keep in touch with the growing points of the music, even if this meant blowing in 'jam sessions' long after the fans had departed, or playing with pick-up groups (among Lester Young's finest solo work are the fragments he played with the Wilson pick-up group which accompanied Billie Holiday in her early recordings). The music of such men, therefore, continued to have an inner life, constantly referred back to and authenticated by standards set and advanced by other skilled performers, or made valid in terms of the feelings and emotions felt by the player himself. Naturally, such men aimed to please their audience—jazz purists are often disconcerted to discover how much this has meant to performers whom they admire.

Jazz may have made compromises all along the way, but it has always maintained the musicians' right to refer themselves to standards and to express emotions other than those set by the commercial market. This sense of integrity in relation to the materials of the art is what has made it possible for jazz—now so long removed from the New Orleans cradle—to retain an independent life of its own somewhere between the folk arts and the commercial assembly line. With pop music, one feels this inner musical life to be almost wholly missing. Its points of reference are almost entirely external—the materials are so stereotyped that they can have little emotional significance for the performer, and the standards of excellence seem to exist essentially in the record companies' charts and the wild responses of the audience. Changes, when they occur, are swings of the fashion trends, not forced forward by the performers themselves—as was the case with Lester Young or Charlie Parker or any of the company of jazz innovators. Even in the jazz world, Miles Davis represents an extreme, but his comments seem so alien to the whole climate of the pops, and so close to the attitudes of jazz, that they are worth quoting in this connection:

Look, if I go to a club and hear a good friend take a solo that I like, I don't applaud him. It's silly, I had a girl friend once who always used to look at me as if I should applaud her. Hell, if she didn't know I liked her, that was *her* problem. I don't mind if the boys in the band bow and all that, but I figure I'm doing the best I can with my horn, and anybody out front who has ears knows that. What am I there for if not to try and make people like what I'm doing? I have to bow too? I pay attention to what counts—the music. People should give me credit for that. I try to make sure they'll have something *to* applaud.

(interview with *Playboy*, August 1960)

It is the absence of anything even modestly approaching this attitude which makes the prospects for pop music as a genuine popular art so dim.

The difference may simply be the degree of exploitation in relation to the potential merit of what is being exploited. Given the simple volume of stuff recorded, perhaps it is no wonder that quality is so hard to come by. And with the present organization of the pop-music industry so firmly based on strict commercial principles, the industry need only risk money on safe bets, which means in essence finding a selective popular strain and milching it for as long as the fans will take it. The very climate of the pop-music business discourages the nurturing of skill and inspiration. There is a built-in expendability both of materials and artist—neither is expected to last the pace for long. They are designed, one feels, to be here today and gone tomorrow. Pop-music talents blaze—careers are always meteoric—but they never seem to flower. The turn-over is too rapid. And since the performer wants to make as much as he can while he remains in favour, the pop singer is sorely tempted to market his person rather than his musical gift. The world of pop music will not of its own accord give an artist the opportunity to make that deep, memorable impression upon which the really outstanding popular artists depend. The real surprise is that, out of so resolutely processed an industry, occasionally a Presley, a Darin or a Shapiro can make a mark.

Throughout this chapter we have constantly made comparisons between pop music and jazz. This is because, though there are many individual pop songs worth listening to, in general jazz seems an infinitely richer kind of music, both aesthetically and emotionally. The comparison this way seems much more rewarding than the more typical confrontation which is so frequently made between pop music and classical music. The reference to jazz helps us to make comparisons with another entertainment music, which nevertheless has legitimate uses and discernible standards. The point behind such comparisons ought not to be simply to wean teenagers away from the juke-box heroes, but to alert them to the severe limitations and the ephemeral quality of music which is so formula-dominated and so directly attuned to the standards set by the commercial market. It is a genuine widening of sensibility and emotional range which we should be working for—an extension of tastes which might lead to an extension of pleasure. The worst thing which we would say of pop music is not that it is vulgar, or morally wicked, but, more simply, that much of it is not very good.

Note: The Beatles
In the pop-music field, fashions change so rapidly that it is impossible to keep abreast. Already, when we were writing this chapter, we were aware that The Beatles, and groups in their style, were something of a new phenomenon. But it is now clear that they represent a distinctive break with earlier patterns. The pre-eminence of the singer has faded before the 'group'. The introspective, wistful, romantic mood has given way to a much more affirmative, extrovert, uninhibited style. Love is still the dominant theme, but it is no longer expressed in a 'moony' way. There is still a remarkable conformity in the texture of the sounds produced, but they seem less relentlessly 'tooled' and manufactured. This stylistic shift is more than a simple trend-change: like each of the previous phases it relates to changes in the audience. The new sound was created, first, in the clubs, and the dances devised on the spot: the movements are, in fact, adaptations of the groups' performance—the jerking on the spot (because the singer cannot move from the microphone?) and the thrust with the shoulders (because the guitarist's left shoulder is free?). In accent, in texture, in inflection, in attack, something of the native quality of life comes through; audiences and performers seem less shielded from one another by the screen of publicity or Big Business. The Beatles belong to Liverpool in a way in which Cliff Richard never belonged anywhere. Their zaniness seems a kind of defence—but it is also a quality of liveliness and energy, without devious complications, frankly indulged. Something of this quality invests the audience and qualifies the disturbing elements of mass hysteria. The fans 'play' at being worshippers as The Beatles 'play' at being idols. Yet the mass hysteria *is* there and the playfulness is a quality which can be, and has been, marketed.

Many critics are concerned about the 'masturbatory quality' of the audiences' response. But the striking thing about The Beatles, and some of their imitators, is that they are essentially childlike, androgynous, pre-pubertal. In their film, *A Hard Day's Night*, they are surrounded by beautiful girls, but they seem quite unaffected by them. They are much more 'themselves' running wild over an empty field. They are not 'sex images': they are 'dolls', 'poppets'.

II

The Big Bazaar

In its benevolence, the Big Bazaar has built the rhythmic worship
of fashion into the habits and looks and feelings of the urban mass:
it has organized the imagination itself. In dressing people up and
changing the scenery of their lives, on the street and in the bedroom, it has cultivated a great faith in the Religion of Appearances.
C. WRIGHT MILLS, *White Collar*

Advertising is usually discussed as if it were possible to make a
neat separation between its economic and cultural functions. As
an economic activity, we are told, it is an indispensable support to
modern consumer society. It is a natural extension of the system
of mass production and mass consumption. Its purpose is, of
course, to capture a section of the market for a particular manufacturer, and thus indirectly to enhance his profitability: but in the
process it stimulates sales generally, and therefore production, it
keeps money in circulation and factories working, and it introduces a wide range of choices to the consumer. This, it is argued,
is so vital an economic service that we cannot afford to do without
it, whatever its cultural costs.

If modern advertising were concerned primarily with bringing
the 'good news' about new products to the consumer—if its
content was essentially *information*—then this argument might
seem more valid. In fact, the main trend within modern advertising is away from information and towards persuasion. It provides
less and less of the basic information about quality and performance which assists the customer to make a rational choice, and has
become more and more involved with the manipulation of social
attitudes. 'It has passed the frontier of the selling of goods and
services and has become involved with the teaching of social and

personal values' (Raymond Williams, 'The Magic System', *New Left Review* 4: the most authoritative critique of modern advertising). The point about advertising is that it serves both an economic and a cultural function: what is more, the economic function cannot be served until the cultural attitudes have been mobilized by advertising through our systems of mass communication. Thus, as Raymond Williams points out, it is not enough to say that advertising reflects the growing materialism of modern society, since, if this were true, 'beer would be enough for us, without the additional promise that in drinking it we show ourselves to be manly, young in heart, or neighbourly'. In some senses advertising shows that we are not materialistic *enough*—or, at any rate, that we can only be persuaded to place our materialism at the service of the manufacturer when it is being appealed to alongside other, more acceptable, social aspirations.

. . . objects are not enough but must be validated, if only in fantasy, by association with social and personal meanings which in a different cultural pattern might be more directly available.

Raymond Williams, ibid.

The central question about advertising, then, is how and why this validation in fantasy is made.

The first task of modern advertising is to organize the market. It is in this way that the growth of advertising and the growth of the mass media are connected. For the media have helped to organize the public into groups and categories of 'audiences', and this process has streamlined the communication between the producer and the consumer. Advertising makes use of all the media—indeed many of the media are financed largely by becoming advertising channels: this is true of one of the two main television channels, the press both local and national, every type of magazine, and the printed circular. Every reader or viewer is a potential consumer: every audience is also a potential market. The function of advertising is to convert 'audiences' into 'markets'. Television, journals and newspapers, which are generally considered as media for carrying news, information, features and stories, opinion or instruction, are transformed by advertising into means for the penetration of particular markets. The general effect of this is only too clear. Advertising comes increasingly to dominate the format and presentation of the media: it dictates the disposal of news on the page in the popular paper, and its rhythms interrupt the viewing pattern of commercial television: in the glossy magazines and the women's magazines it affects the whole tone of the publication. What is more, advertising reinforces the grading of audiences and readers. Advertisements for the more expensive products appear in those papers and journals which are able to develop a reputation for reaching the wealthier type of reader, the 'decision-maker', 'the opinion leader' or the 'trend-setter'. Household goods, consumer durables, cosmetics and sweets are more heavily advertised in the mass-circulation magazines and papers. In each case the advertisement will be adapted in style, appeal and sophistication for the appropriate readership or audience. The stratification by 'brow' within the media is therefore reinforced by a process of grading for income and taste. If the same product is advertised right across the market, each advertisement will reflect in its style the demands of the appropriate medium. A Bri-nylon fabric is advertised in a gay, carefree manner in *Woman's Own*, but in a suave, modish and expensively restrained way once it reaches the pages of *Queen, About Town* or *Vogue* (Plate 14). Advertising contributes to cultural stratification in our society.

The second purpose of advertising is to reach the right audience with the most effective appeal. But, as in other kinds of mass art, the source and the agent of the communication are not the same. The source of the advertisement is the manufacturer, who has designed his product and selected the 'selling points'. The advertiser then becomes the agent, acting on behalf of his client. He is employed to speak to the consumer on the manufacturer's behalf, and he has therefore to make certain assumptions about the audience and about the relationship of the audience to his client. In advertising, as in television and the press, there is a speaker-audience formula, and this formula prescribes a certain view of what the audience is like in order to make communication easy. In some kinds of television, as we saw, the communicator assumes for his purpose an undifferentiated 'mass audience'. The popular journalist often assumes an 'average reader'. These assumptions contain important descriptions of people, and these descriptions in turn govern to some extent what is said and how it is said (see Chapter 9).

The 'mass audience' and the 'average reader' are, of course, crude categories, and rarely correspond to the actual audience for any television programme or popular paper. As the Pilkington Report authoritatively argued, most people in fact will form part of the majority and also parts of different minorities at different times in their lives. These categories serve the purpose, however, of massing people together for the sake of swift and 'effective' communication. They are convenient formulae for dealing with people in a complex society.

Exactly the same point can be made about advertising. It chooses to regard men and women in society as divided into two categories, producers and consumers. Advertising is one-way transmission—from the first to the second of these groups. This relationship carries certain premises with it. For the purpose of advertising it is assumed that consumer and producer can never be descriptions of the same person, that their interests are quite distinct and usually irreconcilable. This is taken to be an accurate generalization about modern industrial societies—yet it is in fact only *one* of several possible descriptions, and an intrinsically false one too. In complex societies such as ours, no one person can produce all the things he wishes to consume, nor does every consumer wish to buy all the things in the many ranges produced. Yet we are all both producers and consumers—we all produce some goods and services, and we all consume goods and services which we need but cannot produce for ourselves. That is the consequence of the division of labour. The question is how to establish a balance between the supply of goods and the demand for them. In our society this relationship is expressed in terms of the market, and the market does set producer and consumer off against one another as competitors at the point of sale. And since the producer is autonomous, with the means of production at his disposal, taking decisions about production as it affects the profitability of his business, and the consumer is assumed to be the private individual making personal choices about the consumption of goods, advertising must legitimize the market relationship and define society in terms of its commanding images. Implicit in advertising as a communication process, then, is the alienation of the sphere of work from the sphere of consumption. Advertising sees us as individual consumers making private decisions at the expense of others in the universal super-market, the great bazaar: it cannot see us as users of a common stock of produced goods and services which we both help to create and, in our turn, need. In these terms, advertising is an extension of the market system and can legitimately be described as the official art of a capitalist society.

A market which is organized by this kind of art has the advantage of leaving open a wide range of choices. But it has the disadvantage of highlighting the personal, as against the social, consumption of goods and services. It defines all needs in terms of personal consumption, though it is clear that many of the real and pressing social decisions in our society cannot be adequately taken in this way: certain individuals can, if they have enough money, 'shop' for an adequate education for their children, but the question of a decent system of public education for all cannot be resolved by private competition and consumption in the market sense. Nor can the question of housing or transport. These are social decisions—they involve the society as a whole and can only be arrived at at the expense of the market. One of the charges against advertising is that, by investing only those choices which we make as private individuals with the glamour of art, it depresses in the public consciousness major areas of life where social decisions are urgent.

The fundamental choice that emerges, in the problems set to us by modern industrial production, is between man as consumer and man as user.

Raymond Williams, ibid.

Advertising exploits, but cannot reconcile, this real contradiction, since its primary purpose is always to 'cash' needs in terms of personal consumption and the consumption ideal: social needs require us to go outside this ideal altogether—to make decisions which relate not to the personal choices but to wider social purposes in the community. 'Advertising, as we see it now, operates to preserve the consumption ideal from the criticism inexorably made of it by experience.'

We have said that advertising is obliged to see us as 'consumers', and that this is a way of seeing a social process, a communication formula, such as we are already familiar with in other spheres of mass communication. But it would be more apt to say that advertisers see us as *reluctant* consumers. Presumably we know what we need, and the decision to spend in order to satisfy our needs is a complex process, determined in part by how much money we have, and whether we choose to spend or to save, in part by a set of priorities between competing needs about which we can only decide in the context of our whole lives. But advertising assumes we are only good for what we spend—and more particularly, since producers of the same kinds of commodities are competing with each other for our custom, that we are only good for what we buy of a particular product. Advertising serves both a general function—to induce us to spend liberally—and a particular function—to induce us to spend on the product which a particular manufacturer is advertising on the market. The general impulse to consume, based on needs and rational choices, is not enough for the advertiser: he must provide the motivation for spending, and to do this he must find a way of making us see our priorities in a different light. He reorders the elements contained in our choice to buy, strengthening the propensity to consume, weakening our sense of alternate needs or competing priorities, which the advertiser must regard as forms of 'sales resistance'. The appeal to consumption is not enough to counter this resistance, for the very good reason that most of us are perfectly capable of placing consumption in the context of our whole lives and of judging such appeals against the background of other, often more pressing, priorities. The advertiser, then, must turn to other areas where we are more vulnerable, and make his appeal either in terms of the established human meanings and values which we have validated in our own experience or culture, or to those social and human aspirations which are not adequately expressed or fulfilled in modern life. The purpose of advertising is to establish a link between the consumption of goods and the satisfaction of these needs. And since this link is very often a meaningless one (if we are weak-willed, beer will not make us 'manly'), or at best provides only a substitute for what is really desired (if we are lonely, a cigarette may make us temporarily forget but it will not give us the consolations of friendship), it can only be forged in fantasy. The art of advertising is the art of fantasy, and fantasy of this order always indicates an area of confusion in our lives, tensions which we can only resolve by dreaming or by the regular displacements of magic:

> If the meanings and values generally operative in the society give no answers to, no means of negotiating problems of death, loneliness, frustration, the need for identity and respect, then the magical system must come, mixing its charms and expedients with reality in easily available forms, and binding the weakness to the condition which has created it.
>
> Raymond Williams, ibid.

In any culture one of the most significant ways in which meanings, aspirations and values are made active is through the language and images of art. In the practice of modern advertising, we see the growth of a kind of bastard art, whose purpose is to mobilize human aspirations and values, not in order to handle them with imagination or to set them to work in a human context, but specifically to attach them by sleight-of-hand to the sphere of consumption.

We said earlier that advertising is communication with an

undisclosed source. No matter how carefully designed, every advertisement has its 'selling point', though the best advertisement leaves this undeclared except to the most critical eye. The approach to the consumer has to be made with considerable discretion, for once the advertiser enters the area of attitudes on behalf of his client, he is dealing with very personal kinds of experience. It is much easier to understand the process if we listen to the advertiser when he is speaking to his client directly, for here many of the inhibitions on his art are relaxed. When advertisers are encouraging manufacturers to make use of their services, a harsher, more calculating and aggressive tone of voice is usually in evidence, particularly in the trade papers where the agencies advertise advertising, and the media offer themselves as 'outlets'. Take media-advertising in a single copy of the *Advertiser's Weekly* (for 1 June 1962). In the field of the provincial press, the *Telegraph and Argus* compares its 'all powerful coverage of the industrial Aire Valley' with the '3 per cent penetration' of other Leeds papers combined into 'bustling Bradford'. The *Sunday Times* speaks of the 'mass impact on the quality market' of its colour supplement. The recently established Wales (West and North) Television 'will generate the warm, personal loyalty of Welsh people, who will welcome your message in the same spirit'. A hint of what the atmosphere is like in the advertising trade is given in the RCN advertisement: the copy, below a picture of a hand squeezing a lemon into a dish, reads: 'The pressures which arise in this business of advertising, far from reducing us to a pulp at RCN, bring out the best in us.' The London & Provincial Poster Group's headline is 'Impact *plus* Repetition'. The *Radio Times* offers its pages as a means of gaining the 'highest coverage of all ABC 1 housewives with maximum economy'. The double-page spread for *Woman* says, openly: 'In the weekly partnership of readers grouped around the magazine *Woman* you have 8,380,000 customers *conditioned* to delight in COLOUR' (their italics). The *Scotsman* reminds readers that 83 per cent of its readers are 'in the ABC social classes'. The *Angling Times* simply says: 'Get your hooks into the angling market.'

These examples are instructive. They show how journals which are generally considered to be media carrying news, features, opinion, information, or devoted to specialized hobbies, become transformed into means of selling products and penetrating markets. In the *Woman* advertisement, the 'reader' actually becomes a 'conditioned customer' before our eyes.

Early analyses of advertising have dealt mainly with the persuasive use of words and language. But, since these studies appeared, changes in advertising techniques have revolutionized its practice. The most significant feature of this revolution is a shift in emphasis from language to images. Most display advertising today is a composition of different elements—picture, drawing, slogan, copy, design and typography. The total 'impact' of the display will depend upon the effect of these component elements working together upon the consumer. But the image or picture is, most frequently, the real point of sale, carrying the burden of the 'message'. The language or copy reinforces the appeal of the photograph, extends the mood of the picture in words, and rivets the name of the brand or product in the mind.

An emphasis upon images has two advantages. In the first place, a visual appeal is more direct. It conjures up a mood quickly. In advertising, speed is essential. The advertiser has to reckon with the rate at which we turn over the pages: he must attract our attention and use the minimum time to put his message across. A great deal of the exaggeration present in advertising is due to this need to create a quick response.

The picture also effectively creates the mood or establishes the social context which the advertiser hopes we will associate with his product. The social setting is most important of all. In most advertisements, the primary appeal is to some desirable social situation, some pleasurable feeling or emotion, or some socially approved attitude. Most display advertising works by arousing these feelings or appealing to these emotions, getting us to associate them in some way with the product advertised so that we transfer the feelings from context to product. It creates a blend or conflation of the two in our minds. The most successful advertisement is the one which achieves this shift most smoothly.

The image, then, is a kind of visual metaphor: a symbol of the total appeal, realized with the help of line, photography and colour. It is possible, for the purpose of analysis, to isolate the linguistic from the visual components of an advertisement, but, in the end, in order to see 'how it works' we must return to the whole artifact—picture, language and design working together.

In the full-page ad reproduced (Plate 15) the *primary emphasis* is upon the head and shoulders of the couple, taken in close-up. The girl has her back to the camera, her sleek hair is being caressed by the strong, possessive hands of the man. In the main photograph there is no hint or suggestion of the product. The *second emphasis*—and the 'line of argument' is controlled to some extent by the skilful layout and positioning on the page—is upon the slogan to the left of the 'image', which also does not mention the product: 'How long since this happened to you?'—with the words 'How Long' and 'You' in heavy capitals. An arrow then directs you to the copy below (the *third emphasis*). It is only at this point that the copy introduces the product.

The copy itself has three stages. The *first stage* 'extends' the mood and appeal of the photograph: it is the linking passage, answering the question:

Too long? Then look to your hair. Does it invite his touch? It will when you use Vaseline Brand Liquid Shampoo! At once your hair takes on new interest. Becomes lustrous. Soft. Exciting. Adorable. Vaseline Liquid Shampoo is good for hair, leaves it so easy to set and styles. Let Vaseline Liquid Shampoo do fascinating things for your hair. Then your hair will do things for you!

Then, at the side of the first piece of copy, line-drawn in a style which contrasts with the photographic realism of the photograph, is the bottle of Vaseline shampoo. The potential customer has come to the product late, but with the approach properly prepared.

Below the first piece of copy is the *second stage*: information and health care:

Everyone knows the high standard of purity and quality represented by the famous trade mark VASELINE. Care for your hair with the shampoo that maintains hair health and gives irresistible glamour.

Finally, picking up the suppressed echo of the argument above, the copy (in the *third stage*) returns us to the picture with a slogan in bolder type:

FOR THE LOOK THAT GOES STRAIGHT TO HIS HEART!

Let us look at the three kinds of language more closely. The first is a continuation of the 'argument' of the picture: if you want to be loved and caressed, you must have beautiful hair, and you can't have beautiful hair without using *this* shampoo. Notice how the language echoes the photograph: 'Does it invite his touch?'—the hands caressing the hair, the couple embracing. Then the use of assonant adjectives, graded to a carefully staged linguistic climax: 'Becomes lustrous. Soft. Exciting. Adorable'. These adjectives are syntactically detached. They come in the sequence of the gently caressing speaking voice. They contain a suppressed line of argument: 'Lustrous' (quality of the hair which has been shampooed), 'Soft' (quality of the hair as handled in the photograph), 'Exciting' (quality of the emotions aroused in the woman so handled, the man who handles), 'Adorable' (the ultimate desirable quality being striven after). The same concealed message lies behind the last two sentences of this part of the copy: 'Let Vaseline Liquid Shampoo do fascinating things for your hair' (or, in other words, 'if a girl looks after her hair') then 'your hair will do things for you' (. . . 'her hair will look after the girl').

Once the product has been introduced, the style of the language changes in tone. The appeal is now a more 'rational' one, stressing health-care, the guarantee of high quality and the recognized prestige of the trading firm. However, the reader must not be allowed to slip away from the primary appeal. The last phrase of this section of the copy returns us mentally to the picture—'gives irresistible glamour'—and thus makes way for the final slogan, which recalls the total effect of the display:

FOR THE LOOK THAT GOES STRAIGHT TO HIS HEART!

It is important to see that the advertisement has a line of argument, though it has no reasoning or facts in the accepted sense. Secondly, the whole shape of the 'argument' is governed by the photograph. The picture of the couple is the *master image*: the language more often than not evokes the mood and associations of the picture, rather than describing the product. Behind the whole appeal lies the pressure of metaphor and simile, a familiarity with persuasive tones of voice and with 'creative writing'.

The language of much advertising cannot be understood except as a kind of verbal invocation. The 'slogan' is itself a distilled and compressed form of speech—like a headline. So are the mood-phrases which frequently recur—the newly minted adjectival compounds, or the coupling of adjective-and-noun or adjective-with-adjective. These work in the same way as the compounded nouns in Anglo-Saxon poetry (e.g. 'king-sword') or the ideogram in Japanese poetry. They are modern 'kennings': 'Foot-fabulous' ... 'Wash-white'... 'The Born-beautiful look'... 'Tomatoful'... 'Youthliness Long-legs' . . . 'Teenfresh' . . . (some actual examples).

Much advertising copy is a form of mood-writing, heavy with adjectives:

Foot fabulous in silk. East meets West serenely in the gentle Shantung court shoe. Blaze of noon to moonlight serenade, this is a shoe to take you through shimmering summer days and nights. Smoothly bowed, in a gamut of colours from delicate to vivid . . .

(advertisement for satin shoes)

In such advertisements there is a rush of language to the head, a loose, bastardized poeticizing.

Part of the purpose of the language of copy-writing is to echo and re-create in words the experience of having and enjoying the product. The tone is adjusted accordingly. So is the rhythm of the piece of prose and the choice of descriptive phrases. In the copy for a new kind of heating in the home, the mood is cosy, intimate, domestic:

Having a quiet night at home for once—and very nice too. You'll browse through magazines, he'll try to read his paper, and you'll both enjoy the sheer comfort of your new —— Fire.

The language of an advertisement for stockings or girdles is more seductive and caressing. The adjectives are of touch, shape, physical comfort:

Get that controlled yet blissfully comfortable feeling with —— [stockings], honey-coloured favourites of the —— range. They mould you and hold you, slimming your thigh line with the lightest free-est touch imaginable, while hidden suspenders do away with bulges.

You can see where the copy in that ad. begins to break away from reality, begins to soar and sing ('free-est')—an effect, however, which is destroyed when the copy brings you back to earth with a rather ungainly bump ('do away with bulges'). Or:

Every inch, every muscle, lifted, moulded, controlled . . . every movement free, but cradled with gentle firmness. Just wait till you feel the bliss.

If, on the other hand, the advertisement is pitched towards dreamy glamour, the language will echo this mood, either in an evocative slogan at the head of the picture:

Rarely there comes a great fragrance . . .

or, explored in more detail, within the copy itself:

O wonderful, wonderful, at last . . . she cried
It was what she had always longed for
It was prettier than salt-sea-green emeralds
more perfect than pearls, rounder than wave-stroked pebbles
It was new as the slim crescent moon
It was a jewel . . . above all others
And it was *hers*. Her treasure.
To uplift her heart.
To carry her, in all the pride of her beauty,
to magical places,
To gilt-edged invitations,
to midnight masquerades and wild beach balls.

She shimmered in its white foam embrace,
gentle and close as a lover's arms around
her. She shivered with delight in her new
beauty, in her very own, very beautiful bra.

THIS WONDERFUL ——— BEAUTY SHAPE
A whole new bra sensation.

This piece of 'creative' copy is set out on the page like a piece of *vers-libre*. It contains the appeals of a 'new bra sensation' but these are in the sensuous and suggestive similes and the rhythm and movement of the prose itself. It is susceptible to analysis only as a piece of bad poetry is, and the intention is, clearly, that it should work on the reader in the same way that poetry does: by evoking mental images and investing the subject matter and product with meaning by tone, rhythm and association.

When the appeal is made more directly to social status, the prose rhythms are likely to be firmer and more authoritative:

People judge you by the cutlery you keep.

This example makes use of a common saying. Its appeal is attached to some well-worn, familiar groove in the reader's mind ('People judge you by the company you keep'). But notice the shift in intention which goes on in the process. The sentiment is simple and Victorian, but there is moral meaning in it. And a moral principle is involved—the old-fashioned one of probity and personal reputation. In the advertisement the sentiment has been drained of moral meaning and adapted to a persuasive purpose. Its air of certainty, and the echoes of traditional moral wisdom that go with it, help the reader to accept the newer attitude without qualification. It has become pure status-appeal.

Similar phrases can easily be found. One—'Beauty from the neck up'—suggests the popular phrase 'Dead from the neck up', which, considering the glazed look in the eyes of the model, is unfortunate. The next example is similar, but its tone is different:

> I do care what people think, when they come to my house!
> I like things to be just so, especially when guests are coming. Peter never stops teasing me about it—but any woman would understand. When guests admire our —— cutlery, it's marvellous to know that they'll never see more elegant cutlery anywhere.

This is the firm conversational tone of a woman who knows her own mind. Though she flatters the 'little weaknesses' of women which men, naturally, don't understand, in the end she knows she commands the assent of that company of women who judge ind demand to be judged.

The voice of authority reaches, perhaps, its apogee in the single sloganized statement—flat and unqualified—which accompanies an advertisement for a very expensive cigarette: 'When only the best will do': or, better still, the advertisement for an elegant settee, with a small cricketer in action in the background, which says, starkly

> . . . for the British way of life.

Advertisements can be graded roughly in style according to three principles: (1) the 'class' of magazine or newspaper in which they appear, (2) the 'class' of readership or audience which is being reached, (3) the sophistication of the readership or audience. The third point includes the recognition that, for the more sophisticated, the advertisement appeal has to be more subtly offered because sales-resistance may be greater. Thus advertisements on television, which must be designed for a highly variable audience, and in which—to use the language of the advertising trade press—there is not much 'control' over the response, are relatively simple. More animation and voice or catchy tune, less mood and atmosphere. The standard of television advertising is very low indeed —repetitive, insistent and gimmicky compared with the best magazine advertisement; yet highly successful (sales of a product leap noticeably after it has appeared on TV or when it is offered as 'the TV ——') and very costly to produce.

We could say that there are four rough categories of display advertising which we have labelled (1) *simple*, (2) *compound*, (3) *complex* and (4) *sophisticated*. In the *simple* kind the product is advertised in an attractive setting, pitched slightly forward in tone or 'idealized'. The settings are easily recognizable—the kitchen, the new home, the bedroom—only tidier, more expensively equipped, better planned than the setting in real life. In this *simple* version, the product may even dominate—a close-up of a can of fruit or a bar of chocolate.

In its *compound* version, the product is firmly placed in an attractive and desirable social setting, and the advertiser is working for a fairly simple transfer of feelings from one to the other. The example analysed on page 322 is a compound advertisement, with a simple switch from the head and shoulders of the girl to the shampoo.

In the *complex* advertisement the background begins to take over. The images and the copy concentrate upon the feelings of luxury or the desirable status pictured; the product takes second place. In a great deal of fashion advertising and expensive consumer durables it is the whole image which is the point of sale, rather than the specific dress or carpet or bedroom suite. In the famous P & O series, with the drawing of the men in evening dress sipping cocktails in the first-class lounge and the slogan: 'How many Chairmen at this Table?', the ship itself is an insignificant detail: in some advertisements, it is an inset run vertically up the page, hardly noticeable. The ad. works because the whole setting or context works. Another version of this type is the prestige and company advertisements in the weekly journals and the 'serious' press. These advertisements are not selling a product, but a 'service to industry' or 'to the nation' or maintaining the prestige of a great industrial firm. It is the context which, in the very long run, sells.

The *sophisticated* style is an extreme development of the *complex*. Here hidden psychological feelings are being explored, subtle associations are made, strange, dream-like transformations enacted (Plate 16). 'Dream' colours are used (pinks and blues) or the photographs are deliberately blurred to re-create a trance-like state in the reader. Frequently in the *sophisticated* style there is an appeal to feelings which are deeply subconscious. They would not normally escape the censor of social custom had they been more directly treated. Such advertisements depend upon sexual moods; the use of recognizably Freudian symbolism (e.g. the bed and the dark wood, or the girl in the nightdress posed on the rocks, her bare feet dabbling in the gushing stream); violence and aggression (e.g. the full-page ad. of the man's hand on the carpet, reaching for a revolver, with a sharp stiletto heel biting into his knuckles, advertising 'wicked ... elegant —— Paris points'); self-indulgence (e.g. those elegant débutantes stroking for ever their well-sheathed thighs); exhibitionism (e.g. the brazen look in the eyes of those four girls who 'dreamed they flew the Atlantic . . .'); occasionally, even a touch of masochism (e.g. the attractive girl in evening gown, with a smile of pleasure on her face, pinned to the wall by throwing-knives: this ad., interestingly enough, promoting an advertising agency).

The *simple* style is, frequently, unobjectionable. It rarely gives much hard information, but it concentrates on selling the product. It emphasizes time-saving devices, convenience, usefulness, efficiency, low cost, and so on. The *compound* version is more subtle, but the transfer of feelings is relatively obvious. The *complex* style, on the other hand, makes a straight bid for social attitudes, and certainly accepts as legitimate the actual status feelings associated with money, wealth, elegance, luxury and the desire to display these things publicly and win esteem from one's peers for possessing them. The *sophisticated* style plays directly up-on psychological areas of experience, upon the most intimate and private feelings, exploring the subconscious and probing the mind.

With certain exceptions, the same product can be advertised in any of the four styles roughly distinguished. A fabric like Acrilan, which has a modish four-page display in *Vogue*, can also be treated in the *simple* manner—a simply drawn or photographed dress for a teenager, bright, gay and convenient—in *Woman's Own*. A simple article like toilet paper can be given the full *sophisticated* treatment in *Queen*—evocative mood, subtle colour, blurred-focus photography, etc. (as with Andrex).

Advertising also seems to depend upon mobilizing certain clusters of feelings, which can appear in either a direct or an extreme form. These can be divided into three main groups:

(1) *The cluster connected with status and social striving to outdo your neighbour or peer*

Advertising which depends upon this group of attitudes always pitches its 'sell' forward. It never appeals to the estimated status and income level of the readers, but to the status or income level to which they aspire. It flatters their self-image.

A *simple* version of this appeal would be the advertisement with the woman who turns to the reader with a look of undisguised envy on her face, her lips drawn together by a sharp, admiring intake of breath, with the slogan: 'Here comes the Joneses' new TV'. The famous *Times* series, 'Top People Take *The Times*', is a *compound* version of the same appeal. The transfer from 'top people' to '*The Times*' is pretty straightforward. (An interesting variant of this advertisement, pitched slightly lower down the social scale, is the version which reads: 'We Are All Self-Made Men'.) A more *complex* version would be the *Vogue* advertisement for Ryvita, which is dominated by a picture of an elegantly turned-out and made-up career woman, with the slogan: 'Witty Editor—Wise Woman'. The copy reads: 'Brains, of course, are essential. But she's got something more—a glowing, magnetic personality that keeps her in the centre of a talented circle.' Here the image of the wise editor dictating letters in the Fashion department of a busy magazine is doing most of the work in the ad. The background has taken over, been articulated, and the 'sell' is made within that context. The packet of Ryvita even seems a little incongruous. A *sophisticated* version of this appeal would be the deeply coloured picture of the couple in evening dress, the woman in furs with a cigarette holder, relaxing into the leather upholstery of a Rolls or a Bentley, with the simple, restrained slogan already quoted: 'When only the best will do.' The ad. is pregnant with status feelings, but these have been wholly absorbed into the image. They need to be touched or 'triggered' off, but the advertiser would not be so vulgar as to refer to them directly.

(2) *The cluster of appeals related to glamour and luxury*

In the *simple* variants, the pitch is directed towards the conspicuous use of money. In more advanced instances, 'luxury and elegance' take the place of wealth (e.g. the woman with the opera glasses: 'The most elegant gloves for cocktails and evening wear in the newest muted and brilliant colours from Paris'). In the most extreme cases, the appeal to glamour becomes an invitation to 'indulge yourself'—to give yourself the thrill of simply spending (e.g. the woman seated on the floor, leaning her body on the bed and gesturing towards the pillow, with the caption: 'It's just as I wanted it'). In most *sophisticated* examples of this appeal, the feeling of elegance and luxury is communicated directly by the cold, haughty expression on the model's face, the withdrawn eyes, hard line of the mouth and restrained superiority and class feeling familiar in the fashion pages.

(3) *The appeal associated with dreaming and fantasy*

Dreaming is a state of mind which advertisers are often anxious to induce, because it is the state in which the rational judgement is suspended, and the indulgent instincts closest to the surface. This, too, can be attempted at any level of sophistication. A popular women's magazine recently carried a black-and-white ad. of a girl, with her eyes closed, dreaming, and the slogan (for cosmetics) 'Only three steps to bliss . . .'. In the more *complex* versions an attempt is sometimes made to reconcile dream feelings with economy—not usually successful. As in '——— Keeps Dreaming Down' or '——— the Dream you can afford'. The state may also be invoked directly (e.g. in the name, Dreamform, or the slogan 'I dreamed of a ——— axminster carpet'). At the extreme, the advertisement is actually designed *as a dream*, the objects become symbols, the rational connection between setting and real life is consciously broken (e.g. the girl soaping herself in the bath which has been set up on an exposed sea-shore; the woman in the négligée posed on the rocks; the woman with the helicopter which has landed on a carpet on the lawn of her stately home; the girl whose body below the neckline dissolves into layers of powder puffs; or the girl with the nude back whose image shimmers in a blur between waking and sleeping on the page). Some of these examples are so bizarre that they deserve the title 'Nightmares'.

It is worth looking out for further clusters of attitudes and feelings, and their development in various styles:

(4) advertisements which play upon the desire for *social security*, the fear of being socially ostracized, loneliness, fear of old age and anxiety.

(5) those which appeal to a *sense of national prestige* or the service which the industry or firm is providing.

(6) appeals to people in the '*middle income*' *brackets*—'go-ahead people like you', young married couples, ambitious young men, the young 'Span-flat' housewife or the fast sports-car bachelor.

(7) advertisements which make use of the *social occasions familiar to teenagers*—parties, motor-cycling, bowling alleys, coffee-bars, holding hands in the woods, etc.

(8) the group, excellently analysed by Miss Marghanita Laski

in her article, 'Advertising: Sacred and Profane' (*Twentieth Century*, February 1959), which attempts to place the product in a flattering relation with what she calls *'numinous' objects*—objects, persons or situations that are deeply respected or valued, and about which mystical or near-religious feelings of awe are engendered. Such 'numinous objects' Miss Laski calls 'triggers' (e.g. religion, royalty, art, culture, natural beauty, childbirth and childhood). Art-objects and culture generally appear in this context. One recalls the EMI ad. in the *Observer* which yoked a Maria Callas record and a Cliff Richard release in the same advertisement. Miss Laski analyses the example of the Goya painting hanging on the wall—a gentleman with his back to the Goya holding a glass of Harvey's sherry: the copy reads:

> The Gentleman has no eyes for the painted lady
> Only for the lady's national drink.

Another excellent example of this group was the *Daily Sketch* middle-page spread (23/3/60) in which the newly-born Prince Andrew was surrounded by advertisements for baby foods, baby cream and knitted woollies.

Certain themes and situations have become the staple diet of some kinds of advertising. Sex is one such theme: love is another. Such examples are almost too common to mention: 'I'm in Love with A ——' (a rug), or the famous 'People Love Players'. In these advertisements the images exploit the extensive connotations of the word 'love'. In the Players example a shift was involved, not simply from the boy and girl holding hands to the cigarette, but *in the meaning of the word 'love' itself*. The 'love' in the picture was between the people: the 'love' in the slogan was between 'the people and cigarettes. These are not—to put it mildly—the same thing.

An advertisement for a car shows a couple holding hands, sitting in evening dress at a candlelit table; contrasted with this is the line drawing of a car. (The example works in exactly the same way as the shampoo ad. analysed above.)

They've discovered each other, and they're wonderfully happy . . . as you will be, when you discover the ———. Let your eye linger on elegant lines and lovely colours, single or two-tone . . . the sumptuous interior . . .

Here we see new feelings and moods being associated with the concept of love. The image of love is dreamy and 'romantic' in a conventional, banal manner. The language borders on the sensual; the feelings are transferred to the possession of things (perhaps we ought to stress that the idea of possession is really at odds with the mature notion of love). In this example the word is being robbed of one set of associations and endowed with another. The concept is both emptied and filled.

It is worse when the word 'love' continually appears in a selling context, linked with other appeals to status, money, prestige and social competitiveness. Here a real corruption of the feelings is taking place—or at least being aimed at. Eventually, the appeal to love can become as ritualized as the appeal to 'luxury'. Some of the values of these newer appeals spread over into the concept of love, giving it loose and false meanings.

Of course, one advertisement, or even a series, cannot be held responsible for a deep change in human feelings. But a culture which is shot through with devaluations of this kind can, in the long run, begin to fall short on its meanings, particularly where fundamental values are concerned. Look at the way in which similar values are handled in advertising: friendship, neighbourliness, pleasure, happiness, sexual feeling.

It is part of the purpose of education to cleanse the language, to deepen the relevance for the maturing child of these fundamental human feelings and emotions and to prevent their devaluation.

Look at the following examples. What are they advertising?

Outside the airport, palm trees rustled in the breeze and brilliant February sunshine flooded Hawaii. . . .

A travel ad?

Ian and Nonnie were as absurdly proud of their cottage as a couple of young robins with a first nest.

An ad. for a new bedroom or living-room suite? Furniture?

As soon as he saw her coming down the garden path he could tell she was in one of her 'let's save up to get married' moods.

Anything from furniture to interior fittings.

Once we have learned the trick, all of us can play the advertising game. We could by now devise a suitable slogan for each of these pieces of copy and a photograph to go along with it. The first might have a stunning length-ways photograph of Hawaii in colour, palm trees, sea and sand, and in the foreground a girl with new leather kit and elegant travelling clothes. The second would, surely, be taken inside the 'cottage', the couple holding hands, a look of 'bliss' on their faces, a new sparkler on the girl's left hand. The cottage would be neatly and cosily fitted out with new gadgets in formica or steel and a snug fitted carpet. The 'tone' of the advertisement would be bright and chirpy, domestic and 'convenient'. The third example offers even more possibilities. The photograph could be shot from behind the lover's head, so that his clean British profile, slim suit and eager, waiting eyes appeared in close-up. The girl might be taken, instead, coming down the path to him, an exalted but resolute look on her face . . .

The only trouble is that these are not examples of advertising; they are the opening paragraphs to three stories taken from the women's magazines—the new popular media which have become such powerful 'outlets' for advertising to the housewife. They are pieces of popular literature which, however, take over many of the tricks and style of advertising. The prose is very similar to the more developed ads. which surround the product with a 'fictional' situation. It is obviously 'creative', but superficial: either a sale or an emotional romantic adventure could be taking place. In each case the tone has been adjusted to the mood, as we saw the advertiser doing in the examples quoted above. The prose reveals the 'pitch' at which the story is cast, and we could fit quite conventional pictures to each with little effort.

The line between the language of advertising, the language of popular literature and the images of the commercial cinema is fast disappearing. And the shift is, undeniably, towards a blander, more persuasive use of prose, a conventional use of romantic clichés and images.

Advertising is not, as we sometimes hear argued, simply reflecting the quality of life in our society. It is teaching society new ways of feeling and thinking, and new ways of giving expression to human values in its imaginative work. Of course, judged as corrupt art, advertising is no worse than a great deal of other kinds of mass art. But often, in the past, popular art has been bad because of its crudity, its exaggerated realism. Popular writing today, touched by the methods of advertising, reflects its fantastic quality. Its keynote is the absence of reality, the irredeemable presence of fantasy and dreaming.

It would have been simple to counter arguments in this chapter by a balancing and objective offering of good examples of advertising. If it were possible to draw a distinction between the aesthetic and the social function of advertising, this would have been all too easy, since a great deal of modern advertising is skilful, witty, beautifully composed, with an excellent use of colour, line, typography and illustration. Moreover, there are examples which, apart from their aesthetic qualities, describe the product advertised without exaggeration or false appeal.

But the main body of display advertising does not fall within this category. Here social attitudes are being used for the purpose of selling goods and the artistic skill involved only makes the process of manipulation more effective—and, by the same token, socially more damaging. It is often said in its defence that we have to bear with these social effects because the service of advertising to the economy is so great. This is a reasonable position for an advertiser or a manufacturer to adopt, but it is quite indefensible to a teacher or an educationist. Curiously enough, some defenders use precisely the reverse of this argument—people, they say, make too much fuss about advertising, since it probably has little effect. But this too is a deceptive line to take. Since the trend towards display advertising is growing every year, one can only suppose that this is because it brings clear rewards to the manufacturer and the advertiser: in some sense it must *work*. Advertisers cannot argue both that advertising is necessary in order to sell goods and that it has no effect. Of course, advertising does not have precisely the effect that the advertiser himself uses as the premise of his work: we do not actually suppose that we are top people simply because we take *The Times*. Yet the very success of advertising is an indication that we are all peculiarly exposed to the language of fantasy when it declares an interest in the sphere of human attitudes and values:

when a magical pattern has become established in a society, it is capable of real, if limited, success.

Raymond Williams, ibid.

Words and attitudes *do* depend on the context in which they are habitually used. They can lose their shape and meaning. Concepts and feelings which we value can be overworked and corrupted by false associations. The continual manipulation of language, and the manipulation which this implies of one group in society by another, is an unhealthy and dangerous trend. A free society means, inevitably, a society in which people are encouraged to search for the truth without mystification, substitution or distortion. Advertising is certainly not the only indication that social manipulation is extensive in our society, but it is an active part of a major social trend.

PART THREE

Social Themes

12

The Institutions

In point of fact it is only the people who conduct newspapers and similar organizations who have any idea quite how indifferent, quite how stupid, quite how uninterested in education of any kind the great bulk of the British public is.

CECIL KING

. . . the incredible evil, my Lords, as I thought it, of putting the ether at the power of money.

LORD REITH.

They ruin your stories. They massacre your ideas. They prostitute your art. They trample on your pride. And what do you get for it? A fortune.

Hollywood writer's refrain

In talking about the impact of the mass media it is most useful to concentrate our attention on particular things—a film, a television programme, a magazine story, etc., rather than to make generalizations over the whole field. But a look at the broader picture is also necessary and students should know something about the organization and history of communications and the way the media operate in society today.

We will confine ourselves to some general points which apply to all media and then concentrate attention on the cinema. We have selected the cinema partly because facts about the press and television are already easily obtainable from the two recently published Reports of the Royal Commission on the Press and the Committee on Broadcasting. More important, the cinema has demonstrated its capacity to produce art of a high order and it is here that we can see most clearly the tensions between the artist and the business man.

341

The sheer amount of activity, the number of words and images manufactured day after day and the vast numbers of people at whom these are directed, is formidable in itself. It has been estimated that nearly 30,000,000 newspapers are bought each day. Two national morning papers, the *Daily Express* and the *Daily Mirror*, account alone for almost one-third of this figure. Many people read more than one newspaper each day but about 90 per cent of the population reads at least one. Over 15,500,000 broadcasting licences were held by the end of 1963, over 12,000,000 being for television. The latter figure has leapt up from 1,500,000 in 1952. Eighty-eight per cent of the homes in the country have television and in its 1963 Handbook the BBC claims that its services reach 99 per cent of the population. In an average day in 1963, 36,000,000 watched television, and 26,000,000 listened to radio. The typical viewer spends over two hours each day watching television. Audience figures for individual programmes are even more striking, and a programme like *Coronation Street* can gather over 20,000,000 viewers. The figures for 'minority' programmes like *Monitor* (3,000,000) and *Panorama* (10,000,000) force the use of the inverted commas. The significance of these figures is revealed in a comparison with the theatre made by Mr Norman Collins, who has pointed out that one of the great record-breakers, *Chu Chin Chow*, which ran for 2,238 performances, was seen by only 3,000,000 people. To get a complete picture, newspaper circulation and TV ratings should be set alongside the 8,000,000 weekly admissions to the cinema, the £480,000,000 spent in 1962 on advertising and the enormously increased sales of magazines, books and records.

The way this vast network of communications is financed is significant. Most of the media are sustained by advertising and could not in their present form exist without it. The sums of money involved are very considerable. £82,500,000 was spent on TV advertising in 1962 and £220,000,000 on the press in the same year. A peak viewing thirty-second spot on Sunday evening on London Area TV will cost over £1,300 and the magazine *Woman* charges £3,750 for a full-page colour advertisement. Leaving aside the matter of prestige advertising in the smaller-circulation press, the effect of this dependence on advertising is to put immense pressure on the providers to get a mass audience. Hence the preoccupation with circulation figures and TAM ratings. Only by showing large circulation figures or high ratings can these considerable sums be charged to advertisers. This is the way advertising affects the content of the press and television. The influence of the advertiser is frequently denied but usually with reference to direct interference over specific items. While such interference in fact does take place, what we are concerned with here is how the need to capture a mass audience to get advertising revenue produces in turn the formula presentation designed to appeal to such an audience. The programme that is not successful on these terms will have to go or be relegated to an off-peak period. The newspaper that similarly fails will have to shut down even though it may have by 'normal' standards a very high circulation.

When we turn to the question of ownership we see that alongside the enormous and rapid rise in the volume of newsprint, TV programmes, etc., the number of major owners has diminished. This is particularly striking in the case of the press where for many years now the trend has been for independent papers and magazines to pass into the hands of a few big combines. The national press is dominated by three groups—Beaverbrook, Rothermere and King, the last having almost a monopoly of the women's magazines.

The cinema industry has long been dominated by two big concerns and, as we will see, this has not changed. The breaking up of the BBC monopoly by the introduction of commercial television has not seriously altered the position; rather than spreading power into new hands it has increased the power of those already holding it. More than half the resources of commercial television are owned in part by newspapers, the film industry and theatrical interests:

. . . the viewer has found himself offered a service that is the expression of the combined experience of those men who for years have run the nation's theatres, cinemas, concert halls, and newspapers. It is also a healthy and democratic thing that financial interests in the Independent Television Companies should be spread so widely. It is gratifying that so many branches of industry, the press and entertainment can participate in Independent Television.

Norman Collins, *Twentieth Century*, November 1959

These are the same facts presented from a different point of view by Mr Norman Collins. Mr Collins has also said:

We should not be satisfied until we have achieved in broadcasting the same richness, variety and competition of which we are so justly proud in the British press.

ibid.

One final point that emerges from these facts and which applies over the whole field is worth stressing. Communication has become one-sided. A few have access to the means of communication with the many. It is difficult for the majority of people to answer back in any very effective way. Even a very rich man could not easily start a new newspaper. It is still possible with relatively modest sums of money to publish a pamphlet, but if costs of publication can be met the problem of distribution remains. For example, the British Council, after repeated attempts to get the Beaverbrook press to report on its work fairly, was in the end forced to publish a pamphlet, but it is doubtful whether this succeeded in reaching many readers of the *Daily Express* and the *Evening Standard*. The same difficulties arise even more obviously with television, the cinema and the advertising business. In the matter of communications we do not participate as equals.

FILM AS AN INDUSTRY

1. *The Main Structure*
The organization of the film industry is like that of any other large

commercial undertaking with the typical three-part structure, called in this case Production, Distribution and Exhibition. The function of the producers and exhibitors is obvious. The distributors (also called renters) handle the films once they are produced, renting them to the cinema exhibitors and organizing the publicity. As will be described in greater detail later, they also play a key role in financing production, based on the fact that producers must make films that the distributor will be willing to take, publicize and hire out. Again, as in other industries, there are strong tendencies towards monopoly. Although there are many independent producers, a number of small renters, whose activities are confined to distribution, and companies owning only one or a few cinemas, the industry as a whole is dominated by two large combines, the Rank Organization and the Associated British Picture Corporation. Both of these have important production facilities and distribution organizations, and own substantial chains or circuits of cinemas. Another prominent organization is British Lion, with capital owned by the Treasury through the National Film Finance Corporation. But British Lion does not own cinemas, and at the time of writing its future is extremely uncertain. The additional major distributors in this country are American companies like MGM, Columbia, United Artists, 20th Century Fox and Paramount. These companies usually have an arrangement with either Rank or ABC for the release of their films.

The power of the two big circuit-owning corporations rests on the fact that unless a producer is able to negotiate a *circuit deal* and get his film released on either the ABC (Associated British Cinemas, the Exhibition subsidiary of ABPC) or the Rank chain he will find it very difficult to get his money back.

Because of the decline in film-going the pattern is a changing one, but in 1962 the position was as follows:

Total number of cinemas	2415 (estimated)[1]
Rank Cinemas	359
ABC	242

1 Note: Because of closures and reopenings, estimates vary.

Of the 1,814 cinemas not controlled by Rank or ABC many, of course, are grouped in circuits like those owned by Granada, but these are much smaller in number and are usually confined to one part of the country. As well as having national coverage, the Rank and ABC cinemas are frequently well appointed and in the best positions and therefore the approximate figure of 25 per cent of all cinemas owned by the two organizations does not reflect their true power. In particular, the circuits have a dominant position in the London release area which provides about 25–30 per cent of the total receipts in the UK. Because of this power these organizations are able to attract the films with the greatest commercial potential.

2. *The Audience*

The following two tables classifying cinema-going come from the 1959–60 IPA (Institute of Practitioners in Advertising) Survey:

Class	Regularly %	Occasionally %	Infrequently %	Never %
AB	7	12	39	42
C1	10	13	32	45
C2	14	10	26	50
DE	16	7	19	58

Regularly: means once a week or more
Occasionally: ranges from less than once a week to once a month
Infrequently: means less than once a month
AB: upper and middle class   C1: lower middle class
C2: skilled manual workers   DE: working class

Age	Regularly % of age	Occasionally % of age	Infrequently % of age	Never % of age
16–24	44	24	21	11
25–34	14	14	34	38
35–44	6	8	34	51
45–64	6	6	26	62
65 and over	5	3	15	78

It will be seen from the first table that, as is well-known, the cinema-going habit is less well established with the upper middle class and that working-class attendance is the highest. The distinction here, which in any case may become less if middle-class standards spread, is less sharp than that revealed by the second table which shows quite clearly the youthfulness of the cinema audience. These facts, of course, are present in the minds of film producers and their interpretation of them is one of the things that influences the kinds of film produced. The major fact about the cinema audience is, of course, its decline. The following table shows cinema attendance and revenue for selected years since 1946:

Year	Weekly Admissions in millions	Gross Takings in £millions	Net Takings in £millions
1946	31·4	118·3	75·9
1951	26·3	108·3	68·9
1956	21·2	104·2	64·9
1960	10·1	65·5	59·5
1962	8·0	58·9 (provisional)	55·1 (provisional)

It will be seen that net takings have not declined in proportion because of the adjustment in seat prices and the cuts in, and eventual abolition of, entertainments tax. In 1962, attendances were only a little over a quarter of the 1946 figure. This is the crisis. In considering the reasons for this decline we should first note that attendance in 1946 was inflated because of post-war austerity. There was bound to be some decline as the pattern of social life changed with the economic recovery, but a substantial part of the later decline can be attributed to the spread of TV which became more effective as it grew beyond the London area and as set ownership permeated all social classes.

Dr Mark Abrams estimated in 1957 that about 100 admissions per year were lost with every new broadcasting licence issued. Two other factors must be taken into account. The fall in attendance has led to cinema closures and these in turn accentuate the decline. John Spraos in his book *The Decline of the Cinema*, from which many of the facts in this chapter are taken, estimates that when a cinema closes 50 per cent of the audience are lost to cinema-going. The second factor is the decline in American production:

Production of long films (over seventy-two minutes) in UK (inc. Commonwealth) and USA

Year	UK	USA	Total
1945	40	179	219
1950	74	260	334
1955	82	200	282
1960	79	142	221
1962	71	117	188

This shortage of product was one of the reasons for the Rank reorganization in 1958 discussed later. British cinemas have, of course, always been dependent on US production.

3. *Effects of the Decline*

In this book we are concerned primarily with the quality of screen entertainment but the economic facts affect this very directly, which is why anyone concerned with films should know something about the way they are produced. The cinema industry has tended to see the crisis almost exclusively in terms of the threat of TV and of providing the kind of entertainment that cannot be given in the home. This has meant, for example, a number of block-busters—large, very expensive, often spectacular films that have specialized showings for long runs and are very heavily publicized. Examples are: *The Ten Commandments*, *Ben Hur* and *South Pacific*. At the same time advantage has been taken of the relaxation of censorship and, as we noted in an earlier chapter, a great many films have been produced which exploit sex or the now permissible nudity.

In addition there has been the interesting and encouraging emergence of a number of independent producers, partly because the big companies are now less interested in fully financed production. The independents are frequently controlled by the creative film-makers themselves. For example Richard Attenborough (actor) and Bryan Forbes (script-writer) formed Beaver Films and produced *The Angry Silence*. Woodfall Productions was formed with the director Tony Richardson and John Osborne. The most interesting recent productions have in fact come from this sort of set-up: interesting because they seem more contemporary in spirit and because behind them one feels something of a personal involvement. The achievement varies, and a number of the independent films are merely cashing in on the fashion for an industrial environment and a working-class hero. Others are rather superficial problem pictures about teenagers, the colour bar and so on, while many seem only to impose on their material a rather flashy American style. Of the films made in recent years, *Taste of Honey, Saturday Night And Sunday Morning, A Kind of Loving* and *The Leather Boys* are among the more serious independent productions. It is clearly important to distinguish films like Karel Reisz's *Saturday Night and Sunday Morning* and Lindsay Anderson's *This Sporting Life* (made by an independent group for the Rank Organization) from, say, *Violent Playground* (melodramatic fantasy) or *Flames in the Street* (problem-play moralizing). It is notable that all these films, including the earlier *Room at the Top*, were first of all successful as plays or novels. The tradition within which film-makers work in this country is still a limited one.

Quite apart from the aesthetic tradition and the question of talent, these independent products are limited financially. They are still dependent on raising money in the orthodox way, and their films can only get to the audience through the old system, which maintains its essential hold, so that they must be successful in terms of that system to allow for a continuing programme.

Against the emergence of the independents we must set the fact that, in other respects, the power of the big corporations has increased. For example, although there were 861 Rank and ABC cinemas in 1957, 260 more than in 1962, this represented only 20 per cent of all cinemas compared with 25 per cent of all cinemas in

1962. The reason is that many *more* cinemas owned by other companies and groups were closed down. Another and perhaps more striking indication of the growing power of Rank and ABC is the fact that between 1952 and 1962 they increased their share of cinema seats by 10 per cent. Everything in fact favours the companies vertically organized to include all three sections of the film business. A loss in one section can be balanced against a gain in the other. In addition the Rank Organization, in particular, has many interests outside the cinema—including Bush Radio, Rank Precision Industries, Victor Silvester Dance Studios, etc., whereas many of the independent exhibitors are wholly committed to the cinema. In 1958 an important reorganization within Rank took place. Up to that time there had been two Rank circuits, the Odeon and the Gaumont, with a government ban on their amalgamation; there were therefore three major release systems for first-run films. In 1958 the ban was lifted and the best of the Odeons and Gaumonts were grouped together in the Rank circuit, so that the main first-run circuits were reduced to two. This increased the pressure on independents because of film-booking arrangements and the lack of good commercial films from America. When one of the big circuits books a film it can impose a ban on that film being shown in a competing cinema. Thus if an independent cinema in any town existed alongside an Odeon or an ABC cinema it could not show their first-run films. It could, however, take the first-run Gaumont film and would for that film be part of the Gaumont circuit. With only two major circuits this is not now possible and the independent is reduced to showing second-run films or films of less commercial potential. The position has frequently been summarized sharply by saying that two men decide on the films we shall see—the bookers for Rank and ABC.

A further crisis developed in 1963 with a bottleneck in distribution holding up British features for as long as twelve months. The delay in getting a return on the money invested in these pictures increased their interest charges, diminished the finance available for new films and caused unemployment. In the view of ACTT (Association of Cinematograph and Television Technicians) and the independent film-makers, this crisis grew out of the dominant role of Rank and ABC and especially of the booking policy of those organizations which favoured their own films and those of their American associates. The two big companies deny this and argue that the problem has arisen because the industry has moved away from a period of 'product shortage' and that it is now, given the number of cinema closures, suffering from over-production. Certainly on the face of it it seems unlikely that the circuits would deny themselves films of commercial potential although they could, as they have in the past, make a mistaken estimate of such potential.

Many years ago Sam Goldwyn tried to persuade Bernard Shaw to work in Hollywood. In his letter Goldwyn appealed to Shaw as an intellectual, stressing the qualities of film as a serious artistic medium. Shaw refused the offer and in his reply said to Goldwyn: 'The problem is that you are only interested in art and I am only interested in money.' The British Independents tend to put up the same sort of smoke screen as Goldwyn. It must be made clear therefore that the struggle is between two different sets of commercial interests and not between the independents who are only interested in art and the circuits only interested in money. Apart from a mere handful of films the independent productions have been just as routine as those of the big companies. The independents were notably coy about naming particular films held up in the distribution bottleneck but there was nothing to suggest that their release would usher in a renaissance of the British cinema. This is not, of course, to argue that the continued existence of independent production is unimportant.

One further feature of exhibition is the rise in the number of foreign films shown and the success of the smaller cinemas running an art house or semi-art house policy. In part this is a reflection of the decline in US production but it is also a sign of the change in public taste for which the Film Society movement, film journals, etc., can take some credit. Immediately we must note that many of the continental films, good and bad, have been exploited in sensational ways.

Excluding American films, the following table shows the number of foreign films released for selected years.

1951	1953	1956	1962
11	16	38	131

4. *Government Intervention*

The government has for a long time paid special attention to the cinema, presumably because it is a very persuasive medium which reaches all sections of the community and is also important in presenting the *British Image* abroad. The affairs of the industry are governed by a series of Film Acts of which the last was in 1960. Intervention takes three main forms:

(i) *The Quota*

British production is protected by a regulation that 30 per cent of the films (features) shown in the cinemas must be British.

(ii) *British Film Fund Agency*

This agency collects a levy imposed on the cinemas, the money going to producers. This scheme to help production, traditionally the weakest section of the film business, was first of all voluntary but became statutory in 1957. It yields over £3,500,000 in the year and the amount paid to individual producers is calculated on the basis of box-office earning so that the more a film earns, the more it can claim from the levy.

(iii) *National Film Finance Corporation*

The NFFC was formed in 1948 to make loans to producers on the basis of a Treasury Guarantee. It started out with a capital of £6,000,000 and one of its first tasks was to attempt to rescue British Lion from bankruptcy. As a result of the collapse of British Lion the NFFC lost almost £3,000,000. It took over a controlling interest in the distributing side of that company. British Lion also owns studios at Shepperton but does not itself engage in production.

In the period 1957–9 the number of films assisted totalled ninety-seven. In the year ending March 1963 twelve short and forty-one long films received NFFC support to the sum of £1,687,964.

5. *Changing Pattern*

Before going on to look at the financing of films and the effects of the economic system on creative work, there are some general features to be noted. We have already seen that the film crisis is altering the nature of film exhibition. The audience is now more selective if not always more discriminating, and this has led not only to blockbusters and cheaply made films exploiting sex, violence and horror, but to some stimulation of more creative work at home and to the showing of more quality films from abroad. We should not be sanguine about the prospects but it is perhaps more possible now for creative film-makers to persuade the financiers that even a good film might make money. As one character remarks in the film *The Great Man*, 'If integrity sells soap, let's have integrity.' There have also been changes in production and in the world pattern of film-making. The most striking of these is the decline of Hollywood. Films, it has been said, are now produced somewhere between Rome, London and New York. While it is true that American films have lost something of their dominance of British screens, and home-produced films now appear regularly at the top of the list of box-office successes, the American influence is still very strong. There are important American distribution offices established in this country and American money plays a big part in financing production here and in Europe generally. Warner Brothers, for example, have substantial holdings in ABPC, and MGM have studios at Elstree. Many American film-makers live abroad to avoid income tax, American films are made in Europe where costs are lower and American money is frequently behind the production programmes of other countries. The various kinds of co-production arrangements add to the international flavour of big-time film-making today which leads some people to worry about the loss of the national character of the films themselves. Many films which are registered as British have in fact been made possible by American support. *Bridge on the River Kwai*, for example, was geared to the American pattern through financial control, its American producer and box-office star William Holden; although technically British, it is discussed as an American film by Arthur Knight in his book *The Liveliest Art*.

6. *Film Finance*

We have considered the main features of film economics, the role of the big corporations, the decline in attendance, the extent of government intervention and the increasingly international character of production. This provides the background to the more specific question of financing production. Films are very expensive to produce. *Saturday Night and Sunday Morning* cost £120,000 and at that was a cheap film, the average cost being higher. Second-feature costs are of course very much lower, below £20,000; at the other extreme *The Ten Commandments* cost, as someone put it, half a million pounds per commandment. The real facts about costs are obscure. It depends what is included in the budget. One film may be required to carry the entire overheads of the studio, and although the wild days of Hollywood have passed the film business is still, in its higher reaches, a bizarre world. The following is taken from a report in the *Daily Telegraph* (17/5/62) of a meeting of Twentieth Century-Fox shareholders:

> It emerged during the meeting that Miss Taylor was reported to be getting well over £357,000 from the company for her work in *Cleopatra*. A woman share-holder thereupon nominated her as a director, saying that anybody getting that amount of money ought to be on the Board . . .
>
> Mr Skouras forecast that the film would be the biggest money maker in the industry's history. It would be released in February and he expected that eventually it would take more than £54 million. The company had lost £8 million last year. Of this £1,300,000 was lost on the first version of *Cleopatra* abandoned because of Miss Taylor's illness. Mr Skouras said that drastic economies were coming.
>
> He was cutting his own salary of £50,000 a year by £11,500. Judge Samuel Rosenman, the chairman of the company, also came under

criticism. He agreed that he received a salary of nearly £27,000 for a 15-hour week.

It is well to remember when we hear of a film losing money that this is often after expensive salaries have been paid; the people hit by the film crisis are the technicians without jobs and the projectionist out of work because his cinema has been closed. Accusations about inflated costs at the top are met by counter-charges of union restrictions. The latter, although more understandable, are hampering at the lower level of production particularly where creative work is being attempted on a very tight budget. But in any case film-making is inevitably expensive and therefore hazardous for the independent producer.

The breakdown of costs will vary enormously depending on the size of the budget, the relative importance of the stars and story, the amount of location work and so on. Two things are worth noting, however. First, a substantial proportion goes in finance charges, as much as 10 per cent. Second, the largest single item will be labour costs and salaries if taken together. This means that the most expensive item is in fact time, and therefore the shooting schedule must be carefully prepared; great importance is placed on keeping up to schedule.

How does the independent producer go about getting his money? In the first place he will have to put up some money of his own which will probably take the form of story rights, payment for treatment and perhaps salary for himself and his immediate colleagues which may take the form of a *paper* payment. He will then negotiate a bank loan on the basis of a guarantee from a distributor that he will take the completed film. The remainder of the money will probably be obtained from the National Film Finance Corporation. The proportions will work out as follows:

Producer's own money	5 %
Bank Loan on Distribution Guarantee	70 %
NFFC	25 %

What must be kept in mind is that of the money thus raised not all is available for direct production costs. There are the finance charges mentioned already, which will include interest charges not only on the bank loan but on the NFFC loan as well. In addition he must raise what is called a Completion Guarantee from an organization that guarantees the bank it will step in and finish the film if it steps seriously over schedule and budget. This in itself might add £6,000 to a £130,500 picture.

When the money returns, the producer is paid last. After the exhibitor has taken his share, the distributor recovers his 70 per cent plus interest but also plus something like 25 per cent for distribution services, and then the loan plus interest is paid back to the NFFC. The producer also suffers from the way the levy mentioned earlier is administered. The sum raised by the levy which was supposed to go straight to the producer is in fact partly paid by him, since it is calculated on the sum collected at the box office *before* the exhibitor pays his hire charge and not calculated on exhibitor profits. Therefore about 30 per cent of the levy is paid for by distributors and producers.

The significance of this system of film finance is that it makes independent production, especially of the more adventurous kind, especially difficult. The Board of Trade figures show that only a small proportion of box-office takings came to British feature producers. For the big combines these problems are a matter of internal accounting.

Division of Gross Box-Office Revenue 1960

	%
Exhibitors	62
British Film Production Fund	6
Distributors	13
Foreign Producers	12
British Producers	7

This then is a general picture of how the film industry works. What effect has the system upon the creative film-maker?

The first point of pressure comes from the distributor who,

before he offers his guarantee essential to financing, will vet the script and the production plans. He will be looking for some assurance of commercial success and the tendency will be to think very much in terms of a formula drawn from past experience. As one producer said, 'It is the only industry where last year's models are thought the best.'

If the film is a low-budget second feature, the emphasis will be on the need to finish it quickly. There will therefore be a demand for the type of story that can fit into routine shooting procedures in the studio, a reluctance to have a lot of location work involving unpredictable risks and the desire for seasoned second-feature players and a director well drilled in the mechanical techniques of this level of film-making. This is the main reason why it is difficult to think of second features as an area for new experiment or trying out new talent.

If the film is an expensive first feature the pressures are, of course, greater and in particular there will be a demand for big stars to *carry* the picture. At this level also it will be difficult to film an original subject since the guaranteed success of a known novel or play is preferred.

It has also been difficult to allow a film to find its natural budget level. The tendency is either for it to be cut back to second-feature status by not allowing for the extra time inexperienced people might require, or for it to be blown up to a major film with all the ensuing pressures of big star names, etc. This is perhaps a little less true now that the film backers are beginning to realize the star system is not what it was and that subject is an important consideration with the public. *A Kind of Loving*, for example, had no stars, nor indeed had *Saturday Night and Sunday Morning*, since Albert Finney only became really well known by his performance in the film.

There are also other considerations such as the possible American market which may call for an American star or adjustments to the story. The NFFC will have views on the proposal which are likely to be similar to those of the commercial industry as the Corporation has a directive not to lose money and inevitably draws its standards from the industry. If the film is being made by a major company, similar pressures will operate from the so-called Front Office (i.e. the business heads of the company). Financial decisions made at this stage of production, decisions on the story, casting, etc., are also creative decisions. Small companies exist making films as cheaply as possible (often for television) with such disregard for quality that even simple technical standards are abandoned. This creates in the craftsmen involved a mixture of frustration and cynicism. In the larger or more responsible studios high-quality standards are maintained and can even be emphasized against the grain of more creative considerations. Here the problem is the imposition of a formula. Many big-company films look alike, becoming studio pictures rather than creations of the individual. Again this is perhaps becoming less so with the growth of the independents who use the facilities of the big studios. But even these can be influenced by the studio ethos which is in part a product of the use of the same small number of key craftsmen over some years. The director of photography and the art director can play a significant role in giving a picture its quality; if coupled with a strong producer they may make it very difficult for a younger and less experienced director to break free from what he regards as restrictive conventions.

Although in writing about films we usually regard the director as the major creative artist this is more often an ideal than an actuality. Of course, this varies from country to country and in general European film-makers suffer less restriction than Americans. Orson Welles has said that only once has his own editing of a film been the version put into release. Lillian Ross wrote a book called *Picture* about the production of *The Red Badge of Courage* which strikingly illustrated the situation in the big American studios. She records that while John Huston, the director, was still filming, the chief MGM editor who was not even on his production team was, unbeknown to him, making editing decisions about the material already shot. When Alexander McKendrick made *Sweet Smell of Success* for Hecht Hill and Lancaster he had to give four alternative endings, leaving it to the

Hollywood producer to choose which would be used. Details of the many ways in which intervention works are difficult to obtain because for obvious reasons the people involved are reluctant to talk about them. Of course it should not be assumed that interference is necessarily wrong. Film-making is a complex business depending on the creative contributions of many people. It is made more difficult because the film only pieces itself together bit by bit and an imaginative grip on what the whole will look like is difficult to maintain. For these reasons a sensitive producer can play a genuinely creative role.

But the overall picture is of an industry in which the creative talents are kept in a strait-jacket, and the decision-makers are frequently men who are out of touch with the public. The power of the two big circuits governs not only which pictures will be seen but, to a large extent, what kind will be produced. The independent film-maker, seeking to use his chosen medium imaginatively, can easily become worn out in the struggle to finance production. Yet it is the independents who have been making not only the most interesting films but often the most commercially successful.

In terms of keeping in touch with changing tastes and attitudes, it is they who have made the running rather than the big companies. It therefore came as a surprise to many people within the industry when a decision was made which, in effect, seemed to favour the duo-monopoly against the independents. Late in 1963 the National Film Finance Corporation decided to exercise its option to buy out the British Lion directors (David Kingsley, the Boulting Brothers, Frank Launder and Sydney Gilliat) with the intention of re-selling the company. The government money in British Lion has provided economic and psychological support for independent production. The company has acted as a buffer between the independents and the big companies and provided a stable centre around which the various independent outfits have been able to operate.

After much discussion and some heavy 'in-fighting', the company passed into the hands of a group headed by Sir Michael

Balcon. It is too early yet to say how this will affect British Lion policy but it was certainly the opinion of many experienced people, at the time of the negotiations, that it would be difficult for the company to maintain its independence returned to exclusively private ownership.

Apart from its own financial difficulties, the NFFC has been motivated by its dislike of the independence it was set up to promote. Its managing director, Mr John Terry, has said:

> This running battle between the directors [of British Lion] and the two circuits is not in the best interests of independent producers. I think the policy of British Lion will have to be reviewed.
>
> quoted in the *Sunday Times*, 22 December 1963

The NFFC was created to stimulate independent production and it acquired its share of British Lion because it was felt important to maintain some kind of competition in the film business (Rank and ABC do not compete, i.e. an independent cannot bargain for a circuit deal), but the men who run it now do not hold to these principles. 'I cannot,' said Sir Nutcombe Hume, K.B.E., M.C., Chairman of the NFFC, 'conceal my conviction that HMG has no business to be in British Lion' (reported by the Boulting Brothers in the *Spectator*, 3/1/64). But even if British Lion were to receive further government money or in some way to maintain its independence, the real problem—the dominance of the two circuits— would remain. It has been suggested that we should adopt the American strategy and legally separate exhibition from production and distribution, but there is no certainty that an independently operated circuit would be more imaginative in its booking policy than the present set-up.

Another solution designed to weaken the power of the big circuits has been put forward by the Federation of British Film Makers in a memorandum (see *Daily Cinema*, 6/2/63) submitted to the Sub-committee appointed by the Cinematograph Films Council to investigate the structure and trading practices of the industry. The FBFM suggested that for booking purposes the circuits should be broken down into local area groups of not more than twenty-five cinemas controlled by an independent local manager. The Sub-committee in its Report (see *Daily Cinema*, 14/8/63) rejected this proposal on the grounds that without the assurance of a major circuit booking, producers would find it difficult to finance first-feature films. Such an argument, and there is no reason to quarrel with it, indicates the importance of providing producers with some sort of guarantee. Granting this, the only alternative to breaking up the existing circuits is to create a viable Third Release. The idea has been much discussed but without any practical outcome since to create such a circuit which was at all viable would mean taking over cinemas at present owned by Rank and ABC. The key is the vital London area where the two combines have a stranglehold. A solid base in London would be essential to the success of any third circuit. Even then it is possible that such a circuit would require a subsidy, in which case it might be as well to go the whole way and create a nationalized circuit based on the purchase of certain London area cinemas from Rank and ABC. The cinemas within the chain could well be operated by the local authorities. Given such an outlet, a programme could be organized around government-supported production and distribution facilities, a reconstituted Government Film Unit for documentary (like the old Crown Film Unit or the National Film Board of Canada) and a plan to use second features for more imaginative work and as a training ground for younger film-makers. But of course the trend is in the other direction with the government selling British Lion, the company which might have provided the anchor for such a programme.

It would be misleading, however, to paint a picture of a wealth of film-making talent frustrated by the wicked system. A new production company recently formed to attempt more adventurous film-making complained that there were few writers of talent interested in working on original scripts and that they were unable to find directors who had scripts they passionately wanted to make. What in fact is striking about the British scene, compared with France, for example, is how few young people there are who think of cinema in terms of a creative career. No doubt the rather corny show-biz atmosphere of the industry puts many people off, but probably more important is the sharp distinction we make between art and entertainment. The fact that in this country we are still a long way from having a Bergman, a Kurosawa or a Truffaut is probably more a reflection of a set of intellectual attitudes than a result of the way the film industry is organized.

We could re-structure the industry, but can we organize talent? Certainly something can be done. There is first of all the question of training. Significantly Britain has no national training school, yet there is one in almost every other film-producing country including Chile and Formosa. There are major schools in the Soviet Union and Poland offering courses lasting five or six years. The exciting work produced in Poland since the war is very largely due to the school at Lodz. There have been various discussions and proposals about forming such a school but there is no immediate sign of activity. Clearly some form of properly organized training is essential and an imaginatively directed school would provide a great creative stimulus.

Many people have pointed out that the way the production levy operates is unsatisfactory, as the money in general goes to those who need it least and is not used to encourage adventurous production. The Cinematograph Exhibitors Association have proposed that an equal share be given to all producers with a safeguard against *Levy Quickies* (films made cheaply just to catch the levy money), and the union (ACTT) has suggested blocking some part of levy funds and only releasing them for new productions. These ideas, however, hardly meet the real need, which is to find a way of supporting films that break with the accepted commercial formula. As we saw, even the NFFC operates in a purely commercial capacity. The proposal has been made that a system of prizes similar to the one in operation in France be adopted where films of quality are eligible to receive a government interest-free loan. The awards are given after a jury has seen the films, but the money is only paid out if the box-office takings are low. Short films are also eligible and a number of distinguished

French film-makers have been supported in this way. The cry of cultural dictatorship is usually raised at this point. But any system has its dangers—not least one which is based on the preferences and intuitions of a few anonymous men in Wardour Street. Surely it is preposterous that government money should be used not for creative work which requires support but in bolstering up a commercial operation?

To get ideas moving in this area would of course call for some new thinking within the unions who are in many respects as backward-looking as the big companies.

The more fundamental, if more intangible, question is that of intellectual attitudes to the cinema in general. To build into informed opinion some recognition of the serious claims of the cinema is a long-term task for education. It is a task which, because it involves our basic thinking about the role of art in the society, cannot be set aside from wider social and cultural changes.

It is the mistake of some left-wing critics of the mass media to suppose that a change in ownership, organization and control will solve all our problems. No doubt such changes are necessary, but unless they are accompanied by some greater concern for the experiences that art and entertainment have to offer we shall find that we have changed the form while the substance remains the same. Good films, like good art and entertainment of any kind, will come only from individual artists excited by the medium and anxious to communicate through it. What we can do is to create the climate for such commitment to flourish and the conditions for communication to take place.

13

Mass Society: Critics and Defenders

> The triumph of mass education is to be found not simply in the increment of those who can read, write, add and subtract. It is to be found in a much more profound and enduring revolution: the provision of opportunities to express the self, and pursue the self's values, opportunities not limited to the children of a leisure class, or an aristocracy, or a landed gentry, or a well-heeled bourgeoisie.
>
> LEO ROSTEN in *Culture for the Millions*

The growth of communications must be placed in the wider context of all the changes stemming from the Industrial Revolution and from the political ideas associated with it. These have altered and are altering our whole way of life, destroying traditional forms of work and leisure and replacing local and regional communities by larger political and economic organizations. The society emerging from this upheaval is usually called by its critics the Mass Society to distinguish it from the democratic society which nineteenth-century Liberal ideas supposedly created. The term is usually applied to the Western countries and above all to America, but other critics see its main features as being typical of all highly industrialized societies regardless of their political system, and therefore apply the term to the Soviet Union also.

In this chapter we want to examine some characteristic attitudes to the new society. We will consider the views of:

1. *The Providers*
Those who own and/or control the means of communication and through them provide us with information, comment, art and entertainment.

2. *The Traditionalists*
Those who reject the present order, but who judge it in terms of the society that has passed and the values it is replacing.

3. *The Progressives*
Those who believe that the present society has positive features and that its failings will be eliminated with time and reform.

4. *The Radicals*
Those who reject the present order but who judge it in terms of a society to come and of the values it frustrates.

Before discussing these attitudes it will be useful to catalogue the general indictment of the mass society. Some of these criticisms are implicit in earlier chapters but are presented here in a deliberately simplified and sharpened form. It is doubtful if any one person would adhere to all of them. It should not be assumed that the writers who have been quoted in support of particular points would do so, and it should be clear that the present writers do not. The following could rather be regarded as the doctrines of an imaginary composite critic of mass culture.

1. *Power*
Power is concentrated in a few hands, and methods of maintaining it have been refined by the techniques of manipulation. Armies of people are employed to test and analyse, to seek out needs and hidden desires and to create needs where they do not already exist:

> Before high-pressure salesmanship, emphasis was upon the salesman's knowledge of the product, a sales knowledge grounded in apprenticeship; after it, the focus is upon hypnotizing the prospect, an art provided by psychology.
>
> C. Wright Mills, *White Collar*

But the ethics of salesmanship have infected every area of life. Politics has become a branch of public relations. Persuasion has been substituted for debate and the search for the right image has replaced the search for the right policy.

2. *Mass production*

Cultural products are mass produced to a formula that allows no place for creativity. Experiment and growth have been replaced by gimmicks and fashion. Mass production demands an audience so large that it can only be held together by appeals to people's most unthinking responses:

> When we are dealing with figures like this, we are no longer considering a mass audience at all: it has ceased to be an audience, in the sense that one can ever hope to communicate with a majority of it in any but the most superficial way.
>
> Henry Fairlie, *Encounter*, March 1962

3. *Consumers*

People are not seen as participators in the society but as consumers of what others produce. Their needs and attitudes as consumers are assessed and analysed but their judgement as men and women is not called upon. They are asked to distinguish between washing powders but not whether they would prefer schools to strip clubs. Their role is passive and they play no part in the world of decision-making. The language of persuasion can be soft and subtle but when the persuaders speak to each other it becomes harsh and aggressive. The people are 'masses' awaiting exploitation:

> To other people, we also are masses. Masses are other people. There are in fact no masses; there are only ways of seeing people as masses. . . . The fact is, surely, that a way of seeing other people which has become characteristic of our kind of society, has been capitalized for the purposes of political or cultural exploitation.
>
> Raymond Williams, *Culture and Society*

4. *The pseudo-world*

Increasingly the media define our sense of reality and organize our experience into stereotypes. We cease to believe in events until the media sanction them. We come to believe more in the pictures of life than in life itself and in the end may accept the distorting mirror of the media as a portrait of our true selves:

> The studio audience, I should say, provides the perfect image of mid-20th century democracy. At the time of Suez, I saw a photograph of troops by the Canal, all looking very glum, except for one small party, which was being televised: thumbs up and smiling, as required.
>
> Malcolm Muggeridge, *New Statesman*, 14 February 1959

5. *The unambiguous world*

Mass culture makes us more alike. It does this not merely by manufacturing standardized products but by trivializing the important things until they are reduced to the level of the commonplace. Magazine pages and television programmes flicker past us—religion and quiz games, criticism and gossip columns, art lovers and animal lovers, all cemented by colourful advertising. Communication and salesmanship become inextricably intertwined, so that there is a continuous blurring of distinctions:

> Not all celebrities have equal value and the same symbolic status. This simple fact is the basis for one of Mr Murrow's most fascinating wiles: *Person to Person* consists of two 'visits' on the same night, and he strives for incongruity rather than harmony. An early programme epitomized this strategy—Krishna Menon and one of the Gabor sisters within the same half hour. Such a juxtaposition, while it tickles our fancy, also manages to blur the distinction between the meaning of a Krishna Menon and a Gabor; by giving both equal value it trivializes the significance of one . . . if you throw a Krishna Menon in with a Gabor, bill the entire 'package' as entertainment, and sell it by way of television, you have gone a long way towards creating an image of an unambiguous world.
>
> Murray Hausknecht, 'The Mike in the Bosom' in *Mass Culture*

6. *The break with the past*

Mass culture destroys folk art, dehydrates popular art and threatens fine art. It has little sense of tradition, of values being modified by change. Instead there is an obsession with fashion and novelty; to be the latest thing is thought in itself a sufficient recommendation:

> . . . most people are subjected to a sustained and ever-increasing bombardment of invitations to assume that whatever is, is right so long as it is widely accepted and can be classed as entertaining. This and the older sense that it is important to 'enjoy y'self while y'can' are connected. To these a third element attaches itself, that of 'progressivism'. Progressivism assists living for the present by disowning the past; but the present is enjoyed only because, and so long as, it is the present, the latest and not the out-of-date past; so, as each new 'present' comes along, the others are discarded.
>
> Richard Hoggart, *The Uses of Literacy*

7. *Corruption of the feelings*

The media exploit rather than satisfy our needs and desires. Not only are appeals made to our worst instincts, such as greed and snobbery, but our best instincts are distorted and our finest feelings squandered on objects unworthy of them:

> The history of popular taste is largely bound up with the discovery by the writing profession of the technique for exploiting emotional responses.
>
> Q. D. Leavis, *Fiction and the Reading Public*

8. *The flattery of mediocrity*

This is the age of the Common Man, the Ordinary Person, the Man in the Street. He is interviewed, researched and polled, and no issue is thought too complicated to be judged by a counting of heads so that in the end the controllers and manipulators go in fear of the Mass Man, the monster creation of their own fantasies:

> The characteristic of the hour is that the commonplace mind, knowing itself to be commonplace, has the assurance to proclaim the rights of the commonplace and to impose them wherever it will.
>
> Ortega y Gasset, *The Revolt of the Masses*

9. *The cult of personality*

In an age of conformity, in which the mass replaces a community of publics, a substitute for true individuality is found in the glorification of personality. This emphasizes not what a man is or what he has done but his image, his public face. The stars of the world of show business have taken over, and in politics grooming the personality becomes as important as brushing up the facts:

I wish men who call themselves public relations counsellors and have three coronets on their notepaper would stop ringing me up and saying in carried-away voices: 'Decca have just signed Fannie Bloggs. She's receiving the Press at the Savoy, 5.30.' I wish that after I have told the men with the three coronets to drop dead, I could come back from lunch and not find a note from my secretary saying Decca have just signed Fannie Bloggs . . .

By the time I get to the Savoy, I find that Fannie Bloggs, whom nobody ever heard of before that morning, is already famous, anyway. Or as good as.

Next morning some hay-haired girl, grasping a guitar by the throat leers up at you from the breakfast table.

Unconsciously you start to believe in her, reasoning innocently that since her picture is in the paper she's sufficiently important to have her picture in the paper.

That's all Fannie needs. With this aberration of logic, which works time after time in our purblind community, the men with the three coronets have you nailed.

Leslie Mallory, quoted in the *News Chronicle*

10. *Escape from reality*

The audience receives the products of the mass media, and is encouraged to receive them, in a state of dream-like passivity:

Why encourage the art that is destined to replace literature? But still, there is a kind of soggy attraction about it. To sit on the padded seat in the warm smoke-scented darkness, letting the flickering drivel on the screen gradually overwhelm you—feeling the waves of its silliness lap you round till you seem to drown, intoxicated, in a viscous sea—after all, it's the kind of drug we need. The right drug for friendless people.

George Orwell, *Keep the Aspidistra Flying*

The media provide us with an endless series of dreams through which we can escape from the reality of the world and ourselves. We are invited to identify ourselves with fictitious characters whose conflicts are resolved by magical solutions, and to indulge in corroding fantasies:

This car is very personal property: once you get the feel of it, you won't want to hold back. Behind the wheel a man feels power—and a woman feels freedom. Turn the key and feel the Capri spring to life, gliding like a panther, hugging the road, clinging to the curves, responding instantly . . . a sleek and elegant extension of your own personality.

(advertisement)

These ten points make up an unambiguous indictment. Before we proceed to set other points of view against this, the words of the late C. Wright Mills might be quoted as a general summary:

The media tell the man in the mass who he is—they give him identity. They tell him what he wants to be—they give him aspirations. They tell him how to get that way—they give him technique. They tell him how to feel that he is that way even when he is not— they give him escape.

The Power Élite

1. THE PROVIDERS

Initially we are thinking of providers as the *owners* or *senior controllers*. One of their responses to criticisms of what they do is to define their work in strictly commercial terms:

In the commercial world it does not matter whether you are selling a newspaper or a breakfast food, if you chase away customers you will be out of business. I cannot see the point of entering on a commercial enterprise and chasing away the people who provide your bread and butter.

Cecil King at the N.U.T. Conference:
Popular Culture and Personal Responsibility

Some people might feel that there are certain important differences between a newspaper and a breakfast food, differences which would probably become clear to the majority if the logic of commercial competition led to all the papers being owned by Mr King.

Indeed the virtue of variety—and the importance of government intervention to ensure such variety—was the main point used to defend the introduction of commercial television:

> I daresay its programmes are not all wonderful (some are); but the principle has been established that viewers should be given what they want and not what Mr Hugh Carleton Greene or even Tom Driberg thinks is good for them. The sound-monopoly of the BBC now seems to be on the way out. This is a strong reason for looking forward to the Sixties. I cannot restrain my impatience to see the day when Broadcasting House is put up for sale.
>
> A. J. P. Taylor, *New Statesman*, 2 January 1960

This introduces the most common argument, that the media operate democratically giving the public what it wants, and that this can be proved by a reference to circulation, box office and viewing figures:

> The television that is produced will reflect what people do like, not what we think they ought to like, and it is not of great relevance to criticize *television*. If we don't like it, or don't, say, like the kind of newspapers or films we have, it is not these things we should be saying are unsatisfactory. We should have the courage of our convictions, and say that we find people unsatisfactory, and that, as Plato said, we must take matters out of their hands.
>
> Sir Robert Fraser, Speech at Scarborough,
> quoted in *Contrast*, 5

This position is a rather crude one and was critically examined in a brilliant passage in the Pilkington Report. But that did not prevent many newspapers using it in opposition to the Report and as it is likely to be used for some time to come we summarize the arguments against it:

(i) The model of communication offered is a very mechanistic one of supply and demand. Obviously supply not only satisfies people's needs but helps to shape and define them; we did not know we wanted Tony Hancock until we saw him. Inevitably anyone working for newspapers, television and so on must accept the responsibility for creating taste changes and not merely responding to them. He must also recognize that what we (the people) like is not always clear even to ourselves and certainly not easy to measure.

(ii) Of course the public (all of us) cannot be given what it likes all of the time; the phrase means what the majority like. This is why figures are quoted to show that ITV is liked more than BBC, that people like light entertainment more than serious programmes, and so on. It is difficult to give the word 'like' in this context any useful meaning. The measurement is exclusively one of quantity and the fact that large numbers of people buy the *Daily Express*, go to see *Carry on Nurse* or view *Sunday Night at the London Palladium* does not tell us much about the quality of their liking. The BBC have tried to measure not simply the number of people viewing given programmes but the extent of their appreciation. The table opposite is taken from their publication *Facts and Figures about Viewing and Listening*.

This clearly points to the danger in assuming too much from the TAM ratings. The fact that frequently programmes with the lower rating figures are the most enjoyed need not surprise us; we know from our own experience that the things we enjoy most intensely are those that appeal to our specialized interests. A football fan may share with millions the pleasure of watching *The Black and White Minstrel Show*, but may get greater pleasure from a sports magazine programme with a lower audience rating.

(iii) These qualifications bring us to the larger assumption that there are two kinds of audience, the majority wanting light entertainment and the minority wishing for more serious programmes. But minority interests are not necessarily highbrow. A liking for

SHOWING THAT BROADCASTS WITH EQUAL AUDIENCES
ARE NOT EQUALLY POPULAR

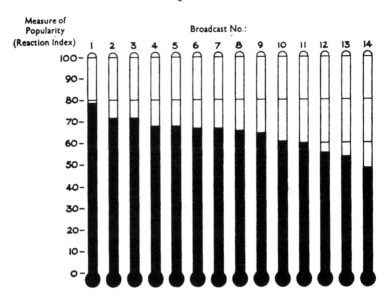

In four typical weeks in mid-winter 1960, fourteen television broadcasts each had an audience of approximately six million people—but their popularity with their audiences varied as shown.

jazz or railway modelling is a minority interest just as much as a preference for poetry or ballet. In any case there are not two distinct groups of people. The majorities are composed of various kinds of minorities. Most of us are members of a majority in some of our interests and of a minority in others. Someone who enjoys *Z Cars, Monitor,* Hancock, athletics and jazz would be an instance of this.

The 'Giving the public what it wants' argument is therefore very shallow and is in fact used to justify going for the biggest audience all or most of the time. When this is carried to the point of putting newspapers out of business and squeezing minority programmes to inconvenient hours we can see that it does not give people what they want. Indeed, the commercial providers share with the authoritarians the conviction that they know what other people should have. Both are undemocratic. A democratic system would aim to provide a variety of choice representing the variety of people's interests and potential interests. Only if there is such variety is freedom of choice meaningful.

If we turn from providers to practitioners we find more reasonable defences. Many journalists, for example, feel that the popular press gives them an opportunity to communicate with large numbers of people which it would be irresponsible to decline and they try to handle important questions in a way which will make them seem relevant to their readers. They therefore resent criticism by people on the outside who judge them in the wrong terms and do not appreciate either the importance or difficulties of popularization. Others go further and say that by dealing in personalities and in the news behind the news they are getting closer to the truth than their colleagues in the quality press or the BBC, who merely present a bleak and official view of the world and mislead people about how decisions are really arrived at. This point was put very effectively by Henry Fairlie in *Encounter*, August 1959:

By divorcing a happening from its origins and its circumstances, the BBC in its news bulletins is as guilty of a gross distortion of fact and truth as any politically biassed newspaper, and almost certainly more consistently so.

It is also said that the quality or posh papers are too subservient to officialdom and that the popular papers often use the techniques of sensational exposure to good purpose. Francis Williams has argued that the popular press acts as 'a mine-field through which bureaucrats tread at their peril' and the editor of the *New Statesman*, John Freeman, has called the *Daily Mirror* 'one of the finest organs of radical opinion in the country'. It will be as well to leave the last word here to the *Daily Mirror*:

The *Mirror* is a sensational newspaper. We make no apology for that.

We believe in the sensational presentation of news and views, especially important news and views, as a necessary and valuable public service in these days of mass readership and democratic responsibility.

Silvester Bolam, quoted in Cudlipp, *Publish and Be Damned*

2. THE TRADITIONALISTS

Many critics attack modern society because of the way it has broken with the past, and set against the present day the traditional wisdom of an older order. This sometimes goes along with the paternalist outlook exemplified by Lord Reith.

The two most distinguished critics of this kind are T. S. Eliot and F. R. Leavis and we shall rely mainly on their arguments in this section. T. S. Eliot has no doubt that cultural decline set in with the introduction of modern democracy:

What I try to say is this: here are what I believe to be the essential conditions for the growth and survival of culture.

If they conflict with any passionate faith of the reader—if for instance he finds it shocking that culture and equalitarianism should conflict, if it seems monstrous to him that anyone should have 'advantages of birth' —I do not ask him to change his faith, I merely ask him to stop paying lip-service to culture.

Notes towards the Definition of Culture

In using the word 'culture' Eliot was referring not to the objects of fine art, not to the group of specialists who know about them, not even to the sum of several activities, but to a way of life. To be cultured in this sense means to be part of this way of life and to draw strength from its traditions. Eliot was preoccupied by the problem of how culture is transmitted:

If we agree that the primary vehicle for the transmission of culture is the family, and if we agree that in a more highly civilized society there must be different levels of culture, then it follows that to ensure the transmission of the culture of these different levels there must be groups of families persisting from generation to generation, each in the same way of life.

ibid.

These groups of families are, of course, classes and this is why he felt that democracy in undermining the class system also destroys culture. At its best the democratic system would produce a society ruled by élites chosen from the whole population on the basis of merit. Eliot's objection is that such a society could not offer stability, there would be no continuity from one generation to the next, and no steady maturing of values contained within a tradition and sustained by ritual. It would be an open and rationalistic society in which men had only a superficial relationship with each other. 'It posits', he said, 'an atomic view of society.' 'Atomic' is to be contrasted with 'organic', and to get an idea of what is meant by an organic community we can turn to Dr Leavis and Denys Thompson. In *Culture and Environment* they make use of quotations from the writings of George Sturt (or Bourne):

> Sturt's villagers expressed their human nature, they satisfied their human needs, in terms of the natural environment; and the things they made—cottages, barns, ricks and waggons—together with their relations with one another constituted a human environment, and a subtlety of adjustment and adaptation, as right and inevitable. . . .
>
> They themselves represented an adjustment to the environment; their ways of life reflected the rhythm of the seasons, and they were in close touch with the sources of their sustenance in the neighbouring soil.

This is a description of what Eliot means by a way of life. But this culture, to continue the argument, is also related to the art of the time:

> What makes the age outstanding in literary history, however, is its range of interests and vitality of language; and here other factors contributed besides the humanism of the Universities and the Court. One of these was the persistence of popular customs of speech and thought and entertainment rooted in the communal life of medieval towns and villages. To some extent the old traditions obstructed the new. But they also combined, inasmuch as the Tudors established a firm

and broadly based national community; and by combining they invigorated the whole idiom of literature.

L. G. Salingar, *The Age of Shakespeare*

One of the criticisms of modern society is that this connection has been broken so that the popular and fine-art cultures of the day, far from nourishing each other, live in increasing isolation. The other criticism is that the modern world has forced a division between work and leisure:

> For the traditions of recreation have died with the old ways of work from which they were inseparable. Men are now incapacitated by their work, which makes leisure necessary as it was not before, from using their leisure for humane recreation, that is, in pursuits that make them feel self-fulfilled and make life significant, dignified and satisfying.
>
> Leavis and Thompson, *Culture and Environment*

There are, of course, important differences between Eliot and Leavis. The latter, for example, sees industrialism rather than democracy as the villain. For Eliot the solution is in a return to the Church and in the maintainance of the class system. For Leavis the answer is in the study of literature as the core of liberal and humane studies and in making the university a centre from which would come the minority dedicated to defending the highest standards against mass society. If the former is a lost cause the latter is, in Leavis's own words, a substitute.

Through the writings of Eliot, Leavis and others in this tradition we are able to see our contemporary problems more clearly. They offer, however, little guidance, indeed little encouragement, to action. Their tradition is essentially defensive, and can encourage a dangerous nostalgia for the past, omitting much that was ugly and mean in it. It is striking that when T. S. Eliot wants a more contemporary illustration of his thesis he goes to Marie Lloyd and the music hall. Even Dwight MacDonald, whose position is close to the one described here, and who is inevitably more in touch (being a professional film critic), believes that, with some eccentric exceptions, the art of the movies died with the introduction of sound in 1929.

3. THE PROGRESSIVES

By progressives we mean those who would themselves make many criticisms about the provision of information, art and entertainment, but would reject the general indictment as being drastically overdrawn. In general they take a more optimistic view, believing that in large measure the problems we face, the lack of acceptable standards and so on, are the products of a transitional period, the growing pains of a new and better kind of society. They emphasize the positive achievements which the sweeping condemnation overlooks and they believe that what does not improve with time can be rectified by reform.

They will note first of all certain contradictions in the indictment. It is not clear, for example, what passivity means. Why should looking at a film be regarded as a passive activity and reading a book not? If arguments are advanced about the lulling atmosphere, the scented dark and so on, they will point out that the log fire, the cigar and after-dinner port can have a similar effect. It all depends on what is being seen or read—looking at *The Battleship Potemkin* is likely to be more active than reading a library romance. The idea that there is something inherently inferior in film-going and television-viewing and that there is a special virtue in the mere act of reading has only a snobbish foundation. With this use of 'passive' eliminated, it is possible to employ the word more accurately to describe the state of mind induced by certain qualities in a work regardless of the means of transmission. In fact, we will be describing one aspect of bad art: 'bad' here meaning the sort of art described by Clement Greenberg as *'pre-digested'*.

Similar reservations might be made at other points in the indictment. In more general terms it would be put that we assume too much. Is there not a danger in drawing conclusions about effects from a study of content only? People do not live at the level of the mass media, and important parts of their lives are not mirrored in the media. A network of interests, associations and personal relationships provides a reality against which the fantasies of mass culture are tested. Some such explanation must be offered of the obvious fact that readers of the *Daily Sketch* or viewers of *Dotto* are not like the image presented of them.

It has also been argued that for many people art (including here advertising and entertainment) plays a marginal part in life, and that if they are unsophisticated in their responses they will be little affected by it. The assumption that the hidden values revealed by the intellectual critic somehow get through to people in a submerged form may not be true. Perhaps critics have been taken in themselves by the claims of the advertising psychologists that their witchcraft actually works. This is a difficult but important point. It seems true that we can be affected by implicit values— especially when they are repeated over and over again in a dramatic form. *Television and the Child* made this clear. But even here the response is not totally unconscious—some ability to organize the experiences of art, some degree of awareness, is implied. This line of reasoning suggests that it is misleading to talk of a training in awareness as a defence against false values. Better to think positively in terms of training a response to the best, because it is only in contrast with the richer values of more creative work that falsity is revealed.

In making qualifications of this kind the progressive critic might modify the indictment of mass culture. Even more important to his purpose would be an insistence on positive achievements, and here he could quote the sales of paperback books on serious subjects, the enlarged public for good music, the increased attendance at art galleries and the use made of the library service. In particular, he might well point out that the audiences for serious TV programmes such as *Monitor* (3,000,000) and *Panorama* (10,000,000) are remarkable. Abuses would be recognized but the modern society would be seen as more open and flexible and more on the move than its critics allow:

Mass society has liberated the cognitive, appreciative, and moral capacities of individuals. Larger elements of the population have consciously learned to value the pleasures of eye, ear, taste, touch and conviviality. People make choices more freely in many spheres of life, and these choices are not necessarily made for them by tradition, authority, or scarcity. The value of the experience of personal relationships is more widely appreciated.

Edward Shils, *Culture for the Millions*

Thinking in such terms of the critics of the mass society the progressives would accuse them of puritanism in their distrust of relaxing entertainment and suspect them of snobbery in their resentment that other people, the mass of the people indeed, were now gaining access to what had previously been the privilege of the few. The abuses are there to be understood, not as inherent defects of a system but as the inevitable accompaniment to this process of making the best available to all. Some measures of reform may be required (lay members on the Press Council would be an example), but the most important steps should be taken in education to make equality of opportunity a reality:

. . . in walking up Fleet Street the other day, my eye caught the title of a book standing open in a bookseller's window. It was—*On the Necessity of the Diffusion of Taste Among All Classes*. 'Ah,' I thought to myself, 'my classifying friend, when you have diffused your taste, where will your classes be?'

JOHN RUSKIN, *The Crown of Wild Olives*

4. THE RADICALS

The radical will accept many of the points made by the progressive critic. In particular he will feel that the old guardians of culture created an exclusive tradition denying people access to what should be part of the common life and that it is a tradition in which the valuable has become dangerously mixed with the meretricious. The movement of the people as a whole towards a fuller participation in society will be welcomed, not feared, and it will be recognized that in the early stages mistakes will be made and standards will seem confused. At this point, however, the radical departs sharply from the progressive. Whereas the latter sees a society evolving, the former sees a society in conflict. The radical's contention is that in this situation what Raymond Williams calls 'cultural inexperience' is being exploited. The mass press, for example, is not the direct result of people's taste but the result of using the new methods of financing newspapers and the techniques of popular journalism to exploit people's uncertainties as they move out of illiteracy. This exploitation of the mind is seen as the twentieth-century equivalent to the political and economic exploitation of the nineteenth century:

> If the active minority continue to allow themselves too exclusively to think of immediate political and economic objectives, the pass will be sold, culturally, behind their backs.
>
> Richard Hoggart, *The Uses of Literacy*

The radical critic sees a conflict between democracy and commercialism and this leads him to demand measures of social intervention and public control, not in the interests of a Brahmin minority against the masses but in the interests of all; not to restrict the freedom of the people, but to enlarge it. This is why the *New Statesman* (normally a progressive rather than a radical paper) could compare the Pilkington Report to the Webbs' Royal Commission on the Poor Law and the Beveridge Report.

The possible methods of social ownership and control have hardly been explored and are obviously more difficult to find in the field of communications than in any other. Raymond Williams has tried, however, to define some of the principles:

> Where the means of communication can be personally owned, it is the duty of society to guarantee this ownership and to ensure that distribution facilities are adequate, on terms compatible with the original freedom. Where the means of communication cannot be personally owned, because of their expense and size, it is the duty of society to hold these means in trust for the actual contributors, who for all practical purposes will control their use.
>
> *Communications*

The objection to this is that, however admirable the intention, it is bound to lead to a bureaucracy and that development, even if slow and fragmentary, towards a greater diversity is preferable to the risk of underpinning the cultural establishment with constitutional forms. The radical's response is that the tendency at the moment is frequently not towards greater diversity but to the opposite. The idea of the open society is itself distrusted and it is argued that the idea of equality of opportunity summed up in the image of the ladder is still a limiting one and that a hierarchy of merit is no less a hierarchy than one of birth or wealth. The second point was given brilliant satirical form by Michael Young in *The Rise of the Meritocracy*. Where the progressive seeks a plural society within which various cultures exist, the radical aims at a common culture based on a community in which the culture at the top is a more refined, more articulated expression of the values shared by all.

Here we come to the basic disagreement between radical and progressive. The objection to the idea of a common culture has been put clearly by Richard Wollheim:

> For it is surely inconsistent with the idea of liberty that men should have their lives limited in any way that is not practically necessary. The liberalized society is one where men fulfil themselves according to their own view or conception of life—provided, of course, that in doing so they do not interfere with, or impose upon, the self-fulfilment of others. To achieve this end, they must be free both of the dictates of established authority and of the subtler but no less effective power of social pressure.
>
> *Socialism and Culture* (Fabian pamphlet)

The progressive feels the society already too much with us, the social pressures already too severe and wishes therefore to stress individuality. The radical believes it is because we do not have a real community that we feel a loss as individuals. Although suspicious of the idealization of the past involved, the radical's aim is to attempt the recapture of the organic community in terms compatible with the gains of industrialization and democracy:

One day we shall win back Art, that is to say the pleasure of life; win back Art again to our daily labour . . . the cause of Art is the cause of the people.

William Morris, *Art and Socialism*

Obviously the views outlined under the four headings of Providers, Traditionalists, Progressives and Radicals are not mutually exclusive, but provided they are not used as labels to classify the views of individual writers they do illustrate different approaches and attitudes. The ideas involved are, of course, more complex than can be made to appear in a short résumé, and the books referred to should be read in full to get a complete understanding.

Clearly many of the ideas are too difficult to discuss except with older pupils and mature students. Yet even for the teacher who cannot handle the ideas directly with his pupils some understanding of these more fundamental issues is necessary. In dealing with them we will, of course, be handling political as well as social and cultural questions about which people are sharply and legitimately divided. The teacher must be ever aware of the danger of using his position of power to impose his views on others. He will best avoid this, however, not by shelving the problems that must concern us all but by dealing with them directly and honestly. People can be indoctrinated in various ways; perhaps the most subtle and penetrating is that which comes from an apparent objectivity in which the teacher's assumptions are concealed from his pupils. We cannot throw off our prejudices by pretending not to have them. If we have larger social objectives we must not hide them; on the contrary, we must be more and unusually clear about them.

Many will disagree over the issues raised by the material in this chapter. But we do not develop our opinions in a vacuum, and by the very nature of the job those working within education are bound to see these problems from a distinctive point of view. We have already noted how, more than others, educationists are inevitably conscious of the pressures of mass society and are likely to be less sanguine about the immediate prospects of change. Against this, however, their view of society is likely to be more dynamic simply because they are concerned with the growth and development of the coming generation. They must believe in the almost infinite possibility of change and feel confident that ultimately all, not merely a few, can share a richer culture. Their faith, particularly for those working in the secondary modern schools, is essentially democratic. It is a faith rather than a programme; but clear enough, we would hope, to reject this doctrine put forward in the *Sunday Telegraph* (11/3/62):

> A free and prosperous society depends on the activities of three distinct classes—a political élite trained by the study of the humanities to take broad and enlightened views about ends and means, a technical élite willing to exercise its skill in obedience to the community's will, and a proletariat with enough mechanical intelligence to respond to managerial direction . . .
>
> More technical instruction for the British working man, so that he learns to understand machines as does his American counterpart, would be an infinitely greater boon than a generation of litterateurs who knew about thermodynamics or a class of engineers who read Dante.

This is not the place to take any further the argument about what kind of society we want. We have tried to put some of the different views as clearly as possible. But for education the debate is not academic. Whatever a teacher's suppositions, he is involved and his ideas and actions will change things. What is more, the changes that education can effect are fundamental. No system can guarantee either freedom or cultural health. Ultimately it is our quality as individuals that will count. This is not to say that we can neglect social action, only that it must spring from the capacities for sympathy and understanding and the powers of judgement and discrimination it is the purpose of education to develop.

Acknowledgments

The authors are indebted to the following for permission to reprint excerpts from:

George Allen & Unwin Ltd., *The Revolt of the Masses* by Ortega y Gasset.

Appleton-Century-Crofts, Inc., *Handbook of Social Psychology* by Kimball Young.

Atheneum Publishers, Inc., *The Image* by Daniel Boorstein.

Basic Books, Inc., *This Island Now* by G. M. Carstairs, and *The Uses of Literacy* by Richard Hoggart.

Cambridge University Press, *An Experiment in Criticism* by C. S. Lewis, and *Elizabethan Tragedy* by M. C. Bradbrook.

Chatto & Windus Ltd., *The Common Pursuit* by F. R. Leavis, *Culture and Environment* by F. R. Leavis and D. Thompson, and *Fiction and the Reading Public* by Q. D. Leavis.

Columbia University Press, *Culture and Society* and *The Long Revolution* by Raymond Williams, and *As They Liked It* by Alfred Harbage.

Felix de Wolfe and Richard Stone, ballads of Peggy Seeger and Ewan MacColl.

Daily Mirror, *Publish and be Damned* by Hugh Cudlipp.

Dobson Books Ltd., *Theory of the Film* by Bela Balazs.

Doubleday & Co. Inc., *Lady Sings the Blues* by Billie Holiday and W. Dufty.

E. P. Dutton & Co. Inc., *One Lonely Night* and *I, The Jury* by Mickey Spillane.

The Free Press of Glencoe, *Mass Culture* by Eric Larrabee and Rolfe Meyersohn, *Reader in Public Opinion* by Walter Lippmann, and *Movies: A Psychological Study* by M. Wolfenstein and N. Leites.

Harcourt, Brace & World, Inc., *Notes Towards the Definition of Culture* and *Selected Essays* by T. S. Eliot, and *Keep the Aspidistra Flying* and *Critical Essays* by George Orwell.

Harper & Row, Inc., *The House of Intellect* by Jacques Barzun.

Heinemann Educational Books, *The Idiom of the People* by James Reeves.

Houghton Mifflin Company, *Raymond Chandler Speaking* by Dorothy Gardiner and Katherine Sorley Walker.

Alfred A. Knopf, Inc., *The Raymond Chandler Omnibus*.

Holt, Rinehart & Winston, Inc., *Hear Me Talkin' to Ya* by Nat Shapiro and Nat Hentoff.

MacGibbon & Kee, Ltd., *The Jazz Scene* by Francis Newton.

The Macmillan Company, *The Liveliest Art* by Arthur Knight, and *Dr. No, Moonraker,* and *Casino Royale* by Ian Fleming.

William Morrow & Co., Inc., *Male and Female* by Margaret Mead.

New Directions, *The ABC of Reading* by Ezra Pound.

New English Library Ltd., *Poor Me* by Adam Faith.

Oxford University Press (London), *Heroic Song and Heroic Legend* by Jan de Vries, and *Television and the Child* by Dr. Hilde Himmelweit, A. Oppenheim, and P. Vance.

Oxford University Press, Inc., *White Collar* and *The Power Elite* by C. Wright Mills.

Pantheon Books, Inc., *Passion and Society* by Denis de Rougemont, *The Nude* by Kenneth Clark, and *The Making of the English Working Class* by E. P. Thompson.

Penguin Books Ltd., *The Pelican Guide to English Literature,* Vols. 2 & 4, and *Communications* by Raymond Williams.

Laurence Pollinger Limited and the Estate of Frieda Lawrence, *Fantasia of the Unconscious and Psychoanalysis and the Unconscious, The Phoenix,* and *Sex, Literature and Censorship* by D. H. Lawrence.

Random House, Inc., *Against The American Grain* by Dwight Macdonald.

Roberts and Vinter Ltd., *Secret Session* by Hank Jansen.

Routledge & Kegan Paul Ltd., *Popular Fiction 100 Years Ago* by Margaret Dalziel.

Charles Scribner's Sons, *Movies for the Millions* by Gilbert Seldes.

Simon and Schuster, Inc., *Television Plays* by Paddy Chayefsky.

Souvenir Press Ltd., *Tommy Steele* by John Kennedy.

Stanford University Press, *Television in the Lives of our Children* by W. Schramm, J. Lyle, and E. B. Parker.

University of Nebraska, *The Popular Novel in England* by J. M. S. Tompkins.

Vanguard Press, Inc., *The Mechanical Bride* by Marshall McLuhan.

D. Van Nostrand Company, Inc., *Culture for the Millions,* edited by Norman Jacobs.

The Viking Press, Inc, *Between Past and Future* by Hannah Arendt.

Trustee of the Estate of Robert S. Warshow, *The Immediate Experience* by Robert S. Warshow.

INDEX

(a raised q indicates a quotation; the Projects for Teaching and Appendices have not been included)